POST-1974 COUNTIES

SHETLAND

ORKNEY

WESTERN ISLES

HIGHLAND

GRAMPIAN

TAYSIDE

CENTRAL

FIFE

STRATHCLYDE

LOTHIAN

BORDERS

DUMFRIES & GALLOWAY

NORTHUMBERLAND

TYNE & WEAR

LONDON DERRY

ANTRIM

TYRONE

FERMANAGH

ARMAGH

DOWN

CUMBRIA

DURHAM

CLEVELAND

ISLE OF MAN

NORTH YORKSHIRE

LANCASHIRE

WEST YORKSHIRE

HUMBERSIDE

MERSEYSIDE

GREATER MANCHESTER

SOUTH YORKS

CHESHIRE

DERBY

NOTTINGHAM

LINCOLN

GWYNEDD

CLWYD

SHROPSHIRE

STAFFORD

W. MIDLANDS

LEICESTER

NORFOLK

POWYS

HEREFORD & WORCESTER

WARWICK

NORTHAMPTON

CAMBRIDGE

SUFFOLK

DYFED

GWENT

GLOUCESTER

OXFORD

BUCKINGHAM

BEDFORD

HERTFORD

ESSEX

W. MID-S GLAMORGAN

AVON

WILTSHIRE

BERKSHIRE

GREATER LONDON

SURREY

KENT

SOMERSET

HAMPSHIRE

WEST SUSSEX

EAST SUSSEX

DEVON

DORSET

ISLE OF WIGHT

CORNWALL

W9-DFG-442

AN AMERICAN'S
GUIDE TO BRITAIN

To Avril, Honor Leigh and Eliot
who travelled so much of it with me

An American's Guide to Britain

Revised Edition

Robin W. Winks

Charles Scribner's Sons
New York

Copyright © 1977, 1983 Robin W. Winks

Library of Congress Cataloging in Publication Data

Winks, Robin W.
  An American's guide to Britain.
  Includes indexes.
  1. Great Britain—Description and travel—1971–
—Guide-books. I. Title.
DA650.W54   1983   914.1'04858   82-42651
ISBN 0–684–17868–0

1 3 5 7 9 11 13 15 17 19   F/C   20 18 16 14 12 10 8 6 4 2

Printed in the United States of America.

Contents

Illustrations

MAPS

LINE DRAWINGS
These illustrations are taken from a series of *Guides* published by Adam and Charles Black in the nineteenth century, with the exception of the following, which are reproduced by permission of the Mary Evans Picture Library: Bath; Cambridge; Ely; Gloucester; Knole; Lincoln; National Gallery, London; Oxford; St Albans; Salisbury; Windsor Castle; York.

The map of the main whisky distilleries of Scotland is based on a map from *The Whiskies of Scotland* by Professor R. J. S. McDowall, published by John Murray.

Introduction

An American's Guide to Britain is intended as a unique guide to a country to which over two million Americans come each year. (This figure is expected to remain steady despite the economy). The guide is meant to be especially American in three ways. Firstly, it makes special reference to those places one may visit which have a specific American association, e.g. Sulgrave Manor (George Washington's ancestral home), Wroxton Abbey (home of Lord North), the ports associated with the Pilgrims (Plymouth, Boston), the American Museum at Bath, and so on. The names of these places are set in heavier type. Secondly, the guide devotes space to the kinds of places and activities that tend to appeal particularly to Americans: exploration of the national parks in Britain, suggestions of places in which tours may be combined with on-the-spot purchasing, and references to literary landmarks in relation to physical features (e.g. Dorchester and Hardy, Broadstairs and John Buchan). Thirdly, the guide combines the features which an American expects to find within a single book: suggested tours, descriptions of places, hours of opening, recommended hotels and restaurants, shopping hints and personal observations.

Clearly, this guide presupposes more extensive travel in the British countryside than do most other guides. Some Americans find driving in London tiring, but once in the country most agree that they encounter no special difficulties in making their way about. For the most part the book, in its organization by self-guided tours, assumes that the best way to see Britain is to leave London by rail and pick up a hire-car at some point an hour or two outside the city, returning the car a few days later to some other point for the return rail journey into London. Generally, the tours themselves consist of a series of circles based on a city in which at least one major hire firm has service.

This guide is not meant to substitute for a standard guide. Obviously it is unbalanced, for to single out a Benjamin West painting for viewing in a gallery when an El Greco hangs nearby, shows a special kind of bias. Clearly one drives to Lincoln to see the great cathedral, not the American-related monuments there. But once there, this guide will point up those monuments. Still, then, the reader will also want, minimally, a compact guide to Britain written to standard tastes – the *AA Great Britain Road Atlas* is good, and contains very clear maps; the *Good Food Guide*, or a similar book, on dining out; and a separate guide to London. Since not everyone will read this book straight through, there is some intentional overlap of information between sections.

Let us be clear. I believe Britain to be a magnificent country in which to wander. Any of a number of reasons can be used to justify wandering. I have collected all the cathedrals, every national park, every county and its principal town, every restaurant or hotel given the highest rating by the *Good Food Guide*, and every Wedgwood blue plaque marking a notable residence in London. To collect them all was less the point than the awareness that, to do so, would open up the whole of the British landscape. Someone else, equally arbitrarily, could decide to collect all the race tracks, surf-boarding beaches, or narrow gauge railways. In pursuing American-related sites by the plan of this book, you will see a great deal of Britain thoroughly, as it has been my joy to do. But do keep what follows here in proportion: *of course* one visits Bath Abbey for itself, not because a former United States Senator is buried there!

To Americans, Britain represents several ties. There is the tie of language. There is the tie of literary tradition – hence my emphasis upon it. There is the waning ecclesiastical/scholastic tie. And there is, for some, the tie of history, of a shared past.

Now if you don't enjoy these kinds of things – if you prefer nightclubs to cathedrals, Ellery Queen to Sherlock Holmes, and the sound of brass marching bands to the skirl of pipes – this book probably isn't for you. If the idea of reading the Brontës while near Top Withens (the original of Wuthering Heights) doesn't appeal to you, why not admit it? For this *is* a biased guide: I like England (and yes, Scotland, Wales and Ireland too); I'll take Stilton over American Processed any day, cider over Coke and Harris Tweed over polyester. Not only do I think good books (and some bad ones) should be read *in situ*, that Britain's cathedrals are all worth seeing – although some more than others, of course – and that even the slums of Glasgow have infinitely more character than those of Detroit, but I am also authoritarian. This guide will tell you where I think you should go and what I think you should see, and even where I think you should eat; in short, it's pretty personal. If I tell you that you're not having real fish and chips unless they're wrapped in a newspaper, then that's the fact, and no chittering arguments about advancing technology and standards of hygiene will change my mind. An excellent writer of science fiction, Ursula LeGuin, has written that the creative adult is a child who has survived. In this sense of the word, this book is meant to appeal to the child in most of us – for when we are truly an adult, we will also be dead. I have a litmus paper test: does the traveller think it foolish to seek out the Pathology Laboratory in St. Bartholomew's Hospital, off the Holborn Viaduct in London, to read there a bronze plaque with these lines? "At this place New Years Day, 1881 were spoken these deathless words: 'You have been in Afghanistan, I perceive,' by Mr. Sherlock Holmes in greeting to John H. Watson, M.D. at their first meeting." If this is foolishness, read no further, for the child is dead. So I am a bit book-bound, nostalgic, romantic, and certainly Anglophilic throughout, and if these are not your biases, why not read this book in your local library before risking your money on it?

Or you may object that you didn't come to Britain to see things relating to America, which you're happy to leave behind. After all, you don't want to get in with a crowd of tourists. Well pause a moment, friend; if you have a camera around your neck, you *are* a tourist, however much you may upgrade your status by calling yourself a traveller. What's wrong with tourists anyway? It is the fact that tourists want to see Ye Olde England that has led hardnosed Town Fathers to preserve good bits of it. There are intelligent tourists – like you – and ignorant ones, and they cannot automatically be distinguished by the guide book they have in hand. Or perhaps it is not your fellow Americans who irritate you overseas as much as the suggestion, insistently made here, that you might find some interest, occasional pleasure, and even a bit of pride in visiting those places in Britain which have close associations with the United States? I, for one, do not feel ashamed to be interested in George Washington while in England, and while I do not wear a ten gallon hat, smoke a cigar, or hang a Hawaiian shirt outside my trousers as I tour, I also do not feel that I must blend into the landscape with leather patch elbows, tweeds, or a rolled brolly. One can tell the difference between the first and second floor, or think the Athenaeum has it all over the Yale Club, and still remain loyal to one's roots. Americans carry their sense of place around with them, and if either my praise for the English countryside over the American, or my singling out an American-related scene with patriotic zeal, bothers your sense of identity, that's your problem, not mine.

So enjoy the book for what it is: an *American* guide to *Britain*.

Robin W. Winks
New Haven, Connecticut

Preface to the second edition

Naturally I was pleased to discover that so many reviewers, travellers, and even some purchasers like this book, which was originally written for the American Bicentennial in 1976. Since then Britain has changed a bit, I have shifted from Glenfiddich to Laphroaig, and we have all grown a mite older. The book was in need of revision, and the publisher offered to restore four chapters that were omitted from the first edition: those on Devon and Cornwall, the Midlands, the Lake District, and Northern Ireland. This revised edition is thereby enlarged by nearly a quarter and at last appears roughly as I originally intended. I have corrected such errors as I have discovered for myself on frequent visits to the United Kingdom since the first edition was prepared and have responded to suggestions from many who have written to me. Obviously one cannot travel again over every road described here, so there is the risk that, on occasions, one must now turn right at the pub rather than left to reach a described goal, since Britain is as mad for one-way streets as we are in the United States. But all information has been brought up to date and here and there a few opinions have been changed. To the acknowledgments I would like to add our dog, stuffily named Bishop Berkeley of Cloyne, though invariably called Berk (and pronounced Bark), who kept me reluctant company as I revised.

R. W. W.

Acknowledgments

For their help I thank them: Julian Bach, my agent, of New York City; Susanne Kirk, my editor at Charles Scribner's Sons, also in New York City; David Gadsby and Richard Newnham, of London; the directors of the hundreds of British historical societies, museums and art galleries to whom I put questions, so cheerfully answered. I also thank my wife, Avril, and children Honor Leigh and Eliot for having been excellent navigators on many a bad road.

How to survive in Britain
The prudence of treating Britain as a foreign country

In having chosen to come to Britain, you may in part have been guided by simple prudence: you speak the same language and should be able to make your way about with little difficulty. The same prudence should lead you to realize that Britain is a foreign country: if not clear on this point before you arrive, you will be within a day or so. Of course, if the British were not a very different people, they would be less interesting, for presumably you would not have ventured out at all if you depended solely on finding a Holiday Inn for the night and a McDonald's hamburger to eat with your Coke.

You will be more likely to survive in Britain if you begin with the simple assumption that the British are (even though they may deny it) Europeans, yet that class, and accent, and a special sense of history still set them apart from the rest of the world, and that part of their fascination lies in this very fact. Indeed, if you are going to be made angry by the discovery that despite the Labour Party, and socialized medicine, and nationalized railways, the British still tend to think in class terms, you had best stay home. For if Britain makes you angry, you are unlikely to survive, much less enjoy, it at all. Most people who know anything about the meaning of the term consider Britain to be substantially more democratic than the United States. But it isn't perfect, and it isn't quaint, and it isn't simply Boston plus Beefeaters. Anyway, if you are inclined to think these things, you wouldn't survive, and the following pages are really of no use to you. Still, assuming that you begin with the cardinal rules of the traveller in mind – take it as it comes; never complain about the weather, since complaint is best reserved for things you can do something about; and assume that bad food, long queues, or indifferent service are all

part of the learning experience – you may find the following suggestions of some value.

Getting oriented (or as the British say, 'orientated')

Pity the poor traveller who doesn't know where he is, or what to see,
or how to get from that lovely restaurant to that intriguing antique
shop spied last night while speeding by in a taxi. Pity also the poor
traveller who, thinking his travel an excuse for paying no attention to
the rest of the world, doesn't understand why people are throwing
bombs at him, because he didn't bother to read the newspaper that
day. Being oriented in a foreign country is more than a matter of maps.

But it starts with maps. The British are probably the best map-
makers in the world. Certainly they are among the most map conscious. You will find a greater variety of maps for Britain than for
any other nation. There are oil company maps (for which you have
to pay) and regional maps, and city and street maps by the hundreds;
there are maps and guides to castles, to cathedrals, to hiking paths,
to fishing streams, to the locations of Scottish clans, to good beaches,
good restaurants, good beds, and good loos (public lavatories). A
fair assortment of these may be found in any of the branches (all over
England) of W. H. Smith's bookshops. If you happen to like maps
yourself and want to sample a wider array, go to the book department
of Harrods, or, best of all, to Map House, on Beauchamp (pronounced 'Beecham') Place in Knightsbridge. (At the least you may
purchase Ordnance Survey 2 cm to 1 km maps if you plan to do much
hiking.)

Three maps are indispensable. You can buy the Geographers'
A–Z London Street Atlas and Index (ask at any news stand in any
Underground station for an 'A to Zed') and with it find any place in
London. Never be without it, for while it is true that London cabbies
(taxi drivers to you) are the best and most thoroughly trained in the
world, even they cannot unscramble your firm command that you be
taken instantly to Gloucester Road, when you have not troubled to
learn which of twenty Gloucester Roads you mean, or even whether
you may not have Gloucester Street (miles away from the others, and
quite major), Avenue, Circus, Close, Crescent, Drive, Gardens,
Grove, Mews, Place, Square, Terrace, Walk, or Way in mind.

If on foot, be certain to have an Underground Map as well. There is one printed in black only, with different symbols for the various lines, on the back of the A to Zed, but it is confusing, and at most Underground ticket offices you can buy a small map with the Central Line shown in red, the Circle Line in yellow, and so on, which will guide you at a glance. The same people, Geographers' Map Company, produce a compact fold-out map of Central London to which the second type of Underground Map is attached, along with location maps of the West End cinemas and theatres. If you plan to travel by bus a good bit, you may also want to add the Geographia London map showing bus routes.

If you intend to travel outside London, even by train, obtain a set of good maps so that you can trace the route across the countryside as you go. All major oil companies sell maps at their service stations; none give them away. Among the best for your purpose are the Shell and the Esso maps, for they are most like those American motorists are accustomed to, and nine separate ones can be bought in a boxed set. Study the legends before using any of them, and make sure you know whether distances are given in miles or kilometres. If you are going to be long in Britain, buy the *National Trust Atlas* (at most bookshops, or from the Trust at 42 Queen Anne's Gate, S.W.1) which locates Trust properties on a standard set of rather bad maps. And if you intend to drive, add a good map of Greater London to your arsenal, for the single greatest driving challenge you will face in Britain is getting out of London and on to the open road. The Automobile Association (always 'the AA', just off Leicester Square) offers an inexpensive and excellent map of this sort; and your membership in the United States is reciprocal.

As an alternative to all the maps mentioned in the paragraph above, buy the *Sunday Times RAC Road Atlas*. Not without errors, it is nonetheless a very good set of maps for the price, with a gazetteer (alphabetical guide book similar to the American Automobile Association regional guides) and a clever and generally well-exercised habit of marking 'picturesque roads' with a special green line. In any event, the guide you are now reading is keyed to it and the *AA Road Atlas* outside London, which is another reason you need one or the other to survive. (Directions in the tours that follow are also keyed to Shell maps.)

Over the years I have arrived in a thousand strange towns with only a few hours in which to find myself, and all that the town offers me, and so I have a few patented techniques in addition to overloading my pockets with maps. Do these.

1 Always buy a local newspaper and read it over your first meal. It not only tells you what is going on in town, but its editorial page, the letters-to-the-editor column, even the advertisements, will tell you a lot about the town.

2 Listen to the local radio, or turn on the local television, when you can. Rental cars in Britain don't have radios, so you can't get the sense of the country while driving across it as you can in South Dakota by listening to Bible preachers, and unless you stay in top-flight hotels, your room may have neither radio nor TV. But the hotel will have a TV room, so be sociable after dinner and take your coffee along and watch the natives watching.

3 If you arrive unprepared in a strange town, or one too obscure to merit a guidebook, you can discover what the locals consider to be the highlights of their city by looking at the omnipresent picture post-cards. But don't try to find postcards in a drug store (don't try to find a drug store for that matter); check at hotel counters, tourist souvenir shops, or news-stands.

Of course, if you don't like to be oriented and are romantically in-clined to think it more fun to let the unexpected sneak up on you (and certainly if you feel no pangs upon returning to Des Moines to discover that you were within three miles of Britain's greatest landed estate, or saw the very Oxfordshire house which was the model for the one in D. H. Lawrence's *Women in Love* without knowing it) then forget all of this. You won't need this book either.

Arriving

Unless you arrive via Ireland, or through Prestwick (Scotland) or Manchester, all decidedly minority routes, your introduction to Britain will be one of the London airports, most probably Heathrow. This terminal is well organized, and even if you are only in transit there is a pleasant, and usually crowded, lounge with a modest duty free shop (which in no way rivals the international airport at Shannon in Eire, however). Your arrival will have a few potential trouble spots for which you should be prepared: the odds are that you may deplane into a bus, to be taken to the bottom of a long ramp, followed by a fairly steep climb, and then an even longer walk through clearly marked but apparently interminable corridors, to immigration control. Try not to have too much to carry, for this can be a wearisome journey. While immigration will be smooth, try to avoid standing in a queue with many Asians or Africans, for the British scrutinize their passports with care. No visa is required (nor a health card unless you are arriving from Africa or Asia). Have your flight number memorized, go down the stairway behind immigration which bears that flight number, and seek out the luggage carousel at the bottom which also carries it. The wait here is likely to be long, but get one of the trolleys (like supermarket shopping carts) immediately, for the supply is low; if there is not one, capture a porter – these creatures are very rare indeed – and have him stand by, even though you will have to tip well to make him your private preserve. With bags in hand, on trolley, or with porter, you pass through the green exit from Customs if you have nothing to declare and the red exit if you do. Immediately outside the Customs' hall you'll find direction signs for taxis, for the airline bus into the city, for car rental agencies, for making direct-line hotel reservations, and a bank. *Do not* take a taxi without a meter, and *do not* take a taxi offered by anyone inside the hall, for these pirate taxis overcharge; go outside and get in the queue, which will move fast.

Money

The moment you step off the plane at Heathrow, *et al.,* you had better know what your money is worth. (It may be less than you think, but any bank can tell you the latest exchange rate.) Equip yourself with a 'tip pack', bought from your bank in America, before leaving; this will get you past the porters, onto the airport bus from Heathrow to London and off again, into a taxi from the bus terminal to your hotel, and past another battery of porters, so that you can study the strange new coins at leisure in your hotel room. (There *are* banks at the airport, of course, but the lines are usually long.) Better yet, bring at least £50 in cash with you (and more if arriving on a weekend) so that you have options: to take a taxi directly from the airport to your hotel, to go out to the theatre the first evening, etc. Your American Express credit card will be accepted at most places in London but may be of little use to you in the countryside, so have travellers cheques as well. Cash these at a bank, for the hotel may take a small fee, and a few country hotels may not cash them at all. Above all, do not suffer from that strange American malady by which you come to feel that all money not like that at home is really play money, or that a pound and a dollar are to be equated emotionally, even if you know damn well that rationally one may be worth twice the other. Always translate prices mentally into American terms before making a purchase, and if you have trouble doing this, carry a computed card supplied by your bank.

British coins are larger than ours and a nuisance to carry. You will get a lot of them. The 10p pieces are useful for many purposes and make a good tip; treat two of them as you would 25 cents. Some of the coins of different denominations look rather alike; study them until you can tell them apart. Small shops, buses, news agents, etc., keep little change; do not always expect them to be able to make change from your five-pound notes. If you change a substantial sum at a bank, take your money in five-pound notes, however, but not tens, for even larger stores and hotels outside London may have trouble changing these. Do not expect stores to take your dollars (although a few will do so) and keep in mind that the day has passed when all Europeans are eager for greenbacks. Currency rates fluctuate, so check the exchange rates daily.

Your hotel

During the hours when service is provided, it is generally better than in an American hotel. But, except in the major hotels in the larger cities, do not expect one-day laundry, assistance in parking your car, or baby sitters. The following points should be kept in mind.

1 Value Added Tax (V.A.T.) will be applied to the cost of your room and meals, so when calculating whether you can afford a particular hotel, find out the current rate in advance.

2 Most hotels charge on a bed and breakfast basis. This means that you pay a single sum for the night's lodging and the breakfast to follow, whether you eat the breakfast or not. The best meal of the day in Britain usually *is* breakfast, and it can be a hearty one, making a light lunch possible, and thus saving you both time and money. If uncertain, enquire when registering whether the charge includes full or Continental breakfast. You often will be charged double the single rate for double occupancy, rather than on a sliding scale, as in America.

3 All meals, except in the larger and fancier hotels, will consist of a set menu with at most two or three choices among the courses. Unless dieting, don't leave a course out, since you're paying for it. But eat what you order, for doggie bags are found only in a few steak houses belonging to a chain that is trying to be American. Lunch may be only three courses, dinner almost certainly will include an appetizer, on occasion a fish course, the entrée, vegetables (very probably including *two* types of potatoes) and a sweet (which is what you mean by dessert) or cheese. The appetizer is often, appropriately enough, called 'starters' where the atmosphere is informal. Coffee will usually be in demitasses and outside London will probably be served separately in the lounge after dinner, and at an extra charge. If you want to drink coffee with your meal you must ask for it. Water will seldom be served at your table automatically, the expectation being that you will order wine or beer, but your waiter will happily bring you water, quite likely iced these days, if you ask for it at the outset. Your coffee, whether at the table or in the lounge, will very likely come accompanied with two types of sugar, white and brown, and on occasion with large brown crystals. These dissolve slowly and turn the coffee into syrup. On the whole, English coffee is not good and the brown sugar makes it more palatable. Do not confuse the English salt shaker for sugar.

4 If you order a full bottle of wine, and do not finish it, and if you are staying at the hotel another day, feel free to have it kept for you with your room number marked on it.

5 Except at table, coffee may be served to you in railway buffets and in coffee shops with hot milk already added, so be quick to say if you want it black. If you really want cream rather than milk you must specify and expect to pay extra. Tea will also come with milk, and will need it, since English tea is served strong enough to corrode a spoon unless you ask for 'very weak tea without milk'. Quite often, whether at table or when having a separate afternoon tea, you will be presented with three pots, which you will come to distinguish by their shapes: one for tea, one for milk, and one for boiling water so that you may dilute to taste. The pots will often be of steel and the handles will burn your hand, so lift them with your serviette (or napkin). Most tea is properly brewed, the more traditional British finding tea-bags an abomination, and rightly so (although they are catching on all too rapidly) and once you have learned the mix between hot water and the tea itself which is proper for you, you will discover that tea is invariably better than coffee.

6 You can usually have early morning tea brought to your room to

help you wake up, often with a daily newspaper, if you order it the
night before. This is more pleasant than a wake-up call (and country
hotels may have no telephone in your room anyway). You can then
have a sip and a read while propped up in bed, before staggering out
to greet the day.

7 You can prop yourself up nicely, since most English beds come
equipped with two large pillows for each occupant, rather than our one
thin pillow. At first you'll find sleeping with two pillows strange, but
persevere, and you'll have fewer gastric problems in the mornings.
And if you're throbbing with good health, throw the damn things on
the floor.

8 Again, outside the large cities, you will not always find hot air
central heating in your room. You *will* find an electric space heater,
which has to be plugged in and switched on, and which will take the
chill off the room. But you will want to sleep under blankets except in
midsummer, for the room temperature will seldom climb above the
mid-60s F and at night will be much colder. You may also find your
bed turned down at night, a truly civilized custom, and, in smaller
country hotels, very likely a hot water bottle will be snuggled down
inside it. If not, feel free to ask for one.

9 In the country, your room itself will probably have a wash basin
in it but it may not have toilet, shower, or tub. The toilet is often called
a 'w.c.' (for water closet). It will be separate from the room containing the bath tub, so that two people may get on with doing their thing
at once. Showers are far less common than tubs – another reason why
that early morning tea is useful, since you can't always take a cold
shower to wake up. Remember to clean the tub after you have used it.
Your towels will be in your room and you're expected to take them to
the bath with you. Bring your own face cloth (flannel) and soap;
hotels do not provide the first and sometimes not the second. Most
bedrooms in London hotels have their own bathrooms.

10 At all times one is quiet – really quiet – in a British country
hotel. No singing in the bath. No loud noises or conversation at the
breakfast or dinner table. (When entering it is expected that you will
return to the same table you occupied for any previous meal, where
you may find your now soiled napkin in a napkin ring waiting for you
– though paper napkins are increasingly common; say a discreet 'good
morning' to the carpet or chandelier and otherwise keep your voice
down. The British are using these moments to order their thoughts.)

11 In restaurants and, less often, in hotel dining rooms, you may be
seated at a table already occupied, or someone may be brought to your

table. The British do not like to waste space by letting a party of two take up a table which will seat four. This startles Americans, who have in this regard a greater sense of privacy than the British. You are not expected to talk with anyone else at your table, however, after the briefest of greetings. (At breakfast, taking your newspaper to the table helps provide a means of getting through those silences which Americans seem to find embarrassing.)

12 You will find dogs are sometimes brought into dining rooms in the country. Merely reflect upon the British love for their pets, and note that the enforcement of health laws obviously differs from society to society. It is quaint of me even to remark on this.

13 The British are wine snobs. This probably stems from the fact that they produce few good wines of their own, since most people acquire a snobbery about knowledge which, when demonstrably mastered, also shows one to have travelled. Don't be put off by this, for you can drink better, and somewhat less expensive, wine in Britain than you generally can in the United States (setting aside some of the California wines) and you would be foolish indeed if you didn't seize the opportunity to taste some really good Sancerre (which doesn't travel well to America at all) or some excellent claret at medium prices for which you would mortgage your house at home. If in doubt, ask the wine steward, who will be helpful and very seldom superior. You can always simply ask for a carafe of the house wine, which will be potable, and the steward will produce an appropriate red or white to go with your main course. One may leave a separate tip for the wine steward, and if the restaurant or hotel is fancy enough to have one with a genuine chain and tastevin about his neck, then by all means do so. Otherwise, play this little problem by ear, but check whether tips are included as a percentage of the bill. Half bottles at lunch leave you sober enough to shop in the afternoon; full bottles invariably lead to foolish purchases. If you are driving on after lunch do not drink at all: British law on this point is severe, heavily enforced, and through the use of a breathalyzer, readily applied.

14 You must book ahead for all good hotels and restaurants. Under no circumstances should you arrive in a country town during the tourist season without a reservation, although if you dine at 12.30 or 6.30 promptly you may find an unbooked table. Keep in mind that the British like to travel too, and they will be on the road during school holidays (three weeks after Christmas, two to three weeks in March or April, and the whole of August) so that you may have problems even outside the June through August peak period. If driving, carry Ashley

Courtenay's *Let's Halt Awhile,* or *Egon Ronay's Guide* or the *Good Food Guide* (one is enough) in order to spot the good places, and the AA Members' Handbook for the run-of-the-mill but dependable hotels, and call ahead to book rooms from a roadside 'phone by lunch time. Tell them when to expect you and whether you will be taking dinner, or will arrive late enough for a cold supper (this means some cold meat and a green salad served between 9.00 and, perhaps, 11.00) to be kept waiting for you. Do not expect to get anything to eat or drink if you arrive after the witching hour.

Indeed, don't count on getting in at all. Outside London, small hotels often lock their outside doors at midnight. There will be a night bell somewhere near the main entrance, and if you push this long and loudly enough someone will come to admit you – usually, and if you are expected. But if you have no booking, the proprietor will probably ignore your rings even if there is a vacancy. Of course, this does not apply to the larger hotels in the bigger cities.

15 Above all, remember that meals are served at prescribed hours. If you arrive for lunch at 2.30, and lunch 'went off' at 2.00, you will not be served. You may be able to make arrangements for breakfast earlier than the set time, but other meals must follow the rules. Restaurants will often advise of 'last orders taken' times, and while you may sit over your coffee well after this time, do not expect to get an order in. In general, it is difficult to find any place in London which will take orders after 11.00; country hotels quite commonly stop serving the evening meal at 9.00 or 9.30. Conversely, do not expect hotels to serve you at 6.00, an uncivilized hour when you should be bathing. Dinner may begin at 7.00 or 7.30. This presents a problem when travelling with young children who find it hard to hold out until then, so keep a small supply of biscuits (cookies) on hand.

16 Only a luxury hotel would think of having a swimming pool or sauna, and, except in resort areas, playrooms are unusual. In such resort areas, the hotels will have anything American hotels do, but you will pay disproportionately more for luxury. In London, a room with private bath will cost twice as much as a room with a wash basin in it; ask yourself whether it is worth the cost of two nights' lodging to you to be able to relieve your bladder in your own room rather than fifty feet down the hall. If so, so be it; if not, don't forget to pack a bathrobe (called dressing gown in Britain) you are willing to be seen in, carry thin slippers, and even if you like to sleep in the altogether (and you won't once you are away from central heating) carry night clothes too. After all, a maid *is* going to come into your room to bring you that

early morning tea. Finally, carry a safety razor; you are likely to find that the bathroom sockets simply will not accept any of those fancy adaptors you brought with your electric razor.

Driving in Britain

Americans take pride in their adaptability, and yet the thought of having to 'drive on the wrong side of the road' robs many of them of much pleasure while in Britain. The British love to drive, think of themselves as among the world's most able car enthusiasts, and provide a landscape which is exceptionally lovely from the road. Drive you must, if you are to take advantage of all the tours outlined in this book, and drive you should if you wish to see Britain. To be sure, you can see more of the countryside from a railway carriage than you would in America, since the British frequently run their railway tracks along an embankment instead of through a trough, as we do. But obviously only the motor car allows you to move at your own schedule, to turn aside for that attractive pub or castle ruin, and to get a real sense of the country. Roads in Britain, while narrow by American standards, are well marked and safe, almost always paved, and, outside the major cities at least, no more crowded than at home.

Don't forget that the steering wheel is also on the wrong side of the car, and this you will quickly find compensates for any strangeness behind the wheel. Indeed, even driving an American car presents no real difficulties, except when overtaking (that is, when passing the car ahead) and when parking. Your rental car will be relatively small, and thus fitted to the narrower roads (it probably will also have manual transmission and will be without a number of those gadgets that you really don't need). You will get more miles to the gallon, both because the car is smaller and because the gallon is one-fifth larger in Britain. And within the first hour of driving, you will find that your sense of confusion will have left. That is, unless you are a confused driver when at home as well.

Of course, there are some differences in highway etiquette and gasoline station routine to which you should be alert.

1 In a large city, such as London, most cars will drive with their running or parking lights on at night, and without headlamps, even when dimmed (dipped). This seems a little mysterious, even romantic

at first, as though all those cars were hurrying to a secret rendezvous and did not wish to attract attention to themselves. If you feel uncomfortable driving at night without headlights on, use them: some drivers will blink their lights at you, but you are entirely within the law, as long as the headlamps are on low beam.

2 The British do not like noise, and they use the horn infrequently. You should do likewise, reserving it for a genuine emergency. Do not expect motorists who are overtaking you to warn you with their horn, and do not expect the use of your horn will make lorry drivers (truckers) move aside.

3 The British are not particularly courteous drivers, and despite their tendency to romanticize themselves when behind the wheel (if all Americans think they are Gary Cooper facing the villain in a shootout in *High Noon,* all Britons think themselves to be James Bond in an Aston Martin) not unusually able drivers. A serious sociological study – to the extent that any sociological study may be called serious – concluded a few years ago that Americans were the most disciplined drivers in the world, and the British stood well behind the Germans, Malaysians, and – yes! – the French. So be a defensive driver. Always come to a full stop at stop signs. Guard in particular against the two most prevalent British vices: they will overtake on hills and curves, at times Americans would regard as suicidal, and they will turn the motorways (turnpikes and thruways) into race courses, streaming by you (lane-hopping the while) even while you cruise a few miles above the speed limit. Let them commit suicide and keep well to the side on two-lane roads to avoid the oncoming steeplechaser. In other respects, the British are excellent drivers to have around: they give way at roundabouts punctiliously – always give way, unless signs state to the contrary, to all traffic from the right – and they keep the traffic flow moving, even in London, so that traffic jams like those experienced daily by New Yorkers seldom occur.

4 They do occur, however, and roads around cities are very heavily travelled. Try to avoid driving on British holiday weekends, and above all on Monday Bank Holidays – lie low in an attractive town and sightsee on foot – and anticipate heavy traffic when getting in or out of London. Do not calculate travel time in terms of miles; ask a knowledgeable Briton the distance to place X, and he will likely as not reply 'two hours' rather than 'fifty miles'. Except on motorways, a mean average of thirty to thirty-five miles in an hour, not allowing for specific stops for sightseeing outside the car, will be about right when calculating whether you have the time for a particular detour.

5 In Britain, you will find very few highway patrols. If you intend to motor far (to Scotland and back, say) or for long (a summer) join the Automobile Association or the Royal Automobile Club. They issue, in addition to the usual maps and listings of hotels, a key to strategically-placed roadside telephone boxes (or kiosks) which can be opened only with their key, and from which you can call their nearest affiliated garage for breakdown service. AA telephone boxes seem to be more frequent than RAC boxes; studies suggest that both respond in about the same time, which is substantially slower than the AAA in America, so be prepared for a wait. Their London addresses are: Automobile Association, Fanum House, New Coventry Street, W.C.2. Royal Automobile Club, RAC House, Landsdowne Road, Croydon.

6 Be prepared for generally poorer highway service than in America. Almost everywhere, highway cafes (kaffs in the vernacular) are truly gruesome. Gasoline stations will sell you gas, if you're patient, but they will not wash your windscreen (windshield), give you road maps, or offer you a clean toilet to use, and very likely they will check your oil and tyres (tires) only if asked to do so. I have driven in over fifty countries, and I have never encountered such surly ill-performance on the forecourt as in England. Service is marginally better in Scotland and Wales but don't count on it. If you do ask for one of these extra services, however normal you may think them in Seattle, be prepared to tip.

7 There are few areas of spoken English where differences between the American and British form can really lead to confusion. You know what a lift is and they know what an elevator is. But the parts of the automobile – our word – or motor car – their words – do provide an often embarrassing series of examples. The important words to know when trying to tell a garage attendant why your car won't run are:

AMERICAN	ENGLISH
hood	bonnet
trunk	boot
generator	dynamo
gear shift	gear lever
muffler	silencer
monkey wrench	spanner
oil pan	sump
fender	wing (and thus, wing mirrors)
license plate	number plate

That gasoline is petrol you know, that a parking lot is a car park you can figure out, and that a lay-by is a place for getting your car off the road you will be able to see. The other terms that you must be able to recognize while on the road are cul-de-sac for dead end, diversion for detour, flyover for overpass, subway for underground pedestrian passage (*our* subway is *their* Underground), level crossing for a grade crossing at the railway, off-side lane for the lane nearest the middle of the road, and near-side lane for that nearest the kerb (curb). Beware of vans (delivery trucks), lorries (trucks in general), articulated lorries (trailer trucks), estate cars (station wagons), and, when at those level crossings, of goods wagons (freight cars).

8 Observe the courtesy of the zebra. This is the striped crossing on the roadway, with blinking lights mounted on poles, that you will frequently encounter. The pedestrian has the right-of-way here at all times, and you are expected to come to a complete stop as soon as anyone puts a foot off the sidewalk at a zebra crossing. This is especially important, because school children count on your doing so.

9 You may either want to buy a British car and use it while abroad, or, more likely, will rent a car. I do not suggest prices here since they invariably change, but on balance they will be lower than in the States, although for a smaller car without power this-and-that, radio, or air conditioning (what would you do with air conditioning in Britain?). Make certain the car does have a good heater and that you understand how to operate it before you take it out on the road. Rental works as in the States, except that you should book your car definitely at least a day or so in advance, and you may be given little choice. You usually pay per the day and by the mile. A few agencies may ask for a deposit but most will not. Lower rates are given for extended rentals if negotiated in advance. Your credit cards will be accepted by most firms.

As to whom you should rent from: the back pages of *In Britain,* the handsome magazine you may subscribe to through the British Tourist Authority, 680 Fifth Avenue, New York City, or buy at a news agent in Britain, list local car hire services, with various vehicles, including vans. If you want a Rolls-Royce for the thrill of it, check the London telephone book. Most firms will provide a driver if you want, although you'll miss half the fun that way. The larger rental agencies can supply the car to you at the airport, although I recommend giving yourself a few days on foot and by taxi to adjust to the traffic. If you intend to drive widely throughout Britain, only three agencies can supply you in the smaller cities: Hertz, Avis and Godfrey Davis. The first two need no introduction. I use the third, for Godfrey Davis is Britain's most far-flung rental network, and although out of some one hundred occasions they failed me badly three times, they have the great convenience of being available whether you are in Salisbury, Leicester, Bangor or Belfast. (Their central booking clerk in London once told me I was their best customer.) Whatever agency you use, do not expect to be able to pick up a car in the middle of the night, and beware of the lunch break. Do not expect the cars to have been serviced as fanatically as in the States – you *will* find ashes in the ashtray. But you *can* drop the car at railway stations in the middle of the night, which is helpful.

10 An International Drivers Licence, available through your local AAA office, may be useful, but it is a bulky document akin to your passport. For the first six months, your American driver's license will be quite sufficient. If you stay longer, you will need to pass the British test, and it is much more strenuous than most American tests.

11 Under no circumstances should you drink and drive. You may as well be caught with heroin on you as alcohol on your breath.

12 In case of an accident do not try to hide behind your American passport. It will buy you nothing.

13 British emergency vehicles use distinctive sirens and bells; they do not sound like their American counterparts. Learn to recognize the sounds and get out of the way instantly.

14 The only time to be genuinely nervous is if you find yourself on a motorway at night in a heavy fog. (This is not uncommon in winter or spring, especially around such cities as Nottingham, or in Bedfordshire.) The British are quite mad at such times, hurtling through two-foot visibility at sixty miles an hour, and someone may ram you from behind. Stay very well to the left and, if possible, get off the road. Chain collisions in fog are unhappily frequent.

15 Picking up hitch-hikers is a good bit safer in Britain than in the States, but there have been enough incidents to suggest that you shouldn't.

16 If you go to Northern Ireland, fly and hire a car there; do not use the ferry. Ditto to the Channel Islands.

17 Buy a Highway Code (from a bookshop) and learn the international highway signs, now in use throughout all of Britain.

18 Most distances on British highways and maps are in kilometres, not miles.

Travelling by rail

Except for the obvious constraint that you must go where the tracks take you, rail travel in Britain is particularly pleasant. Any American, accustomed to commuting on our decaying trains over rough road-beds, peering through unwashed windows, sitting on ripped and stained seats and arriving an hour late at one's destination, will find European trains in general to be great fun. Although the British complain incessantly of the service given them by their nationalized railroad, they have little to complain about – except sometimes on Sundays when 'work on the line' tends to disrupt already reduced schedules. In over a hundred train journeys, only twice was I more than ten minutes late. Even more welcome is the fact that trains leave precisely on time. Stations are well marked, so that you need not guess where you are. And the finest breakfast in Britain is to be found on the longer British Rail runs, such as from London to Edinburgh departing from King's Cross every morning. Again, a few suggestions.

1 British trains generally have both first and second class cars, marked with appropriate numerals. Both will have non-smoking sections, clearly marked. For long journeys, the extra cost of first class is well spent, for the first class carriages offer more privacy, better service, and more comfort. But the second class carriages will arrive at the station at the same time.

2 As on the British Underground (or tube) you are not required to speak to other people and may observe a discreet silence, contemplating the countryside, should you be lucky enough to have a window seat. You may rustle a newspaper, *The Times* softly and the tabloids a bit more loudly, but you do not comment on the news to anyone else unless introduced – and you won't be. Riding in a crowded British railway carriage will give you a sense of being as close to anonymity as if you were to be set down in the land of the deaf. Take a good book – this one for example – to read.

3 A porter or steward will pass through the coach announcing meal times, often in two sittings. Ask for a card for one of them at once, and unless you have recently eaten take the earlier, since at least one course is bound to be 'off' by the second. If the train has no dining car, it may have a buffet car where you can get thin and unappetising sandwiches, tea or coffee, spirits, beer or cider and biscuits. This is also liable to run out of supplies on long journeys. An attendant may also come to your carriage and offer tea or coffee at mid-morning and

mid-afternoon; accept the paper cup offered, and in due course the drink will arrive. There will not be a separate bar car.

4 If you want to be certain of a seat at peak times, you should book it in advance at a travel agency, at one of the railway stations, or at a British Rail tourist office. This is especially necessary for long journeys, or you may find yourself standing, and it also makes it possible for you to arrive just before departure. A booking fee will be charged.

5 If you do not book in advance, be certain to arrive well before departure time, for queues at ticket windows are often long (be certain you are at the right window for both your destination and class) and all of the window seats will be taken at least fifteen minutes before getting under way. Try for a window seat near the dining car (usually at the middle of the train). On the run from London to Edinburgh, sit on the right-hand side of the train for the views of Durham, and, if you can, shift to the left side before Newcastle, and then return to the right.

6 Overnight trains have first and second class berths. They are no more comfortable than anywhere else in the world. Flying is better.

7 If you have much luggage, have your taxi driver put you down where the rare porters are. The porters will put your bags into your compartment on overhead racks and you should tip about 20p per piece. Railway platforms are long in Britain and porters often scarce at arrival; push your window down as the train glides in, shout 'porter' in an imperious voice, and one may appear. They will deliver you to the taxi queue; do not expect them to wait in the queue with you. If you can carry your bags, do so, for it will be much faster and will get you into that taxi queue well ahead of many others. Look for signs pointing to the taxi rank as you get off the train.

8 Trains stand at the platform at intermediate stops for only two or three minutes. Do not get off to buy sweets, cigarettes, or a newspaper, or you will be left behind.

9 On some British railway carriages you may enter directly through a number of doors in the side of the coach, into a small compartment. Half the seating will face backwards, so if that unnerves you, be certain to specify a forward facing seat when you book, or arrive doubly early.

10 In winter you may find the coaches very chilly by your standards so dress warmly.

11 Several cities, and London above all, have a number of railway stations. Do not expect a taxi driver to take you to 'the station', for you must know whether it is Paddington, Victoria, Waterloo, King's Cross,

St Pancras, etc. that you want. (If you forget, London taxi drivers will probably know if you tell them your intended destination, but don't count on it.) If you connect between trains, be certain whether you must get from one station to another. This is especially important in Glasgow, Manchester, Birmingham and, of course, London.

12 British Rail offers a number of special excursion fares and other price reductions. Linger in the railway stations long enough to read the posters and learn of them.

13 Most railway stations will have excellent news agents, and cafeteria-style coffee shops. If trains interest you, explore the book stalls, for the British publish an incredible variety of inexpensive books on old and new railroading.

14 Do not be afraid to ask for instructions. This is especially necessary if your train is made up in sections, with one section to be detached in the midst of a howling wilderness. Don't assume that all coaches on the Birmingham train will reach Birmingham; some may go to Aberystwyth. Ask.

15 If you value your sanity, and perhaps your life, avoid at all costs so-called 'football specials'.

16 Keep your ticket, as you will have to surrender it, either on the train or at the gate as you leave.

17 British Rail is divided into regional services. The Southern Region – south and east of London – does not fully qualify for the above praise about punctuality, cleanliness, and courtesy. Other regions come up to standard except in buffet cars, which have a way of becoming grotty quickly.

18 You can go to Paris, Brussels or Amsterdam by train. Night ferry trains leave from Victoria Station or Liverpool Street Station each evening.

19 If you like, you can arrange to have your car put on a train over the long distance – to Cornwall or to Scotland say – travel with it or a day behind it, and avoid the really long stretches of driving. You must book this well in advance. I do not recommend it.

20 British trains are one of the few places where you may be more comfortable if you do what was essential in the late 1940s: carry a small roll of soft toilet tissue (easily found in chemist shops) with you. British Rail uses two papers, both totally non-absorbent.

21 Whether you travel by train, bus, or air, if you want round-trip tickets, ask for return tickets, and if you are going only one way, ask for a single. When I've written of booking your ticket and carrying

your luggage, I have meant, of course, that you make a reservation and haul your baggage.

22 Combine rail with auto travel. This book is organized on the assumption that you will cover the more congested stretches of Britain by rail, and that having avoided the first fifty miles of driving outside London, you will then pick up a hire car at a railway station. As mentioned, Godfrey Davis has the greatest number of rental points, although their kiosks will generally not be as well placed at the really major rail stations as Hertz or Avis.

The British fascination with their railways is natural. Britain was the first country to be transformed by the train, and today the entire nation is a museum to the industrial revolution, if you keep your eyes open. At Darlington, on the London to Edinburgh run, you will be able to look out of the train and see George Stephenson's first railway engine on the platform. In a dozen places, but notably on the Vale of Rheidol railway from Devil's Bridge to Aberystwyth, in Cardiganshire, you can ride on narrow-gauge steam trains. By writing to The Transport Trust (at 138 Piccadilly, London W.1) you can buy the Transport Museum Register, a guide to over seventy museums devoted to transport. Even if trains don't turn you on but merely get you there, you'll want to see the fine Railway Museum in York and perhaps the Tramway Museum at Matlock, in Derbyshire.

Speaking of transport leads to other museums as well. The London Taxi Cab Museum, while small, is fun (at 1–3 Brixton Road); the Montagu Motor Museum at Beaulieu, Hants., features over a hundred motor cars; the National Maritime Museum in Greenwich is the world's finest museum dedicated to ships; the Waterways Museum at Stoke Bruerne, Towcester, in Northamptonshire, encompasses two centuries of canal boating and is absolutely fascinating; and the Shuttleworth Collection, at Biggleswade, in Bedfordshire, has two dozen aircraft from 1909, many still capable of flying, at least on the last Sunday of each summer month. And pick up a slim little booklet, *Discovering London Railway Stations,* by John Camp (or write to Shire Publications, Tring, Herts.), which provides both a history and a guide to each of the stations, themselves monuments to the transportation revolution.

Travelling by bus

Bus travel in Britain is cheap and efficient. Even if you would not consider travel by bus in the States, you need have no hesitations here. The major touring bus companies operate excellent services to places of most interest to the tourist. Most advertise in *In Britain*, if you wish to write for advance information, and they can also be found in the 'yellow pages'. Frames at 25/31 Tavistock Place, London, and 185 Madison Avenue, New York, is one of the most extensive. You may book seats in order to assure a window view, and if you do not rent a car, and have the time that bus travel inevitably takes, you will find the bus-eye view a closer and more intimate one than the train's.

Generally there are four types of bus service: the strictly tourist, all seats sold for specific tours; the long distance buses to carry you from London to Manchester, etc.; the Green Line coaches; and the London (or other municipal) buses. The Green Line coaches operate out of London into the surrounding countryside and are a pleasant, often meandering, way of spending a day moving from village to village. They may also be the best means of getting from London to a specific site relatively nearby in, say, Sussex, and you can board them throughout the city wherever you encounter green bus signs. In general they operate up to a 40 mile range. You may buy a guide to the Green Line routes at any London tube station.

The London buses are red, as we all know from countless movies. If you can, ride in the front seats on the top deck of the magnificent double-deckers for a superb view of London's busy street life. I often spend my first day in London simply riding, rather at random, these buses, letting the feel of the city soak back into me. You do not pay as you get on (and getting on may require that you queue, at signs for red buses) but rather as the conductor comes through the coach. State your destination and he sells you a ticket priced according to the distance. Keep the ticket until you leave, for an inspector may ask for it. On the newer, single-deck, buses, you enter at the front and pay, depositing the appropriate coin in a slot to release the barrier (although the driver *can* make change, if you lack it). There are now, unhappily, far more single- than double-decker buses. The buses all prominently display their route number and final destination; if you arm yourself with the Geographers' Map of London you should have little difficulty.

Travelling on the Underground

On balance, the British Underground is the best in the world. I collect undergrounds, and have ridden them in dozens of cities. Some (Montreal) are cleaner, and some (Hamburg) are faster, and some (Lisbon) are cheaper. But none are so much fun, so efficiently organized, or so well marked. If you can get lost on the London Underground for long you would get lost in your own back yard. Each of the major routes is marked in red, blue, green, etc., each station is abundantly lighted and posted and full maps of the central area appear in every coach. If the New York subway were not already a disgrace, London would show it to be so.

The etiquette of survival is simple. Either purchase your ticket at a window so marked, stating your destination and paying according to distance, or, if you have the correct change, drop the coins into ticket machines that may stand nearby. If you hold a yellow ticket, you will have to pass it into a slot at the barrier, to have it pop out at you as you pass through. Keep the ticket and surrender it at the end of your journey to the uniformed person at the exit. Usually you will descend by escalator (if so, defy British custom; in this case, keep to the right, so that those in a hurry may run down on your left). Follow the signs to your platform, study the suggestive and even happily indecent advertisements for lingerie that abound only in the Underground – something fitting there – and as soon as the train comes to a stop and the doors open, take a seat or at peak hours struggle to squeeze in before the doors close. They will not close on you, never fear. Watch for stations carefully, especially if you're straphanging, so as not to overrun. If you have a seat, keep it for all except the infirm and ladies with babies in arms, unless you want to be more polite than the British, which in the Underground is not hard. Guard your billfold if in a crush. Do not talk to anyone, avoid trying to read someone else's newspaper, and pretend to be reading the advertisements with care: the Underground is, above all, the place where you must not appear to be interested in your fellow human beings. Rather, show yourself to be a student of this mode of transport by ostentatiously reading one of London Transport's many guides to the Underground, starting with that best-seller, *Sixty Years of the Piccadilly,* which will tell you as much as you really need to know about Cammell Laird trailer cars *circa* 1920.

Travelling by taxi

The London taxi equals the double-decker red bus as the prime symbol of London to the visitor. London's taxi drivers must pass an extraordinarily difficult examination, and they are among the most informed and skilful drivers in the world, making New York drivers look like your twelve-year-old son. They are also generally, although not invariably, courteous. The taxi's engine makes a distinctive noise, like a loud and poorly-oiled sewing machine, and you will know whether one is at hand without looking back. They seat two to three comfortably, and two more on drop seats. You can control your own windows and heat from a switch, and best of all, will have an abundance of leg room, room for your bags (the driver will put large ones in a cubicle up front with him) and be able to sit bolt upright to see the passing parade. All taxis are metered, although there may be a surcharge (if so, a notice of it will be posted on the window) and there are extra charges for bags (if outside the passenger compartment), additional passengers and after midnight. No taxi driver is compelled to take you further than seven miles, and you may have to cajole to get him to do that, especially if late at night.

The taxi is a great friend, but it can also be annoying. A few hints may help it to be the former.

If the driver is going off shift, or is hungry, he may simply sail by and ignore your upraised hand. Shouting Chicago endearments at him will do no good.

To get a taxi, step boldly to the edge of the sidewalk, or into the street, extend your hand or umbrella well into the air, and shout 'taxi'. Several other people more experienced than you may be doing the same, especially if it is raining, so be firm, and also place yourself midway up the block on the appropriate side so that you are seen before they are.

There is no point in going through this exercise unless the yellow light on the top of the cab, which says 'Taxi', is on. One wonders at the number of people (presumably strangers) one sees on London streets raising their commanding hands to darkened cabs.

If you are courteous, and it is not raining, tell the driver your destination before you get in. However, he may then refuse you, and it is harder for him to do so if you are already seated. He may not legally refuse you if it is not after midnight, if your destination is not seven miles away (but he may take your American accent as a give-away that you haven't the slightest notion how far it is from Hampstead to St. Paul's), if you do not have excessive luggage, and if you are not drunk. But he may try to. In such cases, as well as in those not uncommon instances where the driver suggests he will only take you 'all the way out to X in this stinking weather' – a common line after midnight – for double the fare on the meter, simply take his number from the plate prominently displayed facing you as you sit down, and tell him that you will report him to the authorities. This does not always work, but it often does, and you are well within your rights. And then do report him (see the telephone directory under London Taxi Authority).

Do not argue with the driver about the route he is taking, even if yesterday you went from the same place A to place B by a patently different route. London's streets are a maze of one-way paths, and the nature of traffic on them changes markedly depending upon the time of day. Temporary 'road up ahead' (which means under repair) signs change today from yesterday. London drivers may try to charge you double on those long after-midnight journeys, but they do not try to cheat by taking you on the wrong route, and they will almost never shortchange you.

Talk to the driver. Some are fascinating. One told me of a book on Wittgenstein he was writing, another provided me with a succinct summary of IRA activities in Northern Ireland, and a third provided an informed critique of Common Market policy not bettered by *The Sunday Times*.

When you alight, close the door for the driver, check for that collapsible umbrella left behind, and tip reasonably well.

Do not take a taxi at all in the area bounded by Oxford Street, Regent Street, Pall Mall and Park Lane during peak hours, unless you are tired, for you will be able to cover this area faster on foot than the taxi can in driving it.

If you are shy about hailing a taxi, have the hotel ring for one for you.

As everywhere, taxis are hard to find (a) when it rains, (b) after the theatre, (c) when you are late for that important luncheon appointment at Buckingham Palace, and (d) when you want one.

Outside London, taxis are not necessarily of the same type, quite often being normal motor cars with a small illuminated sign mounted on top. The rest of the advice applies, however, except that in such instances you will be appreciated more if, as a single, you are egalitarian and sit up front with the driver. (You may not do this in London.)

Travelling by air

You would be well advised to avoid internal British airlines where possible. I have found the food poor, the service often a blend between nanny-sharp and surly, and the departures late. These strictures do not apply to flying British Airways to Britain, which is a pleasant way to introduce yourself into British cuisine and custom as early as possible, nor do they apply to Aer Lingus. The British like to say that BOAC meant Better on a Camel, but this was hyperbole; the major internal airline, BEA, had rather harsher and more accurate titles attached to those initials. Both are now amalgamated as British Airways, but this has not brought much improvement in conditions. I once had a booking clerk throw my bag at me when I said that he was making me late for my flight by chatting up his girl friend, I have repeatedly been asked to move from a seat in which a stewardess has seen me laboriously installing myself, and one domestic flight out of three departed not just late, but quite late. The image of the pleasantly competent airline stewardess is like that of the polite London bobby, nearly gone. Frankly, I can recommend no survival tactics when you find that you must take to the air internally in Britain, other than that you grin and bear it, do not plan anything that depends upon arrival on time, and take an abundance of reading matter – much more than you think you will need. The usual cigarettes, scarves, perfume and alcohol are sold in flight, to the delay of your meal; there will be no movies; and if you are on a Viscount, you may be seated backwards.

Despite the inconveniences, air travel is fast and sometimes unavoidable. Heathrow airport is intelligently organized, as are some of the smaller airports. You might consider flying from London to Aberdeen, in the north of Scotland, and then motoring south, if you haven't time to drive both ways, and if you mean to get to the Shetland or Orkney Islands, or to the Channel Islands, you will almost certainly want to fly. Definitely fly if going to Northern Ireland or Eire – the ferries are bad news. And on international flights, to Geneva or Paris or Frankfurt, British Airways proves that it can compete very well indeed. In short, one suspects that here is a proof of the theory that service deteriorates where there is no competition, since the airlines must get in and dig when flying overseas, while having a monopoly on most routes within Britain.

Using the telephone

Courtesy on the British telephone is far higher than in America, efficiency far lower. Some delightful services are provided: in London you may ring up (see the front of the telephone directory) to hear a recording on the day's events, or on tourist attractions – this in several different languages – or on the weather, or to obtain the time. You may, for a small fee, have the telephone operator call you even in your own home with an early-morning wake-up call. And you may expect polite and unruffled service which will help you unravel your problem if the directory is of no help. The service will often come with a male voice behind it, which seems to surprise Americans.

Be certain to read the instructions on the box. For the newer telephones have a few 10p coins in your pocket at all times.

Against the courtesy and variety of service, you may cast some disadvantages. The incidence of wrong numbers is high, connections often are bad, you may have a long wait on trunk calls (long distance calls), an extraordinary number of public telephone boxes – those red kiosks you see standing about – will be out of order, will have been used as a urinal, and will lack telephone directories, and you may be disconnected during silent periods unless you whistle, mutter, or murmur into the telephone.

The telephone directory is exceedingly cumbersome and wildly unhelpful. For London it consists of several volumes, and the book for E to K will be precisely the one missing from the kiosk when you need it. (You then ring inquiries, not information.) The idea of 'yellow pages' is growing, but many areas will not have such a directory, so you often must have the precise name of the store you wish to call, and will need to know the country well enough to call Boots the Chemist when you want a drug store, not a chemistry set, and the off licence when you're after a liquor store.

British etiquette on the telephone is courteous but terse, and it is sometimes taken by Americans as rude. Ring a shop to ask whether they have product X and if the answer is 'No' they will say so and immediately hang up; none of this 'bye-bye' bit, and little information beyond exactly what you ask for. People often identify themselves by number, seldom by name. Although they can hear you clearly, they will often say 'are you there?' which is meant as a holding action. You ring up people rather than giving them a call. Speak slowly; your accent may seem strange. And if you fear germs, Britain is one country where you may hire a professional sterilizing service to come and clean your telephone monthly.

In private homes you may see a small box or cup near the telephone. This is meant for your quiet deposit of the cost of the call, for in Britain the home telephone may be billed per call, whether local or not.

Central switchboards at business establishments are often under-manned. Let them ring longer than you would in the States.

In an emergency, ring 999 and state which service – Fire, Police or Ambulance – you want and the location of the telephone kiosk from which you are calling. It will be printed on the telephone directly in front of you.

Going to the theatre

One of the glories of Britain is the theatre. This is true outside London as well as in. The British seem to have an innate sense of acting. Their lower-middle- or working-class comedies tend toward the slapstick and barnyard, and are often based on local terms which befuddle the American, but virtually all other British theatre can be understood by anyone who respects the English language. The British are literate theatre goers and may well laugh at points you find too topical, subtle or obscene for your taste. They place less emphasis on costume and set than New York does and more on relishing the lines, whether of the classics or of modern theatre. At any given time there will be a dozen good plays on in London well worth your attention, ranging from Shakespeare, done only as those whose native tongue he wrote can do it, to frothy bedroom comedies intended for ladies down from Liverpool. Perhaps of all Britain's cultural events, the theatre stands first, and while learned critics, largely American, profess to find the American theatre more alive, you couldn't prove it by me.

It is said that British theatre is cheaper than American. This is so if you purchase the least expensive seats, in 'the gods' (the very upper rows of the balcony, often on a standing basis) or in the upper balconies. But orchestra seats in the middle of the fifth row will cost very little less than such seats in New York. Think about what you will be seeing before you buy: balcony seats are excellent for the many fine Christmas productions for children, the pantomimes and musicals, while you will want to be close to the action if Shaw or Pinter dialogue is what counts.

As a cultural pilgrimage, you should go to the National Theatre at least once. To Sadler's Wells at least once. To Covent Garden (opera) once, and perhaps the Haymarket (classic straight plays), Drury Lane (big musicals) and the Garrick (farce) once. Certainly to the Royal Festival Hall to hear one of the major London orchestras, even if you don't care for music, for the hall is magnificent. Definitely to the Royal Albert Hall. To Gilbert and Sullivan when in season. Perhaps even to see *The Mousetrap,* that venerable record-breaker of all time. And to the Royal Court (avant garde drama). Matinees are considerably less expensive than evening performances, and two plays a day is by no means too much to take.

If you come to Britain on a package tour which provides you with theatre tickets, too bad, for the tickets you will be offered are intended to appeal to the lowest common denominator, defined so low that the fact you can read this book puts you outside that pale. Still, some of your tickets may be for those venerable theatres mentioned, and simply sitting in them, even if in the presence of a vacuous farce, is an Experience to be Cherished.

You should book your seats in advance (although if you are alone, and not going to a red hot hit, you probably can buy a single seat at the theatre booking office). Your hotel porter will do advance booking for you, and booking agents abound. They will charge a fee, of course. You will be given a ticket which often must be exchanged at the theatre box office for the real thing, so arrive a few minutes early. The better and larger theatres will have a so-called crush bar, and often a buffet, so that you may have a snack at the theatre before the play if you wish. At intermissions you may either press to the bar (where you will find why it is called crush) for a drink (here there is no queuing and you simply must be firm and fleshy about it, booming out your order over any little old ladies who are misfortunate enough to be in your way; if you don't, they will) or to a separate counter for coffee. Sellers will circulate down the aisles with cartons of orange squash, ice cream and boxes of candy, so you need not leave your seat. If you order it from one of the ladies in advance, they will bring you tea or coffee on a tray. You should tip them. Cast lists are not usually given away free, and you should buy one if you expect to understand what is going on. As an audience the British will be quieter than Americans unless at the cinema (movies) where they talk more, or unless they are rattling candy wrappers behind you, which is common. A piercing 'Shush' on your part will bring silence rather than a physical attack, as it might at home. Do not expect to be seated, if you arrive late, until an intermission. If you wish to rent opera glasses, you will often find them attached to your seat, removeable by dropping a coin into a slot. Scores for musical events may usually be purchased at a stall in the foyer.

The theatre starts earlier in London than in America, and unless you hurry your dinner, it is better to wait and have an after-theatre dinner in a good restaurant. You must book this in advance, and 10.30 will generally be the latest you can be seated. The curtain may go up as early as 7.00, and certainly by 8.00, in order to meet the demands of public transportation, which runs down rapidly from 11.00 on. In general, the British tend to dress more for the theatre than we do; if you want to flaunt your Americanness, by all means wear a Hawaiian shirt outside your trousers, for no one will enforce a coat and tie rule on you, but expect some searching looks as well. Ladies frequently wear floor-length dresses to the theatre. For the cinema, on the other hand, be as sloppy as you wish. And be prepared to stand in a long queue unless you have bought your tickets in advance – for you may book most movie seats as well.

Need you be told not to applaud between movements at a concert? Certainly not. Neither need you be told that 'God Save the Queen' may begin the concert, to a roll of drums, and that however anti-monarchist you may feel, you owe the orchestra the courtesy of standing. The anthem is seldom heard anymore at the end of a performance in the cinema or theatre, as once was common, and it never has been heard at the beginning of athletic contests, the British not being given to think that they must relate the pledge of allegiance to the flag to the opening of school each day, so your only chance to stand to someone else's anthem may come when the orchestra plays.

Incidentally, the balcony may be called the gallery; the first balcony will certainly be called the upper circle; and the mezzanine will be the dress circle. Nor, despite what I have said, will you be seated in the orchestra, for this would annoy the players; you will take your seat in the stalls.

Your enjoyment of the theatre will be enhanced if you buy, from London Transport, a thin paperback by W. Macqueen-Pope called *Theatregoer's London,* which is a history of each theatre with a guide to what to gaze upon during the intervals.

Words: making oneself understood

Everyone knows George Bernard Shaw's quip that the Americans and the English are two peoples divided by a common language. Actually, vocabulary as such will give you relatively little trouble, for by now the British have moved to a mid-Atlantic position under the influence of much American music, many tourists and all those movies. And Americans from the East Coast have always known that an apartment is a flat and how to pronounce words like 'greasy'. Still, accent, intonation and rhythm will give you trouble, especially in rural areas (and above all in Scotland, in Cornwall and Devon and in Northumberland) and you will give the British trouble, since they think all Americans either sound like the Kennedys, or maybe George Wallace. Just speak as you always would and educate your English friends by using those American words. Call every woman 'Mam', say things like 'I reckon' and 'I allow as how', and 'at this point in time' and 'my statement is inoperable' and they will figure you for the genuine article. But if you expect to be understood in a hurry, there are a few words you had best forget and instead think of Anglicizing your speech for the duration of your visit.

One category of such words has to do with the automobile (see the section on *Driving in Britain*). Another category has to do with shopping (which see). A number of isolated words of importance are dropped into context throughout this guide. A few others remain to be noted.

The British may call you a Yankee even though you may be from Georgia. Don't be offended and don't waste your breath correcting it.

In turn, don't call the English Limeys. Or the Scots Scotch. Scots are the people, Scotch the drink.

Don't expect the BBC, Greer Garson or the Beatles to represent common speech. There is no common British speech. Just listen: it will be perfectly comprehensible if you don't begin by blocking it all out.

The waitress may call you 'luv' or, less often, 'ducks' or 'dear'. She is not propositioning you, and may not even be friendly. Do not reply in kind.

Beware of phrases like, 'It's just a little way along the road'. To the British 'a little way' may mean half a mile.

The important words include 'Could you please?' and 'Thank you' and a crisp 'Sorry' – use them.

The pavement is the sidewalk, the zebra is a crossing, tinned goods are canned, nappies are diapers, teats are baby bottle nipples, a cot is a crib, a pram is a baby buggie, a wire is a telegram, unless it goes overseas when it becomes a cable; a wallet is a billfold, suspenders are garters, tights are pantie hose, plimsolls are sneakers, braces are suspenders, vests are undershirts, while waistcoats are vests; and of course a public school is a private school and a state school is a public school. You want a sticking plaster when a band-aid is called for, a clothes peg for pin, drawing pin for thumb tack, and you will have, rather than take, a bath, after running water from the tap. A socket is a point, sellotape will stick things together while scotchtape will only confuse the issue, and if you want thread, ask for cotton (unless you want a spool of the stuff, when you ask for a reel of cotton). If someone mentions a geyser (pronounced geezer) he will betray that he is over forty, and will be referring to a gas water heater that has to be turned on to prepare your bath water. At restaurants you ask for the bill, not the check, and a cheque is a check. Sweets, plural, is candy, while the sweet is dessert. The garden may or may not have flowers in it – it's merely the yard, and if the British ask whether you have a garden, and you say 'No', despite your rolling acre of green lawn, they'll assume you to be a flat dweller. You play with a pack, not a deck, of cards, the leaves turn in the autumn, and two weeks make a fortnight. The subway is the Underground or, in slang, the tube. The quay is pronounced key. A zero is a nought, the letter Z is pronounced zed, a period on the page is a full stop, and if your trip bombs, it is a total disaster. If you carry a torch (flashlight) you are less likely to bomb.

Functionally, however, the three most important matters to have clearly in mind are: (a) The first floor is called the ground floor in Britain, and if you are directed to the first floor, you should go to the second floor, *et seq.* (b) Do not look for a john, and avoid other silly euphemisms. If you ask for a bathroom you are liable to be directed to a room where you may take a bath. Ask for the lavatory or toilet in a house, a cloakroom in a restaurant, and the public convenience when desperate out of doors. (c) If you want your drink straight, ask for it neat, and if you want your beer cold say so in plain American.

Food and drink

There is a widespread belief among almost all non-Britons that food in the United Kingdom is uninspired, overcooked and plainly bad. This is quite untrue, as this guide attempts to make clear. One can eat exceedingly well while in Britain, and if one uses any of the better guides to dining out, one should have few occasions for complaint. Food in Britain *was* bad in the 1950s, but since then a stream of foreigners have come into the country to give it the most cosmopolitan air of any in Europe. Italian, French, Pakistani and Indian restaurants abound; there are excellent Spanish, Scandinavian, German, Greek, genuinely authentic Chinese of a number of varieties, Malaysian and even American establishments. For variety Britain exceeds France and for cost is cheaper than Germany. To be sure, there is no *vin ordinaire*, and the average meal in a village pub will be well under the standard of the average meal in a French village of similar size. Further, I say that food in Britain can be excellent, not that British food in Britain is necessarily so. It is still true that a really good British meal – of roast beef, Yorkshire pudding, roast potatoes and crisp Brussels sprouts, for example – is very difficult to find. The British overcook their vegetables, they are improving in their grasp of the green salad but still have a long way to go, and the idea of serving two kinds of potatoes, neither very good, persists. Nonetheless, one often finds quite good meals based on this classic English menu, and if you combine these with the use of the many foreign restaurants, you should be able to eat well.

There are distinctive regional dishes, of course, and it is always fun to search these out. Surely eating is one of life's activities to which the advice of 'anything once and nothing twice lest I like it' should be applied. To go abroad and eat hamburgers is uneconomic, cowardly, parochial and several other nasty things. To try regional foods is admittedly a way of having some dishes one doesn't like, but whoever told you life was a bed of roses anyway?

On the whole the best bet in Britain, unless well away from the coast – which is difficult to achieve – and well out of season, is seafood. Dover sole can usually be counted on, and together with a simple green salad (which will probably be truly simple, with oil and vinegar on the side) and a glass of white wine, makes a dependable lunch. The sole is done a variety of ways, and you should tell the waiter whether you want it off the bone or not, for it will not be filleted automatically for you. Try, in particular, Dover sole Walewska, or Veronique, when it is offered. Plaice, an underrated fish, is usually good. And of course you will want to have fish and chips (the latter are French fries, while our potato chips are called crisps), although getting them over the counter and wrapped in the traditional sheet of newspaper is becoming increasingly difficult in an ever-more health-conscious society. Salt them yourself and, as a frightful experiment, do as the British do and add vinegar from a shaker bottle that will be nearby.

Oysters are usually excellent in season, served raw in their shells, and Whitstables above all, although they may be a bit large by your standards. At stalls along the seaside, and from vendors at outdoor markets, you can often sample jellied eel, cockles and mussels and winkles. Don't hesitate to ask how to eat them – everyone knows that Americans don't. You will want to try kippers for breakfast once, although unless you try several times and get the hang of them, their hair-like bones will defeat you. There is also kedgeree, in the Lake District you can sometimes get char, which is not as good as the Arctic char so popular in Canada, and for the name alone have bloaters (most readily found in Essex and East Anglia) which are cured herring. Any shrimps you have will be small; the best are probably from Harwich. On occasion you can find cockle soup, and the scampi are usually good.

Scotland offers two of the best fishes. Salmon is a widespread dish in season, which you can have in England also, grilled, poached, or served cold with fresh mayonnaise (if you see bottles of the stuff sitting about, don't order it). Smoked salmon, sliced very thin, is expensive and exceedingly good, certainly better than the Nova Scotian salmon to which you may be accustomed. And Scotland also offers Arbroath smokies, which are small smoked haddocks and very good indeed.

Meat is generally less good in Britain than in the States, and becoming quite dear (expensive). The cuts of meat are different, and should you have to go to the butcher's, you'll have a difficult time at first. Rather than asking for your usual cut, describe the portion of the animal you're after. When eating out, the meat portions are likely to be small, and very small by Californian standards, so don't omit a course at the hotel under the impression that too much will be brought to you. You will want to have roast beef, of course, cut at your table in the better restaurants, and best eaten as red as possible, although in Scotland it will come in suitably well done. In the poorer places, you'll get a fatty slice or two with a weak gravy and a Yorkshire pudding that looks like a deflated popover, but in the best tradition it will be well raised, light, and quite close to a sopapilla.

On the whole avoid the vegetables if eating British.

Sausages can be very good and come in a variety of shapes and sizes. You can make a good pub meal from the counter, over your beer or ale, off the sausages (on which you add English mustard, which is hot and similar to Chinese), small meat pies and a Scotch egg (a hard-boiled egg covered with sausage meat and fried, served cold). Horse-radish sauce, but not horseradish, is standard. Another obligatory dish is steak and kidney pie, which is often very good, and steak and kidney pudding, which is a suet pudding and about as good as you would expect. Try bangers and mash once too – that's sausages with mashed potatoes. By then you'll be ready for tripe (the lining of the cow's stomach) which the French can do things with and the British can't.

There are some other good things awaiting you, however. Devils on horseback are a kind of rumaki: kidneys wrapped in bacon. Oysters come this way too. A Cornish pasty can be very good, especially in Cornwall itself, served hot. Lamb is generally good in Britain, and with both mint sauce and mint jelly, and new potatoes, makes an excellent meal. The mutton is sometimes local, as are the breakfast sausages, so a happy experience one place does not guarantee a happy one elsewhere – but also vice-versa. York ham is excellent. And in Scotland you will want to inflict haggis upon yourself. This is a pudding made from the heart, liver, and sometimes entrails, of a sheep, with suet, onions and oatmeal, and boiled in the stomach of the sheep. It is not as bad as it sounds, and fortunately for you, is some-times available in tourist restaurants or at the New Year.

There are two high points and one low point in most British meals. The low point comes at the start, for their notion of appetizers, hors d'oeuvres, and even of soups (except for Cockaleekie and Scotch broth in Scotland, and mulligatawny in the ubiquitous Indian restaurants) is uninspired. This may be made up for at the sweet course, however, and almost certainly at the cheese course (only major places will offer both, and you may have to choose, or pay extra for the cheese, which comes last). Caramel custard is usually good, deep dish pies (with a crust only on the top) when berries are in season are excellent, and the various puddings are often better than one has any right to expect. Try gooseberry pie in particular, or gooseberry fool (puréed with custard and cream); summer pudding (bread and five fruits, with blackcur-rants dominant); trifle (sponge cake, custard and fruit jelly) and above all, English strawberries with double cream, over which you will shake sugar from a sugar caster. In the best restaurants there will always be a sweet trolley which you may have brought to the table, so that you can choose visually. And a piece of fruit will usually be at hand as well.

If I must choose, I invariably have cheese. France may have more kinds, and is certainly more famous for them, but I know of no cheese that can rival a ripe Stilton, dug out from the wheel with a silver scoop. Caerphilly is a superb semi-hard cheese from Wales with a taste similar to buttermilk (it is often sold too young, for it should be aged six months). Cheddar, of course, is the staple cheese of Britain and has become standardized. It is often kept too long on the cheese board and is too dry, since it is laid by in quantity. Wensleydale, a cow's milk cheese, is commonly white but may also be blue, when it has a taste of honey. Double Gloucester, a close, crumbly cream cheese cured for six months, is a bit more acid than the slightly pallid single Gloucester. Derbyshire is a moist, thick cow's cheese matured for nine months and will be found in the Midlands, as will Derby Sage. Leicester is a dry, firm, skim-milk cheese cured for three months; Blue Leicestershire is rare. And of course Cheshire is also a major English cheese, although produced in limited quantities and a poor traveller. On occasion you may find a Blue Cheshire, and if so have it and count yourself lucky. Dorset Blue Vinny, once aged in cider, is very hard to find. Most of these cheeses may be purchased in quarter-pound pre-packed cellophane (although Stilton can come in a crock) and one of them eaten while driving, with an uncut loaf of bread, saves time and money and gives one the heady sense of being a free person. If you want to sample the cheeses, go to Paxton and Whitfield, the specialist cheese shop on Jermyn Street in London. And unless the cheese board at the restaurant is lavish and clearly fresh, stick to the English cheeses. You may, incidentally, direct the waiter to give you 'a bit of this and a bit of that', pointing them out, and so need not restrict yourself to a single cheese.

Don't forget tea time. You may save yourself the cost of a meal by having a good tea, and roadside places which advertise Devonshire teas in particular will help to fill you up at little cost, and in places where you might not otherwise wish to eat. A cream tea will include scones and jam; you can also have an assortment of cakes – you pay only for those you eat, not the entire tray brought to you – and less often of sandwiches. A Scottish high tea, on the other hand, truly is a meal, served around 5.00 p.m., and substitutes for dinner (although not for a 10.00 o'clock supper).

Probably you know that sandwiches in England are very thin, emasculated and often unappetizing. You will want several for a meal. They are likely to be made of anything, including scrambled egg, mustard and cress, tomatoes (not as an extra – the tomato is the entire filling) and once (for me) spaghetti. Where possible, get a look at a tray of the things before ordering.

Finally, there are a few highly local foods which cannot be found outside a very restricted area, so that there is no point in being on the lookout for them unless travelling nearby. Of course, the attachment of a placename to a food does not always mean that it is local: Banbury cakes (similar to our Easter cakes with a cross) may be found far from Banbury, Bakewell tarts occur all over the land, and you don't have to go to Melton Mowbray for pork pies, although it helps. You may find soft baps all over Scotland and the North of England (these are soft, floury bread rolls), hard rolls in the South, and shortbread (a form of cookie) and porridge (a form of punishment, but useful on cold winter mornings) all over Scotland. Oatcakes too. But just try to find Kendal mint cake outside the Lake District (except in some health food shops). This is, in fact, simply a slab of hard sugar, minty and often brown. Or try and track down Atholl Brose outside limited areas of Scotland (and this, being a purée of honey, oatmeal and whisky, is well worth looking for); or mead – a drink from fermented honey – outside Devonshire, Cornwall, or a really large London wine shop.

The following books may be particularly helpful. Through the 1982 volume Christopher Driver edited the *Good Food Guide,* which is revised annually; it is much the best. The most recent editions include sections on pubs and wine bars as well as on hotels and restaurants.

Egon Ronay's Guide, also revised frequently, includes a larger number of places and, while less discriminating, is also more valuable when in the Wilderness. Ronay also does an interesting *Coffee Guide to London.*

Ashley Courtenay's *Let's Halt Awhile in Great Britain*, actually a guide to hotels, inns, and guest houses and rather given to making comments on the pattern of the wallpaper, sometimes has useful comments on food as well.

Margaret Costa, herself proprietor of one of London's most interesting restaurants, Lacy's, has written *London at Table,* a guide produced by *Gourmet* magazine. The descriptions are serious and a bit over-long but they make for mouth-watering reading while sitting in Omaha.

Sandy Lesberg's *Economy Gourmet Guide: London,* purports to list low-priced good food places. I gave up at page 31, when I encountered the words 'a surprisingly friendly atmosphere' in the description of the rudest restaurant in London, and the information that Ingrid Bergman frequented the place. But perhaps you like Ingrid Bergman more than good service?

The *Michelin* guide to London is very French and to my view idiosyncratic. This may be a tautology.

Jonathan Routh's *Good Cuppa Guide* tells you where to have tea in London. It's a good read. Routh's other guide is both funnier and more important: *The Good Loo Guide, or Where to Go in London.*

The *Good Pub Guide* is likewise.

And *Harpers Queen Magazine* provides a convenient tear-out Gastrometer in several of its issues, pointing out those places that are particularly 'in' just now. This means they will be crowded, but apart from going to stare, the food ratings are quite accurate.

British beer comes in both bottles and draught; the latter is more fun. The variety is far greater than in the States, and unless you enjoy sampling your way through a number of drinks you don't care for, you may have difficulty in choosing. The British consider our beer to be far too light and aerated; conversely, theirs strikes many Americans as too heavy, bitter, strong, and/or warm. The main species are Mild, Bitter, Stout, Lager, Brown Ale and Pale Ale. The breweries make special brews and usually own the pubs, so that you'll find John Courage or Double Diamond abound. You'll want to try Guinness, of course, and Whitbreads; after that you're on your own. My favorite is Samuel Smith's Old Brewery Pale Ale. India Pale Ale, which can be very good, makes a pleasant starter although it's hardly typical. You may like a shandy, which is a mixture of beer and lemonade or (less often) ginger beer. A lager and lime is refreshing. English cider is true hard cider, not apple juice, and Bulmers or any major line will prove pleasant on a summer day. Perry is based on pears. By all means have scrumpy while in Devonshire – this is the very rough home-brew skimmings of the cider, and a local treat.

Unlike in the States, where one needs to case the joint before deciding whether to take a lady in or not, British pubs have a family atmosphere. The man presses to the bar to get the drinks (don't expect table service) and brings them back to the table where he has placed his lady. You may have to share the table, for every available inch of sitting and standing room is taken up during the lunch break and in the early evening. Unless you're certain of your taste, start with a half-pint of best bitter, or whatever, before moving up to the larger mug.

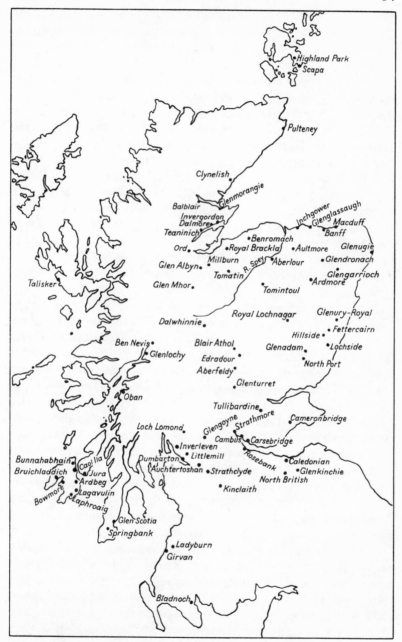

Highland Park
Scapa
Pulteney
Clynelish
Glenmorangie
Balblair
Invergordon
Dalmore
Teaninich
Inchgower
Glenglassaugh
Macduff
Banff
Ord
Benromach
Royal Brackla
Aultmore
Glenugie
Millburn
Aberlour
Glendronach
Glen Albyn
R. Spey
Glengarrioch
Talisker
Tomatin
Ardmore
Glen Mhor
Tomintoul
Royal Lochnagar
Glenury-Royal
Dalwhinnie
Hillside
Fettercairn
Ben Nevis
Blair Athol
Glenadam
Lochside
Glenlochy
Edradour
North Port
Aberfeldy
Oban
Glenturret
Tullibardine
Cameronbridge
Loch Lomond
Glengoyne
Strathmore
Strathmore
Cambus
Carsebridge
Inverleven
Littlemill
Dumbarton
Rosebank
Caledonian
Bunnahabhain
Caol Ila
Auchtertoshan
Strathclyde
Glenkinchie
Bruichladdich
Jura
North British
Ardbeg
Kinclaith
Bowmore
Lagavulin
Laphroaig
Glen Scotia
Springbank
Ladyburn
Girvan
Bladnoch

THE MAIN WHISKY DISTILLERIES OF SCOTLAND

The pub will have a public bar and a saloon bar, and the latter is supposed to be a bit more posh. It may be slightly less crowded; the drink
you get will be identical and more expensive.

Gin and whisky are to be found everywhere. The gin mill of
Hogarth's day may be gone, but it is still a potent drink, and best
taken with something. You may order a martini if you like, but to
insist that it be precisely thus-and-such, straight up, on the rocks with
a twist, shaken and not stirred, etc., etc., is to be disappointed. The
British have begun to learn how to make good martinis, especially in
London, but it still won't be right. Anyway, to persist in your martini
is as bad as to persist in your hamburger and French fries. The British
often take their gin with tonic, or bitter lemon – the last is an ideal
warm-weather drink, while gin and tonic will make you feel appropriately Colonel Blimpish. British gins are (I think) the best in the
world: don't limit yourself to the obvious standbys, such as Beef-
eater's, Booth's and Gordon's – Plymouth gin is superb (it's what
Travis McGee drinks, if you follow that series) and Tanqueray's is
more than just a handsome bottle.

Even if you are not a whisky (or, in Ireland, *whiskey*) drinker,
sample as widely as possible, especially when in Scotland. There are
many distilleries in the Highlands, each making its distinctive whisky
based upon different water and peat and loving care. You can spend at
least two pleasant days driving along the Spey, in northern Scotland,
sampling the best, or you can systematically make your way through
the labels in the pubs. Many of the local varieties are not easily to be
found in England. Proprietary brands sold in England are usually
70% proof, while in Scotland you may escalate to the almost white
Glenfarclas, as unblended malt twelve years old and 104% proof. It
comes from near Glenlivet, a distillery which started in 1834. There is
only one The Glenlivet, although there are twenty-three Glenlivet
whiskies prefixed by another name. The Livet is a tributary of the
River Avon (not to be confused with that of Shakespeare Country)
which enters the Spey between Craigellachie and Grantown-on-Spey,
and in this area you may sample most of the whiskies (visit, in particular, The Blair Athol Distillery, at Pitlochry, which especially caters
to visitors, if you're interested in the distilling process).

If you don't know, you should, that 100% proof in Scotland equals
57% pure alcohol, while in the United States it would be 50%. You
should know that whisky comes in three types: malt, which is distilled
from fermented barley in a pot still, and which is unquestionably the
best (as well as the most traditional) whisky; grain, distilled from

unmalted barley in a patent still; and blended, a mixture of the two. Americans much prefer the last, but the Scots like their Scotch to be an unblended malt, even though it may cost more.

The Scotch whiskies fall into six areas, each distinctive: the Glenlivets; those from Dufftown; the Northern malts (of which Glenmorangie is especially fine); the Lowland malts, which were the first to be drunk in England because they were and are lighter – visit Glenkinchie, near Pentcaitland, in East Lothian, if you can; the Campbeltown malts, a dying breed although Springbank and Glen Scotia survive; and the Island malts. The last are truly different: they are for strong men who stand in driving seas resisting Captain Bligh, and they are distinctly peaty. Drive about on Islay, noting the peat cut out in squares along the roadside, and then try Laphroaig. Talisker is your drink on Skye – a good visit this one. And have a wee sip o' Highland Park, from Kirkwall in the Orkney Islands (but try to get the 100% proof) for the Orkney peat is distinctive. The map will help you find the distilleries, and I recommend that you do a bit of homework, with David Daiches' lively *Scotch Whisky Past and Present* and R. J. S. McDowall's *The Whiskies of Scotland,* both obtainable in any good London bookshop.

Lastly, there are the liqueurs: Drambuie, Glava, Lochan Ora, and the like.

Before liqueurs, you will have had wine. The better restaurants maintain excellent wine cellars, and although prices, especially for French Burgundies and claret, are sky-rocketing, you will still find the wines less expensive than in the States, and available in a far greater variety. If your pocket book doesn't run to the French or Germans these days, try Yugoslav, Hungarian, Portuguese, and Rumanian.

I save for last the very best. If I must choose only one drink, it would be a Pimm's Cup. Served properly in a tall pewter tankard, iced, with a sprig of borage and/or mint, a lengthwise slice of cucumber, a round slice of orange, and a bit of apple, this is the finest drink in the world. But only the better pubs will have it, for many barmen resent having to make 'the fruit salad bit' for it, and it requires time, skill, and on your part willingness to give up more shekels than usual.

Dining out

The *Good Food Guide,* a remarkable publication which, without commercial attachment, provides ratings for restaurants throughout Britain and Ireland, should be among your indispensable five pounds of travel-guide luggage. The guide is not without its biases – some think it places too much emphasis on wine, for example, and for the average American traveller who may not take wine with two meals a day, it probably does. This is not an objectionable bias, however, for you are free to ignore the judgments, if you wish, and to follow them when the mood strikes you. In general, in the better places, wine *will* be taken rather than beer, and if both your taste and pocket book run to the latter, you should eat at least lunch in a pub. You can make an excellent and cheap meal on pub fare, with a pint of ale, and save your wine money for dinner.

There *is* a bias of some importance in the *Good Food Guide,* however. As the *Guide*'s editor has made clear in his introduction (and to me when I have argued with him) the listings are a guide to good *food,* and solely to food (and drink). The quality of the service may be miserable; if the food is outstanding, the restaurant will be listed. The decor may be mid-Victorian Coal Pit; if the food is good, the listing remains. On the whole, Americans place heavier emphasis on atmosphere and service than the British do, and I have accordingly rated the restaurants throughout this book with a balance between service, environment and food in mind. When you use the *Good Food Guide,* as you must, and notice that its ratings differ on occasion from those given here, do keep the difference in mind.

The *Guide* awarded its coveted food and/or wine distinctions to ninety-three restaurants in the United Kingdom in 1982. I have eaten in all of them, always without disappointment, but not invariably with high pleasure. Twelve of the laurel wreaths sit upon London heads, with four others quite near. I have five London restaurants I especially like, one not in the latest *Guide,* any one of which is equal to the best in New York, and I rate them here in order of preference, which has barely made it possible to avoid open bloodshed with my wife. A warning – none is cheap.

1 TANTE CLAIR, at 68 Royal Hospital Road, may be the least known of this favorite five, at least to foreign visitors, for it is still rather new. The food is possibly the best of the lot – certainly the fish can be – and the sense of detail shown throughout the service makes for a pleasant evening, though a hurried lunch (and a disappointment in August, when Tante Claire is closed). Were *Le Gavroche* not so expensive now that one must be from the Persian Gulf to eat there, Tante Clair might seem less fine, but in London today it is a major

dining experience. In any case, the chef from *Le Gavroche* moved here.

2 ROBERT CARRIER'S RESTAURANT, at 2 Camden Passage in Islington, still does not get any ranking from the *Good Food Guide,* though it is highly regarded. The problem may be that the service is not always perfection. Even so, this lovely restaurant continues to offer some of the most imaginative food in London in an atmosphere Americans find elegant though not intimidating.

3 Success did not spoil the CAPITAL HOTEL RESTAURANT, tucked away at 22–24 Basil Street, S.W.1, back of Harrods (meals 12.30–3, 6.30–11). This elegant small hotel aims to please Americans, and it surely succeeds: it is the only one in this list on which my wife and I completely agree. I have never been disappointed, perhaps precisely because the blend of decor, service and food is so American while the quality itself is so English. I particularly recommend the Capital for an elegant lunch (book the day before, even if alone) and this time do have that bottle of wine. Opened in 1971, the Capital may not be able to resist its fame, but one can only hope. Dinner costs about $60 for one these days.

4 MA CUISINE, at 113 Walton Street, is now the most crowded, the most attractive, and possibly the best restaurant in London. This means you must book weeks in advance for lunch or dinner and that it is expensive, but if you want one big night out before you depart for the provinces, this is the place for it. The ambiance especially seems to appeal to Americans and I recommend lunch.

5 Not everyone enjoys Chinese, Greek, or Indian and Pakistani food, and so I have deliberately omitted them from my list. But I would rather eat a really good curry than any other dish, and for those who share this passion, I confess to my top choice, the KHYBER PASS, 21 Bute Street, S.W.7 (meals 12–2.45, 6–11.30). An unassuming restaurant (all authentic Indo-Pakistani places are) which welcomes children, has waiters who will explain the menu with care, and offers a mixture of Afghani, Pakistani, and both South and North Indian dishes, all at quite reasonable cost, makes this both the place for the novice at true Indian food to start and for the expert to finish. If you are nervous, place yourself in the waiter's hands – all will be well. And if you do not like truly spicy dishes they will be spiced to your taste.

Which brings us to elegance. It is not always accompanied by good food. London's most famous hotel, CLARIDGE'S, serves a good table but it is over-expensive. The SAVOY, on the Strand, is hip-deep in tradition, and a meal in the Grill Room will be excellent and nearly worth the cost. By all means eat at both if you are Collecting Experiences. And even if you are not, give yourself two final pleasures before leaving London to eat elsewhere (and the best of all, in my view, is definitely Elsewhere, in Scotland). Have afternoon tea, about 4.00, at the RITZ, simply because tea at the Ritz, like "breakfast at Tiffany's," is something one may dine out on for years. The difference is that you really can have tea at the Ritz, and while it will cost no less than four pounds or so per person for the same assortment of crumpets, sandwiches, and cakes which you may have for half that elsewhere, you are buying a wee bit of England here. Cherish it. And move on for dinner, if your pocket book is a matter of little moment, to the queen of all London hostelries, the only one where the food matches the efficient, distant, even haughty, service in its understated elegance: all Britons think that all Americans eat at the CONNAUGHT HOTEL. In truth, only very rich ones do, and even they may have to think twice about it these days. But why not enjoy Britain to the hilt and go to see what rich Americans, with taste, can do with their money?

As for chain restaurants where you may drop in, often without bookings, and count on a dependable if not outstanding meal, I recommend three: any LONDON STEAK HOUSE, where children are welcome, and you can have a good steak, green salad, and a glass of serviceable Beaujolais quickly; any WHEELER'S, where the seafood will be good and offered up in a bewildering array; and for a true snack, the KENYA COFFEE HOUSES, which serve coffee more to the American taste than any other chain in England. (But do not fail to have at least one cup of slush and grit at a LYONS, one rock-hard hamburger at a WIMPY, and one egg and chips at any smudge-windowed greasy spoon that happens to be near at hand when shopping Portobello Road.)

Americans who really cannot be weaned away from familiar food may have what are truly very good hamburgers, 'East-coast thick' (which means watery) malts, and honest-to-God sesame seed buns with American mustard (and why would anyone crave American mustard with French, German, English and Chinese at hand in London?) at THE GREAT AMERICAN DISASTER on King's Road, or the TEXAS LONE STAR SALOON on Gloucester Road (S.W.7), where you may watch the Brits coming to terms with the New World and be assaulted by a jukebox louder than any I have ever known before.

And you will already know of the two restaurants rated 'most popular' with Americans – SIMPSON'S-IN-THE-STRAND, and YE CHESHIRE CHEESE (truly a pub).

Shopping in Britain

When shopping for unusual items, antiques, paintings, fine furniture, books, unusual foods, and many other items, Britain – and most particularly London – is quite possibly the finest city in the world. When shopping for everyday items, like toothpaste, or a ready-made shirt, or a third scarf to match the two you bought last year that were so admired, Britain – and most particularly London – can be one of the most exasperating cities in the world. There are, therefore, certain facts of British life to keep in mind if you want to shop happily.

In the larger department stores, and outside specialty shops, shop clerks often do not know their stock very well. They certainly do not know their competitors' stock, and the standard American question, 'Where else would you suggest that I look?' will probably be met with a rather indifferent 'I really can't say.' Further, shop assistants are – by American standards – often crisp to the point of rudeness, slow, and ill-informed. Obviously this is not so of the 'better shops', but I have received precisely such service in many shops that think of themselves as 'better'.

Shopping as a whole is slow. Goods are organized on the shelf differently than in America. The relationship between goods is different also: you may be accustomed to finding scissors next to thread, but in London they may be two floors away. Do not try to guess where something will be, for the logic of Associated Use, as employed in the States, appears to take a back seat to the logic of Common Source of Manufacture. Shopping is also slow because of cumbersome methods of adding up and paying bills. It is a not uncommon (although happily receding) practice to have to pick out the item you want, have a sales slip written up by hand for it, take the slip to a cage where you pay the sum due and have the slip stamped, and then return to obtain the parcel, by now wrapped, upon presentation of the slip. (This also leads to your carrying home a bundle that looked just like yours – or so the clerk thought – which turns out to be Henry Miller rather than Billy Graham. I boycott Foyles, allegedly the world's largest bookstore, simply because it is not worth my sanity to try to make a quick purchase there.)

Still, shopping is slow mainly because, outside such department stores as Harrods, you must go to such a wide variety of different shops to obtain what you want. Imagine a typical shopping morning in The Village, if you have settled in for a month or so to a flat and want to stock the larder and the very tiny refrigerator: you buy bread (sliced or unsliced) at the baker; two doors along, you may find a general grocer who will sell you so staggering a variety of items as cold cereal, toilet tissue and tinned soup; but if you want dairy products, the odds are good you must move on again to another shop; and certainly if you want fresh meat you must seek out the butcher, who seldom will have set himself up within the grocery store. (Although the butcher shops may strike you as insanitary, with meat hanging out unprotected and sawdust on the floor, you really needn't worry on this ground. On the other hand, the cuts of meat are quite different, and trying to get a chop that resembles one you are used to can be very difficult.) You want a newspaper too? Don't expect to find it except at a news agent. Fresh fruit and vegetables? Certainly not at the grocery store (or dry goods store) or the dairy, or the meat market – rather, along the way again to the specialist. Yet this may prove rewarding, for, except in winter, the fruit and vegetables available in a British greengrocer's are usually fresher, and offer a wider variety, than in the States. And you wanted band-aids, or razor blades, or lemon soap? To the chemist's, of course, certainly not to a drug store, and certainly not in that grocery store. Finally, some flowers to make the flat look bright. Off once again, perhaps three blocks (streets) away, to seek out the florist who – how odd that you should expect it! – will not be anywhere near the greengrocer.

Now all of this can be fun, and it assures that a half-hour's shopping will take two hours, and that you will be exhausted at the end of it, since each item requires a different transaction, a different queue, and is put into a different (and very thin) paper bag. And you will be on foot, of course, for there will be no place to park, and certainly no supermarket lot.

However, the two most consistently annoying aspects of shopping in Britain remain to be mentioned: in general, the British do not supply you with a single, large, manageable paper bag in which to carry your purchases, but with a series of small breakaway sacks guaranteed to last thirty yards. This is enough, actually, for you are expected to have brought a large plastic, cloth, woven gold, or pure silk sow's ear shopping bag with you. (These cost money and are generally not given away free by the shops.) You may even have a cane one mounted on wheels. A shopping bag you must have, and if you do not, surely you will not be so naive as to think that the shop itself would have anything except a plastic carrier (and not always that) to sell you? No, no! leave the goods there, walk a block in the rain to a hardware store (or a department store) and buy a bag, and then return for your purchases. Don't let the fact that you're losing time better spent gazing upon the Changing of the Guard bother you. You came to learn about British life.

Unhappily, you may not get to fill that shopping basket anyway, for a sales clerk's common refrain is, 'I'm sorry, we're out of stock on that item'. That they were also out of stock two weeks ago, or that even when they obtain new stock they order only one or two of the item, or that the substitute being offered to you is not what you wanted, since licorice soap smells differently from lemon, or that you rather *like* your socks to match your tie, will not move the clerk at all. For British shops stock very little of a given item, do not appear to reorder it until it is completely sold out, and can scarcely be described as vigorous in filling orders once they do set about the task. The rule in Britain, therefore, is – if you want it, buy it when you see it, for it won't be there tomorrow. If told, 'It's on order', forget it, unless you're emigrating.

The British are a people of integrity. This also means they are inflexible where matters of propriety are involved. I once attempted to get a waitress to bring me an order of 'hamburger and egg' with the egg left off, and she refused, since the menu did not list hamburger. The idea that I would pay the full price for half the dish shocked her so deeply, she never found our table again.

The law will also frustrate you. Everyone knows that Boots on Piccadilly is open throughout the night and on Sunday. But you may purchase only emergency items outside regular hours. While the toothpaste will stare up at you from under drapes, salivate all you will, you may not buy it; on the other hand, you may buy a prophylactic across the counter, for clearly this is an emergency. In any event, people would not be interesting if they were logical.

Watch out for 'half-day closing'. On a rotating basis, most towns, or outlying districts of the major cities, close at noon on a specified weekday. Thus, while one village may close on Thursday, the next may have chosen Wednesday. Although this is a convenience when travelling, since you may always find what you want a few miles along the road, it can prove awkward if you see exactly the silver teapot you want in an antique shop and return to buy it the next day, only to find the shop locked up tight.

If you intend to use any of the major American credit cards for your shopping, do not expect to find all of them widely accepted outside the major cities. And do not expect to find your personal cheques, if drawn upon American banks, accepted. If, however, you have established a British external bank account, and have identification of a valid if temporary British address, you may be able to make purchases by cheque. A British bank card is best, of course.

As to the banks themselves, the procedure is very different in Britain. If you have an account, you may have your mail sent via your bank, you may negotiate with the manager for an overdraft (that is, to overdraw your account up to a stipulated limit), and the bank may help you with certain types of purchases. But you will receive less informative statements at the end of an accounting period, will encounter longer lines at the tellers' windows, and will be unable to deposit both 'external' and internal cheques to the same account. In short, if you want to open an account, obtain clear explanations of the limitations on you in advance.

To express a price in guineas (one pound plus five pence) is considered posh. Those branches of business that traditionally price their activities in guineas – doctors, dressmakers and antique sellers – thus set themselves apart from the counter-jumpers of ordinary shops. Of course, antique pricing is an arcane activity in any event.

When antique shopping, do not neglect three areas: the Silver Vaults, off Chancery Lane, where one may view an incredible variety of silver without anyone objecting to your browsing; Portobello Road on Saturday morning (although there are nearby shops open all days) where you may compete with fellow Americans but where, in spite of its reputation, you can still find good bargains; and Camden Passage, in Islington, quite near the Angel Underground station. There is also the Antique Hypermarket (supermarket) on Kensington High Street, although it tends to be over-priced. The really elegant antique shops in the Bond Street area are fair, their prices honest, and their wares so good as invariably to be expensive. There are also antique open-air markets in Church Street (near Paddington Green) on Saturday morning and Cheshire Street on Sunday morning, and on Bermondsey Road (often especially good for copper) on Friday morning.

If you wish to study the price of antiques with care before beginning your shopping, consult the Price Guide series published by the Antique Collectors Club of England, edited by John Steel. In general, as these guides reveal, antique prices have inflated seriously, but they are still less in Britain than in the United States. Pictures, country-style chairs, side-boards, crystal decanters, and any materials sewn or woven have more than doubled in price in the last five years; silver, on the other hand, experienced its price climb about ten years ago and has not gone up in price appreciably since. In relation to American prices, the best buys in Britain continue to be porcelain, silver and clothing. Books are now more expensive in England than in America.

It is always fun to go to a sale of antiques, paintings, or old wines at Christie's or Sotheby's. You may have to pay an entrance fee, for both have had to cut down on the casual browser, but it will be worth it simply to see the auction. British Rail also sells antiques from time to time, and it holds sales of left items regularly. Unless you want to buy a truly superb umbrella at Swaine Adeney Brigg, you might consider going to British Rail's left items shop, where you can pick up a nearly new one very cheaply. And as a final insight into the values placed on things, visit Autographs Ltd on Dover Street, where you can see what autographed letters will bring. (Would you like a six-page letter from Henry James, which simply says that he cannot come to tea? Here is where to find it.)

	ENGLISH	AMERICAN
Dress sizes	10 (32" 22" 34")	8
	12 (34" 24" 36")	10
	14 (36" 26" 38")	12
	16 (38" 28" 40")	14
	18 (40" 30" 42")	16
	20 (42" 32" 44")	18
Shoe sizes	4	5½
	4½	6
	5	6½
	5½	7
	6	7½
	6½	8
	7	8½
	7½	9
	8	9½

A potpourri of general warnings

If you need special medicines, bring them with you. The British will have them, and they will be cheaper, but they almost certainly will be masquerading under another name.

Feel free to go to the National Health Service doctors to see what ails you. They do, in fact, charge a very modest fee. Be prepared to wait a bit, however.

Top-flight British surgeons (called Mister, not Doctor, a nice bit of reverse snobbery) and dental surgeons are among the best in the world; they are also quite expensive. But I would rather have dental work done in London than anywhere else.

Enjoy getting a haircut in one of the 'by-appointment' (to royalty or ex-royalty) barbers. The headiest experience, expensive by British standards and ludicrously cheap by American, is Trumper's, on Curzon Street, which proclaims itself the barber to King George V.

Take no electrical equipment with you. The voltage is different, and a transformer large enough to adapt even a simple toaster will be expensive and weigh fifteen pounds.

If you plan to stay a while, and to put children into school, bring a full set of school records. British authorities will not take your word for it when you say that your twelve-year-old is really ready for the last year in high school. And be prepared to have the headmaster or mistress assume that your children are a year behind. Unless they have had really good schooling, they may be in fact, especially in use of English and mathematics.

If invited out, be prompt. The British mean 7.00 if they say 7.00; they certainly do not mean 7.30. And if you entertain, expect guests to arrive promptly, so you will not have fifteen minutes grace to put on your makeup. Trains scheduled to leave at 8.03 leave about thirty seconds before that. (Only the airways seem to be manned by those who have never heard of 'military time' – which means, five minutes early.) If the invitation reads '7.00 for 7.30' this means to come at 7.00 if you want a drink, and that you will be seated for dinner at 7.30, at which point do not expect to be given a drink to catch up. And if a reception is slated for 7.00 to 10.00, expect it to end at 10.00.

The British like to drink toasts at formal dinners. If invited to such an occasion, it is expected that you will not smoke until The Loyal Toast – the toast to the Queen – has been drunk. You may then be asked to charge your glass for any of a series of other toasts, but you may smoke between them.

The British tend to respect food more than Americans do and, unless your host and hostess do otherwise, you should not smoke between courses, although you may do so before coffee arrives. You naturally will ask permission to smoke a cigar. English ladies are not of the opinion that you show your virility by sticking a fat stogie in your face.

British gaol (jail) terms for being in possession of drugs can be quite long. The American Embassy will not help you if you have violated British law.

Although the British don't in increasing numbers, try going to church one Sunday. An Anglican service can be quite interesting. And an Evensong is often quite lovely.

Both the reception and content of British television are high. Watch it.

If you want to get some sense of a town to which you have no guide, visit its parish church, a pub, the guildhall, and its pleasure gardens.

If you are travelling with children, as we almost always did in Britain, remember that most hotels will serve a 5.00 tea at which the younger children are expected to be fed; querulous children are not happily received in the dining room after 7.30. And equip yourself with publications like *Holidays with Children* (revised annually, and not really very good) or *Children Welcome!* (ditto both) which tell you of hotels that welcome children more warmly. If you have quite young children and would like to travel without them for a few days, an advance booking with the Under-Six Club, Piper's Hill, Byfleet Surrey – which is a children's hotel – will make this possible. (The club will, in fact, take children up to 16 under special circumstances.)

English people, men *and* women, very often shake hands when being introduced. One rises when being introduced, whether you are hostess, older than the introducee, etc.

You won't encounter British titles, most likely. The one that you might is that of a Knight. If he is Sir Robert Smith, you do not address him or speak of him as Sir Smith, but as Sir Robert; his wife will then be Lady Smith. These titles are honorary, not hereditary, and are conferred on sportsmen as well as business tycoons. More than one jockey is a Sir; Arnold Toynbee was not. Do not assume, therefore, that you have to score some kind of egalitarian point in the presence of a Knight, and do not swoon either. They are but like you and me – but better at what they do.

Mail deliveries in Britain are much faster than in the United States.

If you wish to send a telegram, go to the Post Office or use a pay telephone. There are no separate telegraph offices.

As an American you are welcome to pay a visit to your Embassy, on Grosvenor Square. But there is no earthly reason to do so, unless you simply want to see the building.

If you stay in Britain long enough to rent, you will probably take a furnished place. If so, employ an inventory clerk (through the rental agency) to check the inventory with the landlord's agent. Make certain that the clerk notes all scratches and water marks, tears, stains and other defects. If they are not noted on the inventory, you will be held accountable for them when you leave. To have taken the initial rental, you will have been asked for a 'demolition deposit' (a damage deposit) equal to the first unit of rent (whether by the week or month) and this is forfeited if repairs are needed. If you pay rent by the week, remember that this constitutes thirteen months. Your rent may also include the rates – that is, the property tax may be passed on to you in the rental price. Avoid flats heated by electricity if possible, for electricity is far more expensive in Britain than the States, and the heating less efficient.

Are you cold? Wear a sweater. The British consider 65° an excellent indoor temperature, and regard 72° as stuffy. You will pay dearly if you try to close that gap: sweaters and warm socks are cheaper, and you *can* take them with you.

You may not bring animals into Britain except after a lengthy quarantine period. If passing through, they will be quarantined and returned to you – at your point of entry – when you leave.

In London, two reliable baby sitting agencies, which will send sitters to your hotel, are Universal Aunts, 36 Walpole Street, S.W.3 (730-9834) and Babyminders, 32 James Street, W.1 (935-3515). They are expensive and you must book the day before if possible.

Boots, the cash chemist at Piccadilly, is open 24 hours a day.

Dry cleaning is a no-no. If you can, wait until you get back to the States.

Laundry, except in your hotel, may well take a week. Shirts may come back heavily starched unless you specify otherwise.

The British love uniforms, and you will find them on lift attendants, street sweepers and a dozen varieties of functionaries. Learn to distinguish the types quickly.

The fabled, ever-polite, well-informed London bobby (named after Sir Robert Peel, and thus also traditionally, but not actually, called a Peeler, he having reorganized the London police) is a rarer breed every year. They probably can answer your question about directions (and certainly can if on point duty, or otherwise directing traffic) but not about the location of specific shops; they may well be rather offhand with you and less than magisterially courteous; they may be chewing gum. Even so, they won't often be carrying guns and you needn't fear them, so walk right up and ask your question.

Trying to find a 'loo' – British for toilet, lav, w.c., etc. – while out and about can be difficult. Not all gasoline stations have them. There are public conveniences, as we've noted, for men and women (you may be startled to find women attendants in the Men's room) where you may purchase soap, rent a towel and engage in the usual functions without charge, but these will be cold, not very clean and often quite hard to find. Large department stores will have facilities for the public – that is, for those making purchases in the stores – but you may have to ask for directions. Many Underground stations, all railway stations and hotels and pubs will have lavatories, of course, although you will not always be welcome in the last unless making a purchase.

As a final suggestion, you may want to give some thought to how best to organize your day. Having early morning tea in bed may substitute for breakfast and save money, unless you are on a bed-and-breakfast basis. Better yet, having breakfast in your room will save time, for it can be brought while you're dressing (the wait in the average hotel dining room can be quite infuriating at breakfast time, when you're eager to be On the Road, or In Pursuit) and the additional cost is less than in the United States. Time is money is a cliché especially true for the traveller, after all. Read the daily newspapers, keep in touch by radio and television, organize those maps, all before you start the day – or over lunch (although it's a shame to mar a good lunch with work). Avoid really cheap food, for a day in bed with serious indigestion can destroy a schedule. Use Sunday morning, if you don't go to church, to window shop, so that you know what you want to buy in advance. You can't go to the galleries or museums, for they're closed, and a walk through the shopping areas of interest to you will be unhampered by traffic or crowds, so that you can prepare a list of items to purchase on a weekday. During those weekdays, shop in the morning, the earlier the better, to beat the crowds, and go to the museums in the afternoon. Try not to travel on public transport in the rush hours if you want to remain popular with the locals, and preserve your own sanity. Stay in the galleries until they close, then go to the theatre, and have dinner after the theatre, when you cannot be doing anything else anyway.

Enjoy.

A note on survival in the literal sense of the word

Unfortunately, there are few totally safe havens in the world today. Britain is a quieter country, and a safer one, than most, for its crime rate is far lower than America's – there are more murders in a week in New York City than in a year in London. Still, waves of urban terrorism do occur. The risks you run as a tourist are minimal indeed, just as they are minimal (especially in relation to automobile traffic) when you board an aeroplane. Nonetheless, one is sensible to take those precautions one may, especially against the possibility of finding oneself caught in a bomb blast. There are three precautions, in particular, which you may take.

Stay out of other people's quarrels. Do not engage in discussion of the situation in Northern Ireland. Whatever point of view you may lean toward, you should understand that the situation is infinitely complex, not capable of any simplistic solution by any of the parties involved, and not one for you to mess in.

On the whole, you may want to avoid travelling in Northern Ireland just now. If you decide to go, anticipate thorough personal and baggage searches, especially at Belfast airport, and avoid trying to cross the border into the Republic by car. Fly into Belfast, hire a car there, stick to the major roads and the important sights and do not drive after dark. I have travelled in Northern Ireland during this time of troubles under these conditions without incident.

In England and Scotland, avoid pubs or other gathering places frequented by the military. If you find yourself in a pub crowded with uniforms, leave. If the weather is good, why not take your drink outside and enjoy it there in any case?

If you observe these precautions, there is no sound reason why you should not, in all other respects, plan your visit to Britain precisely as you would do in any event. If you travel nervously, you will not enjoy it.

The cathedrals of Britain

Taken as a group, the greatest individual architectural monuments, the most moving man-made sights and the most historically significant ground are combined in the great cathedrals of England. Because they are well spaced across the land, pursuit of all of them assures rather full coverage of the countryside. Any community with a cathedral is, by legal definition, a city, but in truth many of the cathedrals are to be found in attractive small towns, over which they stand in dramatic dominance. One may collect castles in Spain, or châteaux in France, or national parks in America – the great collector's item in Britain (and especially England) is the cathedral. Only those in France can collectively rival the cathedrals of Britain – and to my mind, unsuccessfully.

When one speaks of cathedrals, one usually means those that are Anglican and one associates them with the Middle Ages. Both assumptions are incorrect, of course, for a number have been erected by Roman Catholics since the 1830s, and, of the Anglican cathedrals, four are of the twentieth century and sixteen are parish churches elevated to cathedral status in the nineteenth and early twentieth centuries. But unless you are simply a Collector, most of the parish-church cathedrals are of interest only as a means of drawing you to a community you might not otherwise visit, and only one of the Roman Catholic cathedrals – that in Liverpool – is worth making a special journey for.

There are, in fact, over forty Protestant cathedrals plus York Minster, which is to be viewed as one and which is substantially more significant than most; there are six cathedrals in Wales, each worth a visit; and eleven cathedrals in Scotland, in addition to eight ex-cathedrals, some of which are in ruins. Before exploring any of them,

THE PROTESTANT CATHEDRALS OF ENGLAND, SCOTLAND AND WALES

you may wish to read Alec Clifton-Taylor's excellent illustrated *The Cathedrals of England,* one of the World of Art Library volumes, published by Thames and Hudson or Praeger. It contains summaries and plans of each cathedral, an explanation of its function, and a short history of the emergence of the various architectural styles, from the Norman period through the Early Gothic, the Decorated, the Perpendicular, and the imitative styles which preceded the most recent experiments (as in Coventry) with cathedral architecture. A drier, nonetheless good, guide is Leighton Houghton, *A Guide to the British Cathedrals* (London: John Baker, 1973). You will also be able to purchase excellent, well-illustrated Pitkin booklets on most cathedrals, at each cathedral itself.

There is far more to visiting British cathedrals than in some similar American pilgrimages, whether to visit New England spired churches, or to follow the route marked by the twenty-one Roman Catholic missions of California. The buildings are larger, infinitely more complex, and they require time and attention on your part. Although, to be sure, one may gain some small sense of each on a short visit, the major cathedrals will demand a fair portion of your day (and as they begin to grow upon you, an unfair portion of many days). Cathedrals can be depressing, cavernous and cold, and not everyone is moved by them. But if they are filled with sunlight, whether of the summer or the cold, thin sun of winter; if the rays strike down the great walls and pillars, motes dancing upwards through them; if light stands behind the magnificent rose windows; if there is an Evensong in progress, or choir school boys are hurrying past in their school uniforms, then you will know a little something of why England has endured. Whenever I have visited Durham Cathedral, a massive, even dour, structure of enormous dignity, an unbidden line we all know – England, 'this precious stone set in the silver sea' – comes to me. Edward Thomas, asked in the midst of World War I what he was fighting for, bent and sifted Wiltshire dirt through his fingers, saying, 'This'. So, too, must a similar sense come to those who sit in the meadow downslope from Ely Cathedral, on a summer day, with cows wandering across the view. The cathedrals are essential to an understanding of England.

But you may not have time for all, and so, with an arrogance beyond the rational, I have dared to rate those I think most important for this book, partly because certain architectural features are more clearly illustrated by X rather than by Y, partly because of historical and literary associations which resonate from the cathedral, and partly because of the setting itself. Those cathedrals which must be seen are:

1 St Paul's, London, the second largest church in the world;

2 Canterbury, for its literary associations and its incredible beauty when viewed from a distance;

3 Lincoln, with the most beautiful tower the Middle Ages afforded, dominating a town of great interest;

4 Durham, the finest example in all England of Norman cathedral architecture, and the greatest Romanesque church in Europe;

5 Ely, which rises like a great ship from the flat marshlands;

6 Salisbury, often regarded as the finest building in England;

7 Wells, newly cleaned, one of the most unusual and beautiful of all cathedrals;

8 Coventry, a monument to the British spirit and a triumph of the modern style;

9 York Minster, newly repaired, impressive for its stained glass;

10 Winchester, with an interior of exceptional interest;

11 Liverpool – Anglican – with one of the great towers of the world, the heaviest peal of bells on earth, and the only early-twentieth century cathedral that can stand up to those of antiquity;

12 Gloucester, a fascinating mixture of styles;

13 Bury St Edmunds, more intimate, warmer than many;

14 Exeter, one of the finest Gothic interiors in the world;

15 Peterborough, after Durham the finest Norman church;

16 Norwich, with striking cloisters and handsome detail;

17 St David's, Wales, in the smallest cathedral city in Britain, dating from the twelfth century;

18 Lichfield, for its unusual use of red sandstone, and its literary interest;

19 Southwell, in a charming small town, with an attractive interior; and

20 St Andrews, the only one of the Scottish cathedrals to rival in visual interest those to the south.

The above cathedrals may be said to be worth a journey for the sole purpose of seeing them. I have ranked them in the order in which I found myself drawn to them, and any such approach is so subjective as to be open to instant challenge. But if you have seen these twenty you may feel you have done justice to the cathedrals.

Equal in importance are four of the ex-cathedrals in Scotland, now in varying states of preservation. High on anyone's list of attractions must be a pilgrimage to Iona, to which St Columb went in 563 from Ireland. St Magnus, Kirkwall, now in use as a parish church, is striking in its setting. The ex-cathedral of Elgin, ruined but preserved, contains some of the finest architectural detail in Scotland. And the ex-cathedral of Dunkeld holds a commanding site.

The other cathedrals are: Birmingham, Blackburn, Bradford, *Bristol, Carlisle,* Chelmsford, *Chester, Chichester,* Derby, *Guildford, Hereford,* Leicester, Manchester, Newcastle, *Oxford,* Portsmouth, *Ripon, Rochester,* Sheffield, *St Albans, Southwark* (London), Truro, Wakefield and Worcester in England; *Bangor,* Brecon, *Llandaff,* Newport, and St Asaph in Wales; and *St Andrew's Aberdeen,* Fortrose, Inverness, Oban, *Dundee, St Giles' Edinburgh,* St Mary's Edinburgh, Perth, St Mary the Virgin Glasgow, and *St Mungo's Glasgow,* in Scotland. The other Scottish ex-cathedrals are St Machair's Aberdeen (now a parish kirk), *Brechin,* Dornoch and Dunblane. Those in italics are worth a side journey to visit; the rest merit attention only if you are in the vicinity for other reasons.

Of course, cathedrals are not the only form of significant church architecture in Britain, and some of the abbeys are far more beautiful and impressive than the lesser cathedrals. Bath Abbey, for example, is of great importance and well worth a major journey, while the parish church of Boston – the largest in England – or Beverley Minster are far larger than many cathedrals. There are also several notable chapels and meeting houses associated with the dissenting faiths, the Wesleyans especially, and a number of striking synagogues. Of the nonconformist churches, Underbank Unitarian, in Stannington, Yorkshire and Snaith Methodist, also in Yorkshire, are outstanding, with the most highly developed use of classical design in a nonconformist structure; and several of the churches in Wales are well worth viewing.

Her Majesty's Stationery Office (49 High Holborn, London, W.C.1) issues an excellent small guide to *Abbeys in England and Wales,* from which you may learn something of the purpose and life which was associated with them. In addition to Bath Abbey, there are a number in ruins that are particularly striking. Two, Rievaulx Abbey and Fountains Abbey, are highlights of any visit to England, and five others – Castle Acre Priory (especially), Byland Abbey, Buildwas Abbey, Llanthony Priory and Whitby Abbey – are also of exceptional interest. Children particularly enjoy the ruined abbeys, for they are ghostly and mysterious, often sited in well-tended grassy parklands, and without the restraints on noise placed by still-living cathedrals.

Finally, one must not forget the most famous religious building in all Britain: Westminster Abbey, in London.

Northern Ireland also has its cathedrals of course. They are not generally attractive, however, and only history or sentiment would be likely to carry you to them. There are both Protestant and Roman Catholic cathedrals in Belfast, and others in Newry and in *Armagh,* the ecclesiastical capital of Northern Ireland, contain some excellent memorials; and the Roman Catholic cathedral in Londonderry is handsome.

Whether viewing cathedrals, abbeys, or parish churches, prepare yourself with a small guide to church architecture and furnishings. Two excellent ones are: *English Parish Churches as Works of Art,* by Alec Clifton-Taylor, and *What to See in a Country Church,* by Lawrence E. Jones.

In cathedrals, in particular, you will find it useful to have a lightweight pair of binoculars, for the detail on the roofs, the carved, decorated and painted ceiling bosses, and the glory beams will be far above you. (Some cathedrals have mirrors mounted on table tops which you may roll about, but these do not magnify – they merely prevent a crick in the neck.) In all cathedrals, make a point of examining the monuments, screens, pulpits, and stalls; visit the individual chapels and especially the Lady Chapel; look at the misericords (the carved brackets on the turn-up choir stall seats) and seek out the cloisters, the crypt and the chapter house. Do not take interior pictures, or make brass rubbings, without seeking permission first. And be certain to walk right around the exterior.

Speaking of brass rubbing, the best brasses are not generally found in the cathedrals but in parish churches. In the tours that follow I have singled out some that are especially good (the brasses of Cobham Church, Kent – see Tour 2 – are probably the most famous). One wants to come prepared with the proper paper, crayons, and patience, and it is expected that one will seek permission from someone in the church and probably pay a modest fee.

Brasses are memorials, usually monumental in size, in the form of flat metal plates with incised designs. They are usually inserted into the marble slabs of the floor, although they may also be on walls. They were introduced from the continent in the thirteenth century and were used in England, in particular, from the fourteenth through the seventeenth centuries. If you want to engage in the hobby, write first to The Monumental Brass Society, 90 High Street, Newport Pagnell, Buckinghamshire, from which you can obtain a list of brasses.

Probably the best churches for brass rubbing, in addition to that in Cobham, are the following:

In London, Great St Helen's, in Bishopsgate, and All Hallows, Barking-by-the-Tower, on Great Tower Street. In the counties nearby, St Mary's Church, Chatham, Kent: St Nicholas' Church, Taplow, Bucks.; St Mary's Church, Stoke D'Abernon, Surrey; and All Saints' Parish Church, Acton, Suffolk. A little further out are the parish church of Little Horkesley, near Nayland, in Suffolk, but actually in Essex; and the parish church of Westley Waterless, near Newmarket in Suffolk.

A final word. If you are as entranced by England's cathedrals and parish churches as most American vistors are, you may want to help in some substantial way to assure that they survive. Two societies will be of particular interest to you. One, the Historic Churches Preservation Fund, Inc., receives donations specially from Americans for the preservation of any church or cathedral they wish to name, through Barclays Bank D.C.O., 300 Park Avenue, New York, New York 10022. The other, The Friends of Friendless Churches, devotes itself to the preservation of churches no longer in use and can be contacted by writing to Mr Ivor Bulmer-Thomas, at 12 Edwardes Square, London W.8.

The castles of Britain

One of the most common symbols on a highway map of Britain (and especially of England) is a tiny red mark that appears to have been lifted from a chess set: it indicates one of the several hundred castles, most in ruins, which dot the countryside. There may be other countries in which crenellated towers thrust from the landscape as often, but there can be no others in which so wide a variety of castle architecture is compressed into so small a space. Wherever one travels in Britain, there will be an opportunity to view yet another castle; hence the need for this purely personal short list of the most interesting among them. Unlike cathedrals, I have not systematically collected castles, but all of those I include I have visited, and I can vouch for their interest, by reason of their setting, their associations or their intrinsic nature.

The following are ten great castles of England.

1 Surely Windsor is England's greatest castle; including its grounds, it is certainly the most extensive; it has been the home of England's monarchs for nine centuries; and it is the largest continuously inhabited castle in the world. Open daily throughout the year, Windsor is an essential visit, especially when the State Apartments are available for viewing. Only 21 miles from London, it is readily accessible and may easily be combined with a tour of Runnymede. See Tour 4. Be certain to visit St George's Chapel.

2 The Tower of London has been both palace and castle. From here through the Traitors' Gate, passed Anne Boleyn and Catherine Howard, Henry VIII's second and fifth wives; it is here that the alleged murder of young Edward V and his brother occurred; here Guy Fawkes was tried. The Tower warrants a full morning or

afternoon, especially in order to see the magnificent collection of weapons and, of course, the Crown Jewels. The crowds are intense in the summer, so be prepared for long queues.

3 Bamburgh Castle, north of Alnwick in Northumberland, stands alone on the coast, windswept and exposed as befits so romantic a stronghold. Adopted to many uses – granaries, a school for needy children, a refuge for shipwrecked mariners – this majestic shell is the Ely of castles, awesome for the approach, satisfying in the sampling (open Easter to Sept. 30, daily, 2–8).

4 A great castle-upon-an-island well worth seeking out is Lindisfarne, on Holy Island, midway between Alnwick and Berwick upon Tweed. The cradle of English Christianity, associated with the Venerable Bede and with a romantic setting, Lindisfarne satisfies well anyone's sense of adventure. Do examine the tide tables before driving across the causeway, however. It is open March 28–May 30 and June 22–Sept. 30 daily except Tuesday, 2–6; May 31–June 21, Wed. only.

5 St Michael's Mount, near Penzance, Cornwall, is England's romantic match to France's Mont St Michel. It is not, in fact, nearly so impressive upon investigation, being smaller and without truly first-rate interiors, but the setting, the approach across a narrow spit of land at low tide from Marazion and the tiny isle upon which the structure stands makes for a most satisfying visit. It is open Wed. and Fri. (and Mon., June–Sept.) 10.30 to either 3.30 or 4.30.

6 Tintagel Castle, near Camelford, Cornwall, is a stark ruin high on the cliffs above the sea, well protected, remote, bleak. Associated with King Arthur and the Knights of the Round Table, it is (together with Glastonbury) a place of pilgrimage for those who still seek the Holy Grail. The purely romantic association is no less compelling. It is open May–Sept. 9.30–7, 2–7 on Sun., and 9.30 or 10.00 to 4.30 or 5.30 the rest of the year.

7 Another literary pilgrimage is that to Peveril Castle, associated with Sir Walter Scott's *Peveril of the Peak*, at Castleton, west of Sheffield in Derbyshire. The castle itself is unremarkable, but its history – it was given to William Peverell, natural son of William the Conqueror – and its setting, high above the Hope Valley, provide singular attractions. Be prepared for a stiff climb. (Open as for Tintagel.)

8 Warwick Castle, in Warwickshire, is one of the most glorious of all ancient castles, and having been continuously occupied, mostly by the Beauchamp family, it is exceptionally well preserved. The towers, the barbican, the gates, the curtain walls – all are impressive. A

residence even today, the castle is open April–Oct. weekdays 10–5.30, Sun. 1–5, and at other times (save Dec., when it is closed) Mon.–Fri. and Sun. 12.30–4.30, Sat. 10.30–4.30.

9 Kenilworth Castle is only 5 miles north of Warwick, and the contrast between the two castles could not be finer. Those who have read Scott's *Kenilworth* will need no further reason to visit it. Home of the Earl of Leicester, finally refuge for a colony of weavers, Kenilworth is (together with Corfe Castle) the ultimate in romantic ruins. (Open as for Tintagel.)

10 There are four exceptional castles in Kent, three of them on the coast, which may be seen as a unit in a day. Of the four, perhaps Walmer, just south of Deal, is the most interesting, being the official residence of the Lords Warden of the Cinque Ports (a largely ceremonial post filled, at different times, by the Duke of Wellington, Sir Winston Churchill, and Sir Robert Menzies of Australia). One of the 'Three Castles which keep the Downs' – the others being Deal and Sandown – Walmer is perfectly symmetrical, with a central circular keep, and it contains an excellent small museum. Dover Castle, 'The Key to England', surrendered in 1066 to William the Conqueror, commands one of the most impressive sites in the country. Deal Castle, just north of Walmer, is even more perfect in design and construction than the first. (To these one might add Rochester Castle, immediately above Rochester Cathedral.)

There are many other castles well worth visiting. One of the pleasures of Britain is to stop and walk the well-manicured grounds of one of the castle ruins, however small it may be. For a general description of over fifty major castles, consult Garry Hogg's *Castles of England* (David & Charles, 1979) – a rather cumbersome book to carry – and take with you, if possible, the most recent edition of the annual publication, *Historic Houses, Castles and Gardens in Great Britain and Ireland* which you can get at almost any bookshop in Britain after you arrive.

I am unwilling to leave the castles behind without a word about others which are especially attractive to me. Arundel Castle, in Sussex, with a majestic keep, home of the Dukes of Norfolk, is one of the most beautiful of southern castles. Bodiam Castle, 12 miles north of Hastings has a remarkable moat, appealing to the child in us all, and a pervasive medieval atmosphere. Restormel, south of Bodmin in Cornwall, is a perfect circle with a steep motte. Dartmouth Castle commands the Dart estuary and has been used as recently as 1940. Tattershall Castle, 15 miles southeast of Lincoln, rises as a single great tower block from the flat landscape, and its red brick construction gives it a warmth much needed in this usually damp part of the country. I have a special liking for Ninney Castle – quite small, hidden away in a tiny village southwest of Frome (and even within the village requiring some search) and in its miniature grace particularly appealing. Sandringham House you will not see, for it is one of the royal residences, but a drive through the great parkland which surrounds it, 10 miles north of King's Lynn, is rewarding. Not far away is Castle Acre, where the ruins of a Cluniac Priory and a Norman Castle jointly beckon. Corfe Castle, on the Isle of Purbeck – not actually an island – southwest of Bournemouth, in Dorset (or Wessex if you read Hardy) must be seen against a jagged sky of night lightning, so completely does it fulfil the needs built up in us by the late-late show. And one should visit at least one each of the Welsh and Scottish border castles. I would choose Ludlow Castle, in the Welsh Marches, in Shropshire, property of the Earls of Powis; and Norham Castle, southwest of Berwick upon Tweed, a border castle made famous by Scott in *Marmion*, the poem to that Sir William who resisted Robert the Bruce on the south bank of the Tweed. And thus by stealth we come to Scotland.

The castles of Scotland differ from those of England, as one would expect. There are fewer of them. They tend to be smaller and more widely spaced; yet those that have survived appear, on the whole, larger and more forbidding. A number of them are as fine as any but the very best in England, and in truth the castle I like best of all is in Scotland.

The following are ten major castles of Scotland.

1 If I could visit but one castle, it would be Edinburgh's great fortress, set above the city. One looks down upon a handsome metropolis, one encounters at every step along the cobblestones some living history, the great Tattoo which takes place within the courtyard during the Festival in summer could command no more romantic a backdrop and the many rooms given over to museums are among the finest anywhere. This is the tourist's castle *par excellence*, which means crowds and flying candy wrappers at the height of the season (precincts open 6–9 daily).

2 Glamis Castle (pronounced Glarms) is the picturesque, many-towered (if you climb it, you'll agree that 'to tower' is a very active

verb indeed) seat of the Earls of Strathmore. It was here that Duncan was murdered in *Macbeth*, not far from Birnam Wood and Dunsinane (open May–Sept., Wed. and Thurs., and Sun. July–Sept. 2–5.30).

3 Inveraray Castle, in Argyll, headquarters of the Clan Campbell since the 15th century, contained an excellent collection of weapons, state rooms, and unusual furniture. It was tragically damaged by a disastrous fire in 1975 but has fortunately now been restored and is open to the public.

4 Culzean (pronounced Cullain) Castle, Ayrshire, is probably the best Adam building in Scotland and has close associations with General Eisenhower. The gardens are especially fine (open March–Oct. daily, 10–dusk).

5 Craigievar Castle, Aberdeenshire, is an exceptional tower house, unaltered since 1626, with unusual decorated ceilings and attractive grounds (open May–Sept., Wed., Thurs., Sun., 2–7).

6 Braemar Castle, also in Aberdeenshire, built in 1628, is especially appealing to children, having the kind of towers one associates with fairy tales. There is a *Son et Lumière* show in Aug. and Sept. (open May–Oct. daily 10–6).

7 Certainly the most romantic and startling setting for any castle in Scotland, and one you will recognize at once from British travel posters, is Eilean Donan, in Ross and Cromarty, on the Road to Skye. A 13th century castle rebuilt in 1932, with many Jacobite relics, the castle is a little disappointing inside and the local lore is laid on with a bit o' the trowel. But nothing can take the scene itself away as one looks down from the mountain above onto this 'picture-postcard' castle set upon a tiny islet within the loch. It is open April–Oct., weekdays 10–12.30, 2–6.

8 Stirling Castle, in Stirling, is the only rival in Scotland to Edinburgh Castle in magnitude and sheer mass. The view from it, down upon an old jousting ground, is outstanding, and, if your interest runs to military history, so is the interior (open April–Sept., daily 10–6.45, Sun. 11–6; Oct.–March, daily 10–4, Sun. 1–4).

9 Balmoral is both a castle and a palace. Near Ballater, in Aberdeenshire, it is the Scottish home of Her Majesty the Queen – as the guide books all say, which is their way of informing you that it is not open to the public. You may visit the gardens, and thus view the outside of Balmoral, May–July, daily (except Sun.) 10–5, unless a member of the Royal Family is in residence.

10 Lauriston Castle, Barnton, Edinburgh, is more an overgrown country house than a castle, and you will be disappointed if you are

seeking anything similar to the castles proper listed above. But the grounds are attractive and sweep down to the Firth of Forth; the English Georgian and French Louis furniture styles are well displayed; there is an intriguing, and ugly, collection of wool mosaics; and the collection of Derbyshire Blue John ware is as fine as you will see anywhere (open May–Oct., 9.30–6, Sun. 11–6; Nov.–April, to 5.15, Sun. 12.30–4.30).

This list includes no true Lowland castles, for there are few and they are in ruins. Even so, I cannot fail to mention two, simply because they were the first castles I ever visited in Scotland, years ago, which continue to fascinate: Roslin, a tiny castle reached by rowing a boat across to the middle of the pond in which it rests, 15 miles south of Edinburgh; and Maclellan's, in Kirkcudbright (pronounced Kerr-coo-bree), itself of little interest, but affording a chance to see Broughton House and the Tolbooth in which John Paul Jones, founder of the American navy, was once imprisoned.

Wales also offers a number of striking castles. The following five are outstanding.

1 Caernarvon Castle, at the heart of Welsh consciousness, the birthplace of Edward II, first Prince of Wales, and still the most important of Edward I's castles (open May–Sept. 9.30–7, 2–7 on Sun. and 9.30 or 10.00 to 4.30 or 5.30 the rest of the year). This castle saw the investiture of Prince Charles as Prince of Wales in 1969, and it contains a number of rooms and exhibits well calculated to appeal to children.

2 Harlech Castle, where if you can resist humming 'Men of Harlech' you are a stronger man than I. Built in 1283–9 by Edward I, this concentric structure commands a romantic height above the sea (open as for Caernarvon).

3 Powis Castle (pronounced Pows) at Welshpool, in Montgomery-shire, commands the River Severn. Built of red limestone, it is spectacular in siting, and the grounds contain excellent topiary (open May–Sept. 2–6).

4 Manorbier Castle, 5 miles from Pembroke, is a distinguished semi-ruin, overlooking the Atlantic coast. Here was born Giraldus Cambrensis, author of the Welsh classic *The Itinerary through Wales* (an account of an expedition in 1188) and an unsuccessful campaigner for an independent Welsh church. It is open March 25–April 1, May 13–Sept. 30, daily 11–1, 2–6.

5 Conway Castle, in Conway, is massive, serviceable, and like a rooted Mack truck (open as for Caernarvon).

Again, there are delights such a truncated listing overlooks. One is Beaumaris Castle, on Anglesey, where children may – with care – troop about upon the walls; another is Oystermouth, on the Gower Peninsula outside Swansea – an insignificant castle which helps draw one onto the peninsula; yet another is Carreg Cennen Castle, hidden in the Black Mountains on a delightful and narrow back road from Llandeilo to Brynamman – not open to the public, but offering a magnificent excuse to pursue this lovely route. St Donat's Castle, southwest of Cardiff and now in the hands of the United World College of the Atlantic is charming and offers an unusually effective setting. Nor should one dismiss three quite ugly castles: Cardiff, which you may see with appalling thoroughness; Penrhyn Castle, in Bangor, rebuilt between 1827 and 1840, and not made beautiful by a four-poster bed made of slate, its collections of dolls and pottery, or its Mona marble; and Caerphilly Castle, the second largest in Europe, unappealing but persistent in being open daily.

Northern Ireland is not noted for its castles, and there are none that I recommend.

The country houses of Britain

Country houses, castles, cathedrals: these are the three distinctive forms of architecturally historic Britain. Not that other nations do not have all three; rather, given a punitive taxation system upon the rich, Britain, more than any other country, has country houses open to the public. After the late, great war, the Labour government (followed equally cheerfully by Conservative governments thereafter) blew the winds of change across the estates of the big rich, assessing death duties which in some instances were high enough to be tantamount to confiscation. At first it appeared to some that the English country houses, in particular, might go (and some did). But that especial British pragmatic wisdom, which leads to theoretical justification of policies only after policies have been put into practice, prevailed once again, just as it had done when there was an Empire to be built. The great houses were – in many instances – architectural monuments, potential tourist attractions, even money earners. And so some of the houses became public property, while others remained in private hands, on condition that they would be open to the public for a specified period each year. Nowhere else in Europe may one visit so many great houses, alive with so many literary and historic associations.

For the most part it was not these associations which led to the preservation of a particular house or estate. The preservation movement in Britain is based more on the architectural merit of a structure than on the history associated with it. George Washington may have slept there, precisely *there*, a dozen times; if the building lacks merit, if it is ugly, if it does not mark a high example of a particular style in decoration or a development of significance in construction, it is unlikely to survive in England. Americans tend to be more interested in what happened *in* the building, in its associations, in using its tapestries and furniture to evoke an age, the image of a man, or a work of literature, than they are in the tapestries and furniture for their own sake. Perhaps the British simply have so much history tangibly all about them, that they do not need to foster a sense of the past so specifically. While the United States is setting out systematically to preserve some structure, usually the birthplace, associated with every one of our Presidents, the British apparently would never think of preserving a house simply because a Prime Minister happened to have been born there. Just as Americans carefully preserve the great battlefields associated with their Revolution and their Civil War, the British almost as carefully fail to preserve battlefields, so should one take oneself to Hastings, Flodden Field, or Bosworth, one will find little save a stone slab with an inscription to remind one of the events that occurred there. In this sense, the English country houses are also monuments to the British approach to their collections, and the linking references to personalities are not always made.

But the premise of this guide is that Americans are interested in the sights they see in a peculiarly American way. Our interest often does focus on the historical association. We go to Blenheim as much because of Winston Churchill as because of the size and grandeur of the preserved palace. Perhaps the distinction is best seen in the fact that the British are little interested in ferreting out the houses associated with some of their greatest literature, while Americans find such gentle country seats especially attractive, precisely for those associations. Surely one visits Coole Park, Galway (in Eire) primarily because it was the home of Lady Gregory, and that Yeats came to love it – but then, the house has not been preserved, a crime against literature in the eyes of many Americans, but a natural enough condition in the eyes of the Irish. Hertfordshire contains a number of outstanding houses, including Hatfield and Knebworth, and Shaw's Corner at Ayot St Lawrence. But it also contains Rooksrest, the model for Howard's End in E. M. Forster's novel of that name. Oxfordshire offers us Blenheim, Ditchley Park and Greys Court; it also contains Beckley Park, the model for Aldous Huxley's *Crome Yellow*, and Garsington Manor (in the country southeast of Oxford), the model for Breadalby in D. H. Lawrence's *Women in Love*. The Yorkshires afford thirty-eight listings in the annual guide to *Historic Houses, Castles and Gardens* that are open to the public; Busby Hall, the model for Ford Madox Ford's *Parade's End*, at Carlton-in-Cleveland,

Stokesley, is not among them. To be sure, these rural seats often remain in private hands, closed to the public, and the British would not wish to direct you to them out of their respect for privacy. Yet there are homes with such associations that *are* open to the public, but the rationale for their being so is not usually literary: one can spend weeks visiting the forty homes in Sussex that are open to the public, and may include Uppark, in the South Downs – because it was built by Lord Tankerville in 1690, or because it contains remarkable 18th century interiors, including the original wallpapers, or even because it was built to William Talman's designs – yet no one appears to consider it interesting because it was the model for Bladesover in H. G. Wells' *Tono-Bungay*. The country house is obviously one thing to the British and something else to those who come from elsewhere.

Following is a list of over 150 (out of more than 500) houses which you will enjoy to greater or lesser degrees. Those that have a particular American connection are marked *. A few houses that carry the title of 'castle' are included, when they are, in fact, overgrown houses. The same is true of palaces in Scotland. I also list houses associated with distinguished literary figures, on the assumption that their collections of memorabilia may be of interest to you (names in parentheses). The houses themselves are usually of little distinction. It is *de rigueur* for many of the larger country houses to have a display of vintage motor cars and often a flying machine or two, but I have ignored these attractions. The houses are either chosen because of the distinctiveness of their architecture, the serenity and magnitude of their grounds, the importance of their collection of paintings, silver, and/or furniture, or for a particular association they have. Full descriptions, and times of opening, may be found in the most recent edition of *Historic Houses, Castles and Gardens* which you may buy in any good bookshop in Britain. If the gardens are a principal feature, April through June are the best months to visit; all of the houses will be uncomfortably crowded on weekends in July and August. All charge admission. The pre-1974 county designations are used, as they are still commonly seen and heard. For the county names officially in use since the reorganisations and amalgamations of 1974, consult the map at the end of the book.

ENGLAND

Bedfordshire
Luton Hoo
Woburn Abbey

Berkshire
Ashdown House
Great Coxwell Tithe Barn

Buckinghamshire
Ascott
Claydon House (Florence
   Nightingale)
Cliveden*
Hughenden Manor (Disraeli)
Nether Winchenden House*
Waddesdon Manor

Cheshire
Capesthorne*
Little Moreton Hall
Lyme Park

Cornwall
Cothele House*
Godolphin House
Lanhydrock

Cumberland
Dove Cottage (Wordsworth)

Derbyshire
Chatsworth
Haddon Hall
Hardwick Hall
Kedleston Hall
Melbourne Hall

Devonshire
Buckland Abbey*
Compton Castle*

Dorset
Athelhampton (Hardy)
Clouds Hill (T. E. Lawrence)
Max Gate (Hardy)
Sherborne Castle*

Durham
Washington Old Hall*

Essex
Audley End House

Gloucestershire
Badminton House
Buckland Rectory (Wesley)
Dodington House
Kelmscott Manor (William
   Morris)

Hampshire
Beaulieu Abbey
Chawton (Jane Austen)
Mottisfont Abbey*
The Vyne*

Herefordshire
Eye Manor*

Hertfordshire
Ashridge
Hatfield House
Knebworth House
Salisbury Hall
Shaw's Corner (G. B. Shaw)

Kent
Bleak House (Dickens)
Chartwell (Winston Churchill)
Chiddingstone Castle
Down House (Charles Darwin)
Knole

Penshurst Place
Quebec House* (Wolfe)
Sissinghurst Castle
Smallhythe Place (Ellen Terry,
 Sarah Siddons)
Squerryes Court*

Lancashire

Hall i'th'Wood
Hill Top, Sawrey (Beatrix
 Potter)
Platt Hall
Speke Hall

Leicestershire

Belvoir Castle

Lincolnshire

Epworth (Wesley)
Gainsborough Old Hall*
Woolsthorpe Manor (Newton)

London

Apsley House (Wellington)
Carlyle's House
Fenton House
Hall Place
Hampton Court Palace
Hogarth's House
Kensington Palace
Kenwood, Iveagh Bequest
Lancaster House
Marble Hill House
Marlborough House
Marx Memorial Library
Osterley Park House

Norfolk

Blickling Hall
Holkham Hall

Northamptonshire

Althorp
Burghley House
Cotterstock Hall (Dryden)
Deene Park
Delapre Abbey*
Sulgrave Manor*

Northumberland

Seaton Delaval Hall
Wallington (Trevelyan)

Nottinghamshire

Thoresby Hall

Oxfordshire

Blenheim Palace
Broughton Castle*
Chacombe Priory
Ditchley Park*
Greys Court
Mapledurham House
 (Galsworthy)
Wroxton Abbey*

Shropshire

Boscobel House*
Weston Park

Somerset

Claverton Manor*
Clevedon Court (Thackeray)
Cothay Manor
Montacute House
Nether Stowey (Coleridge)

Staffordshire

Blithfield Hall

Suffolk

Gainsborough's House
Ickworth

Surrey

Claremont
Hatchlands*

Sussex

Bateman's (Kipling)
Battle Abbey
Firle Place*
Lamb House* (Henry James)
Petworth House
Royal Pavilion, Brighton
Uppark (Wells)

Warwickshire

Aston Hall
Charlecote Park
Harvard House*
Packwood House
Shakespeare's Birthplace Trust
    Properties

Westmorland

Levens Hall

Wiltshire

Longleat
Stourhead
Wilton House

Yorkshire

Bramham Park
Castle Howard
Harewood House
Haworth Parsonage (Brontës)
Newby Hall
Oakwell Hall (Brontës)

WALES

Portmeirion

SCOTLAND

Provost Ross' House, Aberdeen
Burns' Cottage, Alloway
Duart Castle, Argyll
Mellerstain, Berwickshire
Carlyle's House, Ecclefechan
Gladstone's Land, Edinburgh
Hopetoun House, Edinburgh
Palace of Holyrood House,
    Edinburgh
Culross Palace, Fife
Falkland Palace, Fife
Barrie Birthplace, Kirriemuir
Abbotsford House, Melrose
    (Scott)
Dawyck House, Peeblesshire
    (Buchan)
Traquair House, Peeblesshire
Scone Palace, Perth
The Binns, West Lothian
Linlithgow Palace, West
    Lothian

NORTHERN IRELAND

Arthur House, Cullybackey*
Castlecoole, Co. Fermanagh
Mellon House, Omagh*
Printing Press House, Strabane*
Wilson House, Co. Tyrone*

Obviously your time will be too limited to visit more than a sample of these, and the list is provided as a guide to houses of especial interest when you are already in the vicinity, or are concentrating on a single area of Britain. But even if you limit yourself largely to houses that can be reached by Green Line bus from London, you will find that you can gain a remarkably full sense of the variety of 'happy rural seats', for not only all those listed under London itself, but most listed under Bedfordshire, Berkshire, Buckinghamshire, Hertfordshire and Kent may be reached by bus from London. Should you have time for only one distant foray into the country, I would recommend Derbyshire, for all five of the houses listed are of major importance, and in two days, using Sheffield as a base, you can see a wide variety of interiors and a reasonable variety of exterior styles and grounds.

Still, some are more important than others, and again, however foolish, let me nominate ten great Great Houses.

1 One begins with Blenheim Palace, outside Woodstock, just north of Oxford. Often called 'Britain's Versailles', although in fact substantially smaller, Blenheim is one of the largest mansions in the land. The gift of the nation to the Duke of Marlborough for defeating the armies of Louis XIV, the palace was designed by Sir John Vanbrugh, built between 1705 and 1722 in the baroque style, and supplied with a remarkable ornamental garden in the manner of André le Nôtre, creator of the gardens of Versailles. The grounds beyond the garden still reflect the more informal English approach of 'Capability' Brown, who was certainly so, and whose landscapes accompany a number of country estates. Other famous names are to be found at Blenheim as well; one may see there something of the best work of Grinling Gibbons and Michael Rysbrack, for example. Winston Churchill was born in Blenheim in 1874. He is buried in Bladon churchyard, nearby. Blenheim is open daily 1–6 March 23–April 2, and (except Fri.) July 6–Sept. 24; April 6–July 2, Sept. 28–Oct. 29, Mon. through Thurs., 1–6; *Son et Lumière* on summer evenings.

2 Knole House, at Knole, in Kent, and also one of the largest of the country houses, may be reached from London on a Green Line bus. Begun by the Archbishop of Canterbury in 1456, granted by Elizabeth I to the poet (and politician) Thomas Sackville, more recently the home of Victoria Sackville-West, the model for Chevron in the *Edwardians* and the house in Virginia Woolf's *Orlando,* Knole is rich in literary associations. It contains an ornamental great staircase which set the fashion for a century, a superb gallery of portraits,

excellent tapestries, and fine furniture. There are better interior collections in other houses, but none so close to London combine such an interesting Jacobean interior with so many associations. Further, the location makes possible a combined outing to Quebec House, Chartwell, Penshurst Place and Hever Castle in the same crowded day (if you have your own transport). Knole is open except Jan., Feb., Wed. through Sat., 10–12, 2–3.30 (winter) 2–5 (summer).

3 Longleat is viewed by some as the Disneyland of country houses. The Wiltshire home of the Marquess of Bath, and 20 miles south of that city, Longleat is a great Renaissance house begun in 1568, with a park landscaped by Capability Brown. When faced with the prospect of selling some of his Reynolds, Lelys, Van Dycks and Titians, his Chippendale and silver, or his First Folio Shakespeare, the Marquess made the defensible decision to put seals in the lake instead and to create a remarkable lion reserve, through which one can drive, with monkeys perching on one's car the while. The carnival atmosphere is kept at a remove from the house, children thoroughly enjoy the lion park, and grown-ups may still see the First Folio in place, rather than in an American museum. In many ways, a visit to Longleat is most likely to be the best obligatory country house tour you might force upon a reluctant family. It is open daily all year, 10–6 (summer), 10–4 (winter). Longleat may be combined with Wilton House in a one-day tour from Bath or in driving between Salisbury and Bristol.

4 Hatfield House, at Hatfield, in Hertfordshire, may also be reached from London by Green Line bus. A Jacobean house finished in 1611, it has been the ancestral home of the Cecil family for 350 years and is judged by many observers to be the finest house in Britain. Among its attractions are a central block attributed to Inigo Jones, a display of arms taken from the Spaniards who were captured when their Armada was destroyed in 1588, very possibly the finest grand staircase in the world, an exceptional Great Hall, a library of 10,000 books and superb tapestries. One may visit Shaw's Corner and Knebworth House on the same day. Hatfield House is open March 27–April 30 weekdays, May 1–Oct. 4 daily except Mon., 12–5 (Sun. from 2.30).

5 The American fascination with Winston Churchill is an intense one, and a focus for this fascination is his home, Chartwell, at Westerham, Kent. It is not a great house in the usual meaning of the word, although one need not insist – as some guide books, reaching for an inappropriate egalitarianism, do – that it is 'modest' either. Churchill lived here for many years, and the house and gardens

(complete with brick wall he laid himself) contain many mementoes of his career. Given his American mother, and his friendship with F.D.R. and Eisenhower, there are also many objects relating to the Anglo-American connection. One may visit Quebec House and Knole on the same day, by Green Line bus. Chartwell is open March–Nov., Wed., Thurs., 2–6, Sat., Sun. 11–6.

6 Chatsworth, at Bakewell, in Derbyshire (where you must seek out an authentic Bakewell tart), was built by William Talman for the first Duke of Devonshire between 1687 and 1707. Built in the classical style, with stunning, warm interiors, Chatsworth is equally famous for its garden, in which four periods of design are nicely illustrated. One may combine Chatsworth with Haddon Hall and Peveril Castle on a day's outing from Sheffield, or with Kedleston Hall and Haddon Hall driving from Derby to Sheffield. It is open March 25–Oct. 4, Wed.–Fri. 11.30–4, Sat., Sun., 2–5.30.

7 Wilton House, near Salisbury, in Wiltshire, is the perfect house to combine with Salisbury Cathedral, Stonehenge and Old Sarum. Built for the Earl of Pembroke, it is small enough to comprehend and large enough to impress. The furniture and plasterwork are justly famous, the design by Inigo Jones attractive, the collection of 7000 model soldiers good fun, and the Rembrandts, Van Dycks, Rubens, *et al.*, impressive. During World War II, the house was used by the British Army as Headquarters/Southern Command, and much of the planning for D-Day was carried out here. Philip Sidney wrote *Arcadia* here, one tradition holds that the first performances of *Twelfth Night* and *As You Like It* were here, and Edmund Spenser and Ben Jonson were frequent visitors. Wilton House is open April–Sept., Tues.–Sat. 11–5.30 (open Sun. at 2).

8 There are those who think Woburn Abbey a bit much, for it now includes a widely advertised 'Wild Animal Kingdom', and in the summer sticky ice cream papers may be thick upon the ground. But it is also a superb 18th century mansion with a collection of Rembrandt, Van Dyck, Gainsborough, Reynolds, Velazquez, Holbein and Canaletto paintings, a fine collection of furniture and silver, fourteen State Apartments and many items relating to the Dukes of Bedford, whose home it is. The Duke was English Ambassador to France at the time of the signing of the Treaty of Paris of 1763 (when Canada became British) and there are other North American reminders, including some dispirited bison. An ugly grotto is hailed as the finest example of 17th century shell rooms; it is handsomely offset by a fine library which includes an elephant folio of John James Audubon's *Birds of*

America. Lord John Russell, the British Foreign Minister who helped keep Britain out of the American Civil War, grew up here. And Woburn also has the famous Armada Portrait of Queen Elizabeth I. When the Duke of Bedford inherited the estate in 1953, he found £5,000,000 in death duties had to be paid, and that the estate has survived at all is testimony to good planning, hard work and a happy location not too far from London. But he prepared for crowds. Woburn is open daily, April–Oct., 11.30–5, Nov.–March, 1.30–4, with grounds opening earlier. One may combine Woburn Abbey with a visit to Luton Hoo, distinguished for its collection of Fabergé jewels, Dresden, Limoges and English porcelain and china, Beauvais tapestries and Rembrandt and Titian paintings.

9 Only one country home is worth visiting solely for its American associations. This is **Sulgrave Manor,** not a stately home but a small manor-house built by a Lancashireman about 1560. The Lancashireman was Lawrence Washington, wool-merchant, mayor, and direct ancestor of George Washington. At the centenary of the Treaty of Ghent, which had ended the War of 1812, British subscribers raised funds for the restoration of the manor, which had become a farmhouse. Opened in 1921, the house was then endowed by the National Society of the Colonial Dames of America. The family arms – to be seen in the spandrels of the doorway – were mullets (stars) and bars (stripes) and there are those who contend that this was the origin of the design of the American Flag. There is an original Gilbert Stuart portrait of Washington, oak furniture of the period, an unusual 200-year-old kitchen and an attractive garden. Both the Union Jack and the American Flag fly here every day. Tours are run from London. It is open daily except Wed., April–Sept. 10.30–1, 2–5.30; Oct.–March, close at 4.

10 My tenth choice will strike the British as idiosyncratic: Speke Hall, near Liverpool. One of the finest Elizabethan half-timbered buildings anywhere, and thus of the style not otherwise included in this list, it contains excellent plasterwork, many secret chambers which the children will enjoy and an attractive courtyard. Although it has no associations with the great African explorer, it is no less romantic for that (open all year, weekdays 10–5, Sun. 2–5).

Some of the country houses of specifically American interest, as shown on the longer list above, are described in the tours. The great houses of London are discussed separately in the section on that city.

The Shakespeare Trust Properties are described under Stratford (see Tour 1).

There are three houses outside England that rank in interest with the ten above.

Falkland Palace, in Falkland, Kingdom of Fife (Scotland) is a 16th century hunting palace built by the Stuart Kings. It was often used by Mary, Queen of Scots, and it is now owned by the present Queen. The gardens have been restored, the narrow streets of the town offer a picturesque backdrop, and the King's bedchamber is properly ornate (open April–Oct., daily 10–6, Sun. 2–6).

The Palace of Holyrood House, in Edinburgh, is the official residence of the monarch when in Scotland, and therefore closed when the Royal Family is there. James IV of Scotland began the palace in 1501; Cromwell's troops occupied it in 1650 and much of it was damaged by fire. Renovated and refurnished several times since, the interior is not particularly attractive, but the grounds, the entrance gate, and the many associations of palace with Scottish history – as well as its location at the foot of the Royal Mile – make it well worth visiting. It is open June–Sept. daily 9.30–6, Sun. 11–6, Oct.–May, close 4.30, Sun. open 12.30.

Portmeirion, in Wales, is not a country home, but a combination of architectural museum, holiday village, pottery industry and Italianate landscaping, dating from the 1920s. It is more successful than one would expect, and as an assemblage of copies of many buildings and monuments dating from 1610 onwards, combined with unusual Mediterranean-style gardens, it provides an exceptionally pleasant spot to visit. The Gwyllt Gardens are famous for their rhododendrons, and the many follies are fun in themselves. It is open Easter–mid-Oct. daily, 10–7, though some structures may be closed for restoration because of fire.

Before setting out to view the country houses and their collections, make a point of reading a superb little book, *The Englishness of English Art*, by Sir Nikolaus Pevsner. The Reith Lectures for 1955, it is a stunningly successful attempt to encompass much in little.

Gardens in Britain

From the 16th century onwards, as the age of exploration and discovery opened up new trade routes and brought new products back into Britain, the British took the lead in botany and gardening, developing new plants and horticultural techniques, and arranging old plants in new ways. Originally, the British preferred the formal gardens now best represented in France. In the 17th century the use of parterres from which one might gain a view of the mathematical certainties of the formal garden, rather than walk within it, the ranking of files of statuary and hedges along avenues and paths, and the development of the art of topiary (the practice of clipping evergreens into shapes, often of mythical animals) reached its height. Then, in the 18th century, William Kent and Capability Brown tore up many of these gardens and replaced them with the informal, natural parkland garden which today is taken to be most typically English. Formal gardens came back into fashion in the Victorian period, and while there were subsequent odd graftings of oriental, Dutch, and other styles, the two main general types prevailed side by side from then onwards. As a result, one may view a wide range of styles of garden as one travels about in Britain.

These gardens are often found in association with the great country estates, and where they are particularly noteworthy, they have been singled out in the section on country houses. Gardens are sometimes open when the house they grace is not. In some cases, as at Westbury Court, in Gloucestershire, noted for its Dutch garden, one seeks out the garden alone, but usually one wishes to see garden and architecture as set in complement to each other. Garden buildings, and especially orangeries, are themselves attractive cynosures. Pagodas, gazebos, 18th century grottos and pergolas add or detract, to or from the scene.

The use of water, in cascades, fountains and reflecting pools; the practice of espalier, against walls; the protection of gardens by ha has (ditches which are invisible from the garden while preventing entry from the public side), knot gardens, mazes and a variety of other artistic expressions, all provide English gardens with a fascination of their own. Above all, the English know what to do with flowers, and whether in a simple country garden, or as a bank of flowers in front of a house, whether a floral clock (as in Edinburgh) or a superb rose garden (as in Queen Mary's Garden, in Regent's Park, London), the display of flowers and flowering shrubs will be superb in spring and early summer. Perhaps the most glorious moment in London is that instant when suddenly Green Park, and the reaches of Hyde Park and Kensington Gardens, are alive with bright yellow April daffodils. Only then can one understand what Wordsworth means to the English.

For a guide to the best gardens, obtain a copy of *Discovering English Gardens*, a slim, excellent paperback by Kay N. Sanecki (through Shire Publications, Tring, Herts.). Gardens are also listed in the annual editions of *Historic Houses, Castles and Gardens in Great Britain and Ireland,* available at most bookshops. In addition to the outstanding gardens associated with the colleges at Cambridge and Oxford; at Stratford-upon-Avon; at Hampton Court; and at such country houses as Blenheim, Chatsworth, Hatfield, Knebworth, Blickling Hall, Chartwell or Castle Howard, there are a number of other major gardens.

The following English fifteen are unusually interesting:

1 Hever Castle, Edenbridge, Kent, probably the finest Italian garden in Britain, with topiary chessmen, a maze, cascades, a huge lake and moat, combining all that the romantic might want, set against the castle that was Anne Boleyn's home (open Easter–Sept. 30, Wed., Sun., Sats. in Aug.–Sept., 1–7).

2 Stourhead, Mere, Wiltshire, is a Palladian house with Chippendale furniture, but the real attraction is the finest landscaped garden in Britain (open Easter–Sept., Wed., Thurs., Sat., Sun.; March–Easter, Oct.–Nov., Thurs. omitted, 2–6; grounds only, daily 11–7 or dusk).

3 Bicton Gardens, East Budleigh, Devon, is Italian in design, with monkey puzzle trees, palm and cacti houses, a pinetum and a garden of North American shrubs. The principal garden was designed by Le Nôtre, of Versailles fame (open March 22–May 31, Sept. 14–30, daily 2–6; June 1–Sept. 13, daily 10–6; Oct., Sun. 2–6).

4 Dartington Hall, Totnes, Devon has many American associations, a large modern garden, fine statuary (including Henry Moore), Irish yews, and a cultural centre. Open by appointment, although there will be no objections if you want to view the grounds.

5 Syon Park, Brentford, on the Thames, reached from London by Green Line bus, is a permanent exhibition, shop and showplace for gardeners, maintained as The Gardening Centre. Syon House, with an Adam interior, is set in a Capability Brown landscape (open late March–early Oct., Mon.–Fri., 11–1, 2–4.15).

6 East Lambrook Manor, South Petherton, Somerset, is a 15th century house with a garden of particular interest to those botanically knowledgeable, as it attempts to contrast leaf and texture in unusual ways (open April–July, Sept., Thurs. 2–5, and by appointment throughout the year).

7 Packwood House, Hockley Heath, Warwickshire, offers the most unusual topiary garden in Britain, representing the Sermon on the Mount (open April–Sept., Tues.–Thurs., Sat., 2–7, Sun. open 2.30; Oct.–March, Wed., Sat., 2–5, Sun. open 2.30).

8 Bressingham Hall Gardens, Diss, Norfolk, while cluttered with a collection of steam engines, also has the finest show of herbaceous perennials in Britain, and dell and water gardens (open mid-May–early Oct., Thurs., Sun., 1.30–6).

9 Compton Wynyates, Banbury, Warwickshire, offers a rather unattractive Tudor house with an exceptional topiary garden (open Easter Holiday, then April–Sept., Wed., Sat., 2–5.30, also Sun. June–Aug.).

10 Lyme Park, Disley, Cheshire, a National Trust property, is a Palladian house in a park of 1300 acres, with a herd of red deer, and a fine, formal Dutch garden. The garden is open all year, daily, 8–dusk; the house, March–Aug., daily 1–6.15, Sept.–Oct., 2–4.

11 Muncaster Castle, Muncaster, Cumberland, contains a fine collection of furniture, but the point of a visit is the extensive garden, with the azaleas in spring and roses in summer and magnificent views of the mountains from the terrace. The garden is open Easter–June 30, daily, July 1–Aug. 31, Wed., Thurs., Sun., 1–6; castle open Easter–Aug. 31, Wed., Thurs., Sun., 2–5.

12 Trengwainton Gardens, Penzance, Cornwall, has fine views to the sea and is famous for its sub-tropical plants, especially magnolias (open March–Sept., Wed., Fri., Sat., 11–5).

13 Tresco Abbey Gardens, Isles of Scilly, Cornwall, associated with

the Valhalla Maritime Museum, is a unique terraced garden of sub-tropical plants (open all year, weekdays 10–4).

14 Compton Acres, Poole, Dorset, has seven gardens in different styles, of which the Roman, Japanese, and heath gardens are outstanding. Valuable marble and bronze statuary abounds (open daily Good Fri.–Oct., 10.30–6.30, and Thurs. June–Aug. to dusk).

15 Ammerdown Park, Radstock, Somerset, 8 miles south of Bath, gets it all together: statuary, fountains, water, terraces, orangery, orchards, yews, pergolas and avenues; the work of Sir Edwin Lutyens, and probably his best (open Sat., 11–7).

SCOTLAND

There are a number of outstanding gardens in Scotland, including those associated with Falkland Palace and Glamis Castle. Five stand above all others.

1 Inverewe, Poolewe, Wester Ross, owned by the National Trust of Scotland, is regarded as one of the finest gardens in all Britain. It is certainly the one I like the best. The views over Loch Ewe are superb, the walled garden is fine and the woodland walk most attractive. There is a special section on America (open daily, 10–dusk).

2 Pitmedden, Udny, in Aberdeenshire, is a reconstructed 17th century garden with fountains, maintained by the National Trust of Scotland, and it is unexpectedly formal for the area (open daily 9.30–dusk).

3 Edzell Castle and Gardens, Edzell, in Angus, is a 16th century castle with an unusual Renaissance garden (open April–Sept., 9.30–7, Sun. open 2; Oct.–March, 10–4.30, Sun. open 2).

4 Branklyn Garden, Perth, is also very fine, with special displays from time to time (open May 1–Sept. 30, Mon.–Sat., 2–5, Sun. to 6).

5 Royal Botanic Garden, Edinburgh, dates from the 17th century, and while not as interesting as Kew, (see page 98) contains attractive rock gardens and the Scottish National Gallery of Modern Art (open daily, weekdays 9–sunset, Sun. open 11; gallery open May–Sept., weekdays 10–6, Sun. open 2; Oct.–April, weekdays 11–6 or dusk, Sun. 2–5 or dusk).

WALES

In addition to the gardens of Portmeirion (see section on COUNTRY HOUSES) there are two outstanding gardens in Wales.

1 Bodnant Garden, Tal-y-Cafn, Denbighshire, laid out in 1875, and regarded by many as the outstanding garden of Britain (open April–Oct., Tues.–Thurs., Sat., 1.30–4.45).

2 Powis Castle, Welshpool, Montgomeryshire, contains fine plasterwork and many relics of Clive of India. The terraced gardens are formal and huge (gardens open May–Sept., Tues.–Sat., 2–6).

NORTHERN IRELAND
There is one garden of great distinction in Northern Ireland: Mount Stewart Gardens, near Newtownards (15 miles east of Belfast, in County Down) where there is fine topiary. It is open April–Sept., daily except Mon., 2–6.

The national parks of Britain

The national park movement has not taken firm root in Britain, and although there are a number of attractive parks, they came too late to preserve large areas in a completely wilderness state. Nor do the British wish to do so, for they argue that a vista punctuated by farmhouse, paddock and fence, even though within a national park, is truer to *their* nature, to the crowded nature of their land, and to a sense of the human in the landscape, than the great wilderness parks of the United States and Canada can expect to be. Americans, accustomed to what they do not always recognize to be the finest national park system in the world (as well as the first), used to finding their great battlefields preserved and carefully interpreted with markers, museums and roadside displays, expecting wildlife, campsites, and National Park Rangers, are often disappointed by the British parks. Yet a visit to one or more of them provides a particularly British set of insights into the nation and its peoples. And the parks *are* worth visiting, for within the more serene, even feminine softness of the English landscape, as opposed to the harsh masculine backdrop of the American West or of Scotland, are large areas of great natural beauty, used yet not spoiled.

In any event, what is a national park? Australia has 156 national parks, so called, and nearly all are administered by the individual states; most would not warrant their title or status outside Australia. (Indeed, the United Nations International Commission of National Parks, which has attempted to set international standards for the use of such a designation, admits only 113 of the Australian parks to its list. On the other hand, 89 *state* parks in the United States are of 'national park' standards by these UN criteria.) If one uses such criteria, the UN admits to 74 areas in Britain – all of them nature reserves – and excludes the 10 areas specifically designated as national parks (in England and Wales) by the British Government, on the ground that they are not under 'total protection'. The National Parks Commission, which operates only for England and Wales, also is responsible for some 15 'Areas of Outstanding Natural Beauty' and 9 'Long Distance Routes', which are scenic roads or trails. There are separate parks in Scotland and Northern Ireland.

In England, there are 7 national parks, listed here by size. Excellent guides to each may be purchased from Her Majesty's Stationery Office, 49 High Holborn, London, W.C.1.

1 Lake District National Park: encompassing the superb lakes of Derwent Water and Windermere, the highest mountains in England – Scafell and the Pikes – and the country in which Wordsworth trailed his clouds of glory behind, is Britain's finest natural park. It can be very crowded at Easter, on Bank holidays, and in midsummer, and the weather is fickle, but it should be the focus for a major visit. There are many walks and climbs, and some 43 ancient monuments, buildings, forts, abbeys, and packhorse bridges have been preserved within the park. There are also the rich literary associations with Wordsworth, Coleridge, Gray, Defoe, Burke, Lamb, Shelley, Scott, Ruskin, Walpole, Southey and Beatrix Potter, creator of Peter Rabbit. The Wordsworth and Potter homes, and the Ruskin Museum, are well worth visiting.

2 Yorkshire Dales National Park offers rugged, isolated, country which requires much tramping to explore at all well. The English regard a drive from Skipton up Wharfedale via Bolton Abbey, to Langstrothdale, through Hawes and Buttertubs and down the Swale to Richmond, as exceptionally wild. And wild it is, as a driving experience, for the road is narrow, isolated, and challenging.

3 Even so, the North York Moors National Park is likely to offer country you will appreciate more. Consisting largely of high, rolling moorland which rises steeply from the Plain of York in the west and falls into the sea from dramatic cliffs on the east, the park is wild, remote, and remarkably attractive. In the winter you can find yourself snowbound here – an unusual possibility for England – and the roads command attention and respect. Rievaulx Abbey, inside the park, and Whitby, just outside, are important sights to visit.

4 Peak District National Park is likely to disappoint Americans, for the peaks have been so much encroached upon from both sides.

5 Dartmoor National Park should be the pilgrimage point of

anyone who belongs to the Baker Street Irregulars or who is even a modest fan of the greatest detective of all time. For it was here that Sherlock Holmes and the good Doctor Watson heard the hideous baying of the Hound of the Baskervilles, it was here that the villain sank (one presumes) to his death in the vile Grimpen Mire, and it was from the great prison in Princetown that the convict who was mistaken for Sir Henry Baskerville escaped.

6 Northumberland National Park is a large area with much of interest within its bounds. From the Cheviot Hills in the north to the Roman (or Hadrian's) Wall in the south, the park offers historic and scenic attractions.

7 Exmoor National Park, the smallest in England, stretches between Somerset and Devon, includes the Lorna Doone country, and attractive backroads.

There are three national parks in Wales.

1 Snowdonia, carved out of Caernarvon and Merioneth shires, is handsome, high country, cold in winter, bleak, and striking. Here is Snowdon, highest peak outside Scotland, at 3560 feet. Much of the area is both roadless and trackless.

2 Brecon Beacons National Park, in south-central Wales, is an impressive, lonely area of stark natural beauty, ruined castles, and waterfalls.

3 Pembrokeshire Coast National Park consists of four separate units of coast, cliff and river, most of which can be reached by car. There are two very attractive walks, one around the Dale Peninsula and the other a coastal footpath in the parish of St David's. Separate guide booklets to these walks may be purchased near the cathedral in St David's and either of them makes for an energetic day's outing.

4 A fourth national park – the Cambrian Mountains, inland from Aberystwyth – has long been proposed but as yet has not been established.

There are no national parks as such in Scotland, although a number of preserves function in this manner.

Northern Island has one national park: Lough Earne. A lough is a lake, and this park in Fermanagh is small.

Art galleries and museums in Britain

Any nation as culturally rich as Britain is bound to have a number of art galleries and museums of the first rank, and to sort out those which must be seen from those that merely provide a refuge on a wet afternoon is not difficult. The great museums and galleries of Britain are world famous, and the many dusty and ill-marked municipal museums in the lesser cities are often, quite justly, unknown. Nonetheless, there may be specific collections of world prominence in an otherwise insignificant gallery, and there will always be those special collections – whether of motor cars, old buttons, or antimacassars – which speak directly to your own hobbies or professional interests. A great country home may be enjoyed variously by members of a party, partly for its setting, partly for its interiors, and partly for its architecture. Museums, except for the largest, are less likely to offer true variety, despite the disparate nature of their holdings, and after visiting several one is bound to feel that all of them consist of variants of the same objects. For these reasons, to offer suggestions as to which museums and galleries (apart from the 'greats') constitute those which must be seen is even more an exercise in individual taste than any listings of castles, country estates, or even shops, may be. Nonetheless, I attempt to distinguish some here.

Two conditioning observations are necessary. Except for the major museums and galleries, the art and technology of display is less well advanced in Britain than in the United States, and you will often encounter a sense of claustrophobia, of crowded aisles and unwashed display cases, especially in the lesser museums. And, as with most galleries, you will also find a good bit of undistinguished lesser art, local painters and examples of idiosyncratic, although often culturally interesting, folk art, from dried flowers to hideous objects made of seashells. Do not be afraid to walk rapidly past such displays, looking for the one room, or the one wall of paintings, which gives the local offering its distinction. And if stuffed animals, snakes in bottles, mounted birds and butterflies, miscellaneous sherds, and the like don't turn you on, you'll be able to move very rapidly indeed in fully half of Britain's local museums and art galleries (often to be found in combination – itself a warning signal).

Paradoxically, you should remember you are in Britain to learn about the British. Just as you will dine in French or Indian restaurants in London, you will also want to see the great collections of Foreign Masters. But remember, if you are moving on to the Continent, that you can see more Rembrandts in Holland, larger and better Rubens in the Altapinakothek in Munich, and more Edvard Munchs in Oslo. Give more time to the great British artists, even if on balance you regard them as lesser, so that you know why Reynolds, Romney, Gainsborough, Turner, Whistler, Moore or Hepworth (to skim across the centuries) are so affectionately regarded. When in a museum, look to the British porcelain first, for you will have other opportunities to examine Dresden; look at the Belleek more carefully than the Lalique – unless, of course, you are not in fact going on elsewhere.

Many British museums and galleries contain artifacts and paintings that are American in origin. But while one might seek out a British gallery to see its Benjamin Wests, presumably one does not go to a museum in Britain primarily to see North American Indian beadwork, even though it may be there.

In any event, this quite possibly misplaced advice will prove impossible to follow, for Britain was, after all, the ruler of a great overseas empire, and for this, and other reasons, the best in Britain is often not British at all: consider the Elgin Marbles in the British Museum, the great Raffles Gamelan at Claydon House, the unequalled Ashanti art in the Museum of Mankind in London. Some view the treasures of Britain's great museums as the plunder of empire; others feel that many of these invaluable objects survived only because the British were interested in preserving them. Whatever the merits of either case, they are there to be enjoyed.

The museums and galleries that are well worth seeing include the following. For details on all except those singled out at the end of this section, consult the guide to *Museums and Galleries in Great Britain and Ireland,* published each July, and available as a slim companion volume to the guide to *Historic Houses, Castles and Gardens* at most good bookshops in Britain. Museums and galleries having displays of particular relevance to the United States are marked *. Museums in association with castles and the major country homes are not included here, having been subsumed under those two previous sections. The names of museums and galleries of the most major interest are set in *italics*.

Bedfordshire
Bunyan Meeting Library and Museum, Elstow Moot Hall, and the Bunyan Collection in the Public Library, Bedford, for those interested in 'Pilgrim's Progress'
Luton Museum and Art Gallery, Luton, especially for displays on the straw hat and pillow lace industries
The Shuttleworth Collection, at Old Warden Aerodrome, Biggleswade, has England's most extensive collection of flying machines. These include American items *

Berkshire
Reading Museum and Art Gallery, especially for medieval metal-work and Delftware
Museum of English Rural Life, at the University of Reading, is compact and informative

Buckinghamshire
Milton's Cottage, Chalfont St Giles, with relics relating to John Milton
High Wycombe Art Gallery and Museum, with a special exhibit on the evolution of the Windsor chair
Disraeli Museum, Hughenden Manor, High Wycombe, with Benjamin Disraeli items
Cowper Memorial Museum, Olney, relating to the poet William Cowper
Waddesdon Manor, at Waddesdon, with tapestries and paintings collected by the Rothschilds

Cambridgeshire

The Fitzwilliam Museum, Cambridge. One of Europe's major museums
Scott Polar Research Institute, Cambridge, with exhibits on polar exploration*
University Museum of Archaeology and Ethnology, Cambridge, with an early American collection*
Museum of Stained Glass, at Ely Cathedral, is new and quite well done.

Channel Islands

Hauteville House, St Peter Port, Guernsey, home of Victor Hugo
Lukis and Island Museum, St Peter Port, a concise introduction to the island
Royal Guernsey Agricultural and Historical Society, is in a building bombed by the Americans after the German occupation of the island*
Hongue Bie, near St Helier, Jersey, combines medieval chapels with an underground museum of the German occupation of 1940–5
Société Jersiaise Museum, St Helier, a useful introduction to the French background

Cheshire

Williamson Art Gallery and Museum, Birkenhead, for its Birkenhead pottery and Liverpool porcelain, and gallery of shipping (the Laird Rams of Civil War fame were built in Birkenhead)*
Grosvenor Museum, Chester, a good collection of Roman antiquities
Water Tower, Chester, reached as one walks the city walls

Cornwall

Helston Borough Museum, Helston, is a folk museum devoted to the Lizard Peninsula
Cornish Museum, Looe, provides a broadly-based display on Cornwall's arts, crafts, and industries, and material on witchcraft and superstitions
Penzance Natural History and Antiquarian Museum, for its tin mining exhibits
Valhalla Maritime Museum, Tresco, in the Isles of Scilly, consists largely of figureheads from ships wrecked in the islands

Cumberland

Carlisle Museum and Art Gallery, offers a quick introduction to the Lake District and a representative collection of Pre-Raphaelite paintings

Derbyshire

Derby Museum and Art Gallery, contains a typical Midlands collection, worth an hour on a rainy day

Devon

Ashburton Museum, Ashburton, includes some good American Indian materials*
Dartmouth Borough Museum, on the Butterwalk, Dartmouth, includes items relating to America*
Honiton and All Hallows Public Museum, Honiton, includes an exhibition of Honiton lace
Plymouth City Museum and Art Gallery, on Tavistock Road, is a good general museum, with several Reynolds portraits and American-related items*
Elizabethan House, Totnes, is as interesting for its siting as for its contents
Buckland Abbey, the home of Sir Richard Grenville, and later of Sir Francis Drake, contains many items relating to Drake; it is actually at Yelverton*

Dorset

Dorset County Museum, Dorchester, contains a Thomas Hardy Memorial room
Royal Armoured Corps Tank Museum, at Bovington Camp, near Wareham, contains over 100 tanks and armoured cars from various nations, and well illustrates the evolution of this form of warfare

Durham

Bowes Museum, at Barnard Castle, 16 miles from Darlington on the A67, includes El Greco, Goya, Tiepolo and Boucher paintings
Gulbenkian Museum of Oriental Art and Archaeology, in Durham, is among the world's outstanding small collections

Essex

Minories Art Gallery, on High Street, Colchester, is in a Georgian house and includes early Constables

Gloucestershire

Cheltenham Art Gallery and Museum, on Clarence Street, includes several Dutch paintings

Hampshire

Montagu Motor Museum, at Palace House, Beaulieu, includes old motorcycles, and is quite interesting to those who like that sort of thing

Russell-Cotes Art Gallery and Museum, on East Cliff, in Bournemouth, is full of often hideously Victorian fun things, and includes oriental items and the best collection of Goldie paintings of Maoris outside New Zealand

Dickens Birthplace Museum, 393 Commercial Road, Portsmouth, is minor

The Victory Museum, at H.M. Dockyard, Portsmouth, offers an exceptionally instructive visit (see below)

Gilbert White Museum, Selborne, relates to the famous naturalist

Southampton Art Gallery, at the Civic Centre, has a good collection of paintings

Tudor House Museum, St Michael's Square, Southampton, is a 16th century mansion with better than average local displays

The Maritime Museum, in the Wool House on Bugle Street, Southhampton, is as interesting for the building as the displays, and includes an intriguing painting of the *Trent* affair during the American Civil War*

Bargate Guildhall Museum, High Street, is above the medieval north gate in Southampton

Westgate Museum, High Street, Winchester, is especially interesting for its medieval weights and measures, and its location

Hertfordshire

Rhodes Memorial Museum, Bishop's Stortford, includes Cecil Rhodes' birthplace; it is less interesting than one might hope

Verulamium Museum, St Michael's, St Albans, is on the site of the

Roman city of Verulamium, includes excellent mosaics, and is the one
Roman museum worth making a point to visit. Easily reached from
London by Green Line bus

Huntingdonshire

Cromwell Museum, Huntingdon, is for those especially interested in
Oliver Cromwell

Isle of Man

Manx Village Folk Museum, Cregneish, includes thatched buildings
and affords a quick introduction to island life
Manx Museum, Douglas: the central museum, and worth a visit

Isle of Wight (actually part of Hampshire)

Ruskin Gallery, Bembridge, contains material relating to Ruskin, and
is open only by appointment
Carisbrooke Castle Museum, outside Newport, contains excellent
island relics
Osborne House, East Cowes, was the home Queen Victoria liked best
and it contains much fascinating Victoriana

Kent

Westgate, Canterbury, includes weaponry in a 14th century gate house
H.M. Dockyard, Chatham, while not a museum, offers tours Mon.–
Fri., at 9.45, 10.45, and 2.45, from Pembroke Gate, which last 30
minutes, and will give you an excellent sense of the development of
the modern navy. If you write in advance to the Secretary of the
Dockyard, you may arrange to see the world's oldest, and still
operable, ropewalk (very cold, so bring a sweater)
Darwin Museum, Downe, shows Charles Darwin's study and drawing
room
Maidstone Museum and Art Gallery, in a 16th century manor house,
has good Dutch and Italian paintings and objects pertaining to the
essayist William Hazlitt
Rochester Public Museum is in Eastgate House, itself interesting, and
there are many Dickens objects and some American association items*
Ellen Terry Museum, Smallhythe Place, Tenterden, was Dame Ellen
Terry's home and is of considerable interest to theatre buffs

Royal Tunbridge Wells Museum and Art Gallery is a representative local collection

Quebec House, Westerham, was the childhood home of General Wolfe, of the Plains of Abraham*

Lancashire

Haworth Art Gallery, Accrington, for those who like Tiffany glass

Lewis Textile Museum, Blackburn, provides a quick overview of the textile industry

Grundy Art Gallery, Blackpool, provides an excellent collection of modern British art for the political party delegates to gaze upon during conference time

Tonge Moor Textile Machinery Museum, Bolton, includes three famous inventions: Crompton's mule, Hargreaves' Jenny, and Arkwright's water frame. Crompton's home, Hall i'th'Wood, on the north edge of the city, should also be visited

Ruskin Museum, Coniston, in that detached part of Lancashire that thrusts into the Lake District, provides a good survey of John Ruskin's work

Walker Art Gallery, Liverpool, contains excellent Flemish and early Italian work, Holbein, Hogarth, and Rembrandt paintings, and Pre-Raphaelites

Sudley Art Gallery and Museum, Liverpool, includes paintings by Romney, Gainsborough and Reynolds

Manchester City Art Gallery, Mosley Street, while less good than it should be, contains a number of secondary works by significant artists

Gallery of English Costume, in Platt Hall, Rusholme, contains excellent exhibits in an interesting house

Fletcher Moss Museum, in the Old Parsonage, Wilmslow Road, Didsbury, at the south edge of Manchester, contains many English paintings, especially Turners

Whitworth Art Gallery, Oxford Road, on the grounds of the University of Manchester. Outstanding 20th century drawings and also Gainsboroughs, Turners and Pre-Raphaelites

Rochdale Cooperative Museum, on Toad Lane, in Rochdale, is the original store of the famous Rochdale Pioneers, the beginning of the cooperative movement

Pilkington Glass Museum, St Helens, illustrates the evolution of glass making. Nearby you may purchase Pilkington glass from Britain's largest glass makers

Leicestershire

Newarke Houses Museum, The Newarke, Leicester, is a good local museum with an interesting exhibit on the hosiery industry
Jewry Wall Museum, St Nicholas Street, includes Roman objects of considerable interest

Lincolnshire

Boston Museum, in the Guildhall, includes American-related materials*
Gainsborough Old Hall, Gainsborough, a 15th century manor house, is now a folk museum, and exhibits reflect this is Pilgrim Country*
Lincoln City and County Museum, includes American materials*
Lincolnshire Folk Museum, Lincoln, contains displays relating to the Pilgrims*
Usher Gallery, Lindum Road, Lincoln, contains some excellent pictures, an unusual collection of antique watches and a Tennyson collection*
Scunthorpe Borough Museum and Art Gallery, includes relics relating to John Wesley

London

Abbey Art Centre and Museum, New Barnet (actually in Hertfordshire, but reached on the Underground) includes pre-Columbian American materials*
The Artillery Museum, The Rotunda, Woolwich Common, is in the tent erected for a visit by the heads of the Allied states in the war of 1812 – to weight its significance improperly to show the quite considerable American interest some of the exhibits display*
Baden-Powell House, Queen's Gate, contains exhibits on the founder of the Boy Scouts
Bethnal Green Museum, Cambridge Heath Road, is a branch of the Victoria and Albert Museum and well worth the Underground ride for its excellent collection of dolls' houses
British Dental Association Museum, 63–64 Wimpole Street, is by appointment only but if dental surgery interests you, well worth the effort
The British Museum is, of course, probably the greatest museum in the world (so see below)
British Museum of Natural History contains superb collections not

displayed as well as one might wish. The museum is on Cromwell Road, in South Kensington, cheek-by-jowl with the Science Museum, and both should be seen together

British Theatre Museum, Leighton House, Kensington, is attractive

The Queen's Gallery, Buckingham Palace, reached off Buckingham Palace Road, to the left (when facing the palace) contains exhibitions from the Royal Collection, and is famous for the Rubens Cartoons

Carlyle's House, 24 Cheyne Row, Chelsea, is handsomely sited and contains much revealing material on Thomas Carlyle

The Commonwealth Institute, Kensington High Street, is the world venue for exhibitions on the member nations of the Commonwealth. The exhibit gallery is strikingly handsome, and the opportunity to see well-mounted displays from many African and Asian countries, from the West Indies, Australia, Canada and New Zealand, is not to be missed unless you have already travelled to those countries. The children will also enjoy this one.

Courtauld Institute Galleries, Woburn Square, and run by the University of London, is a quiet, usually uncrowded, and exquisite small collection of superb works by Cézanne, Manet, Renoir, Degas, Pissarro, Monet, Seurat, Bonnard, Utrillo, Modigliani and Rouault. As a balance to this there are also paintings by Rubens, Botticelli, Goya, Tintoretto and Van Dyck

Cuming Museum, Walworth Road, Southwark, includes miscellaneous odd items, a collection on superstitions, and American associated relics*

The Cutty Sark, at Greenwich Pier, just outside the National Maritime Museum, is the last and most famous tea clipper, fully refitted and rigged, and an excellent reason for taking the Thames River boat trip to Greenwich

Dickens House, 48 Doughty Street, actually lived in by Dickens only 1837–9, but full of fascinating Dickensiana

H.M.S. Discovery, King's Reach, Victoria Embankment (walk down from Waterloo Bridge) was Scott's polar research ship, and you may visit his cabin and the wardroom

Dulwich College Picture Gallery, College Road, Dulwich, is hard to get to, for no Underground stop is really convenient, but the gallery well rewards the effort to reach it. The best approach is from Victoria Station by train. The building itself is handsome, as is the village and the school, and the Rembrandt, Rubens, Poussin, Watteau, Gainsborough, and other paintings are excellent

Fenton House, The Grove, Hampstead, contains a fine collection of historical musical instruments, including Handel's own harpsichord (now owned by the Queen) and the William and Mary house itself is worth the visit

Thomas Coram Foundation Collection, within the Foundling Hospital, 40 Brunswick Square, is a short walk from Russell Square Underground station. There are Handel relics, sculpture, and Hogarth paintings in particular

Geffrye Museum, Kingsland Road, Shoreditch, is a bit out of the way, but on the Underground, and the series of period rooms are well organized and appealing to children

Geological Museum, which is among the Museum Group on Exhibition Road, has a famous collection of gemstones, and many, many rocks

Goldsmith's Hall, Foster Lane, Cheapside, is generally not open, but on occasion it is – watch *What's On in London* – and may be on written application, by appointment. The effort to get in is worthwhile, for the hall holds the largest collection of modern silver in the country as well as much antique plate. Other guild halls may also be open by similar arrangement

Guildhall Museum, 55 Basinghall Street, is mainly interesting for its Museum of Leathercraft

Ham House, Petersham, in Richmond, contains outstanding Stuart furniture

Hampton Court Palace, at Hampton Court, is one of Britain's major treasures (see below)

Hayward Gallery, on the South Bank, is the exhibition hall for the Arts Council of Great Britain, and is always worth a visit for its architecture alone

Hogarth's House, Hogarth Lane, Chiswick, is directly on the road from Heathrow Airport, and whether coming or going, if you are between 11–6 weekdays (or 11–4 in winter) or 2–6 on Sunday (2–4 winter) you can have your taxi stop for 20 minutes, or alight between buses (this is a busy route) and see where Hogarth lived for fifteen years

Horniman Museum, London Road, Forest Hill, is out of the way, but its collection of musical instruments, and the historical nature of its ethnographic materials, make it worth a visit. There are American items, of course*

Imperial Cricket Memorial Gallery, at Lord's Ground, will explain the game to you while telling you much about the English.

Imperial War Museum, Lambeth Road, may not at first strike you as likely to be interesting, but if you want to learn how, and something of why, Britain has survived, you must go.

Kenwood House, technically The Iveagh Bequest, Hampstead, while crowded on weekends, is a must, both for the view of London to be had across the Heath, and for the fine collection

Jewish Museum, Woburn House, Upper Woburn Place, has an excellent collection of Jewish antiquities. If you have never been to a synagogue, you will find the religious objects of great interest, for they are carefully explained.

Dr Johnson's House, 17 Gough Square, was lived in by the acerbic doctor from 1748–59

Keats' House and Museum, Keats Grove, Hampstead, is an attractive Regency house with much of interest concerning Keats and his poetry

Lancaster House, Stable Yard, St James's, is perhaps best pointed out to you by a taxi driver. It is an outstanding example of an early Victorian town mansion, and is used for ceremonial functions, but you may get inside on Sat. and Sun. between Easter and mid-Dec. from 2–6

Leighton House Art Gallery and Museum, 12 Holland Park Road, Kensington, has a fascinating combination of Leighton and Burne-Jones paintings, Persian tiling, and Arabian *objets d'art*

London Museum, which was in Kensington Palace, re-opened in the Barbican in 1976

Martinware Pottery Collection, in the Public Library, Osterley Park Road, Southall, Middlesex, is a very large collection of Martinware

Museum of Mankind, directly at the back of Burlington Arcade, is new and out of the world known to most of us

The National Gallery, Trafalgar Square, is one of the world's great art galleries

National Maritime Museum, Greenwich, is probably the world's largest and best museum of the sea, and why shouldn't it be, given Britain's dominance in this area until the 20th century

National Portrait Gallery, just at the back of Trafalgar Square, once a stodgy place, is now the finest gallery of its kind in the world (see below)

National Postal Museum, King Edward Building, King Edward Street, is small and exquisite, and, except for the postal museum in Stockholm, is one of the few such museums in the world likely to be of interest to those who are bored by the stamps themselves

Osterley Park House, Isleworth, at Osterley Station, is a fine Robert Adam house

Percival David Foundation of Chinese Art, 53 Gordon Square, is a superb collection of Chinese ceramics

The Public Record Office Museum, Chancery Lane, contains the nation's archives and a museum, in which you can view the Domesday Book of William the Conqueror, materials from Shakespeare, Milton and Nelson, and two 13th century copies of Magna Carta. Other research materials are at Kew

Royal Academy of Arts, Burlington House, Piccadilly, hangs Old Masters in the winter, and is most exciting for its annual Summer Exhibition of work by living artists. The price of admission is usually rather high, but if you want to know what's happening now in British art, the Summer Exhibition is a must

Royal Botanic Gardens, usually called Kew Gardens, are the most famous botanical gardens in the world – it was from here that rubber was transplanted to Southeast Asia, and any number of distinguished botanists flourished at Kew

Royal Air Force Museum, Aerodrome Road, Hendon, is the best air museum in Britain. Over forty aircraft are on exhibit, and the Battle of Britain Museum, opened in 1978, is quite fine. In Uxbridge, in the western suburbs, one may also visit the operations room of the famous 11th Fighter Group, where Winston Churchill spent most of the climactic day of September 15, 1940, and from which over 1300 of the 1733 enemy aircraft destroyed were accounted for

Royal Mews, Buckingham Palace Road, contains the royal horses and equipages, and unless you are going to see the Royal Carriage Museum in Lisbon, or will be going to Munich, you should see this one

Royal Water Colour Society, 26 Conduit Street, in crowded quarters, often has attractive changing exhibitions in which the work is on sale

St Bride's Crypt Museum, under St Bride's Church, Fleet Street, is a fascinating (and spooky) place to visit, especially for children, and contains informative exhibits on the history of British journalism

The Science Museum, on Exhibition Road, South Kensington, is one of the world's finest of its kind

Sir John Soane's Museum, 13 Lincoln's Inn Fields, was built by Sir John in 1812–13 to house his private collection, and while his taste is not likely to be yours, it is a place of mixed amusements

The Tate Gallery, Millbank, is London's other gallery of world standing, and is the depository for the national collections of British and Modern Painting

Tower of London (see section on CASTLES)

The Victoria and Albert Museum is, after the British Museum,

London's finest and most varied museum, with exceptional collections of the applied arts

The Wallace Collection, Hertford House, Manchester Square, is a smaller collection, mainly of paintings, furniture and ceramics

Wellcome Institute of the History of Medicine, in The Wellcome Building, Euston Road, contains exhibits of interest to those who care to see how medicine has developed

Wellington Museum, or Apsley House, sits surrounded by roadways at Hyde Park Corner, but you can approach it through the subways. This was the Duke of Wellington's London residence, and it contains his collection of paintings and many military and royal mementoes

Wesley's House and Museum, 47 City Road, is best reached by taxi; it contains a collection of John Wesley's personal memorabilia

William Morris Gallery, Water House, Forest Road, Walthamstow, is in Essex, but on the Underground line. This was the home of the famous 19th century designer, and it contains wallpapers and textiles, as well as an art collection

Norfolk

Old Merchant's House, Great Yarmouth: if old ironwork interests you, this is the place

Norwich Castle Museum, a mixed collection

The Ancient House Museum, Thetford, is in a 15th century timbered house and contains a bit on Thomas Paine*

Northamptonshire

Waterways Museum, Stoke Bruerne, is near Towcester, and provides a fascinating approach to the history of the canals

Northumberland

Housesteads Museum, at Housesteads, is not very interesting in itself, but in relation to Hadrian's Wall it is well worth a visit

Lindisfarne Priory Museum (see the section on CASTLES)

Laing Art Gallery and Museum, Newcastle upon Tyne, is an adequate general collection

Nottinghamshire

Nottingham City Museum and Art Gallery, in the Castle, is an interesting general collection

Oxfordshire

The Ashmolean Museum of Art and Archaeology, Oxford, is one of the world's older and most historically distinguished museums

Museum of the History of Science, on the Broad, Oxford, contains early scientific instruments

The Pitt Rivers Museum, Parks Road, Oxford, is an early ethnological collection of particular interest in the history of anthropological thought

Oxfordshire County Museum, in Woodstock, while tiny, is especially charming, and succinctly illustrates the crafts and industries of the area

Shropshire

The Ironbridge Gorge Museum is a fascinating museum complex in Telford and Coalbrookdale. There is no finer collection of monuments to the industrial age in all Britain, and the seven separate museums are each worth a visit.

Somerset

The American Museum in Britain, at Claverton Manor, near Bath, sounds as though you would be hauling coals to Newcastle if you go, but not so

The Holburne of Menstrie Museum of Art, Great Pulteney Street, Bath, is in an attractive building and contains interesting items

Bath Roman Museum, near Bath Abbey, should be seen in conjunction with the Roman Baths themselves which are, perhaps, the outstanding Roman remain in England

Museum of Costume, in the Assembly Rooms, Bath, shows all aspects of fashion from the 16th century to the present. F.D.R.'s first inaugural suit is included*

Bristol City Art Gallery holds Cranach, Hogarth, Reynolds, Gainsborough, Constable and French Impressionist paintings*

Chatterton House, on Redcliffe Way, Bristol, is the birthplace of Thomas Chatterton, 'the boy poet'

Glastonbury Lake Village Museum, High Street, Glastonbury, while modest, provides the only collection of lake village items in Britain

Coleridge's Cottage Museum, Nether Stowey, was Samuel Taylor Coleridge's home 1797–1800

Wookey Hole is said to be the oldest home of mankind in Britain, and you probably should see it, even though it's all pretty tatty

Staffordshire

Dr Johnson's Birthplace, Lichfield, contains relics relating to Johnson

Izaak Walton Cottage, Shallowford, Stafford, is Walton's restored cottage and a place of pilgrimage for all fishermen

Staffordshire County Museum and Mansion House, Shugborough, near Stafford, has an interesting and varied collection

Stoke-on-Trent City Museum and Art Gallery, in Hanley, is the obvious place to learn about Staffordshire pottery and porcelain

Arnold Bennett Museum, 205 Waterloo Road, Cobridge, Stoke-on-Trent, is housed in Bennett's early home

Spode-Copeland Museum and Art Gallery, Church Street, Stoke-on-Trent, provides an excellent overview of the development of Spode and Copeland ware. A preserved kiln stands nearby, and in the shop you may buy seconds at low cost

The Wedgwood Museum, run by Josiah Wedgwood & Sons in Barlaston, Stoke-on-Trent, is well worth the effort involved in gaining admission, which is by appointment only

Wolverhampton Municipal Art Gallery and Museum is a far better art gallery than you might expect

Suffolk

Christchurch Mansion, Ipswich, contains Gainsborough and Constable paintings

Gainsborough's House, Sudbury, was the artist's birthplace

Surrey

National Army Museum, at the Royal Military Academy, Sandhurst, is well worth a visit, as much to see the famous fount of British military expertise as to view the collection of uniforms, weapons, and so on

Sussex

Bignor Roman Villa Collection, at a villa unearthed in 1911, is the basis for understanding the villa and its mosaics

Potter's Museum, Bramber, Steyning, has an exhibition of illustrations for nursery rhymes

Brighton Art Gallery and Museum, Church Street, is very good, with many lesser Old Masters

The Royal Pavilion, Brighton, is a fairytale (on which see below)

Bateman's, the home of Rudyard Kipling, in Burwash, was used by Kipling from 1902–36, and is an unusually effective memorial to a writer

Royal National Lifeboat Institution Museum, on the Grand Parade, Eastbourne, offers an unusual opportunity to study the evolution of types of lifeboat

The Grange Art Gallery and Museum, Rottingdean, contains material relating to Kipling, and a toy museum

Lamb House, Rye, is a house in which Henry James lived*

Warwickshire

Avery Historical Museum, at Soho Foundry, Birmingham, contains an instructive series of exhibits on the history of weighing

Birmingham City Museum and Art Gallery, Congreve Street, is the best place to go to get a comprehensive sense of the work of the Pre-Raphaelites, as well as to see a good collection of continental artists and an instructive archaeology section. The Department of Science and Industry is on Newhall Street; it is an excellent place to visit if between trains in Birmingham

Barber Institute of Fine Arts, at the University of Birmingham, is a small, well-displayed, and often stunning, collection. Gainsborough and the Pre-Raphaelites are also attractions here. If you have time for only one gallery in Birmingham, I would choose this one.

The Museum of British Road Transport, Coventry, is still growing, but it is already well worth a visit and promises to be a significant museum, worth a side trip.

Shakespeare's Birthplace Trust Properties consist of five separate structures (on which see below)

Harvard House, High Street, Stratford-upon-Avon, is the half-timbered home of John Harvard's mother, and a shrine for all those loyal to Harvard University*

The Royal Shakespeare Theatre Picture Gallery, Stratford-upon-Avon, contains portraits of Shakespeare, material on costume design and pictures of famous actors and actresses

Westmorland

Dove Cottage, Grasmere, was the home of Wordsworth from 1799–1808; you may combine a visit on the same ticket to the Wordsworth Museum, also in Grasmere

Wiltshire

Great Western Railway Museum, Faringdon Road, Swindon, has an exhibition of historic locomotives, together with a room of Isambard Kingdom Brunel relics

Worcestershire

Dyson Perrins Museum of Worcester Porcelain, at the Royal Porcelain Works, Severn Street, Worcester, is the world's largest collection of the work of the oldest factory for porcelain manufacturing in England, which was established in 1751. The museum includes a full set of the work of Dorothy Doughty, one of the great modellers in porcelain of all time, most famous for her incredible series of American and British birds and flowers – figures which now command prices upwards of $30,000 each*

Yorkshire

Castle Howard Costume Gallery, at Castle Howard, attractively displays three centuries of period dress
Brontë Parsonage Museum, Haworth, contains an outstanding collection of Brontëana and is located at the edge of the heath so well described in *Wuthering Heights.* The core of the collection was given by Henry Houston Bonnell of Philadelphia, and the museum represents an Anglo-American effort at its best. The Haworth Parish Church includes a memorial American Window to Charlotte Brontë. You may also wish to visit Oakwell Hall, in Birstall, which has Brontë associations*
Wilberforce House, 25 High Street, Hull, was the birthplace of the great abolitionist William Wilberforce, and is now an excellent small museum to the anti-slavery movement, in America as well as in Britain*
Abbey House Museum, Kirkstall, Leeds, is a folk museum for the whole of Yorkshire
Pontefract (pronounced Pomfret) Castle Museum, Pontefract, contains an interesting set of siege coins
The Green Howards Museum, Gallowgate, Richmond, is a better-than-average regimental museum – there are over 100 such service museums in Britain
Scarborough Museum of Natural History, Scarborough, there being

no Fair – the song to the contrary – to which you may regularly go, offers a substitute in the form of a home of the Sitwell family

Sheffield City Museum, Weston Park, is the place to learn about the development of Sheffield plate and of the cutlery industry which originated in this city; there are numerous obvious associations with the colonial American trade*

Wakefield City Art Gallery contains 20th century work by Henry Moore, Barbara Hepworth, Sutherland, Sickert, and others

Whitby Art Gallery is strong on early English watercolours

Whitby Literary and Philosophical Society Museum is a hodgepodge of curiosa, including objects relating to Captain Cook*

City of York Art Gallery contains representative lesser works by Old Masters and modern English paintings

York Castle Museum is a first-rate folk museum and includes a cobbled street of historic shops, a debtors' prison, a corn mill, and toys – all good fun for the children

The Railway Museum, York, is the finest museum in Britain solely devoted to the railway, and is appealing even to those not turned on by trains

SCOTLAND (alphabetically by location)

Aberdeen Art Gallery and Regional Museum is an excellent local museum

Provost Skene's House, at City Centre, Aberdeen, provides a good opportunity to examine a 17th century Scottish home

Aberdeen University Anthropological Museum includes an American collection*

Burns' Cottage and Museum, in Alloway, is the thatched cottage in which the poet Robert Burns was born in 1759

The Scottish National Memorial to David Livingstone, in Blantyre, Lanark (near Glasgow) is in the birthplace of the famous explorer and missionary

Hugh Miller's Cottage, Cromarty, the birthplace of a famed geologist, is preserved by the National Trust of Scotland and is typical of the work of the Trust

Barrack Street Museum, Dundee, provides a good guide to the shipping and hemp industries of the city

The Spalding Golf Museum, at Camperdown House, Dundee, will fascinate those who are interested in the great game

Andrew Carnegie Birthplace Memorial, Dunfermline, provides a number of telling insights into the nature of the Scots-American tie*

Carlyle's Birthplace, Ecclefechan, where Thomas Carlyle was born in 1795, contains relics

The West Highland Museum, Fort William, contains an instructive display of tartans

City of Glasgow Corporation Art Gallery and Museum, in Kelvingrove, has an excellent collection, including Delacroix, Picasso, Matisse, Rembrandt, Rubens, Degas, and even Salvador Dali, and a very fine display of weaponry*

The Hunterian Museum, at Glasgow University, which includes many Whistlers, is a crowded yet interesting collection*

Mary Queen of Scots' House, Jedburgh, contains items dealing with the unfortunate Queen

Weaver's Cottage, Kilbarchan, contains weaving exhibits from the 18th century

Dick Institute Museum, Kilmarnock, is in the Burns Country, and with its paintings by Constable, Turner and Corot, and its collection of Scottish swords, provides for a pleasing hour or so

The Highland Folk Museum, Kingussie, affords an excellent introduction to Highland life

Kirkcaldy Museum and Art Gallery, Kirkcaldy, offers excellent examples of the work of major Scottish artists

Souter Johnnie's House, Kirkoswald, is the home of John Davidson, on whom Burns based his poem 'Tam o'Shanter'

Barrie's Birthplace, Kirriemuir, is the home of Sir James Barrie, author of *The Little Minister,* and of such plays as *Peter Pan* and *The Admirable Crichton*

Clan Macpherson House and Museum, Newtonmore, Inverness-shire, is a better-than-average clan museum*

Paisley Museum and Art Galleries has a good collection of Paisley shawls

Selkirk Museum, Selkirk, contains a collection of items on Mungo Park, the great African explorer

Hopetoun House Museum, South Queensferry, in the home of the Marquess of Linlithgow, has fine Chippendale furniture

The Bachelors Club, Tarbolton, Ayrshire, contains materials relating to Robert Burns

Edinburgh is, after London, Britain's leading cultural city, and as one would expect it is rich in museums and galleries – most, obviously,

with a special Scottish interest. Unlike London, however, Edinburgh's
museums are sited close to each other, and one may visit several relatively quickly. The following are especially recommended.

National Gallery of Scotland, The Mound, is the national collection of
European art from the 14th century, and Scottish art to 1900

Royal Scottish Museum, Chambers Street, is one of the largest
museums in Britain (see below)

National Museum of Antiquities of Scotland, Queen Street, provides
the finest overall view of Scottish history and art to be obtained
anywhere

Museum of Childhood, 34 High Street, is a unique collection of all
aspects of being a child (not merely toys) and the display of games,
books and costumes is especially fascinating. The museum is not, as
the curator notes, a children's museum; it is a museum about children.

Canongate Tolbooth, Canongate, contains Highland dress and tartan,
and a large collection relating to Sir Douglas Haig

Huntly House, Canongate, illustrates the history of Edinburgh, has an
old kitchen and a copy of the National Covenant

Lauriston Castle (see the section on CASTLES)

Lady Stair's House, Lawnmarket, is a town house of 1622 with items
relating to Burns, Scott and Robert Louis Stevenson

Scottish National Gallery of Modern Art, in the midst of the Royal
Botanic Garden, contains 20th century work

Scottish National Portrait Gallery, Queen Street, more intimate than
its counterpart in London, contains portraits of Scotland's famous
men and women

Royal Scottish Academy, Princes Street, has changing exhibitions,
and during the Edinburgh Festival these will be well worth viewing

Scottish United Services Museum, in Edinburgh Castle, is an excellent
museum of military regalia

John Knox's House, 45 High Street, dates from the 16th century

National Library of Scotland, one of the four largest libraries in
Britain, has a Gutenberg Bible on display

WALES (alphabetically by location)

The National Library of Wales, Aberystwyth, contains displays of
sketches and books, including a substantial collection on Welsh
migration to America*

Museum of Welsh Antiquities, at University College of North Wales,

Bangor, is a quick introduction to Welsh furniture, clothing, and history

The Legionary Museum, Caerleon, displays the material found at the Roman Legionary fortress nearby

Royal Welch Fusiliers Museum, Caernarvon Castle, is an unusually good regimental museum. It was the 23rd Foot, as the Fusiliers then were, that most effectively defended the British position at Yorktown at the end of the Revolution, and the Union Jack flies still over their redoubt in Virginia. John Phillips Sousa, the American march master, composed the Fusiliers march, and the score is on display in memory of the way the U.S. Marines and the Royal Welch Fusiliers fought together in the Boxer Rebellion of 1900*

National Museum of Wales, Cardiff, exhibits many facets of Welsh life, has an excellent porcelain section, superb church plate, and a very rare triton attributed to Severo da Ravenna. You may walk inside a coal mine shaft, too

Robert Owen Memorial Museum, Newtown, contains items relating to the father of Robert Dale Owen, founder of New Harmony, Indiana*

Welsh Folk Museum, at St Fagans Castle, is an excellent folk life museum with reconstructed buildings

Glynn Vivian Art Gallery, Swansea, is excellent for British glass and Welsh pottery

The Narrow Gauge Railway Museum, Towyn, focuses on the narrow gauge trains which served Wales

Wrexham Exhibition Hall, in the Wrexham Public Library, provides exhibits on this border town, including items relating to Elihu Yale, after whom the University is named*

NORTHERN IRELAND (alphabetically by location)

Ulster Museum, Belfast, helps explain Northern Ireland in brief compass

Transport Museum, Newtownards Road, Belfast, includes all forms of Northern Irish transport

Ulster Folk Museum, Craigavad, 8 miles from Belfast, consists of reconstructed houses and exhibits illustrative of life in Northern Ireland, and a spade mill

Outside southeast England, the British complain that London has a monopoly on 'amenities', especially when it comes to museums and art galleries. This clearly is the case, for most of the really great collections have found their way to London, so that, except for Shakespeare's Stratford and the distinctive national collections of Scotland, Wales and Ulster, one may encounter fully representative displays of all that is British without leaving the nation's capital. While Americans, accustomed to their finest galleries and museums being spread across the land, may find this strange, they will also find it convenient. The following list of what I regard as the fifteen most interesting British museums and galleries is organized in descending order as a suggestion of what to see if your time is severely limited. It attempts to balance excellence with variety.

1 The British Museum, London, begun in 1753, is probably the finest museum in the world. Certainly it must be the focal point of a pilgrimage, and even if rushed, you will require half a day here. The richness and variety of the exhibits is staggering, and you must approach the galleries as though on a military exercise, knowing what you are seeking, as well as allowing yourself the luxury of disorganized and aimless browsing. The Magna Carta, Froissart's *Chronicle,* the Rosetta Stone, the log-book of the *Victory,* a 1623 First Folio of Shakespeare, the Elgin Marbles, an array of tombs, mummies, manuscripts, pottery – the exhibits unroll down endless and labyrinthine corridors. The crowds are intense, and the desire to slip away to that handsome reading room in the British library, which houses six million books, will be frustrated by attendants who will ask to see your Reader's Ticket (and so you will not get to see where Karl Marx worked). But it will all be worthwhile (open weekdays 10–5, Sun. 2.30–6). Before going, read Sir Frank Francis, *Treasures of the British Museum,* one of the Thames and Hudson/Praeger World of Art series.

2 The National Gallery, London, is one of the world's great art galleries. Noted for the balance of its collection, it is an especially good art museum for those who are just beginning to come to terms with differing periods and schools, for they are all represented. The Dutch Masters (including nineteen Rembrandts) are perhaps the highlight, but the range across the Western world is enormous, from early diptychs to Seurat – fully 2000 paintings. If possible, study the excellent Thames and Hudson/Praeger guide to the gallery, *The National Gallery of London,* before going (open weekdays 10–6, June–Sept., Tues. and Thurs. to 9, Sun. 2–6). In front is a copy of Houdon's fine statue of George Washington.*

3 The Victoria and Albert Museum, London, contains what is probably the world's outstanding collection of fine and applied arts. The variety is enormous, the size of the V & A so great that you cannot hope to view it intelligently in less than a day and the floors so hard that you will not last that day. In the central exhibit hall you will find the new acquisitions; there is a superb hall of costume, a bewitching collection of Middle Eastern and Indian art, galleries of one-of-a-kind porcelain, silver, cloth, and ornaments from all over the world. Children can also wander here with great pleasure, and the new displays are stunning (open daily 10–6).

4 Hampton Court, near London, was begun in 1514 by Cardinal Wolsey, and was to be the largest house in England. Henry VIII added to it, and William III had Sir Christopher Wren enlarge it further, until it was truly a palace. Grinling Gibbons added his decorative carvings and the leading decorators of the time painted the rooms. Jean Tijou elaborated the magnificent ornamental ironwork. An outstanding garden, with an effective maze, was added: and there stood what is today the greatest palace *cum* museum *cum* art gallery in Britain. One may take a pleasant lunch at the Mitre, on the Thames bank, and wander through the palace seeking out famous details of ornamentation, or merely turn the children loose in the maze, and all will have a good time. Hampton Court is reached from London by boat on the Thames or Green Line bus and is open March, April, Oct. 9.30–5, Sun. 2–5; May–Sept., close 6, Sun. 11–6; Nov.–Feb., close 4, Sun. 2–4.

5 National Maritime Museum, Greenwich, may be reached from the Embankment in London by boat, or by bus, or by train from Charing Cross. (Get off at Maze Hill, not Greenwich Station, and walk back.) The museum buildings themselves are exceptionally handsome, facing the Royal Naval College, on the Thames. The *Cutty Sark* is at hand, and the Old Royal Observatory – from which Greenwich Mean Time is taken – is on the hill behind. Children will enjoy both the trip and the museum, and a picnic in Greenwich Park takes care of *that* problem. Afterwards, see Sir Francis Chichester's round-the-world yacht, *Gipsy Moth IV*. There are numerous exhibits relating to North America and to the Great Migration of the 19th century, as well as to polar exploration and World War II's Atlantic convoys (open weekdays, 10–6, Sun. 2.30–6).*

6 Shakespeare's Birthplace Trust Properties, Stratford-upon-Avon, consist of five separate sites: the great Bard's birthplace, a half-timbered house furnished in the style of the period; Anne Hathaway's

Cottage, just outside the town in Shottery, which is the gem of the lot; Mary Arden's House, in Wilmcote, 3 miles northwest, where Shakespeare's mother lived; Hall's Croft, home of his daughter Susanna and her husband Dr John Hall, with excellent furniture and a fine walled garden; and New Place and Nash's House, with contextual local exhibits. Shakespeare retired to New Place in 1610. You will find a Knot Garden nearby. The houses are open various hours, but not less than 10–6 April–Oct., Sun. 2–6; and Nov.–March, weekdays, 9–12.45, 2–4.

7 The Tate Gallery, London, contains the nation's greatest collection of modern art. Indeed, it covers all important British painting from the 16th century, including outstanding Constables, Hogarths, Turners and William Blakes, together with modern sculpture and paintings from the Continent: Picasso, Kandinsky, Matisse, Braque, Mondrian, everything! The changing exhibits of contemporary artists, for which a separate admission charge is made, are also of major significance in the art world (open weekdays 10–6, Sun. 2–6). There is a fine new restaurant.

8 The H.M.S. *Victory,* Portsmouth, may not seem appropriate appearing on the same page as Picasso, but excellence is excellence in whatever field and this dramatically preserved vessel, Nelson's flagship at Trafalgar, is every romantic's dream of playing at Hornblower. A superior museum, hard by, contains many Nelson (and Lady Hamilton) memorabilia. Unsurprisingly, there are several relics relating to the American Revolution (open at H.M. Dockyard weekdays 10–6, Sun. 1–6, or sunset if sooner).*

9 The Museum of Mankind, behind the Burlington Arcade, Piccadilly, is an extension of the British Museum, and it brings into the open the British Museum's unsurpassed (except perhaps in Berlin) ethnographic collection. The Ashanti bronzes from Africa, the shadow puppets from Indonesia, the devil masks from Ceylon, the American Indian items, and much more, are the finest in captivity. Above all, see the African rooms (open, as for British Museum).*

10 The Royal Pavilion, Brighton, will either be High or Low on any personal list. It's High on mine. Originally built in 1784–7, the Pavilion was redesigned by John Nash, the Prince Regent's architect, between 1815 and 1822, to fulfil the expectations of a British public suddenly, and romantically, aware of India's minarets, domes, and (the public thought, confusing South with Southeast Asia) pagodas. The result might have been grotesque; instead, it is often beautiful.

The interiors – as Chinese as Indian – are of mixed value, but on the whole successful. The Royal Family lost interest in the Pavilion, it was closed in 1845, and only since 1956 has it been restored to its former glory as the original bamboo and lacquer furniture has been returned to it from Buckingham Palace (open daily Oct.–June 10–5, July–Sept. to 8).

11 Imperial War Museum, Lambeth Road, London, sounds repelling to some, and perhaps inappropriately attractive to others. There is, in fact, little blood and quite a bit of courage in the exhibits, and if tanks, anti-aircraft batteries, flags and standards do not appeal to you, then the unexcelled collection of paintings by the official artists of both World Wars may well do so. The displays are unusually effective, the cumulative impact of three hours in the museum both depressing (and who travels to be depressed!) and inspiring. Go, if only to enjoy an awareness of the enormously fascinating, and paradoxical, nature of man (open weekdays 10–6, Sun. 2–6).*

12 National Portrait Gallery, London, has long since become a swinging place, combining special exhibitions of 'The most beautiful women of Britain' and the nation's heroes as measured in terms of the 1980s with the great collection of portraits founded in 1856. The paintings were originally intended to be viewed for the fame of the subjects rather than the artists, and this is still true, but the subjects now seem irrelevant to our present concerns and the artistry is thus enhanced. The gallery is directly behind the National Gallery, just off Trafalgar Square, and if you have no fear of exhibition feet, you can combine the two (open Mon.–Fri., 10–5, Sat. to 6, Sun. 2–6).

13 The Science Museum, London, among the cluster of fine museums along Exhibition Road in South Kensington, is actually a branch of the British Museum. Although specialized, it will be of interest to the most committed humanist, for the exhibits have been arranged with the scientifically ignorant, and even scientifically hostile, in mind. There are dozens of buttons to push and levers to pull, for those who are children at heart, and for those who are children in fact there is a special gallery. A turbo-alternator may not have much appeal, but unless you believe that the moon is made of green cheese, a truly intelligent display on how the steam engine came into being should. It is open weekdays 10–6, Sun. from 2.30.

14 Royal Scottish Museum, Edinburgh, founded in the mid-19th century, is the largest museum of science and art, excluding painting, in Britain. Its most direct rival is the Victoria and Albert, but Scottish

objects are, after all, Scottish, and if you are unconvinced of the fact, visit this museum and seek out the specifically Scottish items. If no single object rivals the distinctive treasures of the British Museum, taken collectively, the Royal Scottish is a most impressive assemblage of the works of man (open weekdays 10–5, Sun. 2–5).

15 Kenwood House, London, officially known as the Iveagh Bequest, is at the crest of Hampstead Heath and is the spot I like best in London on a Sunday afternoon. The house itself is stunning: set in a park of oaks, chestnuts and beeches, remodelled with great success by Robert Adam in the classical style, with everyone's dream of a great library, the house and grounds are half the attraction. The other half is the art collection, which includes works by Vermeer, Van Dyck, Cuyp, Reynolds, Romney, Turner and Gainsborough, and also Rembrandt's 'Portrait of the Artist'. One may walk from Kenwood down through the Heath, or further north to Highgate, and on either stroll, every prospect pleases (open April–Sept. weekdays 10–7, Sun. 2–7, closes 6 or at dusk in winter).

One cannot fail also to mention a lovely museum that will be of particular interest to visiting Americans. **The American Museum,** Claverton Manor, Bath, is included here not only because it is American – after all, you didn't come to Britain to see Pueblo Indian pottery or Hopi Katchina dolls – but because it is genuinely a museum of major significance. Founded in 1961 by Dallas Pratt and John Judkyn, two Americans who wished to provide for a permanent display of the best in American arts and crafts for the British public, the museum is housed in a country home designed by Sir Jeffrey Wyatville, George IV's architect, in 1820. Sir Winston Churchill delivered his first political speech at the Manor in July, 1897, as a plaque attests. Old stables house a folk art collection; the gardens include a replica of Washington's rose and flower gardens at Mount Vernon; and an Indian tepee and Conestoga wagon sit in the grounds, to the delight of children. The interior includes a 17th century New England keeping room, and progressively thereafter period rooms carefully furnished to the appropriate style. Seeing these exhibits in the midst of a British tour provides a unique opportunity to remind oneself of the relationship between American Colonial and British styles. There is a fine display of American quilts, dating from 1777, and even a New Mexican *morada* or private chapel. The British usually express a special interest in the plain Shaker furniture. A country store and herb shop, at which you may make purchases, concludes the tour. Reached in 2½ miles from Bath railway station, by bus or taxi, the museum is open daily, except Mon., 2–5 and is closed in the winter.

Sister cities

The Town Affiliation Association of the United States has helped to arrange a number of matching relationships between cities in the United States and communities in Britain. Such linkages are referred to as Sister Cities. The cities involved usually exchange regalia, the mayor of each visits the other, and a variety of exchanges relating to schools, art galleries, museums, sporting teams, and fraternal organizations are arranged. As a result of these relationships, one will find the American flag, and an appropriate state or municipal flag, hanging in the town hall of a number of places in the United Kingdom. (A typical example is at Machynlleth, in Montgomeryshire, Wales, where in the town hall one may see relics from Belleville, Michigan, on display.) If you are interested in helping your community strike up such a relationship, contact the Town Affiliation Association of the United States, Inc., Suite 206, City Building, 1612 K Street, N.W., Washington, D.C. 20006.

If you want to check whether your home community is already twinned with a British community, the following is a list of some of the Sister City relationships.

ENGLAND

Berwick-upon-Tweed with Berwick, Pennsylvania
Finchley (part of London) with Montclair, N.J.
Glastonbury with Glastonbury, Connecticut
Hartlepool with Muskegon, Michigan
Lewes with Lewes, Delaware
Plymouth with Plymouth, Michigan
Reading with Reading, Pennsylvania

Richmond with Richmond, Virginia
Rugeley with Western Springs, Illinois
Rye with Rye, New York
St Helier, Channel Islands, with Hammonton, N.J.
Scarborough with Scarborough, Maine
Southampton with Hampton, Virginia
Winchester with Winchester, Virginia

SCOTLAND

Grangemouth with La Porte, Indiana
Greenock with Coatesville, Pennsylvania
Stirling with Dunedin, Florida

WALES

Brecon with Saline, Michigan
Flint with Fenton, Michigan
Machynlleth with Belleville, Michigan

Of course numerous other American cities have entered into a similar relationship with a community in Britain without doing so through the Town Affiliation Association. There are special ties between New York City and Bristol, for example. Namesake cities often place a plaque somewhere in their English counterpart, as in Boston, Massachusetts, and Boston, Lincolnshire. If these connections interest you, read a delightful book, *American Place-Names,* by George R. Stewart, which links numerous places in the United States to Britain. These relationships are often largely informal, and no attempt has been made to list them here. The same is true of those communities in Wales, Scotland and Northern Ireland which have produced substantial numbers of immigrants for America. If you are interested in these relationships, you will enjoy reading Terry Coleman's lively book *Going to America.*

The great shops of London

London is an excellent city to shop in, for the major shopping streets are near each other, and the variety of wares from Britain and the Continent is great. Of course, objects imported into Britain may well have paid a high duty, so that the real bargains are British-made goods and antiques. The last are especially good buys in terms of bringing your purchases back into the United States, for if they are truly antique – which is defined by the U.S. Customs as dating from prior to 1830 – there is no duty to be paid. This means that anything Victorian (dating from Queen Victoria's accession to the throne in 1837) is liable to duty, although many Customs officials do not assess it unless the object is patently modern.

Variety is another pleasure of London. Although shops may be out of mass-produced items that in the States would be stocked in quantity, such as your usual perfume or shaving cream, you will not be frustrated when one-of-a-kind shopping is involved. The silver, porcelain, antique furniture, prints and paintings, second-hand books, barometers, rain gear, folk art, jewelry and wine will be well priced in relation to American costs, but more important, there will be a greater variety from which to choose, at a greater range of competing prices, than anywhere in the United States, with the possible exception of New York. Some things will certainly not be cheaper – Persian carpets cost as much in London as in America – and some things will be more expensive.

When making purchases, remember that you pay duty at the wholesale value of the goods purchased, and that each member of your group is permitted $200 in goods duty free. As a practical matter, any books you buy will not be included in the total. On the other hand, buying that new raincoat at the beginning of the journey and wearing it for three months does not render it duty free. Where antiques are concerned, be certain to ask for a receipt or certificate which testifies to the date of the object. You will find you are treated fairly, if not always suavely, by the American Customs agents, and you are more likely to be dealt with gently if you segregate all of your purchases into a single bag so that they can be examined together without pawing through all your luggage (although the official can still paw if he wants to). American Customs agents are knowledgeable, and they will not take well to your declaring an obvious piece of Lalique to be some cheap glass.

When to shop in London? If your schedule permits, try window shopping the busiest streets on a Sunday morning. Downtown London is barren of traffic and pedestrians then, and in three hours or so one may walk all the main streets mentioned below, noting the shops that are of interest. Then return on a weekday, the earlier after morning opening the better, and zero in on the places already chosen. Carry a shopping list of likely items and a large shopping bag. With bulkier objects, keep in mind that most shops will ship them for you – delivery time is about four weeks – and that you almost certainly will pay duty on anything sent in the mails.

Where to shop? The top area consists of two parallel streets, Regent Street and New Bond Street, and of the smaller connecting streets between them, with Oxford Street as a boundary on the north and Piccadilly on the south. One should not miss Jermyn Street, one block below Piccadilly and running parallel to it, or Curzon Street in Mayfair, and the portions of Brook Street and Grosvenor Street running from New Bond Street to Grosvenor Square, as well as Albemarle Street, Dover Street, and Bruton Street. New Bond Street and its immediate conduits is the most posh of all, Regent Street is happily upper middle class, and Oxford Street is solidly in the middle and a bit touristic. It is also the ugliest shopping street in England.

Beyond this area, one must not forget Knightsbridge, with Harrods, the world's most interesting department store, and the streets that cluster around it. There are several interesting antique shops along Brompton Road and in Kensington High Street. A third area radiates from Sloane Square, especially Kings Road – not as fashionable as it once was – and Pimlico Road. Finally, there are the streets that specialize: books, for example, are found in the greatest quantities and range along both sides of Charing Cross Road.

Begin your walk at the eastern end of Jermyn (pronounced Germin – to rhyme with vermin) Street, just south of Piccadilly tube station. Here in a row are most of the top shirt makers, and sellers of ready-to-wear shirts in London, for instance, S. Conway, Harvie and Hudson, Hilditch and Key and Turnbull and Asser. (Beale and Inman, at 132 New Bond Street, is also very good.) If you have shirts made, allow three weeks as a minimum and longer in the summer. Hermes, fine leather and silk goods, is also in Jermyn Street, as is Dunhill (on the corner of Duke Street, and opposite the side entrance to Fortnum and Mason) and Andrew Grima for jewelry. Arthur Davidson, opposite Dunhill, features the schmaltziest antiques in London. Floris is famous for its pomanders, soap and scent and Foster and Son for its slippers. And also here is Paxton and Whitfield, cheese merchants, where you may encounter a wider variety of cheeses – and all of the English cheeses – than anywhere else in Britain.

Jermyn Street runs into St James's Street. Across the way and to the left is Justerini and Brooks, at number 61, superb wine merchants. At the top is Piccadilly and directly across is Albemarle Street; one street to the right is Old Bond Street, leading into New Bond Street. To the left is the Ritz. If the timing is right, treat yourself to a light lunch; shopping on an empty stomach costs money. Here the waiters stand poised like an army in battle waiting for commands, and with a high sense of diplomacy serve up your Pimm's, avocado niçoise, omelette, Chablis and coffee. There were fourteen waiters in attendance on twenty-two diners the last day I lunched there, and the ballet was worth nearly as much as the cost of the lunch. And if it isn't lunch time, have tea, for it is still an Occasion at the Ritz. Then walk west on Piccadilly to Berkeley Street and up into Berkeley Square (you won't hear a nightingale) or below the square left onto Curzon Street, which has a number of useful shops. A haircut by appointment (or just take your chance) at Trumper's is good fun, and cheap by American standards, and Heywood Hill, a pleasant bookshop directly next door, is one of the better ones in London. Further along and opposite is the entrance to Shepherd Market, where prices are too high.

Now walk back up Piccadilly to Burlington Arcade, where a variety of somewhat overpriced shops which cater to American tourists offer up fine cashmeres, silver, ivory-backed hairbrushes, model soldiers and other signs of the good life. On the south side of Piccadilly is the outlet for Spode (Wedgwood is in Wigmore Street) and back towards the Circus is the best browsing book store, both cloth and paperback, in London: Hatchards. Also here are Fortnum and Mason of the fabulous foods; and Swaine Adeney Brigg, where you may obtain a fine umbrella, shooting stick, or leather goods.

On the two Bond streets, visit in particular the shoe shops – Loewe, Ferragamo, Church's, Russell and Bromley, Pinet, and Bally; Asprey's, one of the truly Great Shops, at number 166; Savory and Moore; Herbert Johnson for men's hats; Beale and Inman for shirts; Vidal Sassoon, Gucci and Georg Jensen. Ireland House is on the corner of Bruton Street. Brook Street holds fine art shops, while Morland's is in Grosvenor Street. At 24 South Molton Street is Prestat, for chocolates (but don't forget Charbonnel et Walker, at 31 Bond Street, and Floris, in Soho). At 42 South Molton Street is H. R. Higgins, where one may try any of twenty-six different coffees. Savile Row runs parallel to New Bond Street between Conduit Street and Burlington Gardens. The tailors here continue to deserve their reputation. Having tried three, I unhesitatingly recommend Strickland and Son. Pick virtually any cloth you want, try to have three fittings, expect to wait a month and to spend a considerable amount – $700 or so – and you'll have a suit that still looks new ten years later.

Enter Oxford Street next to the Bond Street tube station. To the left are the mass shops and Selfridges and Marks and Spencer (referred to as Marks and Sparks) and directly ahead is Debenhams – all large Macy's-type operations. Walk along Oxford Street east to Regent Street and turn right. From here into Piccadilly Circus is a wide variety of excellent shops, including Liberty of London, Aquascutum, and a number of art salons. Carnaby Street (now a pedestrian precinct), once famous for the mod look, is behind Liberty's. Burberry's is in the Haymarket. Beyond, at 53 New Oxford Street, is James Smith & Sons, a fascinating establishment where one may simply look at the incredible variety of brollies, or, better yet, buy one.

Now take the Underground to Knightsbridge – Scotch House is across the street from the tube station – and walk along Brompton Road to Harrods. Not all of Harrods is impressive but much is and the range of goods is enormous. (Do you want cleft sticks? With apologies to Evelyn Waugh, they will cleave them for you.) Beyond is Beauchamp Place, with a number of interesting shops (including Map House and a good store for china seconds). A quick taxi now to Sloane Square for a visit to Peter Jones, a department store, The General Trading Company, and David Mellor, a most unusual ironmongery shop; then a walk down to Pimlico Road to see a number of interesting decorator and antique shops and Casa Pupo, which has a wide range of Iberian work. Running out of Sloane Square is Kings Road, with boutique after boutique. Finally, take another quick taxi to Kensington High Street, which has several good shops and the Antique Hypermarket.

To be sure, this means that you have missed shops of considerable interest: Habitat, for example, near Heal's on Tottenham Court Road (though there is also a branch in the Kings Road). It also means that many specialty shops have been passed up. If you want a fine antique or reproduction barometer, for example, take yourself far out to Garner and Marney, clearly the best, at 41/43 Southgate Road (virtually into Islington). Nor has this route brought you to the Silver Vaults, off Chancery Lane. But window shopping here would do no good in any event, and you must go when they are open. As to that, many (increasingly, most) shops are likely to be closed on Saturday afternoon from 1.00 as well as on Sunday. On weekdays, usual hours are 9 or 9.30 to 5.30.

If you are looking for a specialty item as a collector of old maps, coins, war medals, games, stamps, scientific instruments, etc., buy immediately *Nicholson's Collectors' London* (or order it from Robert Nicholson Publications, 3 Goodwin's Court, St Martin's Lane, London W.C.2). They also publish the very good, very compact *London Guide,* as well as *London Girl* and *Students' London.* Another excellent and handy guide is *Antique Collecting with BP. Sheila Chichester's London Woman* (order from 9 St James's Place) is very useful. Fullest of all, although more bulky, is Michael Balfour's *Help Yourself in London* (Garnstone Press Ltd., 59 Brompton Road S.W.3).

All of this has concerned central London. If you want to try another variety of pleasant shops, you might take the Underground to Hampstead and walk about on the hill above the city, sampling the variety of antique, boutique and book shops of this pleasant suburb.

London

London is the second largest city in the world in population, the fourth largest in land area. It shares with most great cities a wealth of entertainment, of distinctive historical places to be visited, and a sense of congestion; like most cities, it requires being lived in to be fully appreciated. But, even on a short acquaintance, it probably has more to offer the tourist than any other metropolis; and so it should, after all, for it is a very old city, as well as a large one, and the cultural as well as political capital of an historic, and artistically rich, people. It is like no other city, in its shops, its galleries and museums, its ubiquitous red buses, its unarmed police, its sense of safety, self-confidence and serenity in the midst of bustle and headline alarms.

London is part of all of us, as is Rome, or Paris, or New York, for it is a world capital – possibly *the* world capital until World War II. The entirety of Britain drains towards London, for it is a true metropolis, an entrepot, in a way that Washington can never be. In America, there are many cities which have reason to think of themselves as 'provincial'; in England, all outside London is 'the provinces'. Thus to know London is, in one sense, to know England, while to know Washington, Bonn, or New Delhi is in no way to know the country over which their bureaucrats think they preside. London must be given time to sneak up on one, for it is a city made for walking in, and any suggestion that one may know the city in a few days is misleading. (There is a short guide book to London with the title *Discover London in 2 Days Leisurely*. One hopes that one can recognize the peculiar English sense of the ridiculous at work here, in the same way as the stationing of the figure of the Angel of Christian Charity, usually mistakenly called Eros, in the middle of Piccadilly Circus is a subtle English pun, for the angelic figure is firing a shaft into the ground, to tell one that the donor of the statue was Lord Shaftesbury.) Even so, one may see much of London in four to five days, and the following material assumes a stay of approximately that duration.

There are many American-related sites in London, as one would expect. That most American of poets, Walt Whitman, said, 'I hear continual echoes from the Thames'. And so we do, whether through ancestry, history, a fascination with the English language, or merely having gone to see *Mrs. Miniver* as a child. To be sure, there is a hint of English arrogance in Samuel Johnson's remark to Boswell, 'By seeing London, I have seen as much of life as the world can show'. But not much, for London has been a world capital for so long, and has served as the head of a large Empire, and later Commonwealth, so skilfully, and has until recently welcomed immigrants so openly, as to be the most cosmopolitan large city on earth. If one wants to find Indian, Japanese, Chinese, Armenian, Iranian, Greek, West Indian, Sri Lankan, Arabian, French, Italian and even American, restaurants, areas of residence, and shops, one readily can, dining out every night in a different foreign country. The Elgin Marbles in the British Museum, those elegant sculptures from the Parthenon which Elgin collected in 1801–3, are symbolic to many of the way in which London salvaged the heritage of others when those others were unable or unwilling to look after it themselves. Yet, they are symbolic too of the way in which London made itself one of the treasure houses of the world, which could also be described as systematic plundering of undefended cultures. The question here is not whether London's riches are the product of rapine and pillage, or of a culture that had a sensitivity to the art of the exotic long before most others did, but that, for whatever reason, it sometimes seems that half the world's movable glories are to be found in this one city.

One does not come to London, then, primarily to see American-related sites. One comes for those Elgin Marbles, or the theatre, or to walk along the Thames and sing softly its sweet song. To suggest that the primary significance of the house on Craven Street in which Benjamin Franklin lived arises from the fact that he did so, is to be as provincial as the Englishman overheard to say of the Crimea, 'It's loaded with history. You get over to Scutari, and Florence Nightingale's hospital is there.' (Perhaps R. F. Delderfield captures this sense even better in the title of his most famous novel, *God Is an Englishman*.) One doesn't visit Syon House because its transport museum includes Al Capone's car (!) or come to London to eat hamburgers at The Great American Disaster, when one can, for the same price, eat a Mughal curry at the Khyber Pass. (Actually, if you must have that hamburger, you can find quite good ones at one of the branches of American Haven – see the telephone directory. There are even McDonald's now, with most of the familiar menu items for visitors who want a strong taste of home.)

Still, this is a guide to American-related sites, some of which are important; it is not a full scale guide to London. For this purpose, you will wish to carry with you one or more other, specifically London-oriented, guides which will supplement the information given here. Of these guides, the best compact one is *The Penguin Guide to London,* compiled by F. R. Banks. The *Blue Guide* to London is also sound and will fit in a pocket. Very valuable is *Nicholson's London Guide,* which is even more compact. If you intend to look for some quite un-usual object, like an antique orrery, consult Michael Balfour's *Help Yourself in London* or *Nicholson's Collectors' London.* For museums and art galleries, David Piper's *London* in the *World Cultural Guides* series is sound, but best read in advance of travel, as is *Kate Simon's London,* a lively book (that is nonetheless well below the standard of her similar book on New York). While in London, make one of your first purchases copies of *Time Out* and *What's On,* weekly guides to the theatre, gallery showings, tours, and current hours of opening of all the major sites.

London is rich in specialized guides as well. If you dislike the Establishment air of some of the above, you may prefer *Time Out's Book of London,* which will tell you which pub is best for pickups (called 'pulling') and the like, or *Alternative London,* which includes a section on abortions. If you want to pursue your best-loved writer, George G. Williams' *Guide to Literary London* sets out a number of good walking tours. Do you want to find the Diogenes Club where Mycroft Holmes had his sherry-and-bitters? It is probably the Athenaeum, a contention argued in Michael Harrison's *The London of Sherlock Holmes.* There is also *The London of Charles Dickens,* which will lead you to the site of the offices of Dombey & Son. Archi-tecture? Try Renzo Salvadori's *101 Buildings to See in London.* Food? The *Good Food Guide* does not publish its London listings as a separate booklet, but the *Michelin* guide does. There is also Margaret Costa's *London at Table,* distributed in the United States by *Gourmet* magazine. Drink? Martin Green and Tony White have done *The Evening Standard Guide to London Pubs.* One should not forget to visit the excellent London wine bars, or the many exotic markets. There is even the *Good Loo* (toilet) *Guide* by Jonathan Routh. And the outlying districts have their own guides, if, having tired of central London, you prefer a day in Dulwich, or Highgate, or Islington. Before leaving home, read in particular Steen Eiler Rasmussen's *London: The Unique City*, revised for 1982, and V. S. Pritchett's *London Perceived*. Having been there, you will then know why Pritchett calls London 'the least nervous city in the world'.

The following material is laid out neither as a strict alphabetical gazetteer (which would require the constant consultation of a detailed map) nor in terms of specific walking tours (which strike me as dictatorial, overly systematic, and generally unworkable in London, since each person will have priorities of his own) but rather as a compromise. I describe briefly a major attraction to which you will surely want to go, and then mention other sites which are in the general area, and to which one might reasonably walk. This organization, used in conjunction with one good fold-out map of London, and a guide to Underground stations, should serve adequately. By and large it is quicker to walk short distances in London than to take a taxi, and better to ride the Underground for the greater distances. The taxi does have two great advantages: it comes to where, bone-weary, you are; and the driver will undertake the responsibility of finding the exact address of your destination. (Even so, some Underground stations post good maps of their environs, which may be sufficient for your purpose.) In figuring distance and time in central London, count the number of Underground stations through which your train must journey and multiply by three, to produce a figure in minutes.

Restaurants in London were discussed above, under 'Dining Out'. One should also consult the sections on museums and galleries before using the material that follows. Carry always a copy of the *A to Z Street Atlas of London*.

If this is a first visit to London, consider taking London Transport's two-hour circular bus tour, which includes the City and the West End. This is a good way to get a sense of where the major sights are.

Historic London presents a special problem. One person may wish to see the site of Geoffrey Chaucer's original home, while another may feel it foolish to merely gaze upon a plaque when one could be walking through Dickens House. It has been estimated that historic buildings take up less than one sixth of one per cent of the total area of greater London; yet, this means that the Greater London Council, in surveying historic structures, has noted 20,000 buildings. And one person may prefer fine Victorian (not a contradiction in terms) to bad Georgian, while another may be interested only in the contents of either. One person may wish to visit the oldest synagogue in England (Bevis Marks) while another prefers a Wren church. Again, therefore, a series of listings have been resorted to here, so that it is possible to pick and choose.

Opinions may rightly differ on who is a historic figure in any event. It is probably salutary for Americans to know that the Greater London Council recently declined to place plaques on the former homes of James Russell Lowell and Gilbert Stuart because they 'would not be sufficiently meaningful to most passers-by in London to warrant the erection of a plaque'. But presumably passers-by do recognize Nicholas Barbon, Muzio Clementi, Sir Philip Ben Greet, Mary Hughes, Charles Manby, Harry Relph and Thomas Wakley, since the Council has put up plaques to them. *That* should keep you in your place. After all, the Greater London Council *has* placed over 300 Wedgwood Blue plaques (some older ones, in fact, are chocolate) on buildings in which famous people lived, provided the original building is substantially intact. If the selections do seem a little odd (Princess Astafieva, ballet dancer, but not James Monroe, diplomat and President) or a little introverted (Willy Clarkson, theatrical wigmaker, but not, until 1967, Karl Marx) and if one may detect a Commonwealth bias (Rabindranath Tagore, but not Robert Frost) it nonetheless is precisely in examining what it is that a people choose to memorialize that one best learns about what they think important. The plaques are always worth paying attention to and sometimes they are informative as well.

A final word. The face of London is changing rapidly, with entire streets being altered in the course of a year. Even when unaltered, a street that was one-way north last month may be one-way south this month, and its whole numbering system may have been changed. The result will be to make some of the precise detail that follows incorrect by the time this new edition has found its way into print, and if a promised plaque – should you in fact, despite what has been said above, still pursue them – is not to be found at the stated number, examine the street for signs of new construction and use a little imagination. Generally the site can be found. Using a guide book is not unlike the experience that the young man in Herman Melville's *Redburn* has when he memorizes his father's old guide to Liverpool and then attempts to walk that city's streets with it in his hands. 'I little imagined that the Liverpool my father saw, was another Liverpool from that to which I, his son Wellingborough, was sailing.' 'Guidebooks', Wellingborough concludes, 'are the least reliable books in all literature;' for, 'the thing that had guided the father, could not guide the son.' Heavier type indicates an American interest.

Historic buildings, parks and streets

Apsley House, 149 Piccadilly, is also 'number 1, London', and the point from which some distances are measured. The house was once the Duke of Wellington's, and it is now a museum to him (open daily 10–6, Sun. 2.30). (See the general section on MUSEUMS.) The collection includes a **John Singleton Copley** oil of William IV. Just south is the Wellington Arch, and beyond – at the west end of Constitution Hill – is the **century of peace arch,** presented to commemorate a hundred years of peace between Great Britain and the United States in 1915.

Armoury House, in City Road, is the headquarters of the Honourable Artillery Company, oldest regiment in the British army. The company started the first American artillery company in 1628, in Massachusetts. Among its exhibits is a cannon ball fired at Bunker Hill.

Baker Street is now a long, rather nondescript thoroughfare, but it is still a sentimental pilgrimage for visitors to London, since Sherlock Holmes lived at 221B. The two leading contenders for the site are nos. 109–11, and no. 61, both more or less matching the descriptions in Conan Doyle's books. The American Ministers **Rufus King** and **Richard Rush** lived at nos. 20 and 51. In George Street, which cuts across Baker Street at right angles, lived **John Singleton Copley** from 1775 until his death in 1815 (now nos. 8–9). His son became Lord Lyndhurst, Lord Chancellor of England, and died in the same house in 1863.

Bank of England, 'The Old Lady of Threadneedle Street', remains one of the most important banks in the world, handling the Sterling exchange for a once-powerful Empire, now Commonwealth. The British gold reserves are here, and one may, by prior arrangement, sometimes tour the more public parts of the bank. There is a memorial to **Thomas Harriot** inside the entrance; he was the author of the first account of exploration in Virginia, in 1588.

Battersea Park has a fun fair the children will enjoy. It also has a fine open-air sculpture garden. On Battersea Church Road, facing the river, is St Mary's, the parish church. **Benedict Arnold,** who died in London in 1801, is buried here.

Belgrave Square, one of the most handsome in London, is the epitome of Belgravia, a fashionable residential area also filled with smaller embassies. Greater London Council plaques abound here. The historian **George Bancroft** lived at no. 90, Eaton Square, when American Minister to the Court of St James's. **George Peabody** died at no. 80 in 1869. West Halkin Street provides a handsome walk into Lowndes Street, where **James Russell Lowell** lived at no. 37. To the left is Cadogan Place, with the American-owned Sonesta Hotel, on the site of a school attended by **Edgar Allan Poe.** William Wilberforce, the opponent of slavery, lived at no. 44. Just north is Lowndes Square, where Lowell and **Edward J. Phelps,** also American Minister, lived at no. 31. The Grenadier, an interesting pub, is in Old Barrack Yard at the end of Wilton Row (Sunday licensing hours extend to 3.00). On Wilton Place is the fine new Berkeley Hotel, drawing upon an old name and offering a superb dining room.

Berkeley Square, where the nightingale was said to sing, was the Gaunt Square of Thackeray's *Vanity Fair.* It is in the heart of Mayfair, perhaps the most fashionable of London's districts, and a stroll through the area is rewarding in good architecture, historical associations and pleasant shops. At the southwestern corner of the square stood Landsdowne House, where **Joseph Priestley,** the chemist who emigrated to Pennsylvania in 1794, discovered oxygen. At no. 45 Lord Clive, conqueror of India, lived and committed suicide. Horace Walpole also lived on the Square. In World War II the **British War Relief Society of America** was located here. In Charles Street, which runs from the southwest corner, lived Sydney Smith, editor of the *Edinburgh Review,* he who scornfully asked, 'Who reads an American book?' Also in Charles Street, at Dartmouth House, is the headquarters of the English-Speaking Union. John Ruskin lived at no. 6. The square is connected with Piccadilly by Berkeley Street. The old **Berkeley Hotel,** now moved to Wilton Place, Belgravia, stood here. It was the haunt of many American tourists, and always the choice of Amy Lowell. **Lord Shelburne,** British Prime Minister at the end of the American Revolution, died here in 1805.

Bloomsbury Square is a small square near the British Museum. The area gave its name to an entire intellectual clique, although its members in fact lived in others of the several handsome Bloomsbury district squares, and one should walk north to explore Russell, Woburn, Tavistock and Gordon Squares. **Gertrude Stein** and her brother Leo lived at no. 20 Bloomsbury Square.

Bond Street is perhaps the most elegant of London's shopping streets, especially at its southern end, where it becomes Old Bond Street. Just east is Cork Street, where **Gertrude Atherton** lived at a hotel during her many visits to London, while **George Peabody,** the American philanthropist, settled at no. 15 (now nos. 21–22). Grafton Street runs west from Bond Street; **Lord Cornwallis** lived at no. 16, while **Charles James Fox,** a defender of the American colonists, lived in the street when Foreign Secretary. South from Grafton Street runs Albemarle Street, in which **Lord North** of the Intolerable Acts was born. Brown's Hotel (q.v.) can be entered from either Albemarle or Dover Streets.

Brompton Road, running from Knightsbridge into Cromwell and Fulham Roads, offers an array of interesting shops along its northern face, and in Beauchamp (pronounced Beecham) Place (which runs into Walton Street) to the southwest, there are more good shops. Harrods, the great department store that one must visit whether intending to purchase anything or not, is here. Just opposite is the area in which several of the British **Loyalists** settled upon their return to England during and after the American Revolution. **Thomas Hutchinson,** former Governor of Massachusetts, died here in 1781.

Brown's Hotel is a sedate, handsomely appointed hotel that would not appreciate having hordes of tourists trooping about. It is a good place for a quiet afternoon tea, when one may think about the hotel's historical associations. For, like Claridge's, the Connaught, the Ritz and the Savoy, the hotel is worth viewing in its own right. Here since 1837, it has provided hospitality to **Mark Twain,** Rudyard Kipling, **J. P. Morgan,** and **Alexander Graham Bell. Theodore Roosevelt** stayed here when getting married, and **Franklin** and **Eleanor Roosevelt** honeymooned here. There are memorial rooms to T.R., Bell, and Kipling, and, if one asks, one may be able to see the first of these. Brown's was the *Bertram's Hotel* of Agatha Christie's murder mystery, and **Thomas Bailey**

BUCKINGHAM PALACE

Aldrich has written entertainingly of it in *From Ponkapog to Pesth.*
Oliver Wendell Holmes stayed at no. 17, Dover Street, nearby.

Buckingham Palace, not open to the public, is where the Queen lives.
One will probably want to see the Changing of the Guard (no
longer a daily event, so check before going) but it will be crowded
and the ceremony is a modest one. Inside, where you cannot see
them (although the Queen places her art on exhibit from time to
time in the Queen's Gallery, around the corner on Buckingham
Palace Road) are nine **Benjamin Wests** and a copy of a **Gilbert
Stuart** Washington. **James Bryce,** British Ambassador to the United
States and author of *The American Commonwealth,* lived at no. 3
Buckingham Gate. The **American Squadron** of the Home Guard
was based at no. 58 in World War II.

Burlington House, Piccadilly, next to Burlington Arcade, is the home
of the Royal Academy. There are usually art exhibitions, and in
May the members' show is quite fine. **Benjamin West** helped
found the Academy and was its second President. The Academy
owns eight of his paintings. Many American artists have exhibited
here, some few have been members. One may view the reference
library and collection of drawings only by appointment.

Bush House, Strand, is flanked by Australia House and India House.
Designed by an American architect and erected by Irving Bush of

New York, the building is dedicated 'to the friendship of English-speaking peoples'. On the arch is a group of statuary representing England and America bearing the torch of freedom. During the Blitz a bomb fragment took off the American's arm, and it has been left off as a memorial to the survival of the bombing of London. Across the street in Aldwych was the Olympic Theatre, where Harriet Beecher Stowe's *Uncle Tom's Cabin* was performed for the first time in England in 1852. Opposite and to the east is Norfolk Street, where **Washington Irving** stayed at no. 35 on his first visit to London. **William Penn** lived in no. 21, the last house on the right. Adjacent is Arundel Street. **Josiah Quincy** lived here for a time. The tune of the Star Spangled Banner is said to have originated in the Crown and Anchor Tavern here, beginning as a drinking song for the Anacreontic Society that met within. John Stafford Smith's 'To Anacreon in Heaven' was used to end group proceedings.

Carlton House Terrace is a fine set of buildings by John Nash, with a contemporary arts gallery facing The Mall and the Duke of York's Column dividing the two piers of terraced houses. **Joseph Choate** lived in no. 1 as American Ambassador – this was the home of Lord Curzon – and **John Hay** lived in no. 5.

Charing Cross Road, a long street running from Trafalgar Square to St Giles' Circus, is lined with both new and second-hand book shops.

Chelsea Royal Hospital, built by Wren in 1682, is a handsome building on Royal Hospital Road. The Chelsea Pensioners can be identified by their red coats. In Tite Street, which runs northwest from Royal Hospital Road, **James McNeill Whistler** lived at nos. 13 (1881–5) and 46 (1888). **John Singer Sargent** lived at no. 31 (now nos. 39–40) for twenty-four years, and died there. There is an elegant stone tablet to him. Oscar Wilde wrote his major works at no. 34, and **Edwin Austin Abbey** died in no. 42. The street runs into Tedworth Square, where **Mark Twain** stayed at no. 23 in 1896–7 (there is a plaque). These numbers have been in a process of change.

Cheyne Walk, or at least the section of it just back from the Chelsea Embankment, is the most famous literary street in London. Here George Eliot died at no. 4, three weeks after marrying John Cross, an American banker. Bertrand Russell lived at no. 14, Dante

Gabriel Rossetti at no. 16 (where he was visited by Whistler) and J. M. W. Turner, the painter, died at nos. 118–19. This house was taken over in 1907 by the American journalist **Richard Harding Davis**. **James McNeill Whistler** painted the famous picture of his mother while living at no. 96. Elizabeth Gaskell was born at no. 93. In Carlyle Mansions, **Henry James** died, and **T. S. Eliot** and Arnold Toynbee lived. The Royal Historical Society's quarters are here as well. In Cheyne Row, which runs north from the Walk, is Thomas Carlyle's house, where he lived for 47 years (open 10–1, 2–6, Sun. 2–6). **Ralph Waldo Emerson** stayed with Carlyle here, while **Whistler** lived in nos. 96 and 101, and died in no. 74. In Oakley Street, which bifurcates Cheyne Walk, Robert Scott the Antarctic explorer lived in no. 56, while in no. 87 Lady Jane Wilde held her literary salon, and was visited by **Oliver Wendell Holmes.** In Lawrence Street, which runs parallel to Cheyne Row, **Henry James** lived briefly. (The house numbers are changing.)

Churchill Gardens, Grosvenor Road, were built between 1946 and 1962. They represent the best of modern London. These flats are heated by waste hot water from Battersea power station. There are two children's 'adventure' playgrounds, a concept which the British pioneered.

College of Arms, on Queen Victoria Street, is a fine 17th century building in which are kept the official records of English and Welsh heraldry, and much material on American genealogy as well.

Thomas Coram Foundation for Children, 40 Brunswick Square, which grew from a foundling hospital, is now a child welfare building. It houses a unique Picture Gallery, where one may see fine Hogarths (he supported the hospital), a superb **Benjamin West** (he was a Governor of the Foundling Hospital) and a **John Singleton Copley** sketch. Coram lived in Massachusetts and helped in the settlement of Georgia.

Covent Garden, rebuilt, is not what those of us who remember "My Fair Lady" want to see, but it does have a handsome set of new shops, there are flowers to be had, and the city fathers have done a bit better in their official vandalism than the Parisians did with Les Halles.

Craven Street, running off the Strand, is intimately associated with **Benjamin Franklin,** who lived at no. 36 during the time he was representative of the Pennsylvania Assembly (1757–75). Built about 1730, the house is being refurbished. Adjacent, running from Trafalgar Square, is Northumberland Avenue. The Royal Commonwealth Society (exhibits) is here, and at no. 10 is the Sherlock Holmes pub, which is virtually a museum of Holmes material assembled by the Holmes Society of London. On the other side of Charing Cross Station is Villiers Street, where there is one of the oldest wine bars in London, Gordon's Wine Cellars – G. K. Chesterton frequented it, and Rudyard Kipling wrote *The Light that Failed* here. John Adam Street runs at right angles to Villiers Street; in it is the Royal Society of Arts, which takes honorary American members in recognition of **Benjamin Franklin's** important role (there is a tablet). **Herman Melville** lived briefly at no. 25, and Heinrich Heine stayed at no. 32. Buckingham Street runs off John Adam Street; **Gilbert Stuart** lived here. The Water Gate, at the Thames end of the street, came from the estate of **General Fairfax** of Virginia fame. **James Fenimore Cooper** lived in John Adam Street in 1828, and in Adelphi Terrace, nearby, **John Trumbull,** the painter, lived in 1779–80. Just beyond is the Savoy Hotel, and below are the Victoria Embankment Gardens (q.v.).

Curzon Street, Mayfair, runs from Park Lane to Berkeley Square. This is a handsome road, which also gives access to Shepherd Market and Hertford Street. Here **General John Burgoyne,** he who lost at Saratoga, lived as a post-war playwright, in no. 10. Richard Brinsley Sheridan lived in the same house, while **Edwin Arlington Robinson** stayed at no. 3 when he visited London, and Edward Bulwer-Lytton wrote *The Last Days of Pompeii* in no. 36. **John Lothrop Motley,** the American Minister and historian, lived at no. 31 (now nos. 19–20). In Down Street, which runs south from Hertford Street, **James Russell Lowell** lived at no. 11 in 1872 and **Ralph Waldo Emerson** at no. 16 in 1873.

Dickens House, 48 Doughty Street (open 10–12.30, 2–5, except Sun.) where the writer lived in the 1830s, contains many Dickens relics, some from the United States. Just north is the handsome Mecklenburgh Square.

H.M.S. *Discovery*, the vessel Captain Robert Scott used in Antarctica in 1901–4, is moored at Victoria Embankment (open 1–4.30).

Downing Street, Whitehall, is where the Prime Minister lives. One may wait outside no. 10 along with other tourists, demonstrators, and the ever-present London bobbies.

Ealing is a suburb on the western edge of London. In **St Mary's parish church** there is a tablet to John Horne Tooke, who is buried here. Tooke raised a fund for the orphans and widows of American soldiers killed at Lexington and Concord, and for doing so he was fined £1,200 and imprisoned for a year.

East India Dock, off East India Dock Road, perhaps the most famous (and also one of the smallest) of the Port of London's docks, begins at Blackwall Pier. The public is not admitted to the dock itself. Here is the **Virginia Settlers Memorial,** commemorating the sailing in 1606 of the *Susan Constant, Goodspeed*, and *Discovery*, with the colonists for Jamestown. In King Edward VII Memorial Park, nearby, is a memorial to 16th century navigators, including Sir Martin Frobisher.

Fenton House, in The Grove, Hampstead, dates from 1693. The gardens are pleasant, and the house contains a fine collection of porcelain, furniture and historical keyboard instruments, including Handel's harpsichord (open 10–1, 2–5, Sun. 2–5, closed Mon.). See also 'Hampstead'.

Finsbury Circus (reached from Moorgate Underground station) is in the midst of the area most devastated during World War II. The new Circus, broad London Wall road south and the cavernous Liverpool Street Station, which can dispatch sixty trains an hour, are worth visiting. The American radical churchman **Moncure Daniel Conway** was minister in South Place Chapel, north of the Circus.

Fleet Street, home of many of the English newspapers, runs past the Inns of Court and Chancery, Prince Henry's Room – the oldest (1610) domestic building in London at no. 17 (open 1.45–5, Sat. 2.45–4.30) – the Olde Cheshire Cheese pub and the entrance to Dr Johnson's house (q.v.) to Ludgate Circus, where a plaque reminds us that Edgar Wallace sold newspapers here as a boy. **Tom Paine** lived at no. 77 Fetter Lane, off Fleet Street, for a time.

Goldsmiths' Hall, Foster Lane, perhaps the most interesting of the guild halls, with a dazzling exhibition of worked gold, is open only four times a year – watch for announcements in *What's On* in order to obtain a ticket.

Gray's Inn, on Gray's Inn Road, is an Inn of Court dating from the 14th century (open 9–6). In the gardens is a catalpa probably brought back by **Sir Walter Raleigh** from America. The Inn had its colonial members, of course. Staple Inn, south, is the only surviving Inn of Chancery; it is an exquisite Elizabethan building.

Green Park, together with St James's Park, both connecting, are the oldest Royal Parks in London. They were laid out in part imitation of Versailles. There are fine views from the parks, especially from the east end of St James's. In a reservoir here, which exists no longer, **Benjamin Franklin** is said to have poured oil on troubled waters to demonstrate the adage. (The Mount Pond, at Clapham Common, makes equal claim to being the site.)

Greenwich, reached down river by a launch from Westminster Bridge, makes a fine day or half-day outing. One must be certain to see the National Maritime Museum (open 10–6), the old Royal Observatory, **the statue to General Wolfe** behind it, the Rotunda Museum (artillery) and the **Cutty Sark,** a great clipper ship that is now a museum which includes American items. The *Gipsy Moth IV*, in which Sir Francis Chichester sailed alone around the world in 1966–7, is also here. **Benjamin Franklin** sailed from this pier for America in 1726. Inland, beyond Greenwich Park, is Blackheath, an area worth exploring. **Nathaniel Hawthorne** lived at no. 4 Pond Road (there is a plaque). West on the Thames is Deptford, from which **James Oglethorpe** and his Georgia settlers sailed in 1732, and **Rotherhithe**, which has many associations with the Pilgrims. Christopher Jones, master of the *Mayflower*, is buried in St Mary's parish churchyard (there is a plaque inside). Rotherhithe Street, running along the Thames, was the site of the home port of the *Mayflower*. The Angel pub, at no. 21, was visited by the Pilgrims. The Mayflower pub, at no. 117, is built on the original foundations of a pub that served the Pilgrims, and a model of the vessel hangs outside. The pub has the unusual right to sell stamps to sailors (including, oddly, American postage stamps).

Grosvenor Square is said to be the heart of 'American London', just as Earl's Court Road is the heart of 'Australian London'. It has been associated with Americans since John Adams, first United States Minister to Britain (and later President of the United States) took up residence on the northeast corner of the square (there is a plaque). The square is now dominated by the American Embassy, designed by Eero Saarinen (who, it is said, was not happy with the result). The huge gilded aluminum American eagle that hangs upon the building was once controversial, but Londoners have become accustomed to its face. One may go inside the Embassy to the main reception area, or enter from Upper Brook Street to see the displays mounted by the U.S. Information Service. On upper floors (generally closed to the public) are fine portraits of previous Ambassadors, American Indian prints and a very good porcelain eagle by Edward Boehm. On the east side of the square is the Canadian High Commission; a plaque on it indicates that it was the American Embassy from 1938 until 1960 and the site of Anglo-American wartime cooperation. A plaque on the north side of the square marks the building that was used as wartime headquarters by General Eisenhower. (CINCNAVEUR headquarters today are a block north.) A fine statue of Franklin Delano Roosevelt, by Sir W. Reid Dick, stands in the middle of the square. It was paid for by public subscription open only to Britishers, with no one allowed to donate more than 5 shillings. The £200,000 needed was raised in twenty-four hours. In Green Street, off North Audley Street, Bishop Berkeley lived upon his return from America in 1731, and Sydney Smith died at no. 56. In South Audley Street is Grosvenor Chapel, built in 1730 and used by the American armed forces during World War II. Washington Irving stayed at no. 4 Mount Street (now nos. 17–18) while Fanny Burney lived at no. 22, Algernon Swinburne at no. 124, W. Somerset Maugham at no. 23 and Winston Churchill at no. 105.

Guildhall, off Gresham Street, is a fine medieval building used for many of the City of London's ceremonial occasions. It contains a clock museum, and a City of London museum that is in the process of being amalgamated with the London Museum from Kensington Palace. Among its holdings are a number of **American bronze medals.**

Ham House, in Petersham, is a fine 17th century country house which may be seen on the same outing as Richmond, Kew Gardens and Hampton Court. It is open April–September, 2–6, October–March, 2–4. In the parish **church of St Peter** is a memorial to Captain George Vancouver, explorer of the northwest coast of America, which was put here by the Hudson's Bay Company. Vancouver is buried in the churchyard.

Hampstead Heath, a great park on the north side of London, is open, hilly, and even a bit wild. There are many literary associations, and the heath has excellent walks and views over London. Kenwood House (q.v.) is here. There are three old pubs along the north-western fringe of the park: the Bull and Bush, Spaniards, and **Jack Straw's Castle.** Washington Irving was a frequenter of the last.

Hampstead Village, perhaps London's most interesting 'village' within the city, has many literary associations, excellent art and book shops, and interesting pubs. Keats' House is here. **Edwin Muir** lived at no. 7 Downshire Hill for a time. Beyond, in Hampstead Garden Suburb (an early planned residential area) is **Old Wyldes,** a weather-boarded house similar to New England timber framed houses. The painter John Linnell lived in it.

Hampton Court Palace, reached by Thames river craft, or by Underground and bus, is a royal palace originally built for Cardinal Wolsey in 1515. There is a fine picture gallery, and handsome state rooms, an orangery, exceptional formal gardens, a good maze, and superb screens. (Note the Yale of Beaufort at the entrance.) This is by far the best of the palaces near London, and if one is not getting into the more distant countryside, the essential great house to be visited (open May–Sept., 9.30–6, Sun. 11–6; Oct.–April, close 4 or 5, Sun. open 2). The Mitre Hotel Restaurant, on the Thames, faces the palace, and it offers an excellent lunch – book in advance.

Haymarket, a handsome wide street running from Piccadilly Circus south to Pall Mall, is a study in contrasts, from the Design Centre to New Zealand House. American Express is here, as is the historic **Haymarket Theatre,** where Tom Taylor's *Our American Cousin* was first performed in Britain in 1861; it was while watching this play in Washington in 1865 that Abraham Lincoln was assassinated.

Highgate, the 'village' I personally like the best, offers commanding views down its hill toward St Paul's. There are many literary associations, a lovely small square, Kenwood House (q.v.) and much of Hampstead Heath (q.v.). A. E. Housman lived at no. 17 North Road, and Samuel Taylor Coleridge and J. B. Priestley lived in The Grove, as does Yehudi Menuhin, whose music school was here. Highpoint Flats (on North Hill) built in 1935–8, were re-garded as a major innovation at the time. Highgate Cemetery is the

HOUSES OF PARLIAMENT

most interesting of London's burial grounds, and its overgrown portion is particularly strange to explore. In the better-kept portion is the great bust of Karl Marx. Before leaving Highgate, have a drink at The Flask, an excellent pub where **Robert Rogers** lived while mapping his search for the northwest passage. At 31 West Hill is the house celebrated by the current Poet Laureate, Sir John Betjeman. Northeast of Highgate and down the hill is Hornsey (the viaduct on Hornsey Lane across Archway Road provides a good view). A memorial window to **Abraham Lincoln** was incorporated in the Hornsey Methodist chapel.

Hogarth's House, Great West Road, is a bit of a journey unless one takes it in when going to Heathrow Airport (leave 20 minutes early by taxi, and ask the driver to wait). This was the 17th century home of the great painter (open summer 11–6, Sun. 2; winter close at 4).

Holland House, in Holland Park, consists of a single remaining wing of a fine 1607 mansion and a modern youth hostel. **William Penn** lived here in 1684, and it received many American literary visitors. Walks in the narrow streets to the east of the house are attractive, and the Commonwealth Institute is nearby. Kenneth Grahame wrote *The Wind in the Willows* in 1908 when living at no. 16 Phillimore Place.

Houses of Parliament, perhaps the best-known sight in London, are a living memorial to the effectiveness of the Common Law. Here were debated the great issues of empire at the time of the American Revolution. One may tour portions of the building; if one wishes to attend a session of Parliament, check that the House is sitting (a light will be glowing above the building) and get into the inevitable queue outside St Stephen's entrance. There are many American associations, of course, together with a good Copley painting and friezes of the departing Pilgrims. One may visit Westminster Hall weekdays 10–4.

Hyde Park is London's major lung, perhaps the most famous park in the world, and is superb for walks along the Serpentine, past Rotten Row, to see the fine **Jacob Epstein** monument to W. H. Hudson, creator of *Green Mansions*, or to move imperceptibly into Kensington Gardens to the famous statue of Peter Pan. Speakers' Corner is opposite Marble Arch on the northeast corner; here one may hear a variety of impromptu speakers any Sunday morning from about 11. (Joining north of the arch is Great Cumberland Place; the **American Chancery** was at nos. 5–7 in the 19th century.) At the southern edge of the park is Albert Gate, where **Mark Twain** lived at 30 Wellington Court, in 1899–1900. Across Kensington Road from Alexandra Gate in **Princes Gate** is the former official residence of American Ambassadors, no. 14, presented by J. P. Morgan. Further west, in Hyde Park Gate, running south from Kensington Road, was the home of American-born sculptor **Jacob Epstein** (no. 18) and of Enid Bagnold, who wrote *National Velvet* here (no. 29). Virginia Woolf was born at no. 22 and Winston Churchill lived and died at no. 28. Further along, in De Vere Gardens, is a plaque to **Henry James** who lived at no. 34. **Twain** stayed at the Prince of Wales Hotel here. On the north edge of the park, across Bayswater Road, is the handsome Hyde Park Square and Hyde Park Gardens. **James Russell Lowell** lived at no. 2 Radnor Place, for a time.

Islington is a relatively large and drab residential area that was badly hit during the bombing of London. **Tom Paine** lived at the Angel Inn, now a shop, near the Angel Underground station. In Camden Passage, off Upper Street, is an excellent antique market. Canonbury, a residential area northeast, is attractive. In **Newington Green,** north of Canonbury, is a Unitarian chapel with close connections with the Unitarian movement in the United States. One of its ministers, Richard Price, was specially vocal in his support of the colonies during the revolution.

Jermyn Street, noted for its shirt makers and Paxton and Whitfield's cheese shop, runs from St James's to Regent Street. At one time **Benjamin Franklin** lodged on this street. **Sinclair Lewis** worked on *Babbitt* and later on *Arrowsmith* while living at no. 10 Bury Street.

Dr Johnson's House, 17 Gough Square, off Fleet Street (open daily except Sun., 10.30–5, winter close 4.30) contains objects associated with the Great Doctor.

Keats' House, Wentworth Place, is in Hampstead (q.v.). Keats lived here when writing his best poetry, and the house is unusually interesting (open daily except Sun. 10–6). His bust was placed in the Hampstead parish church by American admirers. A visit to the house offers an opportunity to walk into the Vale of Health as well.

Kennington stands between the Elephant and Castle, where there is a new commercial development of which the British are rather proud, and Vauxhall Bridge. The Kennington Oval (or Surrey County Cricket Ground) is well known, and Kennington Park is pleasant. In **Christ Church** there is a modest memorial to Abraham Lincoln.

Kensal Green Cemetery, Harrow Road, is, after Highgate Cemetery, the most interesting in London. Many literary figures are buried here; they include **John Lothrop Motley.**

Kensington Church Street is an attractive road connecting Kensington High Street (where one finds good shops and the Antique Hypermarket) and Notting Hill Gate. **Ezra Pound** lived at no. 10 when he first came to London, and across the court from him Richard Aldington lived with Hilda Doolittle ('H.D.') before they were married.

Kensington Palace, in Kensington Gardens, housed the London Museum but this has now been amalgamated with other museums devoted to the history of the city and has re-opened in the Barbican. A portion of the palace is still residential, and thirteen **Benjamin West** paintings are included in the palace collection. The State Apartments are open to the public.

Kenwood House, Hampstead Lane, is virtually in Highgate (q.v.). (See the section on ART GALLERIES AND MUSEUMS.) This is the fine Iveagh Bequest to the city.

Kew Gardens, Surrey, is a 300-acre botanical garden begun in 1759, with fine hothouses where important scientific work has led to the development of a number of colonial economies based on transplants. Perhaps the most dramatic example is the Malayan rubber industry, begun with a plant from Kew that originated in Brazil. The gardens are open 10–8 or dusk, and they include numerous plants of North American origin. See Kew Palace also. Across the Thames via the Chiswick Bridge is Chiswick. In St Nicholas parish churchyard are the graves of **James McNeill Whistler** and his wife.

Lancaster Gate, off Bayswater Road, is a gate, a square, and a street. **Bret Harte** lived in no. 74 (now nos. 34–36) after living at no. 109 (now nos. 32–33). To the north are the once-attractive Cleveland Square and Queen's Gardens.

Lancaster House is a fine Victorian town house with superb painted ceilings (open Easter–Dec., 2–6).

Leicester Square, with its many movie houses, is an area famous for its night life. **Benjamin West** once lived here, and **John Singleton Copley** and **John Trumbull** lived at no. 23, now demolished. On St Martin's Lane, Chatto & Windus, **Mark Twain's** London publishers, developed an exceptionally warm relationship with their favorite client.

Lincoln's Inn, by Lincoln's Inn Fields, is an Inn of Court, and the most interesting of them. See Inigo Jones's chapel. **Judah Philip Benjamin,** Secretary of State for the Confederate States of America, was a member of the Inn after the Civil War.

Lombard Street is London's Wall Street, running from the Bank of England to Fenchurch Street. The lanes of this area are honeycombed with ancient and modern banks, wine bars and pubs, historical markers and derby-hatted clerks. **T. S. Eliot** worked as a clerk in no. 71, Lloyd's Bank. In Birchin Lane, running off Lombard Street, was the Pennsylvania Coffee House, where **Benjamin Franklin** often came, while **Gilbert Stuart** lived in Gracechurch Street.

London Bridge, oldest and most heralded of the Thames crossings, connects the City with Southwark. The present bridge is dull and new. Gullible Americans (and others) can purchase pieces of London Bridge, which are in fact chippings from the re-built 1831 bridge. The old facing stones were taken to Arizona, which now claims to have London Bridge. Actually very little has survived of the famous, older structure, built in 1749.

London Wall is a new thoroughfare built after massive bomb damage in World War II. Just north of its west end are the remnants of a Roman Fort. Here, too, is the attractive new museum of London. The Royal Shakespeare Company now performs in the Barbican, a new center worth exploration. In Aldersgate lived **Sir Edwin Sandys,** a founder of Virginia, and also, for a time, **John Locke,** when he was secretary to Lord Shaftesbury. South of London Wall is the Brewers' Hall, and running southwards from it is Aldermanbury. The **Church of St Mary** here was moved to Fulton, Missouri, as a memorial to Winston Churchill; it was in Fulton that he coined the phrase, 'iron curtain' countries, to describe the Soviet Union and its satellites. John Milton was married in this church. In Coleman Street, which runs south from London Wall just west of Moorgate, was **St Stephen's Church,** where the rector was John Davenport, a founder of New Haven, Connecticut.

Mansion House, opposite the Bank of England, is the official residence of the Lord Mayor of London. Its severe exterior belies the lavish interior. It is open occasionally in the summer (watch for announcements in *What's On*).

Marlborough House, designed by Christopher Wren in 1710, became Crown property in 1817 and has been used as a royal residence by Edward VII (when Prince of Wales), Queen Alexandra and Queen Mary. It now houses the Commonwealth Secretariat, and is open to visitors from Easter to the end of September, provided a conference is not in progress (Sat.–Sun., 2–6).

Marylebone Road runs across the upper portion of central London, parallel to Oxford Street. It is an often handsome, sometimes congested street, with many interesting associations. Friends' House, a fine research library on Quakerism, is near the east end, and there is a handsome bust of **John F. Kennedy** in a tiny park area. Madame Tussaud's Wax Museum and The Planetarium are here. Near the west end, and north off the main road, is the tiny and dignified **Marylebone Station.** During World War I it was a hospital where British and American troops were treated.

The Monument, an ugly hollow column commemorating the Great Fire of London, is just below the Monument tube station. If one can stand the climb to the top, the tower offers a panoramic view of London (open 9–6, close 4 in winter). Billingsgate Market, famous for originating much colorful language, was at the end of Monument Street, east. Parallel, one street north, is Eastcheap. Here stood the Boar's Head Tavern, a haunt of **Washington Irving's.**

The Old Bailey, the Central Criminal Court, is on the corner of Old Bailey and Newgate Street. One may attend a trial here or examine much of the building when the court is not sitting. A memorial tablet inside tells of the trial of **William Penn** for preaching unlawful assembly.

Old Curiosity Shop, 13–14 Portsmouth Street, given fame by Charles Dickens, is now an antique shop of no distinction, but you will feel unhappy if you do not go. Sardinia Street, running from Lincoln's Inn Fields, around the corner, was once the home of **Benjamin Franklin.** The original site is lost.

Oxford Street is a ghastly shopping thoroughfare. Near its eastern end is Newman Street, running north. **Benjamin West** lived at no. 14 (now demolished) for forty years, dying here in 1820. **Gilbert Stuart, John James Audubon** and **Edwin Austin Abbey** also lived in this street, and **Whistler** had a studio at no. 70. **Samuel F. B. Morse** lived at no. 82 (also gone) Great Titchfield Street, which runs north off Oxford Street. At the Palladium, in Argyll Street just off Oxford Circus, one finds plaques to only two stars, both Americans: Judy Garland and Bing Crosby.

Paddington Station, perhaps the most famous of London's great railway stations, retains its fine Victorian glass canopies. On the wall of no. 1 departure platform is a balcony built by Isambard Kingdom Brunel, chief designer of the Great Western Railway, which ran from here. Today 50,000 passengers use Paddington daily.

Pall Mall, perhaps the finest early 19th century street in London, is synonymous with the many clubs that line it. The clubs are not open to the public, and little is to be learned by viewing them from the outside. If you have a friend who can get you in, and a choice, opt for the Athenaeum, Reform, or Travellers (or, if a military buff, the United Services). Among the members of the Athenaeum, for example, were Matthew Arnold, G. K. Chesterton, Joseph Conrad, Conan Doyle, John Galsworthy, H. Rider Haggard, Rudyard Kipling, William Makepeace Thackeray and W. B. Yeats. Nationality is no bar to membership, and many Americans are members of Clubland. In **St James's Square,** just north of Pall Mall, is **Norfolk House,** with a tablet explaining how it functioned as

General Eisenhower's headquarters during part of World War II. The square was the base of American activity in World War I, and the American Legion was founded here in 1919. South of Pall Mall, in front of the Athenaeum, is **Waterloo Place.** The statues here include Sir John Franklin, Arctic explorer; Captain Robert Scott, explorer of Antarctica; Sir John Fox Burgoyne, natural son of General Burgoyne; and Florence Nightingale.

Parliament Square, outside the Houses of Parliament, provides space in which to contemplate Big Ben, the great clock of Parliament. A copy of Augustus Saint-Gaudens' fine Chicago statue of **Abraham Lincoln** is in the square. There are also good statues of Benjamin Disraeli and George Canning, and **Jacob Epstein's** Jan Christian Smuts. On the lawn across the way is a statue of **Sir Walter Raleigh,** donated by an Anglo-American group.

Peckham Rye and Camberwell are inner ring suburbs with more beautiful houses than some. The old Friends' Meeting House in Meeting House Lane off Peckham High Street, was attended by **William Penn.** There is an inscription on no. 180.

Pelham Crescent is a small, exceptionally handsome Georgian crescent off the Fulham Road. **William Dean Howells** lived in no. 18 for a time, while more recently Emlyn Williams occupied no. 15 and Eric Ambler no. 16.

Piccadilly Circus, a roundabout, is garish and overpopulated. Here is London's busiest Underground station, and it is virtually unavoidable. The statue mistakenly called Eros in the middle is overshadowed by the noise and bustle around it. Piccadilly (the street) runs west to Hyde Park Corner, and there are several places of interest, commented on separately, along it.

Piccadilly, the street not the circus, is a handsome thoroughfare running from the circus west to Hyde Park Corner. On it are Burlington Arcade (a Regency shopping promenade, built in 1819, with excellent shops that cater especially to Americans) and Burlington House (q.v.), Fortnum and Mason, book shops, the Ritz Hotel, and St James's church. The Albany (residential chambers) east of the Royal Academy, is a posh address. Among those who lived here are Arnold Bennett, Lord Byron, Edward Bulwer-Lytton, Graham Greene, Aldous Huxley, Thomas Babington Macaulay, Harold Nicolson, J. B. Priestley, Terence Rattigan and Eric Ambler. **John Lothrop Motley,** as American Minister to Britain, lived in no. 17 Arlington Street. In Bolton Street, running northwest from Piccadilly, **Henry James** lived in 1876. In Clarges Street, next to it, **James Russell Lowell** lodged at no. 40, in which Ronald Firbank was born in the same year. E. Phillips Oppenheim lived at no. 13 in the 1920s. There is a blue plaque to Charles James Fox at no. 46. Next is Half Moon Street, where Boswell lived in 1768 when **Franklin** visited him. **Henry James** lived at no. 7, **William Dean Howells** at no. 18 for a month, Lola Montez at no. 27 and William Hazlitt at no. 40.

Portland Place, a handsome, blunted road laid out by the Adam brothers in 1774, runs north from Broadcasting House to the effective Park Crescent (where inside the Industrial Students' House there is a memorial to John F. Kennedy). Portland Place houses chanceries and embassies. For a time the American Chancery was here, and the Minister lived in Langham Place. It, and the Langham Hotel, where Longfellow, Twain, Bret Harte and Ellen Glasgow stayed, are now part of the BBC. Horace Walpole lived in no. 5, James Monroe in no. 23 as American Minister, Edgar Wallace in no. 39, James Bryce (and earlier Henry Adams) in no. 54 (now nos. 23–25) and John Buchan in no. 76. At right angles runs Duchess Street; Ezra Pound stayed at no. 8 on his first visit to London, while Charles Francis Adams lived at no. 5 Mansfield Street, as Minister.

Portobello Road, site of the most famous and best of the Saturday morning markets, runs from Pembridge Road, just north of Notting Hill Gate Underground station. The market is great fun, even if one does not plan to purchase, and amidst the junk one may find much that is worth bringing home. Bargain, and expect that if you are recognized as American – and you will be – some of the barrow people may quote you a higher price at first. In the Greek Church on Moscow Road, east, there is a memorial to **Abraham Lincoln.** Spend the morning at the market, and then have fish and chips for lunch at Geale's, on Farmer Street, or eat a vegetarian meal at Saints and Sinners, 137 Kensington Church Street, both just south of the Underground station.

Post Office Tower, Howland Street, includes a revolving restaurant and viewing gallery at the top. While the food is not good and is overpriced, the view is the finest in London. In 1969 this was the site of the start of a trans-Atlantic air race to the Empire State Building and back, to celebrate the 50th anniversary of the first trans-Atlantic flight. In Cleveland Street, just west, there is a tablet to **Samuel F. B. Morse. Whistler** had a studio at no. 8 Fitzroy Street, east of the tower.

Regent Street, running from Oxford Circus to Piccadilly Circus, is one of the most striking central thoroughfares in London. It is lined with prestige (and some not so prestigious) shops. At Liberty's, on the corner of Great Marlborough Street, there is a miniature **Mayflower,** used as a weathervane. **Gilbert Stuart** lived in Burlington Street, which runs west off Regent Street, for a while. Carnaby Street (now a pedestrian precinct) parallels Regent Street two blocks east, while Savile Row (reached through Burlington Street) parallels it one block west.

Regent's Park, the great green sweep north of Marylebone Road, contains the London Zoo, which is very good, Queen Mary's Rose Garden, and an open air theatre in which *A Midsummer Night's Dream*, or another Shakespearean play capable of being well produced out of doors, is presented nightly during a summer season. **Winfield House,** in the northwest corner of the park, is the official residence of American Ambassadors (closed to the public). The terraces off the Outer Circle on the east side of the park, and again at Sussex Place and Hanover Terrace off the west side, are very fine. In Glentworth Street, paralleling upper Baker Street outside Clarence Gate, are two houses where **T. S. Eliot** lived in the 1920s – first at no. 68 and then at no. 98.

Royal Albert Hall, on Kensington Gore, with the Albert Memorial opposite in Kensington Gardens, has recently been thoroughly cleaned, and it is once more a monument to Victorian taste. One should not fail to attend a concert here. Medieval banquets are served at the Gore Hotel, in Queen's Gate, to the west of the Hall, while in Prince's Gardens, a square to the southeast of the Hall, **Thomas F. Bayard** lived at no. 32 as the American Minister.

Royal Courts of Justice, at the eastern end of the Strand, are well worth exploring; one may use an outside stairway to enter one of the court rooms and listen to the proceedings.

Royal Exchange, between Threadneedle Street and Cornhill, was built in 1842 on the site of the first exchange, opened in 1565 by

Sir Thomas Gresham (he of the law that bad money drives out good). The weathervane is a grasshopper eleven feet long. In front is a good equestrian statue of the Duke of Wellington, and behind it is the figure of **George Peabody,** American philanthropist, who helped make housing available to London's poor. In the interior quadrangle, on the northwest corner, is a bust of **Abraham Lincoln,** the only American to have more than two London memorials.

Royal Festival Hall, and the Queen Elizabeth Hall adjacent, date from the Festival of Britain in 1951. London's great orchestras perform here and the hall is strikingly handsome, especially when approached on foot across Hungerford Bridge from Charing Cross Station. The National Theatre is just beyond the Hayward Gallery.

Royal Mews, at the back of Buckingham Palace, exhibits the Queen's carriages, including the Coronation Coach (open Wed.–Thurs., 2–4).

Royal Mint, near the Tower, offers a fascinating tour to see how money is made. The Mint continues to make the coinage of the Realm, and that of several Commonwealth nations as well. One must apply, in writing, six months in advance for a tour, which makes things a wee bit difficult for the non-resident.

Royal Opera Arcade, the oldest arcade in London, runs off Pall Mall by New Zealand House.

Russell Square is the major square near the British Museum and the University of London. **Thomas Wolfe** stayed at the Imperial Hotel, while in Southampton Row – directly off the square – **Ralph Waldo Emerson** stayed at no. 63 and **Edgar Allan Poe's** family lived at no. 83. Behind the square to the west is the tower of Senate House, the administrative headquarters of the university, and grouped nearby are the **Institute of United States Studies** (Tavistock Square), institutes of legal and Commonwealth studies, and the famous School of Oriental and African Studies. In Boswell Street (east of Southampton Row) was the **Poetry Bookshop** (at no. 35, 1913–26) where Robert Frost took rooms and became acquainted with Ezra Pound.

St James's Palace, at the bottom of St James's Street, is a Royal residence. Built by Henry VIII, it is ugly and forbidding. One may see the courtyards and the Chapel Royal, which has a Holbein ceiling, and there will be a photogenic guard in a busby outside. The palace collection includes two **Benjamin Wests.**

St James's Place, a cul-de-sac running west off St James's Street, was the home of Joseph Addison, Richard Brinsley Sheridan (no. 37), Frederick Marryat (no. 38) and Samuel Rogers (no. 22), patron of the arts, who entertained Byron, Scott, **Washington Irving** and others. When **James Fenimore Cooper** came to London, he stayed in no. 33, as **Hawthorne** did twenty-eight years later. Next to Lobb's, in St James's Street, is a sign to the former independent **Texas Republic.**

St John's Wood is a residential area to the northwest of Regent's Park. Here one finds Lord's Cricket Ground, with its attendant museum. In the parish church is buried **Elizabeth West,** wife of Benjamin.

St Pancras Station, in Euston Road, together with its hotel (now used for offices) has been controversial since it opened in 1873. It is either magnificently Victorian, or horribly Victorian, depending upon one's taste. It has been newly cleaned.

Silver Vaults, off Chancery Lane one street south of High Holborn, are a series of underground vaults from which both fine and less fine silver is sold. One is welcome to browse without buying.

Sloane Square is in a fashionable area. On the square is the Royal Court Theatre, and Peter Jones' department store, built in 1936 and once hailed as an important architectural innovation. Sloane Street runs north from the square. **James McNeill Whistler** lodged at no. 62 when he first came to London. Crossing at right angles to the north is Pont Street, where Rafael Sabatini lived at no. 22. North of Pont Street is attractive Hans Place. Running out of Sloane Square southwest is the Kings Road, once noted for its Chelsea birds, boutiques, and the Great American Disaster. Off Kings Road (the fifth turning to the left) is Wellington Square, where A. A. Milne lived. **Thomas Wolfe** worked on *Look Homeward Angel* while staying at no. 32 in 1926.

Smithfield Market, Charterhouse Street, is the largest meat market in the world. Northeast was the Charterhouse School (now moved to Godalming, in Surrey) where Roger Williams was educated. Southeast is Bartholomew Close, where **Washington Irving** and **Benjamin Franklin** lived. Butcher's Hall is in the Close, which runs into

Little Britain, where Franklin once lodged. Southwest of Smithfield is Snow Hill, under Holborn Viaduct; **Captain John Smith** lived here from 1619–31.

Soho, famous as the 'sin section' of London, is quite safe. Establish-ments here range from the sedate through the useful (Left Handed Only, a shop that includes left-handed scissors in its stock) to the pornographic. On its edge, in Charing Cross Road, is Foyles bookshop, which claims to be the largest in the world. In Gerrard Street, James Boswell lodged at no. 22 in 1776, and Edmund Burke lived at no. 37 in the 1780s.

Somerset House, in the Strand, is a handsome building dating from 1776. It is now the registry office for births, deaths, marriages and wills. In its courtyard stands an unusual statue of **George III,** he who helped his nation blunder into the American Revolution.

Stationers' Hall, off Warwick Lane, is one of the many guild halls. This one holds a **Benjamin West** painting. From here east are a number of other guild halls: the Apothecaries', Cutlers', Painters', Vintners', Innholders', Tallowchandlers', Skinners', Fishmongers', Watermens', Bakers', Clothworkers', Founders', Grocers', Mer-cers', Drapers', Carpenters', Fan Makers', Leathersellers', Armour-ers'| and|Brasiers', Girdlers', Brewers', Pewterers', Iron-mongers', Butchers', Haberdashers', Saddlers' and Goldsmiths' halls. They are generally closed to the public, but most may be viewed one or more days a year (watch for announcements in *What's On*). Vintners', Haberdashers' and Goldsmiths' (q.v.) are especially interesting.

Stock Exchange, Throgmorton Street, has a public gallery where one may watch the proceedings (open Mon.–Fri., 10–5.15). It is less interesting than either Wall Street or the Grain Exchange in Chicago, and you will do better if you can invoke a friend who can get you into Lloyd's, the marine insurers, off Leadenhall Street, where the Lutine bell is still rung when a ship goes down at sea. Off Leadenhall Street beyond Lloyd's to the north, is **Creechurch Lane.** Here is the sign of the Crown and Sugar Loaves, over Davison Newman, the firm that is the oldest tea merchantry in the world. Founded in 1650, this company shipped some of the tea that was thrown overboard in the Boston Tea Party in 1773.

Strand, a wide, busy thoroughfare connecting Trafalgar Square with Fleet Street, is full of London life. Both churches that stand in the middle of the road, St Mary-le-Strand and St Clement Danes (q.v.) are important. (See the entries on Bush House, Craven Street, and Somerset House, above.) Opposite the Savoy Hotel, **John Locke** lived and wrote his best work in Exeter House – the Strand Palace is on the site. In Bedford Street, running northwest from the Strand, **Benjamin West** lived in 1763. At right angles to Bedford Street runs Henrietta Street, where **Washington Irving** took rooms at no. 22, so small that 'a cat could not turn in' them. Henrietta Street runs into the site of the fabled – and now no longer operative – Covent Garden Market.

Syon House, on Park Road in Isleworth, is a bit of a journey but worth it. The garden is by Capability Brown, the interior by Robert Adam, and the rooms are exquisite. There is a good **Gilbert Stuart** on view. The London Transport Collection is in the park, and the grounds include the finest swamp oak from America ever grown overseas. The **gardens** are famous for their big swamp cypress, introduced from South Carolina in 1640. **Pocahontas** lived for a time in Brentford. Kew Gardens is just across the river, Marble Hill House is south of the gardens, and **Twickenham** is just southwest of Syon, so that they may all be combined in a single outing. Stephen Hales, curate of Teddington, Twickenham, was one of the original trustees of Georgia. Lord North lived in Bushey House, at the end of Park Road behind Teddington Station, while William Tryon, governor of North Carolina, is buried in Twickenham churchyard under a tomb restored through American gifts. John Murray, Earl of Dunmore, was governor of New York and of Virginia (1771–6) and Colne Lodge (behind The Green, Twickenham) belonged to his widow.

The Temple, actually Inner and Middle Temples, Inns of Court, are of particular interest, for no fewer than seven signers of the **Declaration of Independence** were members and many other Americans have studied law here. Inner Temple is open Monday–Friday, 10–12, while Middle Temple is open the same days, 10.30–12, 3–4.30. The **Hall** of Middle Temple was used as a dormitory for U.S. Navy men during World War I, and the library contains a book with the names of the naval men inscribed in it. In the Hall is a table made from the timbers of Drake's *Golden Hind.*

Thames Street, Upper and Lower, runs past Cannon Street Station above the Thames, providing occasional views, eastwards to the

Tower of London. Here one finds Fishmongers' Hall, Billingsgate Market, the Custom House, Tower Stairs, and, marked on the wall of a building, the exact measurements of Sir Francis Drake's *Golden Hind*, which was built here. Opposite Cannon Street Station (and slightly to the right) is the London Stone, used for mileage measurements to the City.

Tower of London, which combines a keep, prison and fortress, is best known for its Bloody Tower, Beefeaters, an exhibition of the Crown Jewels (very crowded), a fine collection of weapons and its black ravens. The Tower is often thronged, yet one must not miss it. If possible, go very early in the morning, or on one of the evenings when the Ceremony of the Keys is held (for which one must make prior booking) when both ceremony and tower can be seen. **William Penn** was a prisoner here, and **Sir Walter Raleigh** wrote his *History of the World* while imprisoned here. A first edition is on display, a gift of the librarian of Indiana University. The Tower is open summer 10–5, Sunday 2–5, and less generously in winter. Outside the Tower is the unusual Tower Bridge. (See also Royal Mint and All Hallows, Barking-by-the-Tower.)

Trades Union Congress headquarters, Great Russell Street, is representative of the immediate post-war modern building in London. Some say that Britain is ruled from here. The central courtyard is set off by a good **Epstein** sculpture.

Trafalgar Square, perhaps the most famous square in the world and certainly one of the handsomest, was laid out in 1829. Nelson's Column and Landseer's bronze lions, the probability of an orderly political demonstration and the presence of thousands of pigeons to feed, make this an unforgettable setting. To the north is the National Gallery, to the east St Martin-in-the-Fields, to the south Whitehall and to the west Canada House. In Cockspur Street, just beyond Canada House, is a superb statue of **George III.**

Victoria Embankment offers a fine walk along the Thames for a mile and a quarter, from Westminster Bridge to Blackfriars Bridge, with excellent views across the Thames to the Royal Festival Hall (q.v.) and ahead to St. Paul's. There is a statue of **James McNeill Whistler** by Rodin in the Victoria Embankment Gardens, and at lunchtime in the summer different military bands play here. Near the Savoy Hotel, which looks out across the gardens, is Electra House, which

THE NATIONAL GALLERY

contains memorials to **Hawthorne** and **Irving.** Cleopatra's Needle, which has nothing to do with Cleopatra, is on the Embankment. Its companion sits in New York's Central Park. The Needle was damaged in World War I and has been left unrepaired as a reminder.

Victoria Station, a cavernous barn, is redolent with Victorian and Edwardian sentiment. This was the Gateway to the Continent (as a notice board proclaims) from which departed the connections to the great transcontinental expresses – the Simplon Orient, Engadine, the Arlberg-Orient and the Golden Arrow. At ten o'clock each night the Wagon-Lits still load for the Night Ferry to Paris. To the northwest of the station is **Grosvenor Gardens.** In the Belgravia Hotel here (now gone) was the headquarters of the U.S. Army in World War I, and the American Ambulance was at no. 9. In Ebury Street, which parallels Buckingham Palace Road to the west, **Thomas Wolfe** stayed at no. 75 while writing *Of Time and the River.* Noël Coward lived at no. 111. At **Denison House,** along Vauxhall Bridge Road, was the Society for the Abolition of Slavery and the Protection of Aborigines, which did so much work in North America and Africa.

Waterloo Bridge, designed by Sir Giles Gilbert Scott, is the newest Thames River bridge. Completed in 1939, it was opened in 1944, and, to many, it is a symbol of survival in World War II.

Waterloo Station is London's most impressive monument to the railway age. Even if one is not interested in railways, it warrants a visit.

Wesley's House, 47 City Road, is in a barren stretch of London, but anyone interested in Methodism, dissenting churches in general, evangelism, or the ties between America and England should find it, and the adjoining chapel, of great interest. The house is open daily except Sunday, 10–1, 2–4. John Wesley is buried in the chapel grounds. In **Bunhill Fields,** across the road, are the graves of John Bunyan, William Blake, Daniel Defoe, Nathaniel Mather, Edmund Quincy and Isaac Watts.

Westminster School, the most famous public (i.e. private) school in London, is directly behind the Abbey. Founded in 1560, it occupies restored monastic buildings. One may view portions of it. Among the pupils here were Arthur Middleton, a signer of the **Declaration of Independence,** Richard Hakluyt, the great geographer who popularized knowledge of the explorations of North America, Ben Jonson, John Dryden, John Locke, Charles Wesley, Warren Hastings, Edward Gibbon, Jeremy Bentham and Robert Southey (who was expelled). Mrs Charlotte Lennox, an American-born novelist much admired by Dr Johnson, died in Dean's Yard, adjacent, and Edmund Burke lived there.

Whitechapel Bell Foundry, 34 Whitechapel Road E.1., has always welcomed visitors, but it makes a special point of Americans since the original Liberty Bell – the one that cracked – was made here. The foundry is over 400 years old.

Whitehall, both a place and a synonym for British administrative offices, is a wide street running from Trafalgar Square towards the Houses of Parliament. The Cenotaph divides it, and immediately off it are the Foreign Office, the fine Robert Adam Old Admiralty, the War Office, Great Scotland Yard, and in Downing Street, the site of the old Colonial Office. (New Scotland Yard, incidentally, is not here, but off Victoria Street, well southwest.) One enters these offices only on business, thus missing the fine portrait of George Washington by **Charles Wilson Peale** that hangs in the Old War Office Building off Northumberland Avenue. But one may visit the Horse Guards and the Banqueting House (built by Inigo Jones) dating from 1619 with ceilings by Rubens (open 10–5, Sun. 2.30–6). And if one books in advance by writing to the Chief

Clerk, Cabinet Office, Whitehall, one may join a tour at the Great George Street entrance to the Treasury Building to see the War Rooms, the headquarters of operations during World War II, where Churchill lived and worked. There are two tours a day, Monday to Friday.

Whittington Stone, perhaps a bit of sentimental nonsense, is on the left side (going up) of Highgate Hill, next to the entrance to Whittington Hospital. An effigy of Dick Whittington's cat sits nearby. It was here that the boy is said to have rested while going home from London, to hear the sound of Bow Bells ringing out, 'Turn again Whittington, thrice Lord Mayor of London'. He returned to become precisely that.

Wimpole Street, which runs parallel to Harley Street, famous for its doctors, is probably best known for the Barretts. The house where Elizabeth Barrett lived, no. 50, is partially replaced. From here she eloped with Robert Browning to escape from her tyrannical father. Parallel to Wimpole Street on the southwest is Welbeck Street, where the artist **John Trumbull** lived. From Welbeck Street, Bentinck Street runs at right angles. Edward Gibbon lived at no. 7 from 1772–83 and wrote the first half of his *Decline and Fall* here. Bulstrode Street runs off Welbeck Street north of Bentinck Street; here at present day nos. 28–29 **James Russell Lowell** lived in 1855 as American Minister to the Court of St James's. To the southeast of Wimpole Street is Cavendish Square, on which the colonial American painter **Mather Brown** lived from 1761 until 1831. Chandos Street runs north from the square, parallel to Harley Street; in it **Louis McLane** and **Washington Irving,** American Ministers, lived, the latter at no. 8 while serving as assistant to the then ambassador who had his offices across the street.

The Zoo in Regent's Park is world famous for its fine collection and for its contemporary design. The aviary is especially good, and even if you do not enjoy zoos as a rule, you will like this one. Be certain to see the elephant house, and do purchase a blue plastic key to activate 'speaking stations' for a commentary on the animals. The feeding times are intelligently spaced for viewing.

Churches

St Paul's Cathedral is one of the largest churches in the world and certainly the largest in London, in which there are five great cathedrals and abbeys. The original building was burnt in the Great Fire of 1666, and the present church is Sir Christopher Wren's finest. Opened in 1697, it represents the Renaissance in England at its best. The dome is the second largest in the world and one may mount to it to experience the famous Whispering Gallery. The church contains unusually ugly monuments for the most part, but there are interesting ones to **Benjamin West,** the artists Turner, Landseer, Reynolds and Millais, and Max Beerbohm, Arthur Sullivan and Walter de la Mare. On the north wall of the crypt is a painting of Redemption by **John Singer Sargent.** The choir and baldachino are a bit rich, while the crypt – in which Wren is buried – is heavily solemn, and, truth to tell, several of the provincial cathedrals reflect more serenity. But perhaps one should not ask serenity of a structure that was saved from burning in World War II only by the most desperate of actions. There is a separate **American Memorial Chapel** to the 28,000 American servicemen who died while based in Europe during World War II. The three windows are to Service, Sacrifice and Resurrection. There are also monuments to General Pakenham and Sir Samuel Gibbs, both killed at the **Battle of New Orleans** in 1815, and to General Ross, killed in the **Attack on Baltimore** in 1814. In St Paul's Churchyard, a street on the north side of the Cathedral, was the shop where **Tom Paine** met William Blake.

Westminster Abbey is officially the Collegiate Church of St Peter in Westminster. Completed between 1376 and 1734, the Abbey is the most important church in England that is not a cathedral. England's sovereigns have been crowned here since 1066, and most English kings from Henry III to George II are buried here. Early parliaments met in the Chapter House, and the incredible crowding of the Abbey with monuments attests to the fact that it is, perhaps above all, *the* national memorial. Just inside the handsome West Door is the grave of the Unknown Warrior, from World War I; on a pillar nearby is the **Congressional Medal of Honor,** the highest award that can be given by the United States. Nearby is a memorial to **Franklin Roosevelt.** Among those buried or memorialized here are David Livingstone, Neville Chamberlain, Thomas Telford,

Lord Baden-Powell, William Tyndale, Ben Jonson, John and
Charles Wesley, Lord Clive, the many figures of royalty (do not
miss the brass to the Duchess of Gloucester, the best in the Abbey),
Sir John Franklin, W. E. Gladstone, William Pitt, Lord Palmerston,
Lord Castlereagh, William Wilberforce, Charles James Fox, War-
ren Hastings, Sir Isaac Newton, Charles Darwin, Ernest Bevin,
Sidney and Beatrice Webb, and Spencer Perceval – the only British
Prime Minister to have been assassinated. The Royal Air Force
Chapel is dedicated to those who were killed in the Battle of
Britain. The south transept and aisle is called Poets' Corner, for
here one finds busts, memorials and tombs to John Dryden, **Henry
Wadsworth Longfellow,** Tennyson, Browning, Chaucer, Spenser,
Milton, Gray, Shakespeare, Sam Johnson, Wordsworth, Coleridge,
Southey, Keats, Shelley, Burns, the Brontës, William Blake (by
Epstein), Dickens, Hardy, Kipling, Goldsmith, Ruskin, Scott,
Thackeray, Macaulay, Sheridan, Addison and **T. S. Eliot** – among
others. There are **American tablets** to James Russell Lowell and
Walter Hines Page (in the Chapter House) and a **window** given
by J. W. Gerard, American Ambassador to Germany during World
War I, to the British prisoners of war who died in Germany. Other
windows were given by an American in memory of William
Cowper and George Herbert, poets. **George Peabody's** resting
place is marked by what many mistake for a tomb. In the nave is
a memorial to **Major John André,** the British spy hanged by
Washington, and one to **General Lord Howe,** killed near Ticonderoga in 1758 (this monument was erected by Massachusetts
when it was still a colony). **John Mason,** founder of New Hampshire, is buried here, and **General Burgoyne** is buried in an unmarked grave in the Cloisters. There are memorials to **Admiral
Sir Peter Warren,** who commanded the British ships during the
attack on Fortress Louisburg, and **Colonel Joseph Chester** of
Norwich, Connecticut, who was the editor of the Westminster
Abbey Register. **Charles Wragg,** a Loyalist, is also memorialized.
It is thought that **Richard Hakluyt** is buried in an unmarked grave
in the south transept. A plaque to **Henry James** was dedicated in
1976.

Southwark Cathedral, on the south side of the Thames, was badly
damaged by the war and is much restored. An impressive Gothic
building, it contains a fine choir and retrochoir (a Lady Chapel),
several good tombs, and a memorial to Shakespeare. The **Harvard**

Chapel was rebuilt in 1907 as a memorial to John Harvard, who was born in Borough High Street in 1607; it was his bequest that founded the college. The east window in the chapel is by John La Farge. There is also a monument to William Emerson, an ancestor of **Ralph Waldo Emerson.** From outside the cathedral one may begin the **Pilgrim Trail,** a walk that includes Bankside, the site of the Clink (where dissenters organized a church in a prison which provided us with a generic name); the site of the Globe Theatre; several localities associated with Charles Dickens; the old George Inn – the only galleried inn in London; the site of the Queen's Head Inn, owned by Harvard's family; and, ultimately, on the corner of Great Dover and Spurgeon streets, the **Pilgrim Fathers' Memorial Church,** opened in 1956.

Westminster Roman Catholic Cathedral is the major Roman Catholic church in England. Begun in 1895, consecrated in 1910, the Cathedral has the widest nave in the country. It is a handsome rather than beautiful building, and the interior is relatively restrained. Among several good features are the Stations of the Cross carved in stone by Eric Gill, a copy of Thorvaldsen's statue of St John the Baptist, a chapel to the saints of Ireland, another to the saints of Scotland, a fine Chapel of St Joseph and an altar to the Royal Canadian Air Force men who fell in World War II. The views from the campanile are excellent.

St George's (Roman Catholic) Cathedral, Southwark, is opposite the Imperial War Museum. Built by A. W. Pugin, it was badly damaged in World War II but has now been restored. It was on this site that the 'No Popery' rioters assembled in 1780.

Other churches of importance include:
All Hallows, Barking-by-the-Tower, founded by 675, much restored with American help following the bomb damage in 1940. It has the finest collection of brasses of any London church. William Penn was baptized here, and John Quincy Adams was married here. It is now the guild church of Toc H, and from its lamp all other Toc H lamps are lit. Friends in Texas provided the funds to restore the south aisle.

All Hallows London Wall, at 83 London Wall, is a lovely small church, which now functions as a gallery for church art.

All Saints, on Margaret Street, is regarded as the Gothic Revival triumph of London.

Brompton Oratory, opened in 1884 on Brompton Road, is a focus for Roman Catholicism in London, the cathedrals notwithstanding. Inside is a statue of Cardinal Newman.

Chelsea Old Church, All Saints, on the Embankment, was virtually destroyed by German bombing. It contained a memorial tablet to Henry James, who was buried here in 1916; Anne Washington was also buried here. Now largely rebuilt, it still contains many historic features.

Christ Church, Westminster Bridge Road. The tower of this Congregational Church commemorates the abolition of American slavery. There is a memorial stone, laid in 1874.

Notre Dame de France, 5 Leicester Place, contains a fine Aubusson tapestry and a mural by Jean Cocteau.

St Andrew Holborn, at Holborn Circus, is the largest of Sir Christopher Wren's parish churches. It was restored in 1961 after heavy bomb damage. Wren built over sixty churches in London.

St Andrew-by-the-Wardrobe, Queen Victoria Street, is a fine Wren church, which was also seriously damaged by bombing.

St Anne, Dean Street, Soho, of which only the steeple remains after bombing in World War II, contains the grave of Sir Edmund Andros, Governor of New England, originator of William and Mary College.

St Anne and St Agnes, Gresham Street, is a good Wren church, also restored after bombing.

St Bartholomew-the-Great, Smithfield, oldest church building in London, is Norman. The Lady Chapel was used in the 18th century as a printing house, and Benjamin Franklin worked here. William Hogarth was baptized here, in the only medieval font in London; he was born in Bartholomew Close.

St Benet, Welsh Church, Queen Victoria Street, is another pleasant Wren church.

St Bride, Fleet Street, is a Wren church with a fine spire that was heavily restored after bomb damage. The parents of Virginia Dare, first English child born in America, were married here, as were the parents of Edward Winslow, colonial governor of Massachusetts. When lightning struck its steeple in 1764, George III consulted Benjamin Franklin, and they argued over lightning rods, the king insisting that they should be blunted and Franklin that they should be pointed. Franklin's conductors were eventually used here (as well as on Buckingham Palace). St Bride's is also the journalists' church, and its crypt includes an excellent display on journalism (as well as Roman ruins). There is a plaque from the Overseas Press Club of America. A tablet has recently been added for two Reuter correspondents killed in Vietnam.

St Clement Danes, Strand, was begun by the Danes in the 9th century. Rebuilt by Wren after the Great Fire, totally destroyed by an air raid in 1941, it has been lovingly restored as the church of the Royal Air Force. 'Oranges and lemons' rings out every three hours.

St Dunstan and All Saints, White Horse Road, Stepney, is called 'the Mother Church of East London'. There is a good interior. Governor William Bradford's wife, Dorothy May, was baptized here.

St Dunstan-in-the-West, Fleet Street, continues the name of the church in which George Calvert, the first Lord Baltimore, was buried in 1632. A new church was built in 1833, and the present building is a restoration of this. The reredos is in memory of Edward Winslow, who sailed on the *Mayflower*, and there is a memorial to 'David Brown of Yale'.

St Edmund the King, Lombard Street, was rebuilt by Wren in 1690. It is noted for its woodwork and for being aligned north to south.

St Ethelburga-the-Virgin, 68–70 Bishopsgate, is tiny but fascinating. Henry Hudson and his crew took Holy Communion here in 1607 before leaving in the *Half Moon* on his first voyage. There are three excellent windows, given by the Hudson's Bay Company, the citizens of the United States, and citizens of the British Empire in 1929, depicting incidents in Hudson's voyages. The church survived both the Great Fire and World War II intact.

St George, Hanover Square, has interesting interior features. Theodore Roosevelt, Benjamin Disraeli, George Eliot, Percy B. Shelley, Herbert Asquith, John Galsworthy and John Buchan were all married here. (Hawthorne stayed at no. 24 on the square, while Thomas Wolfe stayed in no. 25. John Singleton Copley lived in present day nos. 8–9. Dickens used to give public readings from his lodgings at no. 3. Arnold Bennett lived nearby, at no. 12B St George Street.)

St George's-in-the-East, Cannon Street, is perhaps the best church by Nicholas Hawksmoor, Wren's pupil.

St Giles, Cripplegate, on Fore Street, contains John Milton's grave, the memorial in Westminster Abbey notwithstanding, and has remains of London Wall in its churchyard.

St Helen, Bishopsgate, on Great St Helen's, contains fine brasses and monuments.

St James, Piccadilly, is a fine Wren church with Grinling Gibbons font and reredos. There are frequently midday concerts and it is also a brass rubbing centre.

St Lawrence Jewry, Gresham Street, has a Wren steeple and ceiling, restored after severe bomb damage in World War II. John Davenport, a founder of New Haven, Connecticut, was the rector here.

St Luke, Chelsea, on Sydney Street, is a very fine example of early Gothic revival.

St Magnus the Martyr, Lower Thames Street, has a fine Wren steeple and is representative of the Anglo-Catholic church's use of baroque.

St Margaret Lothbury, Lothbury Street, has an excellent steeple, Wren interior, and fine screen.

St Margaret Pattens, Rood Lane, Eastcheap, also by Wren, and also with an excellent spire, has good interior features.

St Margaret, Westminster, on Parliament Square, dates from the 16th century and is the parish church of the House of Commons. There is fine modern stained glass by John Piper. A plaque states that Sir

Walter Raleigh was buried here, but certainly his head rests elsewhere. There is a memorial to James Rumsey, American pioneer of steam navigation who is buried in the churchyard, and a window to Phillips Brooks, bishop of Massachusetts. There are windows paid for by American admirers to Raleigh, with an inscription by James Russell Lowell, and to John Milton with an inscription by John Greenleaf Whittier. Elizabeth, daughter of Robert Dinwiddie, Governor of Virginia, and Sir Peter Parker, who lost his life in the War of 1812, are buried here.

St Martin-in-the-Fields, Trafalgar Square, is probably the most famous of the smaller London churches, by virtue of its location, its dedication to the theatre, and its fine spire. It is James Gibbs' masterpiece, dating from 1722. There is a Grinling Gibbons stairway, a fine Rysbrack bust, and both a Royal Box and a box for the Lords of the Admiralty. Benjamin West was married here, and Sir William Washington was buried here. James Oglethorpe was baptized in an earlier church on the same site.

St Martin Ludgate, on Ludgate Hill, is a fine Wren church with an excellent interior. There is a Benjamin West painting of 'The Ascension' inside.

St Mary Abchurch, Abchurch Yard, is another Wren church with a fine reredos by Grinling Gibbons.

St Marylebone Parish Church (Holy Trinity), Marylebone Road, has a fine interior. There is a Benjamin West painting of the Nativity.

St Mary-le-Bow, Cheapside, is the church of Bow Bells, built by Wren in 1680, and now restored after damage in World War II. There is a memorial to Captain John Smith inside.

St Mary-le-Strand, in the middle of the Strand, is by James Gibbs; it is tiny and brilliantly baroque.

St Mary, Twickenham, is the burial place of Sir William Berkeley, early Governor of Virginia, and of William Tryon, Governor of North Carolina. When the Society for the Propagation of the Gospel began to evangelize among the American Indians, four Indian chiefs visited Queen Anne in 1710 and two were baptized in this church.

St Mary Woolnoth, at the corner of Lombard Street and King William Street, is the baroque masterpiece of Nicholas Hawksmoor. Sir William Phipps, a colonial governor of Massachusetts, was buried here.

St Nicholas Cole Abbey, Queen Victoria Street, has good stained glass, not all that common in London.

St Olave, Hart Street, was Samuel Pepys' church. He is buried here, and there is a memorial to him which was unveiled by James Russell Lowell, as well as a monument to John Watts, a Loyalist.

St Peter-on-Cornhill, Bishopsgate Corner, is regarded by many as one of Wren's finest churches.

St Stephen, Walbrook, next to the Mansion House, is anotner major contender for the position of Wren's masterwork. It has a fine interior and good stained glass. There is a Benjamin West painting on the left wall.

St Sepulchre, Holborn Viaduct, was once a Crusaders' church and dates from the 12th century. It was rebuilt by Wren in 1670–7. Captain John Smith was buried here, and Hugh Peters, early colonist, came from this parish.

St Vedast, Foster Lane, is a Wren church where Gilbert Stuart played the organ to add to his insufficient artist's income. The interior is rich.

Museums and art galleries
(See the sections on pages 94–99 and 108–12 as well.)

London is a city filled with superb museums. As one might expect, most contain American-related objects, and it would be fruitless to list them all here. The following suggestions, therefore, are limited to the most significant of the museums, and the most important of the American holdings.

Artillery Museum, The Rotunda, Woolwich Common, contains a fine collection of guns (open daily 10–12.45, 2–5, Sun. 2–5).

Bethnal Green Museum, Cambridge Heath, is especially good on Spitalfields' silks and English domestic art. There is a fine display of dolls' houses and of American toys and dolls. Several good examples of the work of Louis Comfort Tiffany are on display, as well as American ceramics and metalwork (open daily 10–6, Sun. 2). William Bassett, a Pilgrim, was born near here.

British Army Museum, Royal Hospital Road, Chelsea, includes many items of the period 1775–83 which relate to the American Revolution, and also the Guidon of the Hartford Dragoons which was captured in the Battle of Bladensburg in 1814 (open daily 10–5.30, Sun. 2).

The British Museum is one of the greatest museums in the world (see general section on MUSEUMS). (Open daily 10–5, Sun. 2.30–6.)

British Theatre Museum. Once at Leighton House, and promised a place in The Old Flower Market when Covent Garden reopened in 1977, this magnificent collection is still awaiting a home. It is an odd disgrace that Britain, home of perhaps the world's finest theatre, cannot find a place to display its rich collection; which includes much on Henry Irving, Diaghilev costumes and scenery, the Dame Bridget D'Oyly Carte collection, a bequest from Dame Marie Rambert – in all, an estimated £23 million in unique materials. By the time this book appears, relocation may have been achieved.

Commonwealth Institute, 230 Kensington High Street, offers an opportunity to travel to all the nations of the Commonwealth without leaving London (open daily 10–5.30, Sun. 2.30–6). (See page 95.)

Courtauld Institute Galleries hold a magnificent art collection including Copleys, Wests and Whistlers. (Open daily 10–5, Sun. 2–5.)

Cuming Museum, Walworth Road, has a good collection on the history of Southwark; it also holds American prints (open daily 10–5, Thurs. 7).

Dulwich College Picture Gallery, College Road, Dulwich, while difficult to reach is fully worth the effort, for its Dutch and French collection is one of the finest in Britain, and it holds very good works by Rembrandt, Rubens and Gainsborough (open May–Aug., 10–6, Sun. 2; Sept.–April, close 4).

Geffrye Museum, Kingsland Road, has period rooms in 18th century almshouses (open daily except Mon., 10–5, Sun. 2).

Guildhall Art Gallery, King Street, Cheapside, has a good collection which includes two John Singleton Copleys (open weekdays 10–5).

Geological Museum, Exhibition Road, has one of the finest geological collections in the world; it includes gem stones and, of course, many samples from American mines (open daily 10–6, Sun. 2.30).

Hayward Art Gallery, next to the Royal Festival Hall, is interesting for its architecture, as well as for its changing exhibitions of contemporary arts. (Check opening hours for individual exhibitions.)

Imperial War Museum, Lambeth Road (see general section on MUSEUMS) includes many pictures by American artists. Among the large exhibits is an Anglo-American P51 Mustang; there is also a fine case of American decorations and campaign medals. American uniforms are well represented (open daily 10–6, Sun. 2).

Jewish Museum, Woburn House, Upper Woburn Place, has an exceptional collection of ritual objects. There is a pair of portraits of Mr and Mrs Naphtali Franks – Franks having been born in New York in 1715. (Open Mon.–Thurs., 2.30–5; Fri., Sun., 10.30–12.45.)

Kodak Museum, Wealdstone, Harrow, has an unusual collection on the history of photography (open by appointment).

London Museum, which was in Kensington Palace, has now reopened in the new Barbican Center.

Marylebone Cricket Club Memorial Gallery, Lord's Cricket Ground, is rather more interesting than the game. The displays include items presented to M.C.C. touring teams to America (open Mon.–Fri., 9.30–4.30). It says something about the game that the museum is open during match play. Can one imagine a baseball museum that makes a point of being open while a game is in progress?

Madame Tussaud's, Marylebone Road, is a world-famous waxwork museum, and, for those who like such things, the best. Various American figures, including the President, are always represented (open weekdays 10–5.30, Sat.–Sun. 6.30).

Museum of Mankind, actually the Ethnography Department of the British Museum, 6 Burlington Gardens, is one of the finest museums of primitive art in the world. The Ashanti work is fantastic, and the collection of Northwest American Indian coastal art is one of the most extensive outside North America. A Raffles' gamelan is especially exciting. Exhibits change, so if you have not been within the year, go again (open daily 10–5, Sun. 2.30–6).

The National Gallery, Trafalgar Square, is one of the great art galleries of the world (see general section on MUSEUMS). Its collection includes works by such Americans as George Inness and Whistler. But one goes for the Leonardo da Vinci, Raphael, Titian, Rembrandt, Rubens and El Greco works (open daily 10–6, June–Sept., Tues. and Thurs. to 9, Sun. 2–6). A copy of Jean Houdon's **statue of Washington,** which is in Richmond, Virginia, stands in front of the Gallery, a gift of the state of Virginia.

National Maritime Museum, Romney Road, Greenwich (pronounced Grenitch) is the finest naval museum in the world (see general section on MUSEUMS). Among its holdings are numerous American-related items (several to the Revolution) as well as fine paintings by John Singleton Copley, Gilbert Stuart and Benjamin West (open daily 10–6, Sun. 2.30). In Greenwich College there is a memorial to American officers who served in the Royal Navy.

National Portrait Gallery, 2 St Martin's Place (see general section on MUSEUMS) has a fine collection of portraits of historical figures. The gallery includes works by such American artists as Washington Allston, John Singleton Copley, Charles Willson Peale, John Singer Sargent (twenty-one in all), the Sharples, John Smibert, Thomas Sully, Benjamin West and Gilbert Stuart (including an oil of George Washington) (open daily 10–5, Sun. 2). Among the notable Americans represented by portraits here are Benjamin Franklin, Henry James, John Singer Sargent, George Washington, Benjamin West and James McNeill Whistler.

Natural History Museum, Cromwell Road, is open daily 10–6, Sun. 2.30. North America is well represented.

Percival David Foundation of Chinese Art, 53 Gordon Square, has a fine representative collection of ceramics (open Tues.–Fri., 10.30–5, Sat. to 1, Mon. 2–5).

National Postal Museum, King Edward Street, may be the finest such museum in the world, for although small, its displays are unique. Its Berne Collection includes nearly every stamp issued by any postal administration anywhere in the world since 1878 (open Mon.–Fri., 10.30–4.30).

Public Record Office, Chancery Lane, is a national archive. Its small exhibit rooms include the Domesday Book and the signatures of the monarchs of England. There are many American-related documents on exhibit from time to time, including the Olive Branch petition from Congress in 1775, Washington's personal letter to George III and his map of Ohio, and a letter from Sir Walter Raleigh (open weekdays 1–4). The larger record deposit is at Kew.

Queen's Gallery, Buckingham Palace Road, exhibits items from the Royal collections that cannot be seen elsewhere, and usually includes pictures, jewels, tapestries and furniture, as well as the Rubens Cartoons (open Tues.–Sat., 11–6, Sun. 2–5).

Royal Air Force Museum, Aerodrome Road, Hendon, includes forty aeroplanes, uniforms, medals, bombs and associated items, some American. (Reached from Colindale Underground station, and quite a journey, but there is a restaurant of sorts – open daily 10–6, Sun. 2.)

Royal National Institute for the Blind, 224–8 Great Portland Street, has a small museum of Blindiana, which includes an early American Braille writing machine. It is open by appointment only.

Science Museum, Exhibition Road (see general section on MUSEUMS) is open daily 10–6, Sunday from 2.30. The Children's Gallery is especially good, although there is an annoying tendency for moving parts to bear signs that they are out of order. Since the museum is devoted to science worldwide, there are many American-originated displays, including Franklin's frictional machine and the first Singer sewing machine.

Sir John Soane's Museum, 13 Lincoln's Inn Fields, is an eclectic and even peculiar collection (open Tues.–Sat., 10–5, closed August).

South London Art Gallery, Peckham Road, has a fine collection of original 20th century prints, including American (open daily 10–6, Sun. 3).

Tate Gallery, Millbank (see general section on ART GALLERIES) is an exceptional gallery, rich in foreign and modern art, ranging over Ben Nicholson and Francis Bacon to Picasso, Chagall and Mondrian. There is much sculpture, and America is fully represented by Edwin Austin Abbey, Josef Albers, Milton Avery, Charles Burchfield, Alexander Calder, John Singleton Copley, Mark Fisher, Robert Henri, R. B. Kitaj, Willem de Kooning, Roy Lichtenstein, Morris Louis, John Marin, Robert Motherwell, Jackson Pollock, Larry Poons, Robert Rauschenberg, Man Ray, Larry Rivers, Mark Rothko, John Singer Sargent (forty-one!), Ben Shahn, Gilbert Stuart, Pavel Tchelitchew, Mark Tobey, Andy Warhol, Benjamin West and James McNeill Whistler, to name only some. One needs a large chunk of time here (open daily 10–6, Sun. 2).

Victoria and Albert Museum, Cromwell Road, takes up over ten acres and is exhausting (see general section on MUSEUMS). There are many American prints and drawings by such artists as Abbey, Albers, Copley and Frederic Remington, and there are also pictures by Fisher, Marin, Sargent, Stuart, West and Whistler. The Circulation Department has its own collection, ranging from Calder through Kitaj to Claes Oldenburg and Mark Tobey. Open daily 10–6.

The Wallace Collection, Hertford House, Manchester Square, contains Rembrandts, Titians, Rubens, fine French furniture and porcelain, Limoges enamel – and one Thomas Sully (open daily 10–5, Sun. 2). The collection has been handsomely reinstated.

Wellcome Historical Medical Museum, 183 Euston Road, illustrates the history of medicine. It includes an American silver bleeding bowl and George Washington's personal medicine chest – sadly without contents, for those who would like to know what ailed him (open weekdays 10–5, Sat. to 4.30, closed Sun.).

About the tours

The following tours are presented in what I regard as a declining order of preference. I have taken each of them, although not precisely in the order given here, since the routes were often discovered by the travellers' equivalent of a hunt and peck method. When suggested routes deviate from the obvious major highways, or name in passing certain towns, this is done to assure the most interesting tour and in order to include less well-known places. The emphasis is on the types of landscape that I believe Americans come to Britain to find, on scenes relating to the major British writers, and on places with an explicit American association. The names of these last are set in **heavier type.** This does not mean that they are the most important sites, only that they are related to the history and development of the United States. (Obviously, one may debate the question of related-ness. Benjamin West is treated here – and by most art historians – as an American painter, when in fact his best work was done in Britain, and he often imitated English art forms. T. S. Eliot and Jacob Epstein are included as Americans, even though they settled in England. Further, the listing of American-related sites is obviously incomplete; I have limited myself, first to those I regard as interesting, and second, to those I know about. I would welcome information from readers who know of sites that I have not visited.)

Some of the tours provide options and others are divided into separate days. These days are feasible, although they require travelling rather more rapidly and intently than the English like to travel. Material included in parentheses, or set off from the main text with the symbol • requires additional time. Parenthetical material is lesser and suggests a detour within easy reach of the main route, while material with the symbol • represents a side-trip of some substance and, if followed, will totally alter the time estimates. Hours of opening and route numbers are given as of 1982; since travel for this book was carried out between 1969 and 1982, some information has been re-verified only by reference to current standard guide books and maps, not by actually driving the route again. Errors will occur, and I will be grateful to receive any corrections for use in possible later editions. In the case of hours of opening, the more conservative times are given; places may be open later at the height of the summer tourist season.

Suggestions for places to stay and to eat have been tested personally. There are many other fine hotels and restaurants in Britain, and I would not wish this guide to lead Americans to swamp the places specifically mentioned, thus altering their British character. Still, I do not wish to include any place that I cannot personally recommend, for this is meant to be a personal guide. In matters of hotels and restaurants, in particular, tastes differ widely; I prefer smaller, country hotels of a British type, and see no reason to use Holiday Inns except in America. If I must choose, I prefer a good dinner table to a good bedroom. If one must drink before dinner, a good quality neat Scotch, followed by a glass of water, will leave the palate clear. If a clear palate doesn't interest you, some of the restaurants suggested here will be rather too 'precious' and perhaps too dear, and you will wish to seek out others from the several other guides that are available.

No single guide book can provide all the information the traveller needs. This guide book is meant to be an extended inventory of American-related sites in Britain. If other purposes are uppermost in your mind, you will require supplementary guides. Here are some of the best, for a variety of purposes:

On food, the *Good Food Guide, Egon Ronay's Guide,* and the *Michelin: Great Britain and Ireland.* The first is described in the first section of this book, under 'Dining out'. Michelin's guide appeared in 1974, the first since the French abandoned the British field in 1933. While the *Good Food Guide* awards its very highest accolade to thirty-six restaurants and hotels (and Ronay awards 191 stars) *Michelin* finds only nineteen worthy of distinction. Nor do they agree on those nineteen. For accommodation, one should add to these guides a fourth, Ashley Courtenay's *Let's Halt Awhile in Great Britain.* The British Tourist Authority (write to St James's Street, London SW1A 1NF; or 680 Fifth Avenue, New York City) issues a compact brochure, *Stay at an Inn,* which is reliable, as well as 'Where to Stay' pamphlets on different regions.

The British Tourist Authority, through either its London or New York offices, can be very helpful. It publishes *In Britain,* a fine monthly magazine with travel articles and a calendar of coming events. Its brochure on tourist information posts in England will help one find local tourist information quickly. Booklets on farmhouse accommodation, events at historic houses, nature trails, caravans and camping sites, are extremely helpful. It also sells other guide books at its New York office; these include *Holidays with Children* and *Children Welcome!,* the first suggesting places you may want to visit precisely because you have your children with you, the second listing accommodation where you may leave your children while travelling without them. You may also obtain *Holidays on Inland Waterways* from the Authority.

To Britain as a whole there are dozens, nay hundreds, of guides. Four in particular are highly recommended. Least readable, but exceptionally thorough, is the *Blue Guide* series, with separate volumes on England, Scotland and Wales. Edited by L. Russell Muirhead and Stuart Rossiter, these guides make good travelling companions. Exceedingly handsome, more informative, but altogether too heavy to tote about, is the *AA (Automobile Association) Illustrated Guide to Britain.* I study it before making a journey and carry Xerox copies of relevant pages with me. As it has no detailed maps, it should be used in conjunction with the new and quite detailed *AA Great Britain Road Atlas.* The *AA Book of the Seaside* is very good, with fine descriptions and maps. The AA publishes an equally handsome, equally burdensome rival, *Treasures of Britain,* that makes superb pre-departure reading. Good road maps are essential; they are discussed elsewhere. (For prior study, obtain the National Geographic Society's *Traveler's Map of the British Isles,* from the Society, Washington, D.C. 20036.) All but the last, as well as a compact guide to castles, houses, gardens, museums and wild life parks, called *Britain's Heritage,* may be ordered from the Automobile Association, Fanum House, Basingstoke, Hampshire, England.

The National Trust administers many of the great houses, gardens, churches, follies, monuments and parks of Britain. A definitive guide for library reading is *The National Trust Guide* by Robin Fedden and Rosemary Joekes. *The National Trust,* by Peter Ryan, is also necessary planning reading. Both are too heavy to carry with one. There is a *National Trust Atlas* which is unhappily rather poor. Take with you instead, the fine map, 'National Trust Properties', and a copy of the Trust's booklet, revised annually, *Properties of the National Trust,* which lists times of opening, as the other guides do not. These can be ordered from the Trust at 42, Queen Anne's Gate, London. Better yet, help the Trust in its work by subscribing to The Royal Oak Foundation, Inc., in the United States, and receive the booklet free, as well as a pass to all Trust properties (write to 41 East 72nd Street, New York, N.Y. 10021).

There are many series of guide books to the counties and cities of Britain. Two ubiquitous series are quite unsuitable for the serious, and American, traveller: the old *The King's England,* begun by Arthur Mee, and now revised; and Ward Lock's *Red Guide* series. On the other hand, there are two quite useful series: *The Travellers' Guides,* edited by Sean Jennett, and now numbering twelve in all, which may easily be taken about with one; and the *Shell Guides* to Britain, England, Scotland, Wales and Ireland, which are rather over-thorough – one may tire of weed-choked dolmens, burial chambers, cairns, and the like – but good preparatory reading.

Specialist guides abound. Among the best series are the *Discovering* booklets, published by Shire Publications, Tring, Hertfordshire. Especially useful among this series are *Discovering Battlefields of England* by John Kinross, which includes maps keyed to present-day landmarks (better, but heavier, is *The Battlefields of England,* by Alfred H. Burne); *Discovering Schools,* by George Berry; *Discovering Hill Figures,* by Kate Bergamar; *Discovering English Gardens,* by Kay N. Sanecki; and the *Discovering Statues* pocket guides. A compact *Visitors' Guide to Country Workshops in Britain* may be obtained from the Council for Small Industries in Rural Areas, 35 Camp Road, Wimbledon Common, London S.W.19. On literary sites, begin in the library with a World War II publication, *Literary England,* by David E. Scherman and Richard Wilcox (1943) and then go on to Margaret Crosland's very useful *A Guide to Literary Europe.* As the scope of this is so wide, take notes or Xerox pages of the areas of interest to you before you set out. Recent and brief is *A Literary Tour Guide to England and Scotland* by Emilie C. Harting. Also useful are two annual publications, issued by ABC Travel Guides, Oldhill, London Road, Dunstable, Bedfordshire: *Historic Houses, Castles and Gardens* and *Museums and Galleries.*

It may be that you wish to pursue the question of American-related sites further (even though I think the suggestions here press the issue quite far enough). There are books that will help, and I have grate-fully drawn upon all of them when preparing the original journeys during which I visited the sites mentioned here. Old, but still the best, is *America in England,* a gazetteer prepared by Eric and John Underwood in 1949, and now out of print. Frederic Moir Bussy's *Meccas for Americans* (London, 1913) includes much of the original information on George Washington. The 'Discovering' series includes a 48-page pamphlet of high quality, *The American Story in England,* by Eric Rayner (although it is wrong about there being a portrait of George Washington at 10 Downing Street). The more recent *American Britain* (1970) is an alphabetical listing by towns of church windows, memorials and birthplaces, and while it contains errors, it also represents an enormous amount of effective work on the part of its compiler, Gerald Newson (order from him, 31 Southdown Avenue, Willingdon, Eastbourne, Sussex).

In addition to the above listings, the following also make useful reading: H. L. Gee, *American England: An Epitome of a Common Heritage* (1943), J. F. Muirhead, *American Shrines on English Soil* (1925), Alfred T. Story, *American Shrines in England* (1908), Anne Hollingsworth Wharton, *English Ancestral Homes of Noted Americans* (1915), and Marguerite Allis, *English Prelude* (1936). None are light reading but all are interesting if one is ancestor hunting. (For this purpose, read also a 'Discovering' pamphlet, *Discovering Your Family Tree,* by David Iredale.) For a specialized interest, consult H. Clifford Smith, *Sulgrave Manor and the Washingtons* (1933). Finally, there are four delightful books for reading while planning your trip: J. Frank Dobie, *A Texan in England* (1945); Henry Steele Commager, *Britain Through American Eyes* (1974); Stephen Spender, *Love–Hate Relations: English and American Sensibilities* (1974); and Daniel Snowman, *Britain & America: An Interpretation of Their Culture* (1977). The last two are rather more acerbic reading.

Since the first edition of this guide, many new books have appeared, of course, though surprisingly few displace those I have already mentioned, especially for Americans. There is a superb *AA Book of British Towns* which is indispensable, especially if one restricts touring to the middle-size communities reached by rail. Interest in the precise place of a literary scene has grown, and three fine new books are a joy to one who wishes to know just where, in the Malvern Hills, Piers Plowman had his vision of England in the summer season. These are Margaret Drabble, *A Writer's Britain: Landscape in Literature;* David Daiches and John Flower, *Literary Landscapes of the British Isles: A Narrative Atlas;* and Dorothy Eagle and Hilary Carnell, *The Oxford Literary Guide to the British Isles.* The first two are delightful advance reading and the third is the best travel companion. Finally, a rich new book, *Return to Albion: Americans in England, 1760–1940,* by Richard Kenin, provides much additional information on American-related places which could not be incorporated into this revision. Kenin is especially good on American artists and writers.

These days, getting there is no longer half the fun. But reading about it in advance is. And careful planning saves worry, time and dollars. One comes to Britain for so many different reasons; no guide book can ever speak to all needs. For some Americans, England is part of them, whether through ancestry or accident, experience or reading. For others, who would claim Italy or Germany or some other nation as their ancestral land, England is merely a part of our natural curiosity. From this land, once, we grew; from it, now, we have long departed, until we are not just somewhat, but in truth utterly, different. Yet for whatever reason one travels in Britain, there will always be the pleasures of experiencing its tolerance, its complexity and its beauty; of seeing, too, its ugliness, noting its problems, perhaps wishing it well or ill. It is a land of paradox, as all lands are, but the more obviously so for being laid open to us through a shared language. Here one may find tangerine trees and marmalade skies; here too one may find, as that 'first American', Benjamin Franklin, strove to do throughout his life, how to embrace 'the graceful and easy, as well as the Useful'.

The best shorter trips from London

Tours 1–7

If your time in England is limited, or if you prefer to explore the areas you can reach from London and save Wild Wales for another year, you can get a good impression of the variety of the English landscape, historical and scenic, by combining two or three of the classic 'day trips' (as the British say) with two or three overnighters. The following selections are, unhappily, the most popular, which means that you must compete with the crowds during the tourist season and, for your overnight stay, book in advance (a phone call the day before should do the trick except on the first two). But then, some of the crowds will be English anyway, which will give you a good chance to observe the English while they observe you. All of the trips can be made in two to three days by road. I list them in my order of preference.

1 Oxford
Stratford-upon-Avon
The north Cotswolds

The single most congested excursion on the English map, this is the one trip which virtually anyone who ventures out of London will do. Why should you resist? After all, you would make for the Eiffel Tower if you were in Paris, wouldn't you? So don't complain if you find the madding crowd there before you. There are reasons why clichés become clichés, and to miss the classic combination of a great medieval university, Shakespeare, and a preciously quaint countryside would be foolish. Do not make the contrary mistake of assuming you are seeing England, however, for this circuit is John Bull's answer to Disneyland.

Actually it isn't unattractive. Little in England is. And you have your choice of conveyances, if not of routes: all of the tour firms run coaches (buses to you) along some variant of the route I describe, and, with the omission of the Cotswold villages, the train will provide you with quick access to Oxford and Stratford, with the added romance of departing from Paddington Station, just as Sherlock Holmes so often did. In order to allow for a detour or two I will describe the route as though you were travelling by car, however.

Take the A40/M40 out of London. Ignore all that beckons before Oxford (but read up on Tours 4 and 6 below) for if you pause for Stoke Poges, or Cliveden, or the Chiltern Hills, you will find the day already gone. Oxford is about 90 minutes from London by car or by rail. Just before you reach Headington, an outer suburb of the university city, bear right on the B4027, 3 miles to **Stanton St John,** an attractive village in itself, and the birthplace, in the house by the church, on Christmas Day, 1575 of John White, who was responsible for the foundation of the

Massachusetts Bay Company and thus ultimately of New England's most populous colony. Either continue on to Beckley Park, model for Aldous Huxley's *Crome Yellow*, and Woodeaton, another pleasant village, and then follow the signposting to the left for Oxford, or retrace your steps to the A40 (note that in Britain, trunk highway routes are always spoken of as 'the'), turn right, and continue on to Oxford. Before seeing Oxford, you might pursue two literary associations briefly. At Garsington (reached by country road south of the A40 just beyond the Stanton St John turning) is the manor house which was the model for Breadalby in D. H. Lawrence's *Women in Love*. And well beyond Oxford to the west, at Stanton Harcourt, is Stocks, the home of Alexander Pope. Between the two is **Abingdon** – two masts of the *Mayflower* are said to have been incorporated into the school here.

Oxford is high on nearly everyone's list of university cities. Matthew Arnold called it the 'home of lost causes . . . and impossible loyalties'. For the American in particular, who may be unfamiliar with some of the other ancient European universities, it has no rival. The mellow stone gives Oxford a warmth of spirit often lacking in grey Cambridge. The fact that dozens of American universities and colleges have directly imitated Oxbridge architecture at once makes the surroundings familiar and authoritative – going to Oxford for the first time can be, in an emotional way, rather like going home for the American university graduate (especially if he be from New England or the South). And while the Oxford colleges cherish their privacy they also recognize their obligation to humanity by leaving their courtyards (with some signposted exceptions) open to the gaze, and often the footstep, of the tourist, Further, given the traditional tension between town and gown, the evident fact that the university is wedged into the middle of an industrial area and the presence of a major auto works, Oxford has the bustle of an American university town which is so lacking on the Continent. It also has Les Quat' Saisons, at 272 Banbury Road. The *Good Food Guide* finds this one of the best restaurants in all Britain, though the Restaurant Elizabeth at 84 St Aldgates retains its high quality. One of my three or four favorite pubs anywhere is the Turf, tucked up against New College off Holywell, where one may have a Lancashire hot-pot and farmhouse cider while dreaming of Hardy's *Jude the Obscure* (in which the Turf is mentioned).

But you did not come to Oxford to eat, you came to see the colleges. Twenty-seven were founded for men and five for women, which to male chauvinists seems an appropriate distribution, and while all are worth seeing, some are more equal than others. Give Oxford two days and see them all, or give it about six hours and see the best. Virtually nothing is left from the 12th century, when wandering scholars settled upon the site for their studies, but from the 16th century through the Victorian period Oxford is rich in changing styles. *Walk*, do not drive, begin on Broad Street, and work through a short list which must include the follow-

BROAD STREET

ing: Balliol College, which has produced more front-rank historians than any other academic institution in the world; Trinity and Exeter Colleges (the former not to be confused with Trinity, Cambridge, much the grander); St John's and Keble colleges, the latter an atrociously ugly example of rampant Victorianism, with Holman Hunt's 'Light of the World' on view; and Rhodes House Museum in Parks Road, a magnificent library and memorial to Cecil Rhodes, the founder of the **Rhodes Scholarships** which linked the United States, Germany and the Commonwealth to Oxford. Returning along Parks Road past Wadham College you will have the Sheldonian Theatre directly in front of you on the corner of Broad Street – a climb to the cupola is a must (there is a small admission charge); the New Bodleian Library is on your right; and the Old Bodleian (or Old Bodley) through the archways straight ahead. While not, in fact, a particularly large library – any one of a dozen university libraries in the United States is substantially larger than the libraries of Oxbridge – the Bodley is without parallel in its rare books, antiquated cataloguing methods, and sense of the 17th century cloistered scholar bent over his secular devotions. Tread quietly (although if you visit in term time, you will find that the undergraduates do not) and press on to Radcliffe Camera, a masterpiece of the 18th century. Cross the road to look into

All Souls, unique in being without students to teach and the English equivalent of an American 'think tank' for Very Distinguished Scholars, retrace your path past Hertford to a lane on your right and plunge down it to the especially delightful prospect of a well-hidden and charming pub (take the first pathway permissible to your left), the Turf, side by side with what remains of the old city wall and the gate to New College. Inside the yard, which Hawthorne especially praised, you will find a castle mound and inside the chapel some of the finest stained glass in England. John Galsworthy was a student here. Continue along the lane, past **Queen's College** (where each year America's most distinguished historian of American history is invited to serve as Harmsworth Professor) onto the High Street. Bear left to Magdalen College, surely the most exquisite of all, backing onto the River Cherwell, with its deer park and its pleasant walk by the river. Across the road are the Botanic Gardens, not interesting in themselves save in being the oldest in England. Now return up the High past University College, on your left, turn up the next lane to the left for a quick look at Merton (see the library), Oriel and Corpus Christi, and after returning to the High Street yet again, cross the road for Brasenose and Lincoln. The gargoyles that look down upon the High are among the most striking in Europe and you may see them all the way to the Cornmarket, from which, with a left turn, you may find Christ Church. This is the largest college in Oxford, contains the magnificent 'Tom' Tower, one of the best quadrangles in Europe, a fine dining hall and a portrait of **William Penn.** Oxford Cathedral is behind the college, St Catherine's is nearby, and you may also in hunger spot the Elizabeth across the way. Also across the way is **Pembroke;** George Whitefield and James Smithson (founder of the Smithsonian Institution) studied here.

Steady on, you are near the end. Returning along St Aldgate's and past Carfax Tower on your left, you may either move on to the **Ashmolean Museum,** not to be missed (don't neglect the John Singer Sargent and Benjamin West) after seeing Jesus on your right; or if you feel that you simply must do all the colleges, turn left at Carfax and march two long blocks to Nuffield, which is strictly for what the United States calls graduate and the British call post-graduate students, thence in a circle past Worcester (worth the effort), Somerville (maybe) and St Anne's, St Anthony's, St Hugh's and Lady Margaret Hall (only if you are ticking off a checklist).

But wait! What did you see when you hurried through these colleges? As a general rule, head first for the chapel and then for the library, which often has the characteristics of a museum. Do not neglect the dining halls. At each gatehouse there is a map, and a generally reliable set of suggestions of what that college thinks you ought to see while viewing it. And as you move about Oxford one hopes that you will forget the American atmosphere of this book. Surely you have not sought out **Brasenose** because Richard Mather, of the Massachusetts Mathers, studied there, or Frank Aydelotte reorganized Swarthmore on the basis of his experience there? Or remembered particularly that Richard Hakluyt, John Locke, William Penn (who was expelled for non-conformity) and John and Charles Wesley were all **Christ Church** men? (Penn's portrait now hangs inside as does a portrait attributed to John Singleton Copley.) Or even that Sir Walter Raleigh attended **Oriel** (as did Thomas Hughes, author of *Tom Brown's Schooldays*) and that George Calvert (the first Lord Baltimore) attended **Trinity?** Perhaps you will want to see the **tomb of Bishop Berkeley** in the nave of the cathedral, for it is after him that the mispronounced city in California (and the equally wrongly pronounced Yale College) is named. The **chapel of Trinity College** is beautiful for more than the arms of the Washington family which appear in it. Forget things American while at Oxford and think instead of Wren, who designed the Sheldonian, of Samuel Johnson dropping out in poverty, of Carroll's Alice meeting the White Rabbit (by the Sheep Shop in St Aldgate's, actually), of Edward Gibbon and Thomas Hobbes and Oscar Wilde, all happy here, and even of Nathaniel Hawthorne and, yes, thousands of other Americans after him who pronounced, as he did, the High to be 'the noblest old street in England'.

So end your visit to Oxford by buying a book. Back to the Broad, where you will find three of the finest bookshops in the world, crowned by Blackwells, *the* finest. Do not be fooled by its unassuming exterior: enter, pass down the passages toward the back and take that small stairway down, whereupon the truly awesome magnificence of the new underground chambers of the world's largest academic bookstore will greet you.

Too bad. If you had to go by coach you will have missed most of this, being harried along to someone else's schedule. But even the coach tour will carry you on 11 miles north, via the A34, to Woodstock, and to Blenheim Palace, one of the top Country Seats (open April–July, Sept.–Oct., Mon.–Thurs. 1–6; Aug. daily except Fri.). Actually scarcely typical, this gigantic baroque mansion has housed the Dukes of Marlborough since Vanbrugh designed it. Capability Brown laid out the grounds, which are textbook English in their combination of formality and naturalness and across which one may enjoy some of the finest views in England. Americans like Blenheim because Sir Winston Churchill was born here (and he is buried in Bladon, 3 miles southwest on the A4095). Woodstock also has a most pleasant small country arts and crafts museum, and a shop with the best and most reasonably priced English leather gloves you are likely to encounter on your short tour.

Stratford is 34 miles northwest via the A34, but I recommend a modest deviation via **Banbury, Sulgrave Manor,** and **Wroxton,** 50 miles in all. Turn back towards Oxford from Blenheim, and very shortly left on the

A4095 and then left again on the A423 to Banbury, from which Benjamin Franklin's father left for the colonies in 1685. The Banbury Cross is a 19th century one, but the Banbury Cakes you can buy at the bakery will be authentic. (8 miles north on the A423 is **Wormleighton,** which has links with the Washington family.) Right from Banbury on the A422, then left on the B4525, brings one to Sulgrave Manor, the very attractive Northamptonshire home of George Washington's ancestors. Built about 1500, this small manor house is one of the major memorials in Britain to the American connection. To mark the centenary of the Treaty of Ghent, which had ended the Anglo–American War of 1812–15, British subscribers purchased the manor, and the restored house was opened in 1921. It is now endowed by the National Society of the Colonial Dames of America. The arms of the builder's family in the doorway here consist of stars and stripes, and some assert that this is the origin of the design for the American flag. That flag flies every day from the garden. Go also to the village church to see the Washington memorial brasses and family pew. The house is open daily except Wed., 10.30–1, 2–5.30 (closing from Oct. 4–March). Frames' provides a tour from London should you wish to come by bus. 3 miles south of Sulgrave, by country road, is **Marston St Lawrence,** where lived the Reverend Charles Chauncy, later President of Harvard College.

Return to Banbury and leave on the A422 west to Wroxton. Here is **Wroxton Abbey,** with a handsome hall, the home of the notorious Lord North of the Intolerable Acts which helped bring on the American Revolution. The Abbey is now the English campus of New Jersey's Fairleigh Dickinson University, and you should write in advance to the Director if you wish to visit. Beyond Wroxton turn left on a country road and follow postings for Balscott, Shutford and Epwell, to Compton Wynyates. This outstanding country house (open April–Sept. Wed. and Sat., and Sun. June–Aug., 2–6) dates from 1480; the estate has been the home of the Marquess of Northampton and his family for eight generations. Henry VIII stayed here, as probably did Catherine of Aragon. The furnishings are fine, but it is for the topiary garden that the house is best known. Then continue on through Winderton, join the A34 at Shipston on Stour, and thence to Stratford.

Stratford is an Obligatory Town, and it may be that you will even like it. Certainly if you enjoy Estes Park in August, Boothbay Harbor in July, or Aspen in February, you will. You may escape from all this by driving 4 miles north of Stratford to spend the night at the truly delightful Swan House Hotel in Wilmcote, next to the Mary Arden House (Shakespeare's mother) where the food is worth high praise – but you must have booked in advance. They also do a cold pre-theatre supper if you have tickets to the **Royal Shakespeare Memorial Theatre,** which of course you have. (Go to anything, just go.) In the picture gallery there you will find the work of six Americans, including West again.

SHAKESPEARE'S HOUSE, ABOUT 1807

As for Stratford-upon-Avon itself, buy a small guide and use it well. The short list here should include Shakespeare's birthplace, of course; New Place, where he died in 1616; Holy Trinity Church, where he was baptized and buried; **Harvard House,** where the mother of John Harvard, founder of that university, was born; and the 15th century Guildhall. In walking the streets of Stratford you will be joining over one hundred thousand Americans who do so annually, so here perhaps you really should give thought to your countrymen: have a drink at the **Red Horse Inn** in Bridge Street, and raise a glass to Washington Irving, who wrote the *Sketch Book* while staying there; gaze upon the **American Fountain and Clock Tower** on Wood Street, gifts of a Philadelphia publisher; and while at **Holy Trinity,** seek out the American window, with its portraits of Amerigo Vespucci, Columbus, William Penn and Samuel Seabury (the first Bishop of the Episcopal Church of America).

And now you return to London via the north Cotswolds. If you have time to spare you should visit the Great Hall at Charlecote Park (where there is a tradition that Shakespeare was caught poaching) 5 miles east; or Anne Hathaway's Cottage, with its lovely gardens, at Shottery, a mile west. When ready, head south on the A46 and bear left 6 miles out towards Chipping Campden. Turn left for **Hidcote Manor,** where one of the great gardens of the world (open April–Oct., 11–8) was laid out as an American garden by Lawrence Johnston, starting in 1905. Chipping Campden itself is the least spoiled of the large, Cotswold towns with an impressive 15th century church. 3 miles beyond Chipping Campden turn right on the A44 to Broadway. This is the village which all admire, and even though it will greet you with a monumental traffic jam in high summer, go anyway. The Lygon Arms here is an excellent hotel. 4 miles further on, at **Wickhamford,** is a parish church with a floorstone memorial to Penelope, an ancestor of George Washington (again, strictly for Collectors), while 2 miles southwest off the A46, at Buckland, is the oldest rectory in England, which you may see only on Mondays from 11 to 4 and only from May to September. 4 miles further on is Stanway, with a superb view. Return, from Broadway, via the A44 eastwards to Moreton-in-Marsh, and south 4 miles on the A429 to Stow-on-the-Wold, which you would want to visit in any case to drop the name at dinner parties when back home, but which also happens to be the single most charming Cotswold village, hill-set, with delightful pubs and a fine old church, and all of Cotswold stone.

The day will be drawing on and you must make choices. Straight back to London via the A424 south to Burford (in the spring, stop at Burford House Gardens) and then by the A40 through Minster Lovell (lovely village on the Windrush) and Witney. The Old Swan Hotel at Minster Lovell is pleasant. Or southwest from Stow on the A429 to Bourton-on-the-Water, a village along the Windrush, and on to the junction with the A40. Northeast is **Farmington** with a pump house given by the people of Farmington, Connecticut. Thence as described above through Burford – 8 miles longer and 30 minutes more. (Throughout, watch for the unusual Cotswold dry-stone walls.) Or pursue a time-consuming, hill-and-dale journey, which is one I particularly like, solely by country lane, adding miles and many minutes: north from Stow on the A424, left on the B4077 to Ford, left on an unmarked road posted for Temple Guiting and Guiting Power along the upper Windrush. Here is the unique Cotswold Farm Park, dedicated to the survival of rare breeds – Soay sheep, Warwickshire Longhorns, etc. (open May–Sept., 10.30–6). Now left on the A436 for 3 miles, right on an unnumbered road posted Upper Slaughter, and thence by Lower Slaughter to Bourton-on-the-Water. Continue by country road through Little Rissington, Westcote, Idbury, Fifield, Shipton-under-Wychwood and Leafield, through Wychwood Forest to Charlbury, and then along a country road to the back entrance to **Ditchley Park,** in which there is a great house past which you may drive but which you may not enter. (Although you may reflect in passing upon the 30 annual conferences held here on subjects relating to the Anglo-American connection, sponsored by the Ditchley Foundation, and note that it is one of the ancestral homes of Robert E. Lee; and that Winston Churchill met with Harry

Hopkins here at the start of the war, to work out the details of Lend Lease.) Go on to join the A34 4 miles north of Woodstock and thence via the A34 to the A40 and M40 and back to London as you came.

WHAT TO READ Shakespeare, of course. While in Oxford, Max Beer-bohm's *Zuleika Dobson* (does anyone any more?). Shelley's poems. *Alice in Wonderland*, perhaps buying a nice edition on the Broad. Bits of Haw-thorne's *Scarlet Letter* were written while he was in Oxford. Matthew Arnold's *Scholar Gypsy*, which is set along this portion of the Thames. If when in Burford time permitted you to turn south on the B4020 through **Alvescot,** where there is an excellent Anglo-American college, to the B4449, and west, 12 miles in all, to Kelmscott, you would have reason to read William Morris, who founded the famous Kelmscott Press here, and whose *News from Nowhere* is full of local description. (And then you might drive 7 miles west on the A417 to **Fairford,** where lived the once-forgotten, now revived American painter, Edwin Austin Abbey, in Morgan Hall. Together with Howard Pyle, Abbey was regarded as the supreme illustrator of his time. If you do this circuit, return to Burford on the unnumbered country road signposted Southrop, Eastleach and Westwell, to see just how green and pleasant England can be.) And while in the Cotswolds, pause over John Drinkwater's *Cotswold Characters*.

2 Rochester
Canterbury
The Kent coast

One may travel easily from London to Dover by train, with stops in Rochester and Canterbury, for the service from Waterloo and London Bridge is frequent and rapid. But then to trace the Kent coast, visiting Ramsgate and Sandwich, or to include Romney Marsh, Rye and Hastings in the same journey, is quite difficult. An ideal combination, therefore, is to go the first part of the journey, via Canterbury to either Margate or Dover, by train, and then to hire a car for the return journey to London. Kent has much for the Collector and even more for the Obligatory Minded, and while one can travel down to Canterbury and back in the same day, including a Rochester stop for an hour or so, one will want to stay overnight en route. So will thousands of other tourists in the season, so book your room in advance, and if you decide upon one of the restaurants mentioned below, book it as well. This area is especially popular in midsummer and you must be prepared to queue, and also for an impacted countryside which will show at least as much litter as its American equivalents (indeed, there are few more paper-strewn highways than the A2/M2 between London and Faversham). If you have a choice and do not mind some of the gardens and castles being closed, this trip is ideal even in midwinter, when you may even experience a Dickensian fog over Romney Marsh or in the Battle and Burwash areas, a moment of high romance and Victorian adventure well worth the misery.

Take the journey clockwise, so that you have the sea on your left throughout. Leave London on the A2 through some of its dreariest suburbs, and stop for nothing short of Gravesend, 24 miles east of London. An ugly town with little to commend it, Gravesend nonetheless demands your attention. It was here that Benjamin Franklin stepped ashore in 1724, on the first of his three visits to England; it was from here that John Wesley and thousands after him sailed for the New World. But you have stopped here because of **Pocahontas,** the Indian maid who allegedly saved the life of John Smith, and who unquestionably is buried here at St George's Church (follow the road through the middle of the town until you are conscious of going downhill toward the river's edge; look to your right across open space and a car park for the church). The original church burned down long after Pocahontas was buried there in 1617 at the age of 22, while waiting in Gravesend to sail back to America with her husband, John Rolfe (who first introduced tobacco into Virginia). Where she rests now is uncertain, since many were re-interred in a common grave after the fire, but a handsome statue stands outside the church and inside two stained glass windows (given by the Society of Colonial Dames of America), a memorial tablet, and a pulpit given by the state of Indiana, are her memorials. Having once read the lesson before the congregation here, I will be more attached to the place than you, so you may want to justify your sidetrip further by driving two more blocks toward the river, to the headquarters of the Port of London Authority's Harbourmaster, where, if you have written in advance, you may be given an opportunity to see the navigational room from which all river traffic is directed.

Leave Gravesend on the A226 for Rochester, if you wish to pass through the low marsh country intimately associated with Charles Dickens, who set the opening scene of *Oliver Twist* in a churchyard (still there) near Gad's Hill Place – the house which Dickens saw as a boy and was determined to own, and which became his home from 1857 to 1870. (You could then bear left on the A228 to the Hoo Peninsula, across the eerie Thames estuary marshes, if you want to see an area most Englishmen never visit and watch the great ships enter the Thames on your left and the Medway on your right as you stand on the foreshore at Grain, at the very end of the B2001. There is a large, old fort at this point, in a pleasant park, beyond which, as T. S. Eliot wrote, 'The river sweats oil and tar'. But the drive is only worthwhile, since it will take 90 minutes for the round trip, if you are moved by the sound of foghorns, and the knowledge that you are standing at the key defensive point against waterborne invasions of the London area during the wars against the Dutch and French.) Otherwise, leave Gravesend for Rochester by returning to the A2, and divert briefly at the sign for Cobham, to the right on the B2009. Here is a lovely town less than 2 miles off the main road, with typical Kent-style barn roofs, a parish church with the largest collection of medieval brasses in the world set into the floor – excellent place to stop for brass-rubbing, and don't forget to pay a fee – and the Leather Bottle Inn, in which Dickens (and Pickwick) may have downed a few. They do a good luncheon here as well.

Rochester, 5 miles on, stands astride the Medway. Cross on the bridge and turn immediately right to park on the Esplanade. This cathedral city is compact and easy to walk through, although the roaring lorries will pass within inches of you on the narrow High Street, and the middle of the town is unattractive. Begin at the Bull Inn, on the High Street, where Pickwick (and Dickens) stayed; have a drink if you want in one of the self-mocking bars but do not have a meal unless your standard is set at home by McDonald's. Shortly ahead you will see an opening in the old town gate which leads directly to the cathedral in front of which is a surprising Gingko Tree, transplanted from California. Directly opposite is the castle with a massive 12th century keep, definitely to be visited. Continue along the High Street, and cross over it, to **Eastgate House** (open daily 2–5.30) which figures as the Nun's House in *Edwin Drood*, and now a museum which, upon close inspection, is well worth a visit. (The sharp eye will note a number of American-related objects, including a rare Staffordshire figure of George Washington.) After the museum, turn right to Maidstone Road and up the hill to Restoration House, which may be seen by appointment (write one week in advance). It was the model for Miss Havisham's house in *Great Expectations*. Then, with your arms free, return to Eastgate and turn right half a block, to the simple exterior of a famous institution, Reeves, which sells reduced-price seconds from the Spode works, and most other English and Irish pottery, porcelain and crystal manufacturers as well. Here you may find a nearly perfect set of Waterford wine glasses for a third of the price you will pay in London. Fill a basket, explore the attic, have your purchases wrapped in newspaper, and cart it all away yourself.

From Rochester onward you may require a better map than the *Sunday Times* or *AA Road Atlas*. Stop at a Shell station for one of theirs, for they are somewhat better than those of other oil companies. You want their Map No. 2, 'Southern & Eastern England'. Drive on through Rochester to Chatham, directly adjacent to it (bear left if you want to drive by the dockyard). The world's largest still-used Rope Walk is here, and if you have never seen 'naval stores' now is your chance. Open in the summer only, the Rope Walk gives a unique insight into the naval technology of a time only recently past. But if ships are not your thing, continue on through Chatham to the A278 on your right, which in 3 miles will take you to the M2, of which you may as well take advantage for the next 16 miles, by-passing unattractive country, to rejoin the A2 beyond Faversham. (Alternatively, you might follow the A229 from Chatham 6 miles to Maidstone, to see **All Saints Church,** with its memorial to Lawrence Washington, ancestor of George, and then join the M2 via the A249. Or you can drive to the end of the Isle of Sheppey via the A2, A249 – which ends at Sheerness, the naval dockyard Samuel Pepys helped plan – and A250, where at **Leysdown-on-Sea** Wilbur and Orville Wright

ROCHESTER CASTLE

met, prior to World War I, with their British counterparts, including C. S. Rolls.) Thence into Canterbury.

This cathedral city may disappoint you. No English city of great historic worth has been so ill-served by its City Fathers – though the task facing them after the wartime devastation was formidable. Car parks are juxtaposed with ancient ruins, modern architecture with Gothic. But viewed from the hill above the city, it gleams as it must have done for the Pilgrims who made their way here in the late 14th century. (If you share my romantic inclination to walk a bit of the original Pilgrim's Way, be patient – or turn to page 193 now.) Follow the signs to the University of Kent, upon the hill above the city, for from its sweeping campus you will have the best views of the great Cathedral. From a distance, Canterbury cannot disappoint.

In the city you should seek out a car park and walk. Begin with the Cathedral, the heart of English Christianity. You will be hurrying unconscionably if you do not spend at least an hour or two here, for this is a masterpiece which, while not so handsome as Salisbury or so commanding as Durham, must in its combination of faith, literature and architecture, be high on everyone's list of cathedrals. Sit, if you have time, in one of the chairs and read the appropriate passages of Eliot's *Murder in the Cathedral*, which you may buy at the book-stall, and as an American think of the words used in justification of their act by those who killed

Thomas à Becket. Be glad that American money was given the opportunity, in 1947, to help toward the repair of the bomb-damaged structure and drop as many coins as you can spare into the donation box as you leave. Walk along St Peter's Street to West Gate, then return and follow the posted path along the stream on your right to the ruins of Grey Friars, and then walk the outer City Wall, first past the Norman castle, to St Augustine's Abbey. Beyond the Abbey ruins up Longport Street two long blocks is St Martin's Church, the oldest church still in use in England – when St Augustine came here in 597 he found a Christian service in progress within it.

Return to your car and drive back past the West Gate Museum to St Dunstan's Church, on the corner of St Dunstan's Street and London Road, where you may view a vault wherein lies Sir Thomas More's severed head. Two blocks further on Whitstable Road, and to your left, is the Roman Catholic cemetery in which Joseph Conrad is buried.

And now you must make some choices. The Kent coast lies before you. You cannot see it all, and return to London via Hastings, in a single day. If your limit is two days, I would put up for the night either in Fordwich, just outside Canterbury to the northeast, or drive on 16 miles to Dover. If you can add at least half a day to your schedule, staying out of London two nights, I would turn north to Whitstable, having taken the precaution of booking into either Fordwich or Margate by telephone beforehand. In either case, the tiny George and Dragon Inn, at Fordwich (2 miles out of Canterbury on the A28 and bear right at Sturry) is excellent, inexpensive, and provides the best meal within miles. But there are only nine rooms (and only one with bath) so do call ahead. If you would like laurel wreath quality food, however, then leave Canterbury on the A28 toward Ashford – past ruined **Chilham Castle,** where Governor Edward Digges (1655–8) was born – and turn left 12 miles out on a country road posted for Wye. Here is the Wife of Bath, the only restaurant deserving an international reputation in the whole of the southeast corner of England, where you may have a fine meal in country surroundings, and dine on partridge, salmon, or duck, and brown bread ice cream.

Option One Drive directly from Canterbury to Dover, on the A2. Stop at Bishopsbourne, a village on the right, where Joseph Conrad died in 1924 at 'Oswalds'. In **Dover,** the terminus of the greatest number of cross-Channel travellers, head directly for the White Cliffs (not really white) made so famous to Americans in World War II by Alice Duer Miller's book and by Shakespeare long ago: it was to the 350-foot Shakespeare Cliff, now reached by a signposted path, that the blinded Gloucester in *King Lear* was led by Edgar. Here too Matthew Arnold wrote his poem, 'Dover Beach'. Dover is the chief of the Cinque (or five) Ports, and Dover Castle, with gigantic gateways and underground passages, is fun for

CANTERBURY CATHEDRAL

children. Above it stands the Bleriot Memorial, commemorating the first cross-Channel flight in 1909; climb to it for the view.

If you have trouble remembering the five ports, think of Longfellow's poem, 'The Warden of the Cinque Ports':

> A mist was driving down the British Channel
>   the day was just begun . . .
> Sandwich and Romney, Hastings, Hythe and Dover
>   Were all alert that day,
> To see the French war-steamers speeding over,
>   When the fog cleared away.

In World War I the Dover Patrol, a combined British and American force of destroyers, was based here, and in World War II the German air raid on Dover, on August 12, 1940, marked the beginning of the Battle of Britain. Woodrow Wilson, first American President to visit Britain, landed here in 1918.

Option Two Leave Canterbury on the A290 to Whitstable, from which the famous oysters come, and then go east along the sea on the B2205 to Herne Bay to see a particularly horrible example of how the English failed to protect their seaside from the incursion of depressing and tiny beach huts. Lest you think all of England green and trim, a few minutes of this unhappy scene is a necessary corrective. Then by the A299, continuing east, to the A28, thence to **Margate,** where Tom Paine lived and his wife died. Here, and at Cliftonville, you may promenade along the sea front and, in summer, listen to bands play in the Edwardian manner. Continue on, now using your Shell map for detail, via North Foreland and the B2052 to Broadstairs, here to see Dickens' Bleak House. Here too, but unmarked, are the original steps made famous by John Buchan as *The Thirty-Nine Steps*, that greatest of all classics of British spy derring-do. (Driving from North Foreland on North Foreland Avenue watch for a copse of trees on the left, near the cliff's edge just as the road bends slightly inland. A sign reads North Foreland Estate. Stop here and plunge into the grove, where you will find the steps leading down.)

In Ramsgate, which was the town to which the Dunkirk evacuees were brought in 1940, drive to the Hovercraft departure point at Pegwell Bay and watch one of these strange craft rise up and make its eerie way into the sea. (You might take one of its 'flights' – up to sixteen a day in summer – to Calais and back for the day, for a touch of France, and have lunch at the Grand Hotel Clement, in Ardres, ten minutes beyond Calais.) Now follow the A256 south 5 miles to **Sandwich,** where Tom Paine lived. This is the most picturesque of the original Cinque Ports, and yet it is modern too – James Bond played his famous game with Goldfinger here. Nearly everyone knows by now that our *sandwich* is named after the first Earl of Sandwich, who not wanting to leave the gambling table, had his roast beef served to him between slices of bread. Now take the A256 and turn left to Northbourne: the church here has a **memorial to Sir Edwin Sandys,** founder of Virginia. The tomb, in which he was buried in 1629, is particularly fine. Follow unnumbered country roads via Great Mongeham to **Deal** (Deal Castle is well worth a visit). William Penn sailed in 1682 for America, after writing his *Last Farewell to England* here. Just beyond is Walmer Castle, official residence of the Lord Warden of the Cinque Ports. (These were essentially a defensive system of forts built in the Middle Ages to protect the coast against invaders; to the original towns were later added Rye and Winchelsea, which contains an excellent museum.) Thence bear south on the A258 to Dover.

Taking up your journey once again after having spent the night in or near Dover (see option one, above) drive southwest along the coast through Folkestone (note the Martello towers, part of the defensive works along the coast) and Sandgate (where the vegetarian guest house above the beach was once H. G. Wells' 'Spade House', where he wrote *The Invisible Man*) to Hythe. You can swim off beaches at both Dover and Folkestone, although the water will be cold. A mile north of Hythe is Saltwood Castle, where Thomas à Becket's death was planned (open Wed. only, 2.30–6,

DOVER

in July and August) and directly beyond, Sandling Park Gardens. 2 miles further inland, on a country road, is Postling. Here, at Pen Farm, Joseph Conrad wrote *Lord Jim, Typhoon* and *Nostromo*, and received visits from Wells and George Bernard Shaw.

Drive on through Postling to the B2068 and turn left to Lympne. Here are two ruined castles, a massive church tower and the site of a key Roman defensive work. Turn right on the B2067 to Bilsington, where you can turn left onto narrow country lanes which run across Romney Marsh. Famous for its smugglers, this lowland has figured in many a British adventure story (if your children are familiar with Malcolm Saville, they will know of Romney and Rye). Follow the signs for New-church, St Mary in the Marsh – E. Nesbit, ever-popular author of *The Railway Children*, is buried here – and New Romney on the A259, and then across the Walland Marsh on a slow road to one of the gems of England, the village of Rye. (By continuing west at Bilsington, one reaches **Tenterden,** home of the Ellen Terry Memorial Museum which includes many mementoes from American tours by Ellen Terry and Henry Irving.) If you have an extra hour, however, you may want to visit (or revisit, as the case will be for many Americans) some of the sites associated with the **D-Day landings** in Normandy in June 1944. From New Romney go east to Littlestone-on-Sea, where at low tide one may see the concrete pontoons built for the invasion, or go south on the B2075 to Lydd (where the church is known as the Cathedral of Romney Marsh), then to Dungeness, once famous for crab, where you may visit a new nuclear power station (Wed. afternoon only, June–Sept.), two lighthouses (Mon.–Sat. afternoons), and see the terminus of the pipeline laid across the channel to pump fuel to the invading armies. Then return on the B2076 to Old Romney and on to Rye.

Rye is exquisite; if you are here in the tourist season, however, you may find its narrow cobblestoned streets jammed with fellow tourists. It is a lovely December town, and an April one too. The old town gate, St Mary's Church – with the oldest working clock in England – and Mermaid Street must be given attention. Christ's Church, Rye, New York, and Christ's Church here observe the second Sunday in Advent in common. Attention must also be given to **Lamb House,** where Henry James lived from 1898 to his death in 1916 (open Tues. afternoons, and from May–Oct. Wed. and Sat. also 2.15–6). There are a number of charming pubs here, good bookstores and excellent hotels. Not only did James write all his later books here, but Radclyffe Hall wrote *The Well of Loneliness* in 1928, and E. F. Benson, Mayor of Rye, wrote a number of books, now reissued in Penguins, about *Mapp and Lucia* and *Lucia's Progress.* The George Hotel on High Street, the Mermaid and the Hope Anchor on Watchbell Street provide good meals.

Just south of Rye is Winchelsea, one of the most charming hilltop villages in all England, beautifully laid out, ideal for strolling, with excellent pubs and a fine old church. Camber Castle stands in the field below. The A259 winds on to Hastings, the largest of the Cinque Ports. Here one should drive the length of the Grand Parade past the many hotels. The first television transmission was made here in 1925. St Clement's Church, the castle ruin, and **St Clement's Caves,** discovered in 1825 by William S. Golding, developed by an American and used as an air raid shelter in World War II, are worth fleeting visits. Just beyond Hastings is Bulverhythe. Here is the Bo-Peep pub, named after the 18th century nursery rhyme written for the innkeeper's daughter. As the rhyme actually refers to contraband brandy, you might have a drink here – preferably of the distinctive Sussex ale.

Leave Hastings on the A21, and bear right on the A28 to Brede, where at **Brede Place** Stephen Crane, author of *Red Badge of Courage,* lived. The house is well worth a visit even if Crane does not interest you. Berkeley Mather, one of the best current writers of British thrillers, lives in Church House, Brede. Continue north another mile, turn left on the B2089, and follow the signs via the B2092 to Battle. The British have done virtually nothing to preserve the site of the Battle of Hastings, the beginning of 1066 and All That, but one may look down upon the spot where the Norman, William the Conqueror, defeated the Saxons' King Harold and may visit the abbey William built as his victory memorial.

The estate has recently been bought by The Department of the Environment, with financial help from America.

> O Chryste, it is a grief for me to telle,
> How manie a nobil erle and valrous knyghte
> In fyghtynge for Kynge Harrold noblie fell,
> Al sleyne in Hastings feeld in bloudie fyghte.
>
> *Thomas Chatterton*

Drive north on the A2100 until it joins the A21, thence to a junction with the A265, and then 6 miles west to Burwash. Here is 'Bateman's', an early Jacobean house, which was the home of Rudyard Kipling. His wife, an American, presented it to the National Trust, and one may view the study in which he wrote *Puck of Pook's Hill* (open daily except Fri., March–Sept.). In **Heathfield,** 7 miles further west, is the church in which Robert Hunt was vicar. Hunt was chaplain to the expedition that founded Virginia in 1607. Return to the A21, where you must again make a choice.

Option One Continue north on the A21 and divert to Tunbridge Wells on B2169. This is an old English watering place, a Georgian spa, with a good parish church and, in the Pantiles – the 18th century colonnaded promenade – a handsome reminder of a handsome past. L'Hermitage Hotel, at 30–33 London Road, provides a good meal. From here to London it is 37 miles, and assuming that you will see Penshurst Place, Knole, Quebec House, and Hever Castle (q.v.) on a day trip out of London, you may press on via the A21 back to London and your hotel.

Option Two Bear right off the A21 onto the A265, thence north on the A229 to Cranbrook, to the right on the B2189. Here is Sissinghurst Court. A mile beyond, on the A262, are Sissinghurst Place Gardens, and yet another mile further is Sissinghurst Castle, an outstanding example of Tudor-built work. Here lived Victoria Sackville-West with her husband, Harold Nicolson. The gardens (which they created together) and castle are Obligatory (open daily 10–7). Rejoin the A229 and continue north 13 miles to Maidstone. Here, in **All Saints Church,** is a memorial to Lawrence Washington, George's ancestor, who died in 1619. William Hazlitt was born here (Chillington Manor has relics). 5 miles east of Maidstone, via the A20, is **Leeds Castle,** ancestral home of the Culpepers and the Fairfaxes of early Virginia fame. Leave Maidstone northwards on the A229 to join the M20 motorway, which runs to Wrotham, where it rejoins the A20 which will bring you back to London in 30 miles.

To view a portion of the old Pilgrim's Way, as promised, you may either do so now, out of Maidstone, or could have done so from Rye and Ashford. The former stretch is more interesting. At the eastern end of the

M20 come off the roundabout and turn back on the A20 as though for Maidstone. Just past Wrotham Heath a country road, posted for Addington and Trottiscliffe, will carry you back under the motorway. At Trottiscliffe, bear left through the village and begin to ascend the hill. Sharply to the right is a lane, Pilgrim's Way. Follow this to its end and park; for here is a walking stretch for approximately a mile of the original path. The second portion is off the A20 between Ashford and Maidstone. At the village of Charing, turn east on the A252, climbing steeply. Almost immediately the Pilgrim's Way crosses the highway, with a signpost to the right. One may walk for nearly a mile in either direction. While in Ashford, see the museum of the Intelligence Corps (Mon.–Fri., 10–12, 2–4), the only one of its kind.

WHAT TO READ   Conrad, Dickens and Kipling, most clearly, for the many literary associations arising from this journey. John Buchan's *The Thirty-Nine Steps* while in Broadstairs. Henry James and Stephen Crane, although only James was actively writing while resident here. Hazlitt and Christopher Marlowe while in Canterbury (in St George's Church you will see a tablet to him). Malcolm Saville in Winchelsea and E. F. Benson in Rye. Above all, read *Bleak House*, *Great Expectations* and *Oliver Twist* while in Rochester, *David Copperfield* while in Broadstairs, and – most important and obvious of all – Chaucer's *Canterbury Tales*.

3 Brighton

Brighton is probably the goal of the most popular day trip from London; certainly it appears to be so for the British, and you will find the trains to the south coast, and the streets of Brighton itself, crowded in summer. Yet somehow this pleasant city of 160,000 manages to absorb the droves of people who descend upon it, and, except at the Brighton Pavilion itself, you are unlikely to feel hemmed in. If you have time for but one journey out of London, and cannot stay overnight, then choose this one, for the train – and the trip is better done by train, even if you have a car, since the drive south out of London is tedious – passes through some attractive and representative countryside. Leave from Victoria Station on one of the many expresses and you will soon be in the Sussex countryside and stepping out into this fine Regency city 55 minutes later. If you prefer to drive, the A23 and M23 bring you to Brighton in 53 miles; an alternate route, slower but more attractive, is the A22 via **East Grinstead.** (The Hospital bears an inscription to remind you that more American airmen were treated here during World War II than in any other British hospital.) President Kennedy attended Mass in the Roman Catholic church, as a plaque attests. Drive on to Brighton via the A26 and Lewes. Or take the A24 from London, via Epsom and Horsham. In doing so you may pass near **Cheam,** where the parish church contains a memorial to Admiral Hobart Pasha, he who blockaded North Carolina during the Civil War (should you be a Civil War buff) and (by a brief diversion on the A246 just south of Leatherhead) to **Great Bookham,** where the church contains an unusual memorial to a British soldier killed in ambush during the Revolution, showing American irregulars hiding in the

BRIGHTON

woods nearby. South of Leatherhead on the A24 a signpost to your left indicates Box Hill, worth a short stop for the view from its summit and its association with George Meredith. Flint Cottage, in which he lived from 1876, is a National Trust property but it is closed to the public: you may find it at the foot of the steep road to Box Hill, near Burford Bridge Hotel. Meredith is buried in Dorking cemetery, behind the church with the great 200-foot steeple. **Dorking** was the home of William Mullins, who sailed with his family in the *Mayflower*; it was his daughter, Priscilla, who was made famous in Longfellow's poem by the line, 'Why don't you speak for yourself, John?' There is also a pleasant watercress farm some miles west of Dorking on the A25, and while cress may not be your thing, you are unlikely to encounter such a farm back home in Montana. 13 miles south of Dorking, at Warnham (just off the road to the right on the B2199) is the birthplace of Percy Bysshe Shelley and the scene of his unhappy childhood at Field Place. And yet another 9 miles further on, and 2 miles to the right on the A272 brings you to Shipley, where stands a galleried windmill, a memorial to Hilaire Belloc, the great comic writer, and author of those most frankly Imperial lines,

> 'Whatever happens we have got
> The Maxim gun, and they have not.'

Another mile to the west on the same road brings one to **Coolham,** where the Quaker meeting house (known as the Blue Idol) attended by William Penn still stands. To the south was a home – since destroyed – in which Penn lived for 25 years. Continue west to the A29, then south through **Pulborough** where was born Edmund Freeman, one of the original Pilgrims. You may then pass via Arundel (on the A284), seat of the Dukes of Norfolk, where the magnificent castle is well worth a visit (open mid-April–Sept., generally in the afternoon). 14 miles southwest is Felpham where William Blake the poet lived: Brighton is 13 miles to the east – via Lancing, where you may visit the Lancing College chapel, a neo-Gothic masterpiece sometimes called the Cathedral of the Downs. This was the college satirized by Evelyn Waugh.

Despite these temptations, I still recommend the train and a more leisurely day within the environs of Brighton. Plan to look for antiques, even though they are not cheap here, and use Brighton's excellent buses to cover the long stretches of seafront westwards through Hove. And should you be there in November, you can watch the end of the London to Brighton Veteran Car Run.

What to see? First, the Royal Pavilion, built in 1784–7, an odd building in the then-popular mock-Oriental style, which is the grandest product of a royal fantasy in the whole of Britain. (It is open July–Sept., 10–8, and until 5 the rest of the year.) Don't miss the great kitchen, where Carême – inventor of caramel – ruled early in the 19th century. In the area near the Pavilion, and between it and the sea are The Lanes where, in a pedestrian precinct, you will find antique shops, gift shops, restaurants and boutiques. A reasonably good aquarium stands on the foreshore opposite the Palace Pier (worth a visit), but in the matter of aquaria do not expect any place in Europe to rival Florida or California. The **museum** (near the Pavilion) and art gallery are good and include American Indian items. In the spring and summer the gardens on the Old Steine are attractive. Children will appreciate the National Toy Museum in North Gate House, and you may wish to view 6 Eastern Terrace (off the Marine Parade) where **U.S. Grant** stayed on his visit in 1877. Brighton is a city of handsome Regency terraces, and it rewards the walker handsomely.

Now take a taxi 5 miles east to Rottingdean, along Marine Drive. (One passes Roedean School, often referred to as the girls' Eton.) At **The Elms,** in Rottingdean, Rudyard Kipling lived with his American wife – it is open as a museum. St Margaret's Church has good windows by Sir Edward Burne-Jones – he lived at North End House here – and unless you are likely to get to Birmingham or the Midlands, you will see no better of their kind. His work in glass represents the best of British Art Nouveau of the 1880s. Go on to Newhaven on the A259, then north on the B2109 to the A27, then right. At Glynde, off the A27 to the left, is the fine Elizabethan Glynde Place (open May–Sept., Thurs., Sat., Sun., 2.15–5.30). A right turn off the A27 leads to **Firle Place,** home of the Gage family.

Thomas Gage was the Commander of the British forces in North America at the beginning of the Revolution. (22 miles on is the elegant resort city of Eastbourne, with unique Coastal Defence and Royal National Lifeboat museums and several excellent hotels. If you are driving and have given yourself two days, stay in Eastbourne rather than Brighton, at the Burlington, Cavendish, Cumberland or Grand hotels.)

Return west on the A27 to **Lewes** – where Tom Paine once lived – to see the Anne of Cleves House and South Malling Church, where John Harvard was married, and then go northeast on the A265 to **Ringmer.** In the Lady Chapel of the parish church is a memorial to the Reverend John Sadler, father-in-law of John Harvard; there is also a monument to Sir William Springett, Penn's first father-in-law. Return to Lewes and follow the A27 back to Brighton. On this return circuit is the University of Sussex, Falmer, which has won numerous architectural awards, especially for the overall conception by Sir Basil Spence. This university is one of the few worth your visit, if universities interest you at all, and you will want to contrast its clean, functional lines and brickwork with Oxford and Cambridge. To the right is **Stanmer,** from which came the regicide William Goffe, who lived in exile in New Haven, Conn.

One comes to Brighton for two reasons other than sightseeing and antiques. One is to go to the opera at Glyndebourne. Here, just outside Lewes, near Glynde, you may attend one of England's more elegant occasions. One dresses for Glyndebourne, and the sight of men in dinner jackets (or tuxedo, if you prefer) and ladies in long gowns seated upon the grass having their picnics from fitted hampers is the nearest thing in Britain to the Harvard-Yale-Princeton tailgating party at a football game. The entertainment is rather better, although expensive, and you must book well in advance. If a picnic on possibly wet grass doesn't appeal, you may book a table at the restaurant.

And one eats in Brighton too. In 1982 the *Good Food Guide* fancied there were six restaurants in this city worth dining in, which ranked it ahead of all other cities in Britain save London, Manchester and Edinburgh. Brighton is not *that* good, actually, but you will eat well at *Le Grandgousier,* (15 Western Street) and comparatively inexpensively at Wheeler's (17 Market Street). If you want an early evening devoted to very good wines, with the food incidental, go to the Market Wine House (20 Market Street). There will be trains to take you back to London running until after 11.00, but check the exact times on arrival.

WHAT TO READ   If children are with you, they will enjoy reading Malcolm Saville's *Brighton Pavilion Mystery* before exploring the place. Belloc, of course, and Graham Greene's *Brighton Rock.* You may want to do justice to George Meredith too: he wrote *The Egoist* and *The Adventures of Henry Richmond* while living at Box Hill. Thackeray's Becky Sharp, in *Vanity Fair*, loved Brighton. But most obviously, Kipling is to be read. His principal house-museum is somewhat afield – at 'Bateman's', a 17th century home in Burwash, about 35 miles east of Brighton. Read Dickens' *Dombey and Son*, which he wrote in the Bedford Hotel (destroyed in 1964) in Brighton. Best of all, experience with Lydia, in Jane Austen's *Pride and Prejudice*, the thought that 'a visit to Brighton comprised every possibility of earthly happiness.'

4 Windsor
Winchester
Salisbury
Portsmouth
Chichester
Guildford

An early start is needed for this trip, which requires two days or more. (One may, of course, go to either Guildford or Windsor easily from London, by rail or Green Line bus, on half-day outings, but to combine the several points noted here, more time and a car are essential.)

Leave London on the M4 motorway, as though for Heathrow Airport, to exit 6, thence by the A4 to the B416 north in Slough (pronounced to rhyme with 'now'). Short of reaching Stoke Poges one passes, on the left, the church by which Thomas Gray wrote his 'Elegy in a Country Churchyard'. The church also contains the pew of the **Penn family**: John Penn erected the memorial to Gray. At the **Stoke Park** golf club is the home of William Penn's grandson, John, built in 1789; a piece of the elm tree under which William Penn signed his treaty with the Indians is preserved in the club house. Return to Slough, drive west on the A4, and north on the B476, to **Cliveden House,** given to the National Trust by Viscount Astor to promote Anglo-American friendship (grounds open April–Sept.). The mansion is now the English campus of Stanford University. Continue on the B476 to the A4094, then left into the A4155 to **Marlow.** Izaak Walton often fished the Thames here. The parish church shows the Washington coat of arms. Edgar Wallace, the thriller writer, is buried here. Mary Shelley wrote *Frankenstein* in Albion House on West Street.

Following the A4155 one reaches Henley-on-Thames, site of the famous annual regatta. Take the A321 to **Twyford.** William Penn died at Southcombe Farm here in 1718. Turn east on the B3024 to the A330 north, sharp right on the A308, and almost immediately sharp left on the **Bray** road.

• If you prefer to omit Windsor Castle, or wish to move more deeply into the countryside, take the A4 from Twyford to **Reading** (site of the Reading Gaol of Oscar Wilde's Ballad). Penn worshipped here at the Quaker Meeting House – it is now converted into a store. County town of Berkshire (pronounced Barkshire) with a population of 135,000, Reading is an industrial city. King's Road diverts right from London Road (in which William Penn once lived); another right into Forbury Road leads to the ruins of the Benedictine Abbey, once the third largest in England. The first music composed for several voices, 'Sumer is icumen in', is commemorated by a tablet on the chapter house; the gatehouse was a school which Jane Austen attended. Reading Gaol is adjacent; Wilde wrote 'De Profundis' here. **Reading Museum and Art Gallery** contains some American Indian materials. South on the A327 is the University of Reading (1926); on the campus is the interesting Museum of English Rural Life (open May–Oct., weekdays except Mon. 10.30–5, Sun. 2.30; Nov.–Apr., Wed., Sat., same). Beyond Shinfield, further south on the A327, turn left on the B3349 to **Barkham.** There is a crucifix to an ancestor of George Washington in the parish church.

• Northwest of Reading on the A329 is Pangbourne, where Kenneth Grahame lived in Church Cottage. West of Reading on the A4 to Newbury, thence south on the A34, brings one to the area Richard Adams called *Watership Down* for his modern tale of rabbit adventure; the map supplied with the book coincides with land roughly bounded by the A34 on the west, the A339 on the north, the B3051 on the east, and the B3400 on the south. Southwest of Reading via the A33 and A30 is **Dummer,** where George Whitefield, the person most responsible for the Great Awakening in America, began his practice.

If you ignore this diversion you may have a fine meal at the **Hindhead Hotel** at Bray; the inn contains interesting plaques to its American guests and Robert H. Davis of the *New York Sun*. You may wish to see Windsor Castle and then return here for a late lunch.

Follow the A308 into Windsor. Just to the north is **Eton College,** on the playing fields of which it is said the British Empire was formed. One signer of the Declaration of Independence, Thomas Lynch, was a pupil here. Windsor Castle is the goal, however, for it is the largest inhabited castle in the world. The State Apartments are very fine (usually open daily, March–Oct., 10.30–5, Sun. 1.30; Nov.–Feb. close 3) and Queen Mary's Dolls' House and exhibition is fun, as are the drawings by old masters (open same as above except closed Sun.). But the highlight for most people is St George's Chapel, with stalls, brasses, and banners of the Knights of the Garter (open weekdays 11–3.45, Sun. 2.30–4, closed Jan.). The Castle grounds open at 10.00 and remain open until dusk, but you will find everything closed on the first day of any State Visit, and the State Apartments close for six weeks at Easter, three weeks at Ascot,

WINDSOR CASTLE

three weeks at Christmas, and when the royal family otherwise wishes. It is their home, after all.

To the south of the Castle is Windsor Great Park, fine for walking in. At its southern edge is an excellent Spanish restaurant, the Bailiwick, which is noted for its gazpacho. The restaurant is at the park's entrance, so one may walk afterwards and the Virginia Water section is especially attractive. One of the tallest totem poles in the world stands here, a gift from British Columbia. (Just north of Egham via the A30 and the B376 is **Wraysbury.** William Pynchon, founder of Springfield, Massachusetts, is buried in the parish churchyard.)

In the triangle formed by the A30, the A308 and the A328 is **Runnymede,** a shrine to English (and American) liberties. The barons who withstood King John had not dreamt of democracy, to be sure, but nonetheless one may trace our rights and privileges from the signing of the Magna Carta here on a tiny island, in 1215. It was an Anglo-American couple, Lord and Lady Fairhaven, who presented the site to the National Trust. Just up the hill is a moving memorial to John F. Kennedy, and on the hillside above is the Commonwealth Air Forces Memorial to 20,000 airmen who have no known grave. In the parish church of **Egham** are reproductions of the barons' shields, tracing their descendants in America as well. (South of Egham on the B388 is **Chert-**

sey; an American poet, Rose Hartwich Thorpe, wrote 'Curfew Must Not Ring Tonight' to commemorate the heroism of Blanche Heriot, who in the Wars of the Roses prevented her lover from being executed at curfew by climbing the church tower and hanging onto the clapper of the bell.) Ambassador Joseph P. Kennedy lived in **Sunningdale** in 1940.

South of Windsor Great Park, drive west on the A329 to Ascot, scene of Britain's most elegant race meeting, and thence south on the A330 to rejoin the A30, right to **Bagshot.** This is upper class commuterdom (Westport, if you will). The **Museum of the Royal Army Chaplains' Department** contains many American presentation items. Further along the A30 is **Camberley:** Bret Harte died here in The Red House in 1902, and the museum contains mementoes to him. Between here and Sandhurst is the Royal Military Academy for army officers, the West Point of Britain, founded in 1799. The **National Army Museum** (open weekdays 10–5, Sun. 11) in its grounds is very good, especially for Indian Army materials and items relating to disbanded Irish regiments. There are numerous American-related objects, including the Colour carried into battle at Saratoga.

From Sandhurst go south on the A321 through **Frimley** (Bret Harte is buried in the churchyard) to reach the vast cemetery of **Brookwood.** In the southwest corner is an American World War I burial ground for 500 men. Turn south on the A324 through **Pirbright** (Henry Morton Stanley, the American who uttered those immortal lines, 'Dr Livingstone, I presume?' is buried in the churchyard here) to **Aldershot.** This is a military town, and there are four interesting specialized museums: the **Airborne Forces Museum** at Browning Barracks, which has a section devoted to American airborne soldiers; the **R.A.M.C. Historical Museum** at Keogh Barracks, Ash Vale (right on the A321 before entering the town) with several items relating to the Revolution; the **Museum of the QARANC Training Centre** (Queen Alexandra's Royal Army Nursing Corps) at the Royal Pavilion on Farnborough Road, which holds objects relating to visits to America by Matrons-in-Chief; and, for those who care, the Museum of the Royal Army Dental Corps on Evelyn Woods Road. Unless your interest in military matters is intense, limit your visit to the first of the four.

Follow the signs for **Farnham.** William Cobbett, apostle of Free Trade (and soldier in Florida), was born in the Jolly Farmer Inn (when it was a house). Between 1817 and 1819 he edited his *Political Register* from America. His classic traveller's account, *Rural Rides*, makes leisurely reading. His memorial is in the church. **The Farnham Museum** in Willmer House holds a good John Singer Sargent. Continue on the A31 to **Alton;** in the parish church is a tablet to John Murray, founder of the Universalist Church in America. Just south at Chawton is the home of Jane Austen (open daily all year 11–4.30); here she wrote *Mansfield Park, Emma* and *Persuasion.*

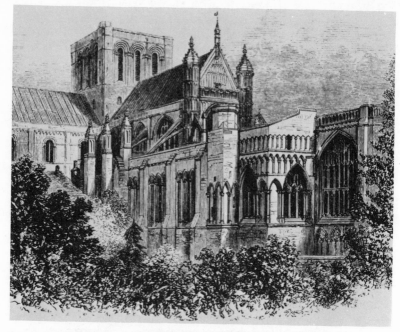

WINCHESTER CATHEDRAL

It is time for the night. Two pleasant places are at hand: the Swan Hotel, High Street, Alton, or southeast on the B3006 in Selborne, the Queen's Hotel. The famous naturalist Gilbert White lived here and made the village a household name; his home is now a museum (open daily except Fri., Sun., 2.30–5.30, also 11–1 Apr.–Oct.). Or if a really fine dinner is wanted, check in to the Swan Hotel to claim your room, and then drive on the A31 to Alresford, where O'Rorkes offers dinner only from 7–9.30 to 35 people.

• If you can spare some extra time before making for Portsmouth, strike southwest (on the A31 from Chawton) for a brief glimpse of Winchester, Salisbury and Stonehenge.
• Winchester city and Cathedral are both world famous. Anyone of literary bent knows them well, for this was Thomas Hardy's Wintoncester of *Tess of the D'Urbervilles*. It was the home of Izaak Walton (who died at 7 The Close at the age of 90) and important to Keats and Thackeray (*Vanity Fair*) alike. Jane Austen died in College Street. England's capital for centuries, Winchester still has the air of a royal city and its handsome Cathedral, one of the longest in Europe, is on everyone's short list of

SALISBURY CATHEDRAL

major sights in Britain. From the station, drive into the High Street until
the Cathedral is passed on the right, and then use the car park directly
behind it. The Cathedral was being built from 1079 until 1404. There are
seven chantry chapels, fine medieval wall paintings, a superb carved font,
excellent tombs (including King Cnut and William Rufus) and tablets to
Jane Austen and to Walton, both of whom are buried here. The stalls
have strong misericords, there is an incredible reredos, and St Swithin's
shrine, while new, is quite effective. Ask to be allowed to see the library,
which contains copies of the Venerable Bede's history and the Winchester
Bible. Although not my favorite cathedral, Winchester is possibly the
most interesting and consistently instructive.

• Walk through the Cathedral Close, out of King's Gate and then left
into College Street to Winchester College, founded in 1382 by William
of Wykeham. It is the oldest of the major public schools, and the buildings

date from 1394. See the chapel (open 10–4, Sun. from 2). There are tours of the college at 10, 11.45, 2, 3 and 4.30, except Sunday. The great destruction brought to Britain by World War I is attested to by the War Memorial Cloister, which notes the names of 500 Wykehamists who died in the War.

• **The Museum of the King's Royal Rifle Corps,** in Peninsular Barracks, a quarter of a mile west of the Cathedral, contains several Revolutionary items.

• A mile to the south of the city, via a path along the River Itchen, is the Hospital of St Cross (open daily except Sunday, 9–5) which was founded in 1136. Pensioners here may be seen wearing their traditional gowns and caps and Trollope's *The Warden* springs from here.

• From Winchester, take the A272 and the A30 westwards again to Salisbury (ignoring all temptations to divert along the way – although you may be intrigued by seeing Nether Wallop on the signposts).

• Salisbury, the fine small city that is the county town of Wiltshire, is famous for its Cathedral, for nearby Stonehenge, and as Trollope's Barchester. In its architectural mass, it is probably the finest cathedral in Britain, and perhaps in Europe. Its spire – read William Golding's *The Spire* if you can – is the tallest in Europe. Begun in 1220, the Cathedral is full of wonderful features: superb vaulting, elaborate strainer arches, an ancient choir screen, a 13th century cope chest, several fine tombs, the oldest clock in England and the oldest and largest cloisters. There is a tomb to **Sir Thomas Gorges,** of the family that first settled Maine. Be certain to visit the chapter house. The Cathedral Close is unusually fine, and the grounds are interspersed with modern sculpture, some by the late Barbara Hepworth. Laid out on a grid pattern, Salisbury is an easy city to walk in and well repays any effort spent.

• Leave Salisbury north on the A345 for Amesbury. On the left is Old Sarum, the extensive and intriguing ruins of the Roman fortress of Sorviodunum. The first cathedral was begun here. Old Sarum acquired more recent fame as one of the rotten boroughs against which the Reform Act of 1832 was directed; William Pitt represented it – not rottenly. Amesbury is the gateway to Salisbury Plain. (Just north off the A345 is Milston, birthplace of Joseph Addison; the baptismal font may be seen in the church.) West on the A303 and A344 is Stonehenge, a Bronze Age site, dating from before 1800 B.C. Mystery still surrounds Stonehenge, and the argument goes on as to its original purpose. It is probably the most famous prehistoric site (and certainly the most visited) in Europe. (From here one may continue west on the A303 and A36 to Warminster, there to join the Bath and Bristol tour.) At Stonehenge, one is at the heart of England's prehistoric and Roman ruins: 80 sites within a 40-mile radius. These, as well as those in the rest of the country, are described in a fine paperback book by Jacquetta Hawkes, *A Guide to the Prehistoric and Roman Monuments in England and Wales.*

Should you not have managed to make this expedition, you should now – from Chawton – drive the next 20 miles through the rolling South Downs, via the B3006, the A325 and the A3 to Portsmouth. (Just below Petersfield the B2146 east reaches South Harting, where Anthony Trollope is buried, and **Uppark,** open Wed., Thurs., Sun. afternoons. The great house, now a National Trust property, was the 'Bladesover' in H. G. Wells' book *Tono-Bungay*. There is a portrait by Benjamin West of Uppark's owner, Sir Harry Fetherstonhaugh. On the nearby hill is the **Vandalia Memorial,** a ruined tower erected to commemorate the syndicate formed to establish a colony in America, a scheme destroyed by the outbreak of the Revolution. One may continue into Portsmouth on the winding B2146 and B2147, and the A27.) South of Petersfield is the village of Buriton, where Edward Gibbon lived as a boy. If, just before reaching Portsmouth, you turn northwest on the A333 for about 7 miles you will come to **Wickham.** The flour mill here was made from timbers from the American *Chesapeake,* captured in the War of 1812.

Portsmouth, a city of 210,000, is the main base of the British navy. There is much to see here for naval buffs, and there are many associations with America. Charles Dickens was born in a house, now a museum (open weekdays 10–5, at 393 Commercial Road) while George Meredith was born at 73 High Street. There is a tablet (erected in 1784!) to the founder of New Hampshire, **John Mason,** in the Garrison church (one block left from the High Street at the Grand Parade) – he lived at Buckingham House, 10 High Street (which runs from the Cathedral). The **Cathedral** was founded in 1927 and is still unfinished; it incorporates elements from a church of 1188. In the south tower transept a 48-star American flag is hung. The **City Museums,** on Alexandra Road, are good; their holdings include Blackfoot costumes. Along Clarence Esplanade are many monuments, including one to the *Chesapeake*; an information bureau; and Southsea Castle. Off the Eastney Esplanade, at Eastney Officers' Mess, is the **Royal Marines Museum** (open Mon.–Fri., 10–4; Sat., Sun., 10–12) which contains despatches from the Battle of Bunker Hill, a recruiting poster for the American War and other Revolutionary objects, as well as association items (specially for the Boxer Rebellion) with the U.S. Marine Corps. There is a superb regimental medal collection.

Above all, one comes to Portsmouth to see the *H.M.S. Victory* (open weekdays 10–6 or dusk, Sun. at 1) in the Royal Dockyard. Launched in 1765, this was Admiral Horatio Nelson's flagship at the Battle of Trafalgar in 1805. The *Victory* has been brilliantly restored, and however little interest one may have in naval architecture, a visit here is certain to effect a conversion.

Lunchtime will be at hand. Portsmouth is a good place for a pub lunch – try the Lone Yachtsman, on the Point (beyond the Cathedral, at the entrance to the harbour, from High Street), to watch the warships – or drive on to Chichester, 17 miles east, and eat on the terrace at the Little

CHICHESTER

London Restaurant, or at the Cattle Market Inn, a pub overlooking the market square. Just south off the A27 between Portsmouth and Chichester is Bosham, where King Cnut ordered the tide to stop. Before reaching Chichester one passes Fishbourne; a vast Roman palace has been excavated here, and the museum is well worth visiting.

Chichester is a fine, small cathedral city. The Cathedral itself, while badly crumbling in places, has several magnificent features including a fine spire, perhaps the best medieval carvings in Britain, an Aubusson tapestry designed by John Piper and the splendid Arundel tomb. At Roussillon Barracks is the **Royal Sussex Regimental Museum** which holds several items relating to the French and Indian wars. The regiment suffered in the massacre at Fort William Henry, when the commanding officer was the Colonel Monro of James Fenimore Cooper's *Last of the Mohicans*. The regiment also took part at Bunker Hill, and in the battles for Brooklyn and White Plains. There is a good painting by John Smibert and a large diorama of the Battle of the Plains of Abraham in 1759. Also here is the Museum of the Royal Military Police. Just northeast of Chichester, off the A285, is Goodwood House (open April–Oct., Sun. and Wed., for luncheon tours beginning at 11.15 and tea tours beginning at 3.00) which contains a good collection of paintings, including Van Dyck and Canaletto, and excellent English and French furniture. Call ahead to reserve a place in the tours (no reservations needed June–Aug.).

Now strike for London, north on the A285. At Petworth (15 miles) is Petworth House, one of the most stunning in the whole of Britain (open April–Oct., Wed., Thurs., Sat., 2–6, with extra rooms shown on 1st and 3rd Tues.; park open daily). The grounds are by Capability Brown, the house by Salvin, the deer park by God, and the paintings by Turner, Reynolds, Gainsborough, Holbein, Rembrandt and Hals. Turn west at Petworth on the A272 to Midhurst, through the best of the Sussex country-side, and then north on the A286 to **Haslemere** where James Edward Oglethorpe, the founder of Georgia, was Member of Parliament. Each July the Dolmetsch Musical Festival presents medieval music played on old instruments. Tennyson lived here, and the path he followed to Black Down is still maintained; his last home, Aldworth, can be seen on the hill. Take the A286 northeast towards **Godalming,** a pleasant old town; the Meath Home for Epileptics, near the railway station (watch for signs left) was once the home of Oglethorpe. Just northwest is **Charterhouse School,** at which Roger Williams, and such figures as Addison and Steele, Lovelace, Barrow, Blackstone, Crashaw, Wesley, Thackeray, Baden-Powell, Ralph Vaughan Williams and Max Beerbohm studied.

The A3100 carries on to Guildford. The new University of Surrey is here and there is an attractive High Street, but it is the new Cathedral, begun in 1936 and completed in 1964, that draws visitors. Stark and institutional on the outside, the Cathedral contains several interior features of interest.

The A31 running west of town along the Hog's Back offers excellent views, or if time and inclination have run out continue to London on the A3 through **Esher,** where Thomas Hooker, the founder of Hartford, Connecticut, was the rector.

WHAT TO READ   Jane Austen, of course, Tennyson, Hardy and Bret Harte. But also Scott, who wrote *Waverley* after a visit to the ruined abbey in Elstead, near Guildford, and *Daniel Deronda,* which George Eliot wrote while living in Witley, near Godalming. Dickens collected much local color for *Nicholas Nickleby* in Portsmouth, and Sir Arthur Conan Doyle began his medical practice there: Dr. Watson is modeled on a Portsmouth friend of Doyle's. *A Study in Scarlet, The Sign of Four,* and *The White Company* were written there.

5 Knole and nearby Kent and Surrey

A particularly popular day trip out of London takes one to Knole, one of the most interesting of the country estates, and into the sections of Kent and Surrey that are immediately adjacent to London. If you do not have time to press further into the countryside, this trip offers an opportunity to see something of the nature of London's suburbs, to sample a few American-related sites and to be back in London comfortably by dinner. With careful attention to timetables, you can also make the entire circuit by public transport, first by train from Charing Cross Station to Seven-oaks, and then by Green Line buses through moderately built-up sections of the countryside. You may have a pleasant pub lunch at the Spotted Dog in Penshurst or at the Castle Inn in Chiddingstone, and in the evening either return to London to try a restaurant on the south side of the Thames or have a leisurely meal at the Dorincourt Hotel in Warlingham, coming back afterwards by train from Croydon. Or sacrifice Croydon – no great loss – to stay in Westerham to dine at Le Marquis de Montcalm, back-to-back with Quebec House (must book).

If driving, leave London on the A21 through Lewisham and Bromley to **Sevenoaks.** Jeffrey Amherst lived here, and he is buried in the parish church. Passing through the town, you find Knole (open Wed.–Sat., 10–12, 2–3, closed Dec.–Feb.) on the left, just after a junction with the A225. Seat of the Sackville family, this is probably the largest baronial mansion in Britain with a reputed 365 rooms. Begun in 1486, it is closely associated with the Sackville-West family, and with Virginia Woolf's *Orlando*. The deer park is attractive, and the fine collection of furniture and paintings (Van Dyck, Holbein, and others) is worth seeing. A few miles east on

KNOLE

country roads is Ightham Mote, a handsome old manor house (open April–Oct., Fri., 2–5) and a further mile southeast is **Shipbourne.** Sir Harry Vane, a Puritan, went to America from here in 1635 and became governor of Massachusetts. He later returned to England, and in the Civil War was executed for taking the Cromwellian side.

Continue south to Tonbridge and turn west beyond it on the B2176 to Penshurst. Here is Penshurst Place (open Easter–Sept., Tues.–Thurs., Sat.–Sun., 2–6), in the possession of the Sidney family since 1552. Sir Philip Sidney was born here; there is a good collection of art. 2 miles west is Chiddingstone, an almost too-perfect Elizabethan village that has been kept much as it was; the entire town is under the care of the National Trust. 2 miles further west is **Hever Castle** (open Easter–Sept., Wed., Sun., 2–7) where Henry VIII met Anne Boleyn. It has a working draw-bridge, handsome gardens, and was the property of the Astor family, the American millionaires. You can walk on country paths, well posted, from Penshurst through to Hever in an hour and a half, or follow the winding B2176 and well-marked country lanes.

Carry through via the B269 and right on the B2026 to **Chartwell.** This was the country home of Sir Winston Churchill (open March–Nov., Wed.–Thurs., 2–6, Sat.–Sun., 11–6). Churchill's studio, his garden, and several American mementoes, as well as black swans from Western Australia and the brick fence Churchill laid, make this an interesting (and frequently crowded) place of pilgrimage.

The B2026 enters Westerham. In the village are statues of Churchill and General Wolfe. The latter was born here, and he lived in **Quebec House** (open March–Oct., Tues.–Wed., Sun., 2–6) as a youth. The house was preserved through the intervention of Joseph Learmont of Montreal. Many relics relating to Wolfe may be seen in **Squerryes Court** (open March–Oct., Wed., Sat.–Sun., 2–6). The **parish church** also contains a memorial window to Wolfe. Follow the A25 west from Westerham to the A22, and then turn right into **Croydon.** Here was Bethlem Royal Hospital, the oldest hospital in the world for the insane – it was popularly called Bedlam. John Singleton Copley, the painter, is buried in St John's Church in Croydon, and Thomas Hutchinson, controversial governor of Massachusetts in the 1770s, is also buried here. The Selsdon Park Bird Sanctuary contains benches in memory of American benefactors. Return to central London on the A23.

WHAT TO READ   There is little time for reading on an outing such as this. But the delightful and lighthearted guide, *Here's England,* by Ruth McKenney and Richard Bransten, makes a good companion on a bus. Penshurst and Knole are rich in literary, and related American, associations, of course. Since E. M. Forster went to school in Tonbridge, this might be the appropriate moment to read *Maurice.* A superb novel for reading in hunting country, which reminds us of what we like most and dislike most about the British, is Isabel Colegate's *The Shooting Party.*

6　St. Albans and the Chiltern Hills

Both St Albans and the Chilterns are popular outings from London. One may do either without a car, depending on the Green Line buses, although to combine them in a single day requires having wheels of your own. The line that divides this trip from number 4 is the M40 motorway.

Leave London going north on the M1 to exit number 6, then right on the A405 to St Albans, entering on the A412. The cathedral here was originally an abbey, founded in the 8th century by Offa of Mercia; it received its present status in 1877. The nave is the longest in any Gothic cathedral in the world. Mural paintings from the 13th century, an exceptional reredos, and the fine Ramryge chantry are among the best features. One of the finest brasses known, of Thomas de la Mare, is in the chantry. To the west is the Roman city of Verulamium, with extensive excavations, a theatre, hypocaust and museum. Ye Old Fighting Cocks, once a monks' fishing lodge, is east of the dig; it is one of the oldest inns in Britain. North of St Albans are Ayot St Lawrence (Shaw's Corner), Knebworth House, and Stevenage. 2 miles west is Gorhambury House (open May–Sept., Thurs. afternoons) which contains relics of Francis Bacon and beyond is **Hemel Hempstead,** a well-planned satellite town from which the founder of Topsfield, Massachusetts, emigrated. (Just south is **Kings Langley,** according to Debrett's the ancestral home of President Jimmy Carter.)

North of Hemel Hempstead the A4146 enters the low Chiltern Hills. To the left is Little Gaddesden and the Ashridge Estate, an attractive drive, while ahead and to the right on the B4506 is Whipsnade Zoo, the country zoo for London and one of the most pleasant in Europe. Southwest on the

B4506 is Berkhamsted, an attractive town with a ruined castle and moat. Follow the A41 west to **Tring.** The baptismal register here refers to the Washington family. At Aston Clinton, beyond Tring on the A41, there is one of the most famous restaurants in England, The Bell, which warranted a top entry in the *Good Food Guide* for 25 years. Westwards again is Aylesbury, to which the duck is no longer limited, and which is a good town for walking in once one has found the middle. West on the A41 is **Waddesdon Manor** (open Easter–Oct., Wed.–Sun. 2–6), designed like a French chateau and built in the 19th century by Baron Ferdinand de Rothschild. It holds the rolltop desk that belonged to Baron de Beaumarchais, on which the title pages of two pamphlets of the Revolutionary War are reproduced in marquetry on the writing slide. South on country roads at Lower Winchendon is **Nether Winchenden House.** This was the home of Sir Francis Bernard, colonial Governor of Massachusetts.

Return to Aylesbury on the A418 from just beyond Lower Winchendon, follow the road right into the A413 to **Wendover,** and then right on the B4010. Left at Butler's Cross is Chequers, the country residence of the British Prime Minister (not open to the public). It was presented to the country in 1921 by Lord Lee of Fareham and his American wife, Ruth Moore of New York. The road turns into the A4010 to **West Wycombe,** joining the A40 at West Wycombe Park, which is a National Trust property of 300 acres; Benjamin Franklin visited here as a guest of Sir Francis Dashwood in 1773 (open daily, July–Aug., 2.15–6). In High Wycombe the **Castle Hill Art Gallery and Museum** (open Mon., Tues., Thurs.–Sat., 10–5.30) contains a fine exhibit on the evolution of the Windsor chair and a portrait of Lord Shelburne, by Sir Joshua Reynolds. Shelburne was the British Prime Minister who made peace with the former colonies. Just north off the A4128 is Hughenden Manor (open Feb.–Dec., daily except Tues. 2–6, Sat.–Sun. open 12.30), home of Benjamin Disraeli. It is now the Disraeli Memorial Museum; he is buried in the nearby churchyard.

Retrace your route to High Wycombe and leave again going northeast on the A404 to Hazlemere. 2 miles southeast on the B474 is **Penn;** the church contains brasses thought to be associated with William Penn, and there are Penn tombs in the nave. Beyond the church take the second road to the left, just before entering **Beaconsfield** (Edmund Burke is buried in the parish churchyard and G. K. Chesterton lived here for years – his memorial is in St Teresa's Roman Catholic church), go across the A335 and straight on a further 2 miles to **Jordans.** William Penn is buried at the Quaker Meeting House here. There is also a famous old barn reputed to have been built from timbers taken from the *Mayflower.*

Continuing north on a country road through Jordans one comes to Chalfont St Giles; here is the 'pretty box', a cottage (open Feb.–Oct., daily except Tues., 10–1, 2.15–6, Sun. at 2.15; Nov.–Jan., Sat.–Sun., same hours) in which John Milton sought refuge from the plague in London. The cottage is dark and Milton was already blind when he moved here, to

ST ALBANS

complete *Paradise Lost*. Across the A413 is **Chorleywood,** where William Penn was married; then to the right on the A404 is **Rickmansworth,** where Penn lived at Basing House in the High Street. The A412 south carries one into the A40, which brings one back to Regent's Park. If dinner outside London is wanted, the Magnolia House in Beaconsfield (43 Aylesbury End) offers an excellent late meal.

WHAT TO READ   This has been William Penn country, of course, and any good biography of the founder of Pennsylvania makes a suitable travelling companion. Milton should be at hand. A fresh experience might be Disraeli's novels, especially *Sybil* and *Coningsby*, both of which wear very well today. Berkhamsted is Graham Greene country, however, and I confess to not following my own advice: I never read a biography of Penn, but instead put up at The Bell at Aston Clinton for two nights and revisited Greene's early books.

7 Bath
Bristol
The south Cotswolds

It is possible to see both Bath and Bristol in a single day from London by leaving early and returning late, travelling both ways by train. Two days are obviously better, especially if you wish to see anything of the surrounding countryside, and three days better yet. There are several excellent restaurants in Bath and Bristol, one of the most striking of all cathedrals is only 21 miles from Bristol by car, while Longleat, one of the outstanding English country houses, is the same distance from Bath. I strongly recommend that you give yourself three days, therefore, since this is one of the loveliest sections of England, with cultural possibilities second only to London and Oxbridge, and with a number of American-related sites as well. Further, Bath in particular requires exploring on foot. You can, if you wish, also include Cheltenham and Gloucester in an extended circular tour, if you hire a car and add a day or so more. You can journey to Bath from London by train and on the second day hire a car there (booked in advance, of course). Upon completion of your journey you may drop the car in Bristol or Bath and return to London by train. Or, if you prefer, you may drive directly from London on the M4 in two and a half hours.

The frequent trains to Bath leave from Paddington, the station noted as Sherlock Holmes' most common point of departure from London, and for the children's stories of Paddington Bear. There are better reasons than these for arriving a few minutes early so that you may look at the station, however, for it is the most individual and romantic of London's terminals. Built in 1854, it is redolent of the Victorian age. There is a plaque to Isambard Kingdom Brunel, designer of the Great Western line which ran from Paddington to Bristol, on the wall opposite number 1 platform. Once under way, if you watch carefully from the left side of the train, you can see the Uffington White Horse, a huge pagan figure cut into the chalk downs in the Iron Age, shortly before Swindon. (And a stop for an hour and a quarter between trains in Swindon would enable you to visit the excellent Great Western Railway Museum there. The **North Star,** a broad-gauge locomotive on view here in replica, was built for the New Orleans Railway, which did not accept delivery, so that it became the Great Western's first major locomotive.)

Bath comes high on nearly everyone's list of cities. Small – 85,000 – and elegant, it captures the best of Georgian England, as well as offering Roman ruins worth visiting even though you may be going on to Italy. Badly bombed during World War II, much of the city has been rebuilt. It has good museums, one of the most beautiful abbeys in England, and a handsome surrounding countryside. It also has exceptionally good restaurants, and since Beau Nash, a leader of London society, took up residence there in 1705, it has enjoyed continuous popularity as a spa. The Bath Festival, under the direction of Yehudi Menuhin, is held here each summer. **American associations** are numerous: among the most interesting are those with Major John André, who was hanged as a spy near Tappan, New York, in 1780, on the orders of George Washington; and scenes from Booth Tarkington's *Monsieur Beaucaire.* Sir Henry Frankland, collector for the Port of Boston prior to the American Revolution, is buried here, and at nearby Claverton Manor is the American Museum.

Upon leaving the railway station, proceed on foot directly up Manvers Street and left at the circus. Here is Bath Abbey with its back to you. (Opposite the Abbey is the information bureau where, from 10 to 5.15, you may obtain a map of the city.) Founded in 1499, the handsome Abbey merits close study, for it is both ostentatious (especially when viewed from the front) and also serenely aware of the history around it, as embodied in the many interior monuments. Particularly interesting are the carved figures of ascending and descending angels on ladders, on the west front exterior; the very fine fan vaulting inside; the memorial to Arthur Phillip, as 'founder and first governor of Australia'; and the wrought iron screens. There is a monument to **Senator William Bingham,** a Philadelphia-born banker who, in 1781, founded the business which became the Bank of North America. He served in the Continental Congress and the Senate and was the founder of Binghamton, New York. Bingham died in Bath in 1804. **Thomas Pownall,** Governor of Massachusetts 1751–60, is buried in the Abbey.

Near the Abbey are the ruins of the Roman Baths, after which the city takes its name (open daily 9–6, winter close 5). A statue of the Emperor Hadrian gazes down upon the Great Bath, one of four baths now to be seen. They and the museum behind them provide the best understanding

of Roman Britain you can obtain south of Hadrian's Wall. You can have
a drink from the Roman reservoir by visiting the Pump Room (open 9–6,
winter close 5), where there is a fountain or, if you prefer, you can have
morning coffee to music. From the Baths you may then walk north, into
Union Street, and carry on up Milsom Street to George Street. Here, if you
have booked in advance, is a restaurant regarded by many, at least until
recently, as one of the best in Britain: The Hole in the Wall. Whether the
ham soufflé with champagne and orange sauce and the salmon *en croûte*
with ginger are served well or not, this restaurant at 16 George Street will
still be better than most. A taxi ride to the Priory Hotel on the A431 will
also produce an excellent meal. (This is, incidentally, an attractive small
hotel for the night, if you do not plan to go on to Bristol so soon.) Two
blocks to the north of George Street are the Assembly Rooms, where the
world's largest **Museum of Costume** will demand an hour or more of your
time (open 9.30–6; winter 10–5). A number of American heiresses married into European nobility, and they are credited with introducing the
Gibson girl look, nicely shown in the museum, to Britain. There are
several items relating to America here, and the most unusual room is the
one devoted entirely to women's underwear. You will also see the costume
worn by F. D. R. at his inauguration in 1933, donated by Eleanor and the
Marchioness of Reading.

A block west is **The Circus,** on the way to Royal Crescent: at nos. 7 and
8, lived William Pitt, Earl of Chatham, America's closest friend during the
Revolution (whose statue a group of titled British sought to give to the
United States as a Bicentennial gift), while the luckless Major André was
at no. 22. David Livingstone lived in 13, Clive of India in 14, and Gainsborough in 24. Thomas Pownall also stayed at no. 22.

The single handsomest street in Britain is usually said to be Royal
Crescent, a magnificent sweep of 114 Ionic columns and 30 houses, on
which a number of the doors are marked with small notices of the famous.
You may go into no. 1 to see a Georgian interior. Having seen Lansdown
Crescent too, you will agree with America's William Dean Howells, that
Bath's houses are the handsomest in the world. Unhappily, a number fell
under the bombing of World War II.

Returning to the Abbey, and bearing left along the Grand Parade, one
reaches the **Art Gallery** (open daily except Sun., 10–6). Then right across
the River Avon via Argyle Street, you come into Great Pulteney Street
(**Admiral Lord Howe** lived at number 71) at the end of which lies the
Holburne of Menstrie Museum and Gallery (closed Wed.). They hold a
miniature of George Washington by Henry Bond, after Gilbert Stuart, and
two Joshua Shaws. Jane Austen lived for a number of years at 4 Sydney
Place and several houses are marked with discreet brass plaques along
these streets, indicating famous literary and historical figures who lived
within. This is true also of North Parade, which crosses the Avon by the

ROYAL CRESCENT

next bridge to the south; here, at no. 11, lived **Edmund Burke,** the friend of the colonies during the approaching Revolution. (Oliver Goldsmith lived there too.) Another American-related address of note is 5 Trim Street, in the middle of the town, where **General Wolfe** once resided.

By rental car or taxi leave Bath on the Salisbury road, the A36, to Claverton, thence right to **Claverton Manor, The American Museum in Britain** (for a description, see section on ART GALLERIES AND MUSEUMS). Even if you are not interested in America while in England, this excellent museum – which provides eighteen rooms furnished in different American regional and period manners, as well as an herb garden – is rewarding. Its journal, *America in Britain,* is useful reading. Founded in 1961, the museum is associated with the John Judkyn Memorial, which provides for travelling exhibits of Americana to go out to British schools and shows. Between them they own over forty American paintings, including a Thomas Sully and a Benjamin West. (Why not help by joining the Friends of the American Museum, Halcyon Foundation, 228 East 49th Street, N.Y.?)

You can return to central Bath past the Bath University of Technology, and carry on by the A4 west to Bristol, or continue south on the A36 for a circle tour through Warminster to Longleat House, Frome, Wells, the Cheddar Gorge and into Bristol.

• Warminster is 18 miles along the A36, at the edge of Salisbury Plain. It is here that the greatest number of British UFO sightings have been reported, and the village is associated with such sci-fi movies as *The Village of the Damned*. You can carry on toward Salisbury, to join with Tour 4, or turn right on the A362 and then left to Longleat House, one of the most interesting of the great country estates (see section on COUNTRY HOUSES) and probably *the* most rewarding for children. If you have time for only two or three visits to country houses in Britain, this should be one of them, for as George III said after his visit in 1789, 'Everything at Longleat is very good.' Go boating on the lake – with any luck a seal will leap into your boat. And don't fail to walk in the great park, planned by Capability Brown (open daily, 10–6, winter close at 4).

• A few miles further on is **Frome,** from which came the Cabell family of Virginia, perhaps best known from James Branch Cabell's *Jurgen*. Turn left on the A361, and do not by-pass Nunney, for here is an attractive village with a lovely, small moated castle. (North 4 miles is Mells, where the church contains a memorial to the Horner family of Little Jack Horner fame.) Further along the A361, at Shepton Mallet, are two excellent examples of how good small English country hotels can be, and if you can arrange a night in either, preceded by dinner and/or followed by break-fast, do so: Bowlish House, off the Wells Road on the far side of town, and Charlton House Hotel, on the Frome Road as you enter, with four and thirteen rooms respectively, so you must book. The church here has 300 bosses, none of them repeated. And one of England's most interesting restaurants lies 10 miles ahead, the Miners' Arms at Priddy, beyond Wells. Leave Shepton Mallet going north on the A37, then left on B3135, and you will come to it; a lonely whitewashed restaurant open only for dinner (and then not on Sunday) except for lunch on Sunday. The owners main-tain a snail farm, experiment with frozen foods, and behave quite indi-vidually. The best Cheddar in England, which comes from nearby Chewton Mendip, is served here, as is draught cider from an agricultural research station, and dishes with names like Priddy Oggy and Priddy Oyster. Nearby are the St Cuthbert Lead Works, the most extensive remains of lead smelting in England, which closed in 1908. Take care if exploring these and other examples of industrial archaeology in the Mendips.

• 4 miles southeast of Priddy, or 6 miles west of Shepton Mallet, is Wells. The cathedral here is unusual and immensely appealing. Its West Front merits closer study than any other in Britain, for it is the richest of all in medieval sculpture. A medieval close has survived almost without change, and the chapter house is unusually fine. Children will enjoy what may be the most famous clock (save for Big Ben) in England: made in 1390, it sends armed horsemen into rotation as it strikes, with a knight being felled at each rotation of the men. Needlework on the stall seats and backs is unusual, and the library is delightfully medieval with its chained books. But it is the nearly 400 statues of the West Front, called 'the richest receptacle of thirteenth-century sculpture in England', that brings one to this tiny cathedral city, which is often compared to Anthony Trollope's Barchester, of the *Chronicles of Barsetshire.* Just beyond Wells are the **Wookey Hole Caves,** of which much is made; unless you are deeply interested in Iron Age artifacts, you will not find much to interest you, even with its exhibit of fairground carved animals (including American), and the best course is to turn south for Glastonbury.

• For here, along the A39 at Glastonbury, is one of the sites in Britain most intimately associated with King Arthur and the legends of the Round Table (the other most important is Tintagel). The ruined abbey, said to have been founded by Joseph of Arimathaea, who brought the Holy Grail here, is of great interest. The abbot's kitchen, dating from the 14th century, is the most complete medieval kitchen to survive in Europe. Sir Bedivere lived in the abbey as a hermit after Arthur's death, if one follows Sir Thomas Malory's *Morte d'Arthur.* Glastonbury was built on platforms out over the water between the 2nd century B.C. and the coming of the Romans, and one may visit the Lake Village Museum to see what one otherwise sees best in Switzerland: remnants of the ancient Iron Age lake villages. Glastonbury is regarded as 'the birthplace of English Christianity' for you may walk in the footsteps of St Joseph of Arimathaea and St Dunstan, and visit the Blood Spring (also called the Chalice Well) where the Holy Grail was buried. As Alfred Lord Tennyson wrote:

> The cup, the cup itself, from which our Lord
> Drank at the last sad supper with his own.
>
> Arimathaean Joseph journeying brought
> To Glastonbury, where the winter thorn
> Blossoms at Christmas, mindful of our Lord.

• On a country road southeast of Street, on the A39, is **Barton St David.** From here emigrated the first member of the Adams family, ancestor to John Quincy. There is a tablet in the church. In **Bridgwater,** 15 miles further west on the A39, in the Admiral Blake Museum, one may see relics of the Confederate ship *Alabama,* the famous scourge of the seas during the American Civil War (open daily 10–1, 2–5, closing at 1 Tues.). (West on the A39 at Nether Stowey is the cottage once occupied by Samuel Taylor Coleridge – open daily except Sat.) South on the A38 11 miles is **Taunton,** famous for its cider. The Shire Hall contains busts of Somerset figures, including Henry Fielding, to whom James Russell Lowell wrote his line, 'Who loves a Man may see his image here'. The Somerset County Museum includes ships' flags captured by men of the XIIIth Light Infantry on Lake Champlain in 1813. Further on is **Wellington,** whose monument crowns a nearby hill. In the parish church is a memorial to Sir John Popham, who ordered exploration of the Maine coast.

• From Wells one may otherwise turn toward Priddy and descend the Cheddar Gorge on the B3135, or drive west on the A371 and then ascend the gorge. Either drive is an attractive one, although the gorge is very modest by most standards, and rather over-commercialized. Axbridge, just past the Gorge on the A371, is an interesting old town. Turn right on the A38 for Bristol and right again on the A368 for Burrington. At the gorge here one may seek shelter within the cleft rock in which Augustus Montague Toplady sought protection from a thunderstorm. After this experience this 18th century clergyman wrote the words to the hymn 'Rock of Ages – cleft for me,/Let me hide myself in thee.'

• Return to the A38, turn right, then left on the B3133, then right, bringing one to **Wrington;** here, in 1632, John Locke was born, as were two of the Pilgrims' wives. One may continue on to the A370, and by turning right reach Bristol, via **Long Ashton.** Sir Ferdinando Gorges, the 'father of colonization in America', who founded two Plymouth companies to aid settlement in New England, and who, in 1639, was named proprietor of Maine, was born and is buried here. Further on is the A38 once again, which leads you into Bristol.

Bristol is a handsome city of nearly half a million. When Americans are asked where in England, after London, they would most like to live, many of them choose Bristol. It has a great university, a fine theatre – the Bristol Old Vic – good restaurants, an excellent art gallery and museum, and a happily compact central area so that one may see much fairly quickly. Bear left at the roundabout, through the handsome Queen Square, past the floating dock, to College Green, where you may park opposite the cathedral.

If you are hungry, Bristol offers five restaurants in the *Good Food Guide.* Certainly the most interesting is very near you: from College Green, return toward the dock, then turn left into Denmark Street, where at no. 12 is Harvey's (not open for Sat. lunch or on Sun.). Run by the house of Harvey, one dines in a wine cellar, sampling one's way through a fine variety of sherries, to end with Harvey's Bristol Cream, surely one of the most satisfying of pre- and after-dinner drinks (if you want to flaunt your Americanism, you *can* get it on the rocks since Harvey's has taken to advertising it that way).

Bristol Cathedral was the first great 'hall-church' in Europe, and it is architecturally one of the most interesting in England. The choir, and the view from it, are regarded as finer than any in Europe of the same period (1298–1330). Richard Hakluyt, who compiled the first accounts of North American exploration and, as the creator of the *Reader's Digest* of his day, stimulated much interest in America, is memorialized in the Cathedral's north choir aisle. The chapter house is one of the finest Norman rooms in England, while the arches in the Lady Chapel are the tallest. Many memorials attest to the close connection Bristol had with the West Indian trade (and the slave trade). The Rumsey candlesticks which stand on the altar in the eastern Lady Chapel, dated 1712, were a thank-offering for the safe return of two ships which voyaged around the world, one of which brought back from the Juan Fernandez Islands Alexander Selkirk, who was Daniel Defoe's Robinson Crusoe. The Cathedral lost its library in the Reform Riots of 1831.

Now step out into the city. Many communities in the United States have taken their name from it, for it was one of the major points of departure for emigrants. The first all-steam crossing of the Atlantic, by Brunel's *Great Western* in 1838, was from Bristol to New York. Brunel's railway provided the journey from London and one overnighted at his hotel in Bristol. Many places relating to America – as well as a great deal else – were destroyed during the seventy-seven bombing raids the city sustained in World War II, but much remains. From Bristol came the family of **James Russell Lowell;** from here came the American cotton textile industry in the person of **Francis Cabot Lowell;** from here sailed **John Cabot,** explorer of the Atlantic, who reached Cape Breton Island in 1497; here may have been born **Sebastian Cabot,** founder of the Society of Merchant Adventurers; **Elizabeth Blackwell,** one of the first women doctors, who was to organize hospitals in New York, was born here. And a New York-born man, **Henry Cruger,** was mayor of Bristol and M.P. during the American revolution.

Opposite the Cathedral, across the green, is the Lord Mayor's Chapel (to the left is the curving facade of the Council House), the only church in England owned by a city corporation. Of no special note when viewed from the outside, the interior contains the finest collection of monumental church sculpture in Britain, a fine floor of Spanish tiles and a dazzling array of stained glass, including some from William Beckford's 19th century Gothic dream, Fonthill Abbey. Upon leaving the chapel, turn right up Park Street. To the left is the **Merchants House** museum and, just beyond, Brandon Hill, on which stands **Cabot Tower,** erected in 1897 for the 400th anniversary of John Cabot's discoveries. A tablet here is dedicated to peace and friendship between Britain and America. The Thomas Chatterton house, birthplace of the boy poet, lies further up Park Street (open Wed., Sat., 3–5). At the top one reaches the university, the museum, and the **art gallery,** all excellent. On the outer art gallery wall is a plaque to **Colonel Henry Washington,** grandson of Lawrence Washington, who on July 26, 1643, attacked the Parliamentary defenders of Bristol from near here, effecting a breach which allowed the entry of the Royalist troops. The gallery holds the Sharples Collection of ninety-seven works by members of the family, most of them of early American figures, among them the only original profile portrait of **George Washington** in existence, and seven other American works, including one attributed to Gilbert Stuart – a portrait of Henry Cruger. The museum has an excellent collection of toys.

Return now to your car, and head east, then left, to the top of the lengthy roundabout (interesting buildings here) into Marsh, Corn, and Wine streets in succession, where there is a car park. Walk east to **St Peter's Church,** in fact a ruin because of German bombs; here were monuments to the Bristol merchants who purchased Monhegan Island, off the coast of Maine, in 1626. Retrace your steps to the bottom of Corn Street, to **St Stephen's Church.** Here is a monument to Martin Pringe, buried here in 1626, explorer of Maine's coasts in 1603 and a Virginia landholder. The Portland Street **Wesleyan Methodist Chapel** was founded by Captain Thomas Webb, an early leader of American Methodism; within is a stained glass window dedicated to him. In St Augustine's Parade by the roundabout there is a statue of **Edmund Burke,** who was member of Parliament for Bristol 1774–80. From here Cabot sailed in the *Matthew,* when the present gardens were part of the old dock.

Once more return to your car, and follow High Street to the Bristol Bridge and into Redcliffe Street, to the right, thence to a roundabout, beyond which is a car park on the right and the magnificence of **St Mary Redcliffe** directly ahead. This, one of the largest churches in England, would dwarf half the cathedrals in the land. Queen Elizabeth I considered it the most beautiful church she knew, and its lavish north porch and the exceptional array of brasses and monuments inside, set it apart even in Bristol. At the west end is a monument to **Sir William Penn,** father of Pennsylvania's founder; above hang his weapons and pennants. The Chapel of St John the Baptist is known as **The American Chapel,** since it was restored by the Friends of St Mary Redcliffe in the United States; the arms of the thirteen original states and the seven original dioceses may be seen on the kneelers. Below the tower is a rib of a cow-whale, brought by John and Sebastian Cabot after discovering Newfoundland; the brothers can be seen in the south transept window. On the north side of the chancel is a brass, marking the grave of John Brook, who paid John Cabot for his discovery; another is to Richard Amerike, sheriff of Bristol when Cabot returned. Above the outer north porch is a muniment room in which Thomas Chatterton wrote his verses, and in the north choir aisle is a window to Handel. Chatterton is buried in the churchyard. Both Southey and Coleridge were married in this church. Don't forget to look for the grave of the church cat, also in the yard.

Return once again via Queen Square to the Cathedral, and continue past it on the A4. Here is Westbury College, where John Wycliffe, he who launched the first translation of the Bible into English, was a prebend. Beyond is the Clifton Suspension Bridge, based on designs prepared by Isambard Kingdom Brunel, which was considered an engineering triumph when it was thrown across the Avon Gorge in 1831–59. And near the junction of the rivers Frome and Avon, on a shed facing Wapping Road, is a plaque marking the site of **William Patterson's shipyard,** where the

Great Western was launched in 1837. Brunel's second great ship, the *Great Britain*, was floated in 1843; it won all the trans-Atlantic crossing records, brought British troops to Canada during the war scare of 1861–2, when Britain feared a Northern attack on Canada during the Civil War, and it now floats again in Bristol's dock. The present **Wapping Dry Dock,** then called the Great Western Dry Dock, is the site of the launch; it is within Hill's Albion Dockyard and is still in use. An alternative is to leave the middle of the town on the A4018 and make a point of visiting Blaise Castle House Folk Museum, at Henbury, off the A4018 shortly before it connects with the M5; here is a thatched dairy and the fine old Stratford Water Mill (open daily May–Sept. 2–6, Oct.–April 2–4.30, opening an hour later Sun.).

Thornbury is 12 miles north of Bristol via the A38 and B4606. Here is Thornbury Castle, a vast and rambling structure in which may be found the restaurant regarded by many as the finest in Britain. Only dinner is served, except on Sunday when lunch is substituted, and the hours are scanty: 12–2.30 on that Sunday, 7–10 on those evenings. The dining room is chilly, so dress warmly, and plan on a relaxing evening here. On a country road to the west, signposted Littleton, then **Elberton,** is the birthplace of Joseph Sturge, the Quaker who travelled in America with John Greenleaf Whittier, and who was a leader in the anti-slavery movement.

If returning from Bristol to London by train, drop your car at Temple Meads Station – the finest early (1840) railway terminal still in use in England – near St Mary Redcliffe. Trains leave until after 8.00 each evening and take up to two and a quarter hours to reach Paddington Station. Or you may choose to spend another day or two in the West Country and take a circuit north to Gloucester, Cheltenham and Cirencester, thence returning either to Bristol or driving on to Oxford. This circuit is a particularly attractive one, passing through the southern Cotswolds and including a fine cathedral, Britain's most interesting wildfowl refuge, a number of villages with American associations and Castle Combe, to this writer the most perfect of the Cotswold villages. (This village may also be reached easily from Bath, being only 15 miles away.)

• If you do decide to extend your trip, leave Bristol on the A38, past Thornbury. To the left on the B4066 is **Berkeley Castle,** where Edward II was murdered in 1327. The castle has been the home of the Berkeleys since 1153 and the family is closely associated with colonial Virginia. There is a fine Elizabethan garden and ancient bowling alley in the grounds (open Good Friday to Sept. 30, daily except Mon., 2–5.30). Shortly beyond, off the A38 at Slimbridge, is The Wildfowl Trust, where Peter Scott, son of the Arctic explorer, has brought together the largest collection of waterfowl in the world (open daily from 9.30, Sun. from 12). The A38 then brings one to Gloucester, 35 miles from Bristol. (If you wish to omit the above, the new M5 will have you there in 30 minutes.) **Button Gwinnett,** one of the original signers of the Declaration of Independence, was born in Gloucester.

• The **Cathedral** at Gloucester was begun in 1089. In atmosphere, and in its cloisters and Lady Chapel, it is among the best in England; it has the earliest fan vaulting in the country, a fine setting, and a monument to **John Stafford Smith,** son of the organist of the Cathedral, who composed the tune that became the **Star Spangled Banner.** The tombs of Robert, Duke of Normandy, and of the John Machen family, are very fine, as is the tomb of the murdered Edward II. The sculptures of a heavenly orchestra on the choir vault, the so-called Crécy window, the exceptional Great Cloister, and the monks' washing place are worth seeing. There is also a fine monument to Edward Jenner, inventor of smallpox vaccine.

• Gloucester is a compact city, and one may see most of it in an easy walk. The Folk Museum is interesting, especially in its displays devoted to fishing – it is in Bishop Hooper's House, to the west on Westgate Street from the front of the cathedral. **St Mary de Crypt Church** and the City Museum and Art Gallery will repay a visit, as will the **Bell Tavern,** where George Whitefield, the first great missionary to the colonies, was born. Whitefield was regarded as the greatest religious orator of his day, and it is said that when he preached his first sermon, in St Mary de Crypt, fifteen persons were driven mad.

• For a most unusual sight, drive 5 miles west of Gloucester on the A40 and A48 to Minsterworth, on the right bank of the Severn. Here at high tide in February to April and August to October one may see the Severn Bore, a tidal wave sometimes 6 feet high, which roars upstream with great force for 8 miles. (For information on tides, call the Severn River Authority.) And at Newent, 10 miles west of Gloucester on the A40 and B4215 is the unique Falconry Centre (open except Tues., 10.30–5.30) with a museum of world-wide falconry.

• Continue north of Gloucester on the A38. A country road, east, goes to **Down Hatherley,** where **Button Gwinnett** lived. One may carry on on the A38 to Tewkesbury, where alleyways, narrow streets, timbered buildings, and a supremely fine Norman abbey with excellent stained glass, combine to create a particularly attractive town. Some identify George Eliot's *Mill on the Floss* with the old mill here (but see Gainsborough, Lincolnshire). The medieval tombs in the abbey are regarded as possibly the finest in England. 7 miles north on the B4080 is **Eckington,** where George Soule, a Pilgrim, was born.

• From Tewkesbury turn east on the A438, then right to the A435 to Bishop's Cleeve. Here is my chosen restaurant of the many excellent ones on this tour: Cleeveway House, a 17th century creation of Cotswold stone. The food is imaginative and cheerfully served, the wine is excellent, the lawns are well manicured, and the atmosphere is leisurely. You must book, the house is not open for dinner on Sunday and if there for lunch,

GLOUCESTER CATHEDRAL

you have only 12–1.45 available to you. Now take the narrow country
road to the top of Cleeve Hill, on which there is the remarkable Belas
Knapp long barrow, of ancient times. Turn left 6 miles on the A46 to the
handsome Sudeley Castle (open Easter–Sept., daily except Mon., Fri.,
1.30–5.30) or right to follow the A46 into Cheltenham.

• Cheltenham has an air of gentility starting to fade. An old spa, to which
George III and Lord Tennyson both went, it remains famous for Cheltenham Ladies College, oh so nice, and a somewhat esoteric annual music
festival. It is said that more colonels retire to Cheltenham than to any
other place in England. If you wish to enjoy an upper middle class English
meal which won't be half bad, pop out to the Moorend Park Hotel (you
can stay there too) just east of town. Walk The Promenade, for it *is*
exceptionally handsome, and the antique shops are very good. The Public
Library, Art Gallery and Museum, all in one, are good value; there is a
collection of **American coins,** including a 1776 dollar. Just south of the

town off the B4070 is **Leckhampton,** with an excellent view of Cheltenham; here is a memorial to the colonial treasurer of Virginia, Colonel Henry Norwood, who before retirement, was M.P. for Gloucester. 12 miles southeast of Cheltenham via the A40 is Chedworth Roman Villa, one of the finest in England (open except Mon. 10–1, 2–7).

• Follow the A46 south from Cheltenham to Stroud, nestled in a deep valley, and bear left here on the A419 for a most attractive drive through Sapperton (off the main road to the left), home of the poet laureate John Masefield, to Cirencester, the 'capital of the Cotswolds', an ancient Roman town with a fine parish church – the fourth largest in England. The Corinium Museum is devoted to the Roman period. The Thames rises just south of here. Leave town southwards on the A429, then turn left after about 10 miles on the B4040 and watch for a country road, right, to **Garsdon,** where the church contains another monument to Lawrence Washington. Return to the B4040 and turn left, or west, through Malmesbury, where there is a fine market cross. (East on the B4042 is Brinkworth. A mile north was **Penn's Lodge,** home of the Penn family.) Drive on to Badminton House at Great Badminton, where a deer park with fine oak trees sets off a house famous for its English, Dutch and Italian paintings, and annual Horse Trials held in April (house open June to mid-Sept., Wed. only, 2.30–5). Thence on to **Old Sodbury,** where the church contains a memorial to David Hartley, the chief British peace negotiator with the Americans in 1783. Return now on the B4040 towards Badminton to the B4039, bear right, and enter Castle Combe, surely one of the most beautiful of the stone-built Cotswold villages. Indeed, the village won a contest in the 1950s as 'Britain's prettiest', and this nearly ruined it for a time. Jason Love, of James Leasor's thrillers, comes from here. The Manor House, with fifteen rooms, is small, cozy, and the finest example I know of just how good a country hotel can be. It is surrounded by 26 acres of gardens and lawns, and the river is stocked with brown trout. It is in Castle Combe that the harried American may, if off-season, at last come to some understanding of the meaning of Idyllic.

• You may then continue on the B4039 and the A420 to Chippenham, an attractive old town, and turn right toward Bath on the A4 past Corsham – where Corsham Court is worth visiting to see its collection of Old Masters and Capability Brown gardens (open every Sun.; April–Oct., Wed. and Thurs. as well; July–Sept., daily except Mon., Fri., 11–4.30). Alternatively, the A350 south of Chippenham passes through Lacock, one of the most charming villages in England, to the A365, where a right turn brings one to the junction with the B3353. Turn right again to Corsham and the A4 beyond. 9 miles west on the A4 is Bath, the railway station, and your return train to London, taking just on 70 minutes for the journey to Paddington. Or from Chippenham you may turn north on the A420 to join the M4 for a fast two-hour drive back to London via Swindon and Reading.

WHAT TO READ   Sir Thomas Malory's *Morte d'Arthur*, or one of the many modernized renderings of the Knights of the Round Table – Lady Antonia Fraser's is especially good for children – are essential to this journey. And for an examination of the historical and legendary bases of Arthur, read Leslie Alcock's *Arthur's Britain*. As noted above, Trollope on Barsetshire, of course; and Dickens' *Pickwick Papers*, since Pickwick took his holiday in Bath. Jane Austen's *Northanger Abbey* and *Persuasion* are especially appropriate as well. It was in Bath that Henry Fielding found the figure he made into Squire Allworthy in *Tom Jones*, and Fanny Burney lived in Gay Street. And read T. S. Eliot's 'Burnt Norton', for with James, Sargent, Copley and Whistler, he best represents the Anglo-American figure, and his Norton was amongst the Cotswolds through which you travelled.

8 Longer Tours

Based on Leicester:
Nottingham
Peterborough
The Pilgrim Country
Lincoln
Boston

This tour carries you through one of the areas in Britain most densely populated with reminders of the Anglo-American connection. It provides an opportunity to see three large industrial cities which, however, lack the congestion of Birmingham or Manchester; to pay homage to Robin Hood and Sherwood Forest (thus placing reality and fantasy into proper perspective against each other); to pass through the Lincolnshire country-side, with its Dutch-built dykes and, in spring, fields of tulips; to see one of the largest parish churches in England, at Boston; to explore what was, until its disappearance into Leicestershire in 1974, England's smallest county, Rutland; and to see five cathedrals, one of which – Lincoln – is outstanding. It is also, unhappily, an area more than a little barren of good eating, so that you may have the mixed pleasure of risk-taking as you dine. Perhaps most important, the tour covers the area of Britain statistically shown to be the least visited by foreign tourists, so that you are unlikely to meet yourself along the narrow fen roads and will be seeing a highly culti-vated, but relatively thinly populated, slice of the Real England. It is, after Essex and East Anglia, truly muckers country, so should you be travelling under threat of rain – and when does one not so travel in England? – be well shod and brollied. The circuit may, if you are really determined, be traversed in three days, although four would add comfort and leisure.

Leave London from St Pancras Station, that glorious monument to architectural madness, on an early train and enjoy an excellent breakfast, British Rail's great moment of the day. Too few cars are used on this run, so claim your seat early, or reserve one in advance. You will arrive in

Leicester, via attractive and green countryside, and can pick up a hire car at the station. Traffic is bad in this city of 300,000 and you might do best to leave the car at the station, taking a taxi to the Cathedral, and walking the circuit (about a mile) of what there is to see – which one must admit is not a great deal. The Cathedral itself is an upgraded parish church, and on the whole worthy only of the Collector. The **Herrick Chapel** – actually the north choir aisle – was restored by American members of that family.

Next to the Cathedral is the Guildhall. Follow the lane until it emerges on St Nicholas Street: to your left is a church well worth a brief visit – St Nicholas, which incorporates material from the Roman and Saxon periods. Here, and to the left along Castle Street, past the Old Roman Wall and the Castle Gardens, are relics of the Roman period during which Leicester was fortified. Just beyond is the excellent small Newarke Houses Museum which celebrates the industrial history of this city, where the invention of the stocking-frame, and the inauguration of the first of Thomas Cook's tours (a railway excursion to Loughborough) in 1841, marked two stages in the industrial revolution – the mechanization of the textile industry and the freeing of the lower middle class by the expansion of the railroad into the countryside. In New Walk is the city museum and **Art Gallery,** which contains American paintings, including a Sargent and a Whistler, various items relating to the 17th Regiment of Foot during the American Revolution, several Seth Thomas clocks, Indian items, and letters written by George Washington and John Paul Jones, among others (open May–Aug. 10–7, earlier closing other months, Sun. 2–5). A short walk up Newarke Street, behind you, to the bus depot will find you a taxi back to your car at the station.

Before leaving the city, turn out of the station southeast on London Road, then right on University Road, to see the university, famous for engineering, for Victorian Studies, and for the promotion of local history. It is architecturally perhaps the most typical of the mid-period 'red brick', and probably only Birmingham and Nottingham are visually more interesting of this period. Return to London Road, the A6, and turn right (south) to Oadby, and then right (west) on the A5096 (a ring road to circumnavigate Leicester) through Wigston Magna – a tiny village now overwhelmed by the city, and perhaps the most studied such village sociologically in all England – to Newbold Verdon, off the B582. An un-numbered country road south here, posted for **Peckleton,** brings one in 4 miles to that village, the ancestral home of the William Howard Taft family. William Bradford, who was to print the first newspaper in Pennsylvania, came from this area. From Newbold Verdon follow the B585 west to Market Bosworth (easily seen from a distance by its high church spire). It was near here, at Bosworth Field, that Richard III was slain in 1485, his crown found upon a bush, and the Henrican reign of the House of Tudor began. The site is discreetly marked in a tumbled field 2 miles south of the village. Follow the posting for Sutton Cheney, turn right for

Shenton, and at Ambien Farm, with permission asked, you may see in the farmyard the well marking the spot near which King Richard was killed. 3 miles south from Shenton on a country lane is Higham-on-the-Hill, the site of Lindley Hall, where Robert Burton, author of *Anatomy of Melancholy* (1621) was born; yet another 5 miles south, to Nuneaton, and then southwest via the B4112 and the B4102, brings one to Arbury Hall, an 18th century Gothic structure in a 300-acre park (open Easter to October, Sun., 2.30–6). George Eliot was born at South Farm, nearby, and christened Mary Ann Evans at Chilvers Coton church (at the junction of the B4102 and the B4112); she lived for twenty-one years at Griff House, just south of Nuneaton, where there are memorial gardens and a museum The countryside round here is that of most of her novels. But all of this is taking you in the opposite direction to your main journey, and if Burton and Eliot do not interest you, turn north from Bosworth Field on the A447 to its junction with the A50.

• At this point you may opt for industry or for countryside. Bear left on the A50 to pass through Ashby de la Zouch (which the song tells us is 'by the sea', and which so evidently is not) pause a moment for the ruined castle, scene of the tournament in Walter Scott's *Ivanhoe*, then go north on the A453, and left on the B587 to Melbourne Hall, home of Lord Melbourne, Queen Victoria's first Prime Minister and subject of that finest of all Prime Ministerial biographies, *The Young Melbourne* by Lord David Cecil.

• The A514 passes close to Melbourne and carries on to **Derby** (pronounced Darby), home of the Rolls-Royce (here that great motor car is referred to as a Royce, and everywhere else as a Rolls) and Royal Crown Derby porcelain. If you have written in advance you may visit the works, which are fascinating; even if you have not, you may buy seconds in a nearby shop. The city is unattractive, as is the exterior of the cathedral (raised from the status of a parish church in 1927) save for its tower, but the interior is well worth a visit for its screens and monuments. The first English cheese factory was set up at Derby in 1870 by an American, Cornelius Schemerhorn. Derby appears in George Eliot's *Adam Bede* as Stoniton, but today the only really sound reason to visit this industrial city of 220,000 is to get the feeling of a truly working class community grown large. As the A514 will have brought you directly to the Cathedral, past Market Place and via Irongate, you may park nearby and walk from the cathedral along St Mary's Gate opposite, left on Bold Lane, and on your right will be St Werburgh's Church with the Art Gallery opposite. Dr Johnson was married in the church. From Derby take the A52, which is of motorway standard once out of the city, 16 miles to Nottingham.

• Or you may have opted for countryside as the A447 met the A50, and have turned right. In time you will see the MI before you – pass under it. Immediately bear right for **Markfield,** 1 mile, where Thomas Hooker, founder of Hartford, Connecticut, was born. Return to the junction and drive north on the B587 and right on the B591 to the A6. You will pass through Charnwood Forest, now only clusters of scattered trees and a lesson in how to denude a countryside (there is a viewing park at the junction of the B591 and the B5330). Turn left on the A6 through Loughborough, a particularly ugly town not saved by a good parish church and an unattractive university, until the A6 meets the M1, reward yourself with 5 miles of the motorway, and take exit 25 (onto the A52) into Nottingham, to rejoin the Derby option.

If you resisted Robert Burton and George Eliot, and if you have booked your hotel ahead, you have just enough time to see Nottingham, a city of 300,000 with a good traffic pattern and little to hold you. The A52 brings you in close by the Roman Catholic Cathedral (visible to your right, next to the Playhouse Theatre, which is well worth buying tickets for if you are staying the night). Before you reach the city, Wollaton Hall (natural history exhibits) and the massive University of Nottingham, on grounds given by Sir Jesse Boot, of Boots the Chemist fame, are set upon the hill to your right. Bear right on Granby Street, toward the Castle, which you should visit, and stop at the pub reputed to be the oldest in England – the Trip to Jerusalem on Castle Road, built into the Castle wall, where you may try your hand at an old form of the ring toss game and hoist a pint for a pittance. Robin Hood's statue is just beyond. The city museum and art gallery, in the Castle, includes the Regimental Museum of the Sherwood Foresters, which has items relating to the wars in North America from 1760–78, and American Indian items (open daily 10–6.45 or dusk, closes 5.45 Fri., 2–4.45 Sun.). Don't omit a pilgrimage to the Trent River Bridge and the famous cricket ground just beyond. Have a slightly noisy night at the Albany Hotel on St James's Street, or strike for Southwell, 14 miles northeast on the A612, where there is a pleasant country hotel, the Saracen's Head, from which Charles I went to surrender to the Scots in 1647.

• The environs of Nottingham may hold you longer than its crowded landscape suggests. If approaching from Loughborough, you could enter through **Gotham,** just off the road. Here one Dr Andrew Border (said to be the original 'Merry Andrew') wrote *The Merry Tales of the Mad Men of Gotham* in the 16th century. These nursery tales were of people who, while wise, acted the fool to mislead those who thought themselves sophisticated, and it is from this source, through the work of Washington Irving, that New York City became known as Gotham (as surely all readers and viewers of Batman are aware!). To the northwest of Nottingham, on the A611, is Hucknall, technically Hucknall Torkard: here in the parish church is the tomb of Lord Byron, a romantic lamp burning always. Beyond Hucknall north via the B6011 and the B683 to the A60 is

Newstead Abbey (open April–Sept. afternoons), Byron's home, where you may see his bedroom and imagine yourself both poet and mad. 10 miles north is Hardwick Hall, one of the truly fine country mansions (open April–Oct., Wed., Thurs., Sat., Sun., 2–6, open at 12, May–July) and yet another 3 miles leads to the village of Sutton Scarsdale. Ruined Sutton Hall here was dismantled and a room re-created in the Philadelphia Museum of Art from the contents. 5 miles west of Hucknall on the B6009, passing via **Greasley** (home of the Rev. John Robinson, whose preaching inspired the Pilgrims) is Eastwood, unlovely and forgetful of its own. But one wants Eastwood to be unlovely, for here D. H. Lawrence was born in 1885 at 8A Victoria Street, and his anger at his unkempt mining town and the destruction of the countryside by industry is what will, in the long run, make us continue to read *Sons and Lovers* and *Lady Chatterley's Lover*, both set here. If you are to miss Halifax, Huddersfield and Hull, or Preston, Blackburn and Wigan, then see Eastwood, merely to see how bleak it all can truly be. Even Browning could not make April lovely here.
• Enough masochism. East of Nottingham an attractive road carries one through the Vale of Belvoir (pronounced Beever); take the A52 east, turn right at the posting for Cotgrave, then left for Cropwell Bishop, right again for Colston Bassett, and left for Langar. This is the ancestral home of the **Howes.** George Howe was killed at Ticonderoga, fighting the French; Richard Howe was the admiral in command of the British fleet off North America in 1776; William Howe was at the Plains of Abraham in 1759, was the British commander at the **Battle of Bunker Hill,** and commander of the British troops who won at White Plains and Brandywine. Here, too, is where Samuel Butler grew up, unhappily, in the rectory, which he described with bitterness in *The Way of All Flesh.* Country roads south via Harby bring one to Long Clawson, where Stilton cheese is made, and on into the western wolds to Old Dalby and the A46. Country roads east from Langar to Belvoir are especially attractive, and the art collection in Belvoir Castle (open April–Sept., Wed., Thurs., Sat., 12–6, Sun. 2–7) is very good. Further on via the A607 is Croxton Kerrial, a fine wold village. Country roads north from Langar, via Granby, Elton, Orston, Hawksworth, **Screveton** (the parish church has a monument to Richard Whalley, grandfather of Edward Whalley, one of the three Regicides who sought refuge in New Haven, Connecticut, and Hadley, Massachusetts), Kneeton, East Bridgford and Burton Joyce will carry you slowly through attractive landscape and pleasant villages, via **Bestwood,** where Bret Harte did much of his writing on the American West, back to Nottingham, or on to Southwell on the A612. But assuming you have omitted all of these options and have maintained the Basic Tour, you will have spent the night in Nottingham or Southwell, and be ready for another day.

From Nottingham drive to Southwell on the A612. Here is perhaps the least known of the cathedrals (see CATHEDRALS) and one well worth a visit.

SHERWOOD FOREST

From Southwell a country road via Normanton connects with the A617 at Hockerton; turn left to the A614, turn right (north) along it and then left on the B6034 to Edwinstowe, where stands the Major Oak, said to have been a refuge for Robin Hood. A couple of miles east is **Ollerton,** from which early settlers to America are said to have come. East again 5 miles on a country road is Laxton, a unique village in that it retains medieval open fields and strip farms. From the A614 north of Ollerton, turn left to Victorian Thoresby Hall (open June–Aug., Wed., Thurs., Sat., 2.30–6, Sun. 12.30–6). Continue north by winding parkland roads to Carburton and Clumber Park. Here are National Trust holdings and a pleasant, isolated chapel upon a lake, and here stand most of the best surviving examples of the great oaks of Sherwood Forest, where Robin Hood – traditionally thought to be the dispossessed Earl of Huntingdon – and his Merry Men held forth. The area is attractive, and while it is scarcely a forest, neither is New Jersey the Garden State: use a little imagination. On the way, if American associations truly fascinate you, two await collecting: at **Perlethorpe,** adjacent to Thoresby Hall, in the church, is a painting, 'St Peter's Denial', by Benjamin West. And in **Market Warsop,** 6 miles southwest of Thoresby Hall on the A60, was born the wife of the Rev. Richard Clyfton, of whom more shortly. From Clumber

Park join the A57 and turn left for **Worksop,** from which came Richard Bernard, Pilgrim. One gains an unusual hillside view coming into the town. At the junction with the B620, short of the middle of the town, bear sharp right for Ranby and Babworth, where you may begin to seek out Pilgrim-related sites in earnest, if interested.

The communities to be visited are Babworth, Retford, Blyth, Scrooby, Harworth, Austerfield, Doncaster, Adwick le Street, Gainsborough, North Wheatley and Sturton le Steeple. You may wish to impose your own sequence upon them – the total area is about 20 miles square – and so the following list is arranged alphabetically. Afterwards you should move on to Lincoln, so that in fact a circuit taken in the sequence above will be most economical of time. If time is limited, Babworth, Scrooby and Gainsborough are the most important.

Adwick le Street   In the parish church is the tomb of James Washington, ancestor of George.

Austerfield   William Bradford, author of the *History of Plimouth Plantation*, second governor of Massachusetts, was born in the manor here (private). Inside the Norman church of 1080 is the font in which Bradford was baptized; the north aisle was restored in his memory in 1897 by the Society of Mayflower Descendants. (Beyond Austerfield on the A614 is Finningley; here during World War II was a large R.A.F. aerodrome which cast the continuous drone of bombers over the countryside. The Manor Farm here was once owned by Martin Frobisher, the first explorer of North America's far north.)

Babworth   The Rev. Clyfton was rector here 1586–1604. The only Puritan in the area, he drew a special congregation which included William Brewster, and then moved on to Scrooby and the Netherlands with the Pilgrims, dying before the Scrooby Congregation made its way to Massachusetts. The parish church of All Saints at Babworth has been lovingly looked after over the years and has many homely relics relating to the Pilgrims and to the continuing connections between this section of Nottinghamshire and the United States.

Blyth   Here was born Francis Cooke, early Pilgrim.

Doncaster   John Carver, early Pilgrim memorialized in Massachusetts place names, was born here. (The Mansion House, St George's Parish Church and the museum are worth visiting.)

Epworth   John and Charles Wesley were born in the old rectory here, in the middle of the Isle of Axholme, drained by Cornelius Vermuyden and Dutch workmen in 1626–8.

Gainsborough The John Robinson Memorial Church is dedicated to the 'Pastor of the Pilgrim Fathers'. It was built by American and English Congregationalists in 1896–1902. Robinson had intended to sail on, or after, the *Mayflower* but died before he could do so. The Old Hall was used for Separatist (as the Pilgrims at first were called) meetings. Keep this Americana in proportion: John Wesley preached in Old Hall and Henry VIII met Catherine Parr there. Further, Gainsborough – despite claims for Tewkesbury – is most probably the scene of George Eliot's *The Mill on the Floss*, being St Ogg's. The Old Hall is open daily 2–5. (At Epworth 14 miles north on the A161, is the Old Rectory, John and Charles Wesley's childhood home, now a museum; open weekdays 10–12, 2–4.)

Harworth Thomas Morton and George Thornton, Pilgrims, were born here.

Scrooby Here the pilgrimage to America began. In 1606 the Gainsborough congregation divided, Richard Clyfton bringing several Separatists to Scrooby, to meet in the Manor House, home of William Brewster. The Scrooby congregation moved to the Netherlands and, in time, via the *Mayflower* to Plymouth. Two reminders remain: a plaque on the one standing wall of the Manor House, to Brewster; and the parish church, which contains carved pews (one to Brewster) and a memorial tablet from the Pilgrim Society.

Sturton le Steeple Here John Robinson was born. (Littleborough, 2 miles on, has an interesting Norman church.)

East Retford and Gainsborough are the largest market towns of the area. At the Elms Hotel in East Retford you may comfortably eat or sleep, perhaps in the attractive bedroom in which King Olaf of Norway whiled away his period of exile during World War II.

Enter Lincoln on the A57, probably via the A156 along the Trent from Gainsborough. This, the heart of **Lincolnshire,** plunges you deeply into the country which, save for Essex, Sussex and Surrey, probably has more American associations than any other. If you want to pursue them with diligence, you may consult two specialized guides, both of which may be purchased in Lincoln, the first at the cathedral and the second at the museum: *Lincolnshire Links with the U.S.A.*, by A. M. Cook (who has written a similar slim book on links with Australia) and *Lincolnshire Links with North America*, Museum of Lincolnshire Life, *Museum Publication No. 5*. Since these exist, the listings here can be relatively brief. In any event, the larger delights of Lincolnshire lie in the cathedral, in the fens to the east, and in the wolds. The places of American significance are Immingham, Grimsby, Humberston, Gainsborough (described above),

LINCOLN CATHEDRAL

Belleau, Alford, Bilsby, Willoughby, Spilsby, Horncastle, Revesby, Coningsby, Boston, Skirbeck, Fishtoft, Swineshead, Horbling, Sempringham,
Honington and Grantham. Distances are long by English standards, and
the first two and last three places are well off any clear circuit. To these,
for other reasons, should be added Caistor, Somersby and Skegness. Each
is discussed below, alphabetically, after Lincoln, but if you do not have
two or three days for the wold and fen villages, you can follow a circuit
which includes the three most important sites: east from Lincoln on the
A158 beyond Horncastle to a country road just past Hagworthingham,
bear left to Harrington, then left to Somersby, and left again via Ashby
Puerorum to Horncastle once more. Then go south on the A153, and turn
left before Coningsby on the B1192 through New York to a junction with
the A1121, then east to Boston, and thence south on the A16 toward
Peterborough.

Lincoln is a striking city, laced with history and, in the cobblestone
lanes near the cathedral, much charm. Entering on the A46, keep straight
on up the appropriately named Steep Hill to park, if lucky, near the
cathedral, which dominates the city from its summit. Here is an original

copy of the Magna Carta (see CATHEDRALS) and **stained glass windows** to John Smith and the *Arbella*, John Winthrop's vessel. This is a city to walk in: to the castle, northwest of the cathedral, to the Stonebow and Guildhall, the **Usher Art Gallery** below the hill (with several objects relating to America) and through the Arboretum to the remains of the Monks' Abbey. Seek out, too, the **Museum of Lincolnshire Life,** which includes items of American interest. The **Regimental Museum** of the Royal Lincolnshire Regiment contains exhibits relating to the American Revolution – for the first two British soldiers to fall at Concord Bridge were of the 10th Foot, the Lincolnshire Regiment. **The Lincoln City and County Museum** holds items relating to Sir John Franklin, Northwest explorer, and paintings by continental artists who worked in America. You may end your tour here, checking your car back in at the railway station; you may purchase excellent antiques; and there are a variety of good, small second-hand book shops. Doddington Hall, 5 miles south on the A46 and west on the B1190, is Obligatory – a superb Elizabethan manor house with grand gardens and fine tapestries (open May–Sept., Tues., Thurs., 2–6). Or you may leave Lincoln on the A158 to visit any of the following places.

Alford A pleasant Georgian village with an attractive market, is the birthplace of Anne Hutchinson, who emigrated to Massachusetts in 1634. Banished to Rhode Island for her religious principles, she helped to make that colony a truer haven for freedom of worship. John Smith attended school here, and Tom Paine lived here 1764–5.

Belleau From here came Sir Henry Vane in 1635, to become Governor of Massachusetts.

Bilsby From here came the Wheelwright family in 1630.

Boston A contraction of 'St Botolph's Town', which has given its name to one of America's greatest cities. From here in 1607 Brewster, Clyfton, Robinson, and others of the Scrooby Separatists sought to move to the Netherlands. Betrayed by the master of the ship on which they hoped to sail, they were jailed, and returned to Scrooby. The **Guildhall** in which their case was heard, with its original cells, has been restored by the Bostonian Society of Massachusetts. In 1612 John Cotton became vicar of St Botolph's; after twenty-one years he came under attack for his Puritanism and fled to London, then sailing with Thomas Hooker for Massachusetts. However, the city in that state was named by John Winthrop's Puritans, not by the Pilgrims of Plymouth, in 1630. The site from which Winthrop's Puritans sailed is marked by a simple shaft at **Scotia Creek** near the Wash – follow the signposts from the central square through

Fishtoft (from which came Edmund Quincy in 1623). On the square is **St Botolph's,** one of the largest parish churches in England and far more impressive than many cathedrals, and a major American shrine in England. The church was restored in 1857 by Charles Francis Adams and other Bostonians, in Cotton's memory, with the text of the tablet composed by Edward Everett – he who competed with Abraham Lincoln for attention on the occasion of the Gettysburg Address. Americans contributed £11,000 more toward restoration in 1930. The great church tower, known as the 'Stump', was also rebuilt by Americans after World War II. The tenor bell of the peal of ten bells bears the Stars and Stripes. There is also a stained glass window to Anne Bradstreet and John Cotton. The central bosses of the nave roof include one of the *Mayflower*, and, in the north aisle, of John Cotton, and one to Boston, Massachusetts. It was near here that Nathaniel Hawthorne wrote his *English Notebooks*. Next to the Guildhall is **Fydell House** with an American room. The Royal Naval Base during World War II was H.M.S. *Arbella*. Nearby, there are windmills built in the Dutch fashion, which differ from those in Norfolk. The best portions of the fens, drained in the 17th century partly to grow flax and thus drive the Dutch from the cloth trade, lie to the north of Boston.

Caistor   A particularly pleasant village on the A46 between Lincoln and Grimsby.

Coningsby   An attractive village with a great windmill and an unusual church tower, this is the location of Tattershall Castle, dating from the 15th century. It was restored and given to the National Trust by Lord Curzon, with the aid of his American wife. From the castle came Lady Arbella Churton, daughter of the third Earl of Lincoln; she married Rev. Isaac Johnson, who went with Winthrop to Massachusetts, and she died after arrival in America. Winthrop memorialized her by changing his flagship's name from *Eagle* to *Arbella*. John Smith worked at the castle for a time. Benjamin Disraeli named his novel *Coningsby* after the village.

Fishtoft   See Boston.

Grantham   Here Tom Paine lived from 1762–4. But if you go here at all, go because of St Wulfram's Church, with its 280-foot spire, and because of Sir Isaac Newton, who went to the grammar school here.

Grimsby   Prior to 1637, this town sent settlers to Massachusetts Bay. It is now one of Britain's main trawler ports with vast docks. There are excellent views of the mouth of the Humber from Cleethorpes.

Honington   The tiny church here contains a monument to John and William Smith.

Horbling   From here came Simon and Anne Bradstreet, who sailed with the *Arbella.*

Horncastle   The Rev. William Blackstone left from here for America in 1623.

Humberston   From here came the Rev. Hansard Knollys in 1638.

Immingham   As easily reached from Hull as from Lincoln, this village near the mouth of the Humber is the point from which, in 1609, the original Pilgrims left England for the Netherlands. An ugly memorial shaft stands at Killingholme Creek near Immingham Dock.

Louth   John Smith, founder of Virginia, as well as Sir John Franklin and Tennyson were educated here. The King Edward VI school has a portrait of Smith and Pocahontas.

Revesby   Home of Sir Joseph Banks, explorer of Labrador and New-foundland and later scientist with James Cook in the Pacific.

Sempringham   Home of the widow of the third Earl of Lincoln, this estate was the meeting place of the Emmanuel College men who discussed plans for emigration to Massachusetts. The site is 1½ miles south of Billingborough on the B1177, below Horbling, off the A52.

Scunthorpe   The Museum and Art Gallery in Oswald Road holds a collection of Indian arrowheads.

Somersby   Alfred Lord Tennyson was born in Somersby House (then the rectory) in 1809, lived here until 1837, and wrote 'The Lady of Shalott'.

Skegness   This seaside town is always described as bracing. It is.

Spilsby   Home of Sir John Franklin, who lost his life in 1847 in his search for the Northwest Passage.

Swineshead   Supplied Herbert Pelham to Massachusetts in 1638, although there had been a Pelham in the *Arbella* group.

Willoughby   Captain John Smith, who led the colony at Jamestown, Virginia, was born here in 1579, went to school at Alford, and became an apprentice in King's Lynn. It is Smith who named New England. He died in London in 1631. His baptismal entry may be seen in the parish church, dated January 9, 1580.

South of Boston remain on the A16 to Sutterton. Here you may divert southeast on the A17, and then the A101, to Wisbech, through flowering country in the spring, to pay homage to the birthplace of Thomas Clarkson, father of the British anti-slavery movement – but the drive is slow and not recommended at any other time of year, unless you want to carry on toward Cambridge and Ely, to connect with Tour 9, or to Norwich. Otherwise, remain on the A16 through Spalding – where there are spacious tulip fields – bearing left on the A1073 to Crowland and to the magnificent ruined Benedictine Abbey where Hereward the Wake is buried. Follow the A1073 to the A47, then right (west) to Peterborough (again, you may leave your car at the railway station and return to London from here if you like). The cathedral is a keystone of the development of Norman architecture and is Obligatory. You are now in what was the Soke of Peterborough until this portion became part of Cambridgeshire in the reorganization of 1974.

Leave Peterborough westwards on the A47, via Castor, an attractive village with a 12th century church with a fine Norman tower. At the junction with the A1, turn north to Stamford, once again in Lincolnshire. A remarkably preserved market town of 14,000 inhabitants, Stamford is best seen by walking, for there are many historic churches and old buildings. Burghley House (open April–Oct., Tues.–Thurs., 11–5, Sun. 2–5), Elizabethan, contains a fine collection of Italian paintings. There is an excellent hotel here, the George, dating from 1597, with an attractive garden. Sir Walter Scott stayed here frequently, and as it has 50 rooms, you may too.

Leave Stamford on the A606 to Oakham, in the Vale of Catmose, county town for the Rutland that was, until 1974, smallest of the English counties and the heart of the slowly dying blood-sport of fox-hunting. With no surprise, then, you will find a museum of horseshoes within the castle – there is also an attractive market cross and a pleasant church. You may now decide which of two routes to use to return to Leicester: north on the A606 to Melton Mowbray, a market town famous for its Stilton cheese and Melton Mowbray pork pies (which you may still buy at Dickinson & Morris on Nottingham Street) thence by the A607 and the A46 into Leicester. Or go south on the A6003 to **Uppingham,** and then by the A47 into Leicester. My preference is for the latter, for in Uppingham one may see one of the famous public schools of Britain, dating from 1584, with its simple motto, 'Duty, God, Country', and then pass through a number of attractive villages. You may also get a good meal at the Lake Isle, basically a wine bar that takes its themes from Ezra Pound. You can buy a Melton Mowbray pork pie at the Leicester railway station in any case, after dropping your car. Or if you are still madly enjoying yourself, you may drive on south toward Northampton.

WHAT TO READ   Obviously this has been Lord Byron, George Eliot, Robin Hood, Nathaniel Hawthorne, William Bradford, John Smith and Alfred Lord Tennyson country. The appropriate suggestions appear above. The only book which must, I think, be read *in situ* is *The Mill on the Floss*, while in Gainsborough. If Samuel Butler and Bret Harte do not interest you, then turn to D. H. Lawrence while in or near Eastwood, perhaps best choosing *Sons and Lovers*. And do not forget *Ivanhoe*.

9 Based on Cambridge:
Ely
Norwich
The Pilgrim Country

This is actually two trips. You may visit Cambridge and Ely in a single strenuous day and return to London for the night. Or you may add Bury St Edmunds and Norwich and stay two nights or more on the road, spending three to five days profitably in exploring the East Anglian countryside of windmills and sea, and the Suffolk and Essex sites so intimately connected with the Pilgrim Fathers. Cambridge and Ely you may do comfortably by train; for the rest you must have a car. I therefore divide this trip into two sections, the first assuming that you travel by rail, and the second that you pick up a rental car in Cambridge for the continuation of your journey.

FIRST DAY

Cambridge can be reached by train either from King's Cross or, usually more swiftly, from Liverpool Street. Trains run from Liverpool Street twenty-nine times daily (except on Sundays) and return twenty-six times – testimony to the fact that some must find Cambridge so attractive that they never return. The station itself is redolent of the 1890s, and although exceptionally ugly, is also one of the most interesting in London. At the height of its use, 40,000 people pass through the barriers in an hour, and it can dispatch sixty trains every hour. Arrive early, for the station is divided into two confusing sections, joined by a passageway, and you will need a little time to locate your train. The journey to Cambridge takes just over an hour on an express. Given the frequency of service, you may want to stop off at Bishop's Stortford and catch the next train on an hour or so later. An interesting market town, Stortford has a pleasant hotel, The Foxley, that serves a good meal, and an equally pleasant park with a castle mound in the middle. But the primary attraction is the birthplace of **Cecil Rhodes,** founder of the Rhodes Scholarships, on which Americans, among others, are able to attend Oxford. (John Norton, a leading Pilgrim, was also born here.) Rhodes was one of the greatest of the Empire builders, and by energy, guile, duplicity and daring, he prepared the way for British hegemony in southern Africa. Attached to the house in which he was born (take a taxi from the station, for although it is not far, it is not easy to find) is an informative museum. Stanstead Airport, much used for charter flights, is near Bishop's Stortford and 15 miles north is Audley End House – well worth visiting – with a parish church containing an **American memorial.** The site of the old grammar school was the headquarters in World War II of the 65th Fighter Wing of the **U.S. Army Air Force** – a sports complex now stands as a memorial.

Cambridge, a city of 100,000, is more apparently a university town than Oxford, for it lacks the industry and the bustle. Once more famous for science than the arts, Cambridge has now moved to draw marginally more abreast of Oxford in the arts. While Oxford's mellow, yellow stone is infinitely appealing, Cambridge's colder, grey Gothic requires a sunnier day of the kind it too seldom receives. But Cambridge is also more of a whole, and its pleasures become more apparent with exploration – for it requires closer attention and more persistent poking about than Oxford does. Nor does Oxford have any collegiate building quite so nearly perfect as King's College Chapel. The University provided a hundred of the early settlers to New England, which was more than Oxford sent abroad. The individual colleges here, as at Oxford, have alliances with the colleges of Yale and the houses of Harvard, providing yet another Anglo-American educational link.

The bleak railway station – now modernized – is far from anything of interest, and you should proceed immediately to the bus and get off at Gonville Place. To the left is **Downing College,** founded in 1800 with funds provided by Sir George Downing, who made his fortune in America; his grandfather is commemorated in both Downing Street, London, where the Prime Minister resides, and in Downing Street, Newport, Rhode Island – not least, one presumes, because he was the second graduate of Harvard College. Continuing up Regent Street, which changes its name without apparent cause to St Andrew's Street, you will find **Emmanuel College,** the Puritan foundation of Sir Walter Mildmay, on the right. Many of the Cambridge graduates who came to America in the early days were from this college, and it was here that John Harvard, John Cotton and Thomas Hooker (founder of Hartford, Connecticut) studied. There are close ties between Harvard University's Lowell House and Emmanuel, and a window in the college chapel attests to this, with more piety than beauty. Christ's College is next, nearly opposite the post office. Carry on to Jesus Lane, turn right (Sidney Sussex College is on the corner) until you come to **Jesus College** on your left. Well worth a visit, Jesus was the home of both John Eliot, the 'apostle to the Indians', and Francis Higginson, who emigrated to Salem in 1629. East Apthorp, a signatory to the Declaration of Independence, studied here. Beyond is Jesus Green, and below is Midsummer Common. Walk beyond the college, turn left on Victoria Avenue, and left again on Chesterton Road, to gain views across the green. A left turn once more will bring you into Magdalene (pronounced 'Maudlin') Street and Bridge Street. **Magdalene College,** where Henry Dunster, first President of Harvard, studied, is here, and on your left is the Round Church (Holy Sepulchre, 12th century), one of four, and the best, of its kind in England. Shortly, on your right down St John's Street, is **St John's College,** one of the finest in Cambridge. Founded in 1511, St John's has a superb library, a fine chapel, and the most stunning gateway in the city. Peter Bulkeley, a St John's man, helped found Concord, N.H., and John Horne Tooke, whose picture may be seen in the National Portrait Gallery, helped raise a fund for widows and orphans of American soldiers killed in the Revolutionary War, for which he was imprisoned for a year. Be certain to see all three courtyards, which bring you to the Bridge of Sighs over the River Cam. Cross here and, with any luck at all, you will quickly see the special charm of Cambridge: punting on the river, and on the Backs. (To hire a punt, go to the bottom of Mill Lane, off Trumpington Street near Pembroke College, just behind the Garden House hotel. Ask for a punt 'on the lower river' which will take you along the Backs. You can also hire from near Magdalene Bridge.)

Now pause: Cambridge has twenty colleges. By one of those subtle differences so dear to the British, one does not refer to the colleges by that appendage (despite my doing so to this point) – while at Oxford one does. Thus, Queen's College is at Oxford and Queens' is in Cambridge. The particular glory of Cambridge is the Backs, where one may stroll and punt as one wishes. Here in succession is some of Britain's finest architecture, open to view because of the sweep provided by the parkland across the river.

Next to St John's in sequence is **Trinity,** one of the two finest colleges in Cambridge, and certainly the most imposing, with a great central courtyard. An outgrowth of a foundation of 1317, the college itself was initiated by Henry VIII in 1546, and his arms are above the entrance. King Edward's Tower, begun in 1426, is the oldest of the Cambridge gatehouses. The college library is handsome and offers the finest work of the Danish sculptor Bertel Thorvaldsen; Sir Christopher Wren designed the library in 1676, and inside there is some of the finest work of the 17th century woodcarver, Grinling Gibbons. Among those who studied here were Charles Chauncy, a President of Harvard; Thomas Pownall, Governor of Massachusetts 1757–60; John Winthrop, the first Governor of the Colony;

KING'S PARADE

and two Americans who did much to move certain eastern colleges along Oxbridge lines, Charles Astor Bristed (Yale) and William Everett (Harvard).

Next comes **Gonville and Caius** (pronounced Keys) where Thomas Lynch, a signer of the Declaration of Independence, studied. The term used in America to describe classes – as sophomore or junior – originated here. Then come Trinity Hall and **King's**, noted for the finest college chapel in Britain. Perpendicular in style, with outstanding fan vaulting, the chapel was completed in 1515; it deserves careful attention inside – it is the only major medieval English church, except for York Minster, to retain its original glass – and a slow and contemplative viewing from the Cam. An evensong is always attractive here, although you want daylight to view the Rubens, but should you have an opportunity to hear the King's College Choir sing, abandon all other plans in order to do so. You may also walk directly from the chapel on to **Clare,** an attractive college that Lord Cornwallis, commander of the British troops at Yorktown, attended; his portrait is in the hall. A fine gate, designed by Thomas Grumbold, gives access here to a bridge across the Cam and, by a short walk directly ahead and through a newer part of Clare, to the University Library, opened in 1934, home for a million and a quarter books and a major landmark with its tower. Walk round the right-hand side of the library to Grange Road, turn left, and in a quarter-mile **Selwyn** is on your left, followed by Newnham, on the corner of Sidgwick Avenue. Turn down the avenue and left again on Queens' Road to complete a circle back to the pathway leading to the Clare bridge.

Coming out of Clare past King's Chapel onto King's Parade, pause to study the handsomest prospect in all Cambridge, with eight colleges stretched out before you, and the elegant Senate House, designed in 1722, near the head of the street, adjoining Gonville & Caius. **Corpus Christi,** on the east side of King's Parade near Pembroke, is well worth visiting, even if only to pay your respects to Edward Braddock, commander of the British forces against the French in the Pennsylvania forests of 1755; it was under Braddock that George Washington served. John Robinson, pastor to the Pilgrim Fathers, also studied here. Along the road is **Pembroke,** where Roger Williams, the founder of Rhode Island, sought his spiritual education. The first American to study in a British university, John Stone, came here in 1654. The chapel, in a pure Classical style and the first completed design by Christopher Wren, is especially fine. Opposite Corpus Christi is St Catharine's, and just beyond it, on Silver Street, is Queens'. The dial in the Old Court at the college is regarded as the finest sundial in Britain.

Return now to King's Parade, turn right into Trumpington Street, and you will find the oldest of the colleges, **Peterhouse,** founded in 1281. Here studied William Brewster, leader of the Scrooby congregation of Puritans who ultimately made their way to America, and John Norton, a founder of Ipswich, Massachusetts. Little St Mary's Lane passes down the side to the Museum of Classical Archaeology; the church of **St Mary the Less** has a monument of Godfrey Washington with the family stars and stripes. Just beyond Peterhouse is the **Fitzwilliam Museum,** one of the finest collections in England. American items here include sixty-seven Whistlers, three Benjamin Wests, and sixteen John Singer Sargents. Continue on Trumpington Street, turn left on Lensfield Road, and right on Hills Road, and you will be on the bus route back to the railway station. Of course, if you are fortunate enough to be in Cambridge during May Week (which, logically enough, is ten days in early June) you will want to linger. If not, you may return by train to London, remain for the night in Cambridge – unhappily, there are not enough places which can be recommended with enthusiasm – or, madly, press on toward Ely.

You might now hire a car and pay your respects to Dorothy L. Sayers, that greatest of English mystery writers (and a Dante scholar too), for her cottage at Bluntisham, which bears a plaque, may still be seen despite fire damage. Leave on the A604 northwest. On the way you will pass the new Churchill College (1960) and Girton College, well outside the city and both on the right, and just afterwards a posted turning to the left brings you to **Madingley,** site of an American air force base. Nearly opposite the turning is the attractive and well-kept **American Memorial Cemetery,** with the group of 3811 American fliers and other servicemen killed in World War II (closes at 5.00). The chapel contains a mural depicting the war. (If you have no car, a bus from near the Market Square will get you there.)

You might also drive south from Cambridge on the Trumpington Road, turning right in Trumpington for Grantchester, where Rupert Brooke lived in the Old Vicarage for two years. Or you could continue on the A604 beyond Girton College and the Swavesey turnoff for another 8 miles, to Huntingdon, in which was the county of Huntingdon and Peterborough until 1974 – an odd union of old identities now united with Cambridgeshire. 8 miles further northwest is **Little Gidding,** where Nicholas Ferrar, a member of the Virginia Company, established a religious community in which he led the people in prayers for Virginia every day for ten years. Here, too, lived T. S. Eliot for a time, and his poem, 'Little Gidding', uses the church as a symbol of community, of inheritance from the past, and of the pentecostal fire: '. . . the communication/Of the dead is tongued with fire beyond the language of the living.' To read the poem here is to be 'touched by a common genius. . . .' Alternatively, take the A603 southwest of Cambridge 11 miles to **Croydon;** Sir George Downing is buried in the parish church. Another 8 miles is **Sutton,** home of the Burgoynes, including the general who surrendered to Washington at Saratoga.

Cambridge is enormously rich in literary associations, of course, and if there were only a truly comfortable hotel one could hole up for days, pursuing Henry James, Rose Macauley, Coleridge, Kingsley, Pepys, Tennyson, Strachey, Trevelyan, A. E. Housman, Ronald Firbank, or any of a dozen writers about donnish detectives (no, no! not Innes or Crispen; that's Oxford). Dorothy L. Sayers' *Nine Tailors* is based in part on nearby Bluntisham. One had best hole up, for the city is virtually devoid of good food, and one's best bet in a bad lot is a pub, the Fort St George, on Midsummer Common, where one may escape the jukebox into the garden.

SECOND DAY

Assuming that you have not attempted to drive on to Ely craving food, but returned to Cambridge for the night, you should now proceed by hire car out of Cambridge northwards on the A10. You will be passing through the **Isle of Ely,** the lower portion of the marshland drained by the British in the 17th century when, with the aid of a great Dutch engineer, Cornelius Vermuyden, they set out to provide themselves with farm land, partly for the cultivation of flax so that they could drive the Dutch out of their controlling position in the cloth trade. This entire area, ranging north to The Wash, and northwest into Lincolnshire, is closely related to the coming of the American Revolution. For it was as a result of the report of a Royal Commission in 1622 that the British government decided it must compete more effectively with the Dutch, and that in order to do so it must control trade to and from its North American colonies more directly. There was no point in remaking a vast area of England in order to become independent of Dutch linen, cotton and wool goods, if the colonies were allowed to undermine those efforts by trading directly with the enemy. As a result, by 1660 the British had worked out the theoretical justifications for placing severe limitations on colonial trade and manufacturing, limitations which came to be known as the policy of **Mercantilism.** And it was against the 18th century extensions of this 17th century logic – extensions spelled out in the principle of enumerated goods, and ultimately in the infamous Stamp Act – that the American Revolution was fought. In one sense, all that happens in history is interrelated: ten people a year are still killed on the beaches of France by the explosion of buried shells dating from World War II. And the marsh and fen lands of this stretch of English countryside mark the real link between Britain today and the American Revolution. The country is not particularly or obviously attractive, and many other areas are more picturesque, but no land is more relevant to the American story as it relates to Britain.

Ely is 16 miles north of Cambridge. Its magnificent cathedral is one of the finest in Britain, and as viewed across the meadow before it, a meadow often populated with Holstein, Friesian and Jersey cows, it is at once more bucolic and open to grander distant views than any other cathedral. It was at Ely – then literally an isle – that Hereward the Wake, 'the last of the English', resisted William the Conqueror to the end. The cathedral came later, but not much, having been started in 1083. It contains some of England's best Norman architectural features, a unique lantern tower and possibly the finest painted roof in Britain. The highlights of the cathedral include the presbytery and high altar, Bishop Alcock's chapel, the misericords – sixty-two carvings under the choir stall seats, which one is free to turn up to view – and the ceilings and bosses throughout. The cathedral is one of those saved in the last three decades from the ravages of the death-watch beetle, and is testimony to the fact that while the church may be suffering from low attendance today in England, the historical church lives.

Walk along Waterside, an attractive medieval street, and throughout this small cathedral city and the Close (the King's School is worth a visit) before moving on. You may drive directly north on the A10 to King's Lynn if you plan a three-to-four day outing in all, or turn east on the B1382 and the B1104, thence south through Isleham. The bell in the church here is in memory of the **Peyton Family** and its American connections. Newmarket, south, is the headquarters of the Jockey Club and National Stud and site of Tattersall's bloodstock sales, for racing fans.

ELY CATHEDRAL

The A11 leads northeast 50 miles to Norwich. (See the paragraph on Thetford, below.)

However, if you have allowed yourself enough time to explore all the detours recommended here, you should take the following routes.

• From Newmarket follow the A11 signposted for Norwich to the junction with the A45, and turn right 16 miles to Bury St Edmunds, where the Cathedral is particularly fine. King Edmund was killed by the Danes here in 870, and King Cnut, who conquered England in 1016, elevated the monastery that had been founded here in 636 into an abbey, in 1032. A Frenchman was in charge when the Norman conquerors arrived, saving the town from war. One of the most famous abbots of all time, Anselm, was appointed to Bury St Edmunds in 1121, and you may see the fruits of his ministrations all over the western world in the extraordinary **illuminated manuscripts** (the metropolitan Museum in New York has a fine example) which issued forth. Perhaps most notable of all is the fact that it was here, in 1215, that King John's barons met and swore on the altar of the church that they would force John to sign the Magna Carta.

• The town is small enough to explore on foot with ease, and it is one of the few medieval towns left in England in which the old town plan of a square for man and a square for God may easily be seen. The church became a cathedral in 1913, and although its exterior is less interesting than many, there are numerous fine interior features and attractive grounds through the Abbey Gate to the left and rear of the cathedral. There you will find the Magna Carta pillar. Opposite the great gate is Angel Hill (God's square) where you may visit Angel Corner, a Queen Anne house with an exceptional collection of valuable clocks, and the Angel Hotel, which appears in Dickens' *Pickwick Papers.* Moyses Hall Museum is also worth a visit to see its collection of Bronze Age weapons and tools, discovered in 1959. If you now require lunch, drive 2 miles south on the A134 to Sicklesmere, where the Rushbrooke Arms will take care of you nicely and at modest cost. And see **Ickworth House,** 3 miles southwest of Bury St Edmunds on the A143; the park was designed by Capability Brown, and the house is unusual in design and rich in silver, paintings and Regency furniture (open Easter–Oct. 4, Wed., Thurs., Sat., Sun., 2–6). It contains Benjamin West's famous oil, 'The Death of General Wolfe'.

• North from Bury on the A134, left shortly on the B1106, and left again on a country road is **Hengrave;** the Hall here has a window bearing the Washington coat-of-arms. B1106 continues to **Culford,** the home of Lord Cornwallis, the British commander who surrendered an empire at Yorktown, and who sought out a new empire in India to compensate for the World Turned Upside Down. Carry on to a junction with the A11 at **Elveden.** There is a memorial window here to the United States Army Air Force, which operated from this area in World War II. Follow the A11 right to **Thetford.** An ancient, flinty-grey town, said by some to have been made the capital of East Anglia in 575, and one of the five greatest towns in England at the time of the Domesday Book, it has narrow streets and churches well worth wandering within. It was the home of **Thomas Paine,** author of *The Rights of Man* and in 1776 of *Common Sense,* those resounding calls to Revolution. Paine's father is buried in the churchyard of **St Cuthbert's,** and the family attended services there. Opposite the Bell Hotel is Paine's **statue.** Down Bridge Street and across the bridge over the Thet you will come to **The Boys Grammar School,** possibly the oldest such school in England; Paine studied here. Items connected with him will be found in the **Ancient House Museum** (open weekdays 1–4; in winter, Tues., Thurs., Sat.). Walk up White Hart Street, reached from Bury Road, to **Chantry House,** on which a plaque (placed here by members of the U.S. forces stationed nearby) attests to Paine's birth in 1737 in **Grey Gables,** a three-bay, two-floor house directly around the corner. And take time to see Thetford Priory, in Minstergate. In Cage Lane you will find the site of the **Quaker Meeting House** with which Paine was associated. Finally, visit the **Guildhall** to see Paine's portrait.

• By the direct route on the A11, Norwich is 29 miles. Four places of interest intervene. Right on the B1111 is **Quidenham,** where the church has a memorial chapel to the U.S.A.A.F. Left on the B1111 is Wayland Wood, 1 mile north of its junction with the B1077 – this was the scene of the cautionary tale, 'Babes in the Wood' (the house of the wicked uncle still stands at Griston). Right from Watton on the B1108 is **Hingham** – the church contains a bronze bust of Abraham Lincoln, whose ancestors came from here. The village sports a boulder from Hingham, Massachusetts, for one of the early settlers there was the Rev. Robert Peck of this Hingham. B1108 continues to Norwich. Or, if you remained on the A11, you would pass through **Attleborough,** once home of the Rev. William Blackstone, earliest settler in Rhode Island.

• Alternatively, there is the long route. Leave Thetford on the B1107 to Brandon (where stone curlews breed) crossing a portion of Breckland, an ancient name for the wild heathland that once predominated here. There were many airfields throughout this area during World War II from which bombers flew on their dangerous missions. While much of the area is now covered with conifers put in by the Forestry Commission, you may still get some sense of the heath as you proceed on the B1106 to Whitington (watch for the occasional surviving mere) crossing some of the most fertile land in England, and thence by the A134 north to its junction with the A10 and on to King's Lynn, 35 miles in all. If you want to see the modern successor of those wartime airfields, however, then leave Thetford on the A11 going southwest, and at the junction with the A1101 turn right to **Mildenhall,** then north on country roads posted for **Lakenheath,** to the B1112. Between these two towns you will see the largest American air force base left in Britain – a contribution to the NATO commitment. The B1112 carries on across the Feltwell Fens to the A134. If you do not take this detour then you may want at least to take a shorter one in order to get some sense of how the fens were canalized and dyked: when the A134 junctions with the A1122, bear left to Downham Market, right on the A10, and, in a mile, left on an unnumbered country road posted for Stowbridge. This road will carry you across the Ouse, along the Marshland Fen, to Wiggenhall. Turn right, cross the river, and left again to follow the country road to King's Lynn. At Wiggenhall St German's, pause to visit the church and examine the startling carved bench ends of the Vices in the jaws of Hell's beasts.

• King's Lynn is an important seaport. A *lynn* is a pool. You will pass through the South Gate, dating from the 15th century, if you enter on the A10. Bear left into The Friars to see the Whitefriars' Gateway, past the Greenland Fishery to St Margaret's Place, marked by the towers of the church of that name, and thence on past the Guildhall to the Tuesday Market Place at the head of High Street, where you may park. Walk back along King and Queen streets, to see in succession St George's Guildhall, a theatre in which Shakespeare is said to have played; the square-built Custom House, dating from 1683; Clifton House – a merchant's home open to the public – the Guildhall and Town Hall, of flint chequer work; and St Margaret's Church, best known for two huge 14th century Flemish brasses in the south chapel. Directly opposite is Hanseatic Warehouse, a reminder of the power of the Hanseatic League. Then return to the Tuesday Market Place, lined with handsome buildings. If hungry, you can get a reasonable meal in the Duke's Head Hotel there. **George Mason,** founder of New Hampshire and Governor of Newfoundland, was born near here. And George Vancouver, the explorer of the Pacific Northwest of America, was born off New Conduit Street.

• Evening is near. Press on! But first buy a copy of Fanny Burney's *Evelina,* or her *Diary* in the Penguin edition, to read this night, for she was born in Chapel Street, King's Lynn. Leave the town on the A148, and continue straight on an unnumbered but posted road to Castle Rising. A port until the sea receded, the village offers a lovely, pocket-sized 12th century castle sited in the midst of some of the finest earthworks in England. Join the A149 just beyond the village, bear right on the B1439, and pass through the forest preserve of Sandringham House. The gardens are open to the public when the Royal Family is away (open June–Sept., Wed., Thurs., 11–5). The rhododendrons are especially fine. The house is not open, but the parish church, **St Mary Magdalene,** is; there are many decorations here which were begun by Queen Victoria, and also plaques to members of the Royal Family. An American admirer of King Edward VII, Rodman Wanamaker, presented the oak pulpit, silver altar and reredos and bronze altar rail, between 1911 and 1927, as well as the gold communion plate and a jewelled Bible. Leave the grounds north on the B1440 to join the A149 again, and go 4 miles north (right) to **Heacham,** just to the west of the highway. This was the home of the Rolfe family. John Rolfe encouraged the formal cultivation of tobacco in Virginia; it was he who married Pocahontas, daughter of Powhatan, and brought her to England (see Tour 2) where she died, near Gravesend, at the age of 22. Heacham Hall is a Georgian house which incorporates the original Rolfe home, and the parish church contains the font in which John was baptized, as well as a carving of Pocahontas.

• And now hurry on to Norwich, 45 twilight miles east on the B1454, the A148, and the A1067, via Fakenham. If time permits, you may alternatively wish to turn south on the A149, back through Sandringham, then east on the A148 to Harpley, and south by a country road to Castle Acre, where an impressive Cluniac priory stands in ruins (and thus south on the A1065 to Swaffham, with its fine church, and east on the A47 to Norwich). Or beyond Fakenham at Guist, turn right on the B1110 to East Dereham. George Borrow, author of *Lavengro,* and a fife-player in the British army at Bunker Hill, was born at **Dumpling Green** here. Or you might continue at Guist on the A1067 to Bawdeswell. Here a left turn on the B1145 to **Reepham** brings you to the manor house of Booton where, with advance permission, you may see a portrait of Pocahontas, the church here having been built by the Rolfes. A right turn at Bawdeswell on the B1147 brings you to **Swanton Morley,** where Henry Ainsworth, a Pilgrim, was baptized. The village has ancestral links with Abraham Lincoln. The old homesite is owned by the National Trust, and the Angel Inn is the 16th century home of Richard Lincoln. The seal of the family appears on a window in the parish church. But for myself, I would bear directly ahead from Fakenham to Norwich, there to spend the night in a hotel carefully reserved in advance, since Norwich is often fully booked for days ahead. Either the Maid's Head Hotel, near the cathedral, or the Castle Hotel will provide good rooms and service and an adequate meal.

THIRD DAY

Norwich can take a full day, or only a full morning. If you want to see something of the Broads, you will have to opt for the shorter period in the city. (Note that the town is pronounced Nor-itch, and that the Broads are an interlocking system of lakes and rivers, not what you may have thought.) This city of 120,000 is best seen on foot, for the traffic pattern is one of the most complex in England. Begin with the cathedral and its environs, and especially with Elm Hill, the best preserved of Norwich's old streets, which runs off Princes Street. This is an excellent area for antiques. On the corner is St Peter Hungate Museum, a disused church converted into a museum of ecclesiastical art. At the other end of Elm Hill, a right turn brings one into Tombland, a former market place on which is the Maid's Head Hotel, behind a statue of Nurse Edith Cavell. Her grave is behind the cathedral, directly opposite. At the end of Tombland is **St Mary's,** a church with a tablet to a supposed ancestor of the Lincoln family. Another tablet will be found in **St Andrew's,** just beyond the far end of Princes Street (thereby completing a circle back beyond Elm Hill), which was the church in which the Rev. John Robinson, pastor to the Pilgrim Fathers, was a minister.

The cathedral is one of the finest in England, and its precinct incorporates a variety of structures, including an old grammar school, the Bishop's Palace and a cloister with two closes. The cathedral was begun in 1094, and its rarest treasure is two ancient stones which form the Ancient Throne, the oldest bishop's throne still in use in any cathedral in England. The vast interior comes as a surprise after the much-altered 19th century exterior west front, for it is in fact, one of the least changed Norman structures in England. There is much rich, yet well-spaced, interior detail, including 800 exceptional bosses, many in the nave (mirror tables are provided for examining them, but you will need binoculars to do the job properly), fine choir stalls with carved misericords beneath the seats, and bosses in Bauchun Chapel which illustrate the work of Chaucer. The apse is one of the finest in England, and the painted panels in St Saviour's Chapel are unique. The Erpingham Window in the north aisle of the presbytery shows the finest remaining medieval Norwich glass, reassembled in 1963, and to those knowledgeable in liturgical matters the Sanctuary is regarded as the most historically faithful in England. But to the non-specialist, the true glory of the cathedral arises from its cloisters, widely considered the most outstanding in any cathedral. The doors and bosses are especially fine here too. From the cloisters one may pass into an open space called Lower Close, and beyond it a short walk brings one to the medieval water gate, now called Pull's Ferry, one of the most photographed scenes in the city.

Now return to Tombland, bear left (south) along it, then right into Queen Street, jog left and right again into London Street, then left into Castle Street, and you will confront Norwich Castle, on your left, and the old Market Place in front of the Guildhall one short street away to the right. The castle has one of the largest and most handsome of Norman keeps; today it is a fine **museum,** which has some lesser American items, with a good **art gallery** attached. Here one may see many fine paintings, including one by C. H. Cox, the American, and a good Benjamin West oil (open weekdays 10–5, Sun. 2.30–5). The Market Place is one of the most interesting in England. To the left is St Peter Mancroft, a church of major importance, Perpendicular, and dating from 1435. The interior is severely Gothic and worth visiting largely to sense what the light is like in a church without stained glass windows, and to examine the baptistry, into which the font is set – rare in England. The Guildhall is open weekday afternoons and is worth a visit. Beyond it to the north is the Maddermarket Theatre, followed by Strangers' Hall on Charing Cross Street, a 15th century house with rooms furnished to various periods. A left turn at the Guildhall would have brought you into St Giles Street, where at the top stands St John the Baptist Church, a massive structure built at the end of the 19th century. Ordinarily, churches of this period are not interesting, and to see five or more churches of any date at one time may usually represent diminishing returns – although there are thirty-three pre-Reformation churches in Norwich, at least ten of them demanding your attention if time permits – but this one is unusual. It was built in Early English style and may be the most successful modern attempt to capture medieval Gothic in all Britain; the interior is most impressive, the stained glass very good, and the whole is a convincing testimony to the fact that to imitate need not always mean to fail. Alternatively, a right turn from the Guildhall would produce The Bridewell Museum, in the alley of that name. The museum is in a 14th century merchant's house, and its display of local industries provides a quick history of Norwich. Nowhere else may you see a display on the breeding of canaries (open weekdays 10–5).

North of the river are a number of other interesting sites, including four older churches of merit, but unless you can give Norwich a full day you will have to forgo them. Because of her interest in America, you may wish to visit the birthplace of **Harriet Martineau,** the writer and reformer, in the corner house on Gurney's Court. The court is reached from Tombland going north, across the river into Magdalene Street, and right shortly before coming to St Saviour's. And you may find one of England's most interesting nonconformist churches, originally Unitarian and now Congregationalist, on the north side of Colegate, which leads left off Magdalene Street just after crossing the bridge.

The day may now be gone. At the very least, it will be time for a late lunch. There are no places to recommend particularly, although the Royal Hotel is trustworthy, and it is said that you may obtain samphire (samfer) there. Since it is sea grass cooked and buttered, you may not wish to find it. **John Jenney,** a Pilgrim, was born somewhere near the hotel, in 1594.

And now the Broads. These are lakes set into a large fan bounded roughly by Norwich, Lowestoft and North Walsham. It is an excellent area for boating, since there are many rivers and small cuts, or canals, which afford 150 miles of connected, navigable water. The English enjoy houseboating here, and one form of holiday is either to hire a motor-driven craft or to join a water-based tour group. (The area is best seen from the water, but this requires at least three days.) Except for Breydon Water, the second largest lake – near Great Yarmouth – the lakes are artificial, the result of peat digging prior to the 15th century, after which the pits filled with water. The entire area is a birdwatcher's paradise. Fishing is good, and you may buy a permit for a small fee at a post office, or through the tackle dealer from whom you rent equipment. Since the back roads are narrow – the only time I ran a car off the road in thousands of miles of driving in Britain was near Hickling Green – you would be wise to buy a detailed map of the area in a Norwich bookshop or stationery shop before exploring.

But you, harried and hurried, have only three to five hours, so let me suggest a route which I think will show you the best, the typical, and the most interesting. Leave Norwich on the A47 as if for Great Yarmouth until you reach the Circular Road, go left to the B1140, and then right to South Walsham. Here are two churches in a single churchyard. Turn left for Ranworth, where the church – called 'the Cathedral of the Broads' – has the finest screen in East Anglia and a solid tower which you may climb for views across the Broads to the northeast. Continue on to Woodbastwick (just before town a lane to the right will take you to the edge of the river for a pastoral view) thence to Wroxham, a typically cluttered boating area in the summer. Turn right on the A1151, then right on the B1354 for Horning, an attractive village, where a right turn carries you along the river to the church and back onto the main road, thence to Ludham, a village of Georgian houses thatched with reed. The church is a fine one with an excellent rood screen from 1493. In smaller churches such as these, one may often notice details missed in the larger and more elaborate ones: here, for example, a St Catherine's wheel, or in South Walsham the poupée heads on the bench ends – both seen elsewhere but now standing in relief when not challenged for attention.

Carry on to Potter Heigham: to the right is a medieval bridge across the Thurne, to the left the old church with an odd round tower. Turn north on the A149, and almost immediately angle right for Hickling Heath and Hickling Green. Above Hickling Green drive due east for the Stubb Windmill (best reached by walking the last quarter-mile). Then from Hickling Green north via Hickling to Ingham, with a pleasant church typical of the Broads, right on the B1151, and then south on the B1159 along the coast to Horsey. You may view Horsey Mere from the bank here, next to the fine windmill. There are a number of windmills dotted throughout this area, sparsely enough to remind one of Cape Cod far more than of Holland, and to those interested in windmill construction, unique. At West Somerton turn right on the B1152 to Acle and then back to Norwich on the A47 – if time is now running short.

If you have an hour's margin, however, turn left beyond Martham (after Somerton) on the A149 through **Ormesby St Michael,** birthplace of several of the Pilgrims, to Great Yarmouth. The English swim here from the sandy beach off Caister; to all save Americans from Maine and the Pacific Northwest, the water will probably be too cold. Caister Castle, a mile inland west on the A1064, is interesting.

Great Yarmouth is a market town and seaside resort which once was important in the herring industry. Much damaged in World War II by bombing, the main attraction now is the mile of quayside along the River Yare, where Georgian buildings survive, and the seafront, which if you will not be getting to Brighton, Bournemouth or other major seaside resorts, will show you something of the impacted way in which the British pass their summer holidays. Anna Sewell, author of *Black Beauty,* was born in a house next to the parish church. 10 miles south is Lowestoft, another resort, famous for the ware that bears its name. The headland here, the Ness, is England's most easterly point. Or you may return to Norwich from Great Yarmouth on the A47, which plunges straight across the Halvergate Marshes, with glimpses of Breydon Water on the left and the River Bure on the right. The night is again best spent in Norwich.

FOURTH DAY

You will, in fact, require two days if you attempt to see *all* that follows. The assumption is that you will pick and choose. In a direct line Norwich is 115 miles from London. However, the countryside between is Suffolk and Essex, two of the three counties (Lincolnshire being the other) richest in American-related scenes. As a minimum, with early rising, you should wish to see Aldeburgh, Ipswich, Colchester and Chelmsford, and this you can do in a single day, arriving in London in time for a late dinner. This means hurrying past some fine restaurants at other than mealtimes, and not lingering for the festival at Aldeburgh should your visit coincide with it; to do these as well, you would have to end this fourth day at the rail-

way station at Ipswich, where you may drop off your rental car and
return to Liverpool Street Station on an evening train. The tour below
shows all sites off the main Norwich–Aldeburgh–Ipswich–Colchester–
Chelmsford route as side excursions, set off from the main text with the
symbol •

Leave Norwich southwards on the A146, then right on the A144 through
Bungay. Just north, at Ditchingham, lived H. Rider Haggard, author of
She and *King Solomon's Mines;* there is a window to him in the church.
Continue 21 miles to a junction with the A12. Turn left to the A1095 and
right to **Southwold.** This was the home of George Orwell (Eric Blair).
The pulpit in the parish church was a gift of the people of Southold, New
York.

• Or turn right on the A12 and then left on a country road marked
Darsham, carrying on through Westleton to **Dunwich,** a ghost town on
the seacoast. This was the birthplace of Sir George Downing, Harvard
graduate (see Cambridge) and tutor, whose uncle was John Winthrop,
Governor of Massachusetts. Henry James and other writers have been
attracted to this town, which is disappearing under the sea. Return to
Westleton, turn left, and follow the B1125 to the B1122, and thence south
to Aldeburgh.

• Alternatively, just beyond Bungay turn right on the B1062, an attractive
road, to join the A143 at Homersfield, and thence to **Redenhall,** birthplace
of Samuel Fuller, the physician to the Pilgrims. At **Redgrave** – west on
the A143, then right on the B1113 – Sir John Holt, jurist, who declared
a Virginia slave brought into England to be free, thus initiating abolition,
is buried. Proceed southwest through Brockdish to Hoxne on a signposted
but unnumbered road. It was here that Edmund, king of the East Saxons,
was beheaded in 870 by the Danes for refusing to renounce Christianity.
Follow the posting for Chickering, Wingfield and Fressingfield, where
one finds the Fox and Goose, a pub widely debated among gourmets.
Here one should request a menu in advance and order by telephone unless
a steak is sufficient. Then go south on the B1116 to **Framlingham,**
ancestral home of President James A. Garfield, of Josiah Quincy, of the
Danforth family, and of Richard Henry Dana. Right on the B1119, at
Saxtead Green, is the finest old mill in Suffolk. Left on the B1119 is
Saxmundham; go south on the A12 from Saxmundham, and within a
mile left on the B1121 to **Sternfield** where, in the parish church, is a
painting by Benjamin West, who enjoyed visiting nearby. The B1121
carries on to the A1094, thence left to Aldeburgh.

Aldeburgh is an attractive seaside resort. George Crabbe, the poet, was
born here in 1754 and the church of St Peter and St Paul has memorials
to the family. The Moot Hall is still the town hall; it dates from the
early 16th century and is open in the summer. The real point of Alde-

burgh is the famed Music Festival, began in 1948, which is held near here every June. Since Benjamin Britten, the originator of the Festival, lived in Aldeburgh, the Festival was very much his. At Snape, 5 miles northwest on the A1094, is The Maltings, a beautifully restored set of industrial buildings dating from 1859, the major structure now being the highly successful opera house and concert hall for the Festival. The views of the tidal River Alde, the tasteful shop of local craftsmen's work, and the attractive parish church help make Snape unusually pleasant. In 1948 an American, **John T. Appleby,** who served with the thousands of American airmen who flew from airfields in Suffolk, Essex and Norfolk, wrote a moving little book, *Suffolk Summer* (it is still in print, and may be purchased from the East Anglian Magazine, 6 Great Colman Street, Ipswich) in which he declared the English landscape in Suffolk, and especially around Snape, to be 'at its subtlest and best'. (He also nominated the Beccles Marshes, 9 miles west of Lowestoft.)

From Snape, you may avoid the congested A12 again. (A right turn north, then left on a country road to Bredfield, brings you to the birthplace of Edward Fitzgerald, he who wrote *The Ruba'iyat of Omar Khayyam*; he is buried in Boulge churchyard, south.) The A12 brings you to Ipswich in a few miles – if you *are* looking for the railway station, be certain to have allowed enough time, for traffic is both complex and heavy in Ipswich. Just before reaching town, a country road right takes you to Playford, where you may see from the lane the home of Thomas Clarkson, the Great British anti-slavery leader who had such impact in America. The house is private.

Ipswich, a community of 125,000, is rich in Pilgrim – and other – associations. Cardinal Wolsey was born here, in Nicholas Street; Gainsborough lived here; Dickens wrote of the Great White Horse Inn in *Pickwick Papers*; Grinling Gibbons carved a fine pulpit for St Mary-le-Tower. The Christchurch Mansion Museum is disappointing, although there are Gainsboroughs and Constables. Indeed, the entire town is disappointing, and it need not detain you for long, although coffee in the Great White Horse, as homage to Dickens, provides a pleasant break. To reach it, go into the middle of the town on the A1071 to Northgate Street, turn left, then right on Tavern Street; it is on the corner. You may walk in 15 minutes to both St Mary-le-Tower and to The Ancient House, on Butter Market. Proceed up Tavern Street and it junctions with the A12 for Colchester. (17 miles north via the A45, the A140, left on the A1120, and then right on country roads, is **Mendlesham,** where there is a memorial to the 34th Group of the U.S.A.A.F. Richard Hakluyt, who made the New World so well known, was rector of **Wetheringsett,** 2 miles northeast.)

• One may leave Ipswich going west on the A1071 for the Constable Country, well known to many from the great artist's paintings. At Had-leigh the church and castle (which affords fine views from its tower) are worth visiting. Proceed on to Boxford, then right to **Groton.** The manor here was the ancestral home of the Winthrop family, and the American school is named after it. John Winthrop, first governor of Massachusetts, was born at **Edwardstone,** a mile west, via Millbreen; it was he who led the *Arbella* group to the New World in 1630. John Winthrop the younger, founder of Connecticut, was also born here. A brass to the family may be seen in the parish church, and the glass in the east window commemorates John. At **Lindsey,** north, the St James chapel belonged to John Winthrop. (The phrase 'linsey-woolsey' comes from the early cloth trade here.)

• A cluster of particularly attractive Suffolk villages, singled out by John Appleby in his book, is nearby: Kersey, the one Appleby likes the best, is 4 miles northeast of Groton, and Bildeston and Chelsworth lie another 4 miles north. Lavenham, west of Bildeston, often called 'the most delightful village in England', has many timbered houses, a fine medieval market place, one of the best guildhalls in the country and a stunning church said to have the finest bells in the land. It is reputed that 'Twinkle, twinkle, little star' was written at Shilling Old Grange. Yet another 6 miles southwest, by country roads, is Long Melford, on the A134, contender for the 'most beautiful village' accolade (best seen entering from the south). The church is one of the finest 15th century Perpendicular structures to be found; there is much stained glass. Melford Hall, an Elizabethan manor house, may also be visited. 6 miles more on the A1092 brings you to Cavendish, another lovely village. Turn left on the B1064, then right on a country road to **Belchamp St Paul;** the parish church has a memorial window here to the American Golding family. 4 miles south of Long Melford is Sudbury, noted for Gainsborough's house (open Tues.–Sat., 10.30–12.30, 2–5, Sun. 2–5). Just beyond, you enter Essex, linked to America by over 100 uses of place names. Or at Cavendish you may continue on the A1092 through Clare – one of the most attractive villages in West Suffolk, on the River Stour – to the A604, thence right to **Haverhill,** where Nathaniel Ward, who named the city of the same name in Massachusetts, lived. This excursion brings you in an additional 19 miles into Cambridge, where you could drop the rental car and return to London by train.

• From Sudbury you can also proceed south on the A131 to **Braintree,** which produced two men for the *Mayflower*: John Carver and John Bridge. In the town a country road right to **Bocking** brings one to a parish church in which there is a stained glass window to emigrants to America. Nathaniel Rogers, pastor of Ipswich, Massachusetts, was curate here. 2 miles northwest of Braintree, on a country road off the B1053, is **Panfield,** where Edward Bangs, a Pilgrim to Plymouth, Massachusetts, was born. (North on the B1053 is **Wethersfield,** site of an R.A.F. station in World War II at which United States Army Air Force units were headquartered. In **Finchingfield,** slightly beyond, is a church partially repaired with American assistance.) From Braintree continue south on the A131 and the A130 to Chelmsford, or turn east on the A120 for Colchester, to return to the main tour.

The road from Ipswich to Colchester is wide and fast, and the 18 miles pass quickly. (One may divert right at the B1068 to visit Stoke-by-Nayland, a particularly attractive Suffolk village, thence by the B1087 to Nayland and by the A134 to Colchester. Stoke-by-Nayland is in the Constable country, and the great painter gave us many scenes of the Stour between here and Dedham, to the east.) If you stick to the A12 from Ipswich, be certain to divert left twice: first on the B1070 to Flatford Mill, still easily recognizable from John Constable's work, and via East Bergholt, where he was born in 1776; and second, a mile later, on the B1029 to **Dedham,** another mile away. Roger Sherman and General W. T. Sherman trace their ancestors to this village, where there is a house on the main street called 'Shermans'. Then drive south to Ardleigh and right on the A137 to Colchester. (Beyond Ardleigh the B1029 comes to **Great Bromley,** where the parish church contains a memorial window to the emigrants to colonial America. 15 miles northeast on the A604 from Colchester is **Harwich,** where the ferry leaves for Holland and where the captain of the *Mayflower,* Christopher Jones, was married in St Nicholas Church. His house at 21 King's Head Street is marked with a plaque.)

Colchester, birthplace of several of the Pilgrims, has 79,000 people, an oyster festival in October, and a castle with the largest Norman keep in England (open weekdays 10–5, Sun. 2.30–5) in the middle of the town. Park nearby and walk west on High Street and north on North Hill to see the oldest buildings. Shakespeare's Cymbeline was king of the ancient settlement here – Camulodunum; the Romans occupied it in AD 43 when King Cole reigned and established one of their major colonies. Here Queen Boadicea's followers revolted and massacred the Romans in AD 60. The Holytrees Museum is devoted to the archaeology of this early period. The Minories in the High Street is also a gallery, with Colchester clocks and several Constables. There is a memorial bench to American troops on the side of the Ipswich road, and the new University of Essex, just outside the town at Wivenhoe Park (take the A133 southeast to the B1028 and then right) is well worth viewing for its architecture.

Leave Colchester on the A12, which is four-lanes nearly all the way to **Chelmsford,** 22 miles southwest. The road passes through Whitham, long the home of Dorothy L. Sayers. In the last Sayers contest, held annually, Americans carried off the first three prizes. **Boreham,** left off the road just before reaching the city, has a stone memorial to the U.S. armed forces. **Springfield,** on the northeast edge of Chelmsford, sent John and William Pynchon to Massachusetts, where the latter helped found Springfield, Massachusetts. The Reverend Thomas Hooker, founder of Hartford,

Connecticut, was associated with Chelmsford's St Mary's Church – now the Cathedral – and Sir Walter Mildmay, founder of Emmanuel College, Cambridge, which inspired the Separatist movement, was born here. The **Cathedral** is worth visiting, although it is a lesser one, having been elevated from a parish church in 1914. There is a commemorative window to the American air force men stationed in Chelmsford during World War II, and the entire south porch is something of a shrine to the men of the 8th and 9th U.S.A.A.F. If British birds' eggs interest you, visit the Chelmsford and Essex Museum in Oaklands Park. There are then essentially two routes into London.

Option One   Leave Chelmsford east on the A130, then left on the A414, and left on a country road to **Little Baddow,** where Thomas Hooker and John Eliot conducted a school together. At **Danbury** (after which the Connecticut town is named) continue on the A414 to Runsell Green, then left to **Woodham Walter.** It is believed that the brick church of St Luke, in Isle of Wight County, Virginia, was built to the model of the parish church of St Michael here. Carry on through the village, then right to **Maldon,** where there are several old houses. The 13th century tower on All Saints' Church is the only triangular one in Britain; inside is a Washington Window, presented in 1928 by the people of Malden [*sic*], Massachusetts, to commemorate **Lawrence Washington,** great-great-grandfather of George, who is buried in an unmarked grave in the churchyard. Christopher Jones of the *Mayflower* was baptized here, two speakers of the Massachusetts House of Assembly were born here, as was General Horatio Gates who, as an American, defeated Burgoyne at Saratoga in 1777. The town has many links by emigration with New Hampshire and Rhode Island. Go south on the B1018, then right on the B1010 to **Purleigh,** where Lawrence Washington was rector from 1632–43. Carry on to the junction with the B1418, then turn left to **Woodham Ferrers,** where Archbishop Sandys lived, who was the father of Edwin Sandys, so important to the history of Virginia. There is a monument in the church to Cecilie, the archbishop's wife. The B1418 south junctions with the B1012; bear right to the A132, which is to be found after the A130 crossroads.

(Left on the A130, again on the A127, right on the A129 and left on the A13 produces Leigh-on-Sea. Here seaside stands will sell you cockles, eels and periwinkles, and you may make an excellent and hearty meal on such delights and local fish at Oscar's Dining Room, 11 Leigh Hill. If you continue on to Southend-on-Sea [where the world's longest pleasure pier juts into the Thames estuary] and turn left to Rochford on the B1013, then right on a country road, you reach **Great Stambridge.** The parish church contains a plaque to John Winthrop, who was married here, and a memorial window.)

Alternatively, from the A130 crossroads, take the A132 to Wickford,

then right on the A129 to **Billericay**. A timber-framed house opposite the
parish church here was a meeting place for the Pilgrim Fathers. An inscription on Mayflower Hall is to Christopher Martin, governor of the
Mayflower, and three others who sailed aboard the vessel. Just south of
Billericay, to the left off the B1007, is **Great Burstead,** where Martin was
born; he was married in St Mary Magdalen Church here (which is more
interesting for its memorial to George FitzGeorge, illegitimate son of
George IV, who is buried here). The A129 leads on from Billericay to
Shenfield, where Nathaniel Ward is buried. Follow the A1023 to Brent-
wood and turn south on the B186 until you reach the B187; turn right
here to Cranham. James Oglethorpe, founder of Georgia, retired to
Cranham Hall in 1743, where he introduced pecans. He died there in
1785 and the tombs of him and his wife are in the parish church. (The
B186 continuing south passes through **South Ockendon.** In St Mary
Magdalene Church are brasses to Gilbert Saltonstall and a fine monument to Sir Richard Saltonstall, who sailed on the *Arbella.* The *Mayflower's* physician, Samuel Fuller, came from here as well. The B186
continues to the A13, and thence the A1089 and the A128 lead to
Tilbury, of the famous docks. A country road east leads to **West Tilbury** –
William Laud was Rector here – and a fine preserved fort overlooking the
Thames at East Tilbury.) From Cranham the B187 leads on to the A124;
turn right on the A125 to **Romford**. Francis Quarles, who wrote the
early metrical psalms sung in the churches of John Winthrop and John
Cotton, was born here. During World War II some of the Royal Air
Force's most daring pilots, such as Douglas Bader, operated from an
aerodrome near here. Then carry on to London, 10 miles away, on a
choice of major trunk roads.

Option Two   Alternatively, leave Chelmsford west on the A122 through
Ongar to a junction with the A128, then south to Chipping Ongar. A country road left beyond the town takes one to **Stondon Massey,** whose minister, Nathaniel Ward, bequeathed 500 acres to Harvard College before
leaving for New England. Right from Chipping Ongar 1 mile on a
country road is **Greensted.** The wooden church here is the oldest such
in England, the split log walls of the nave dating from Saxon times, and
the white-painted tower with its shingled spire being seen as an ancestor
of the timber houses of New England. Essex's emphasis on clapboarding
(called weatherboarding in England) is, in fact, clearly such an influence
throughout. Return to Chipping Ongar, turn north around the Ongar
circus, onto the B184, and then immediately left on a road posted for
Moreton. Beyond is **High Laver,** where in a now destroyed mansion three
figures famous in American history lived: Roger Williams, founder of
Rhode Island; John Norton, the chief persecutor of the Quakers in Massachusetts; and John Locke, who spent his last fourteen years here, and
who wrote the Fundamental Constitutions of Carolina. His tomb is in the

parish church, marked by the American and British Commonwealth Association in 1957. Williams was married in this church.

Continue north to Harlow, one of the largest and best planned of the post-1945 British New Towns. A portion of the old town has been preserved, and the contrast is instructive. Harlow has been widely studied by Americans interested in the problems of town planning. From Harlow you may turn south on the A11 through Epping, reaching London in 25 miles.

Beyond Epping the A11 passes through the scraggly remains of Epping Forest. A side road to the right leads to High Beach, where at **Lippits Hill** one may see a monument on the site of the first American anti-aircraft gun emplacement that was fired to defend London during World War II. Turn left for **Chigwell.** Charles Dickens wrote part of *Barnaby Rudge* here, and William Penn went to Chigwell School. Just beyond the Underground station, turn sharply right and then left on the first main street to **Grange Hill,** where American construction units worked in World War II to help prepare supply lines for the nineteen American airfields which sprang up throughout what became known as American Occupied Essex during the war. Pass through **Woodford Green,** where one may see an American flag flying behind a wall at the home of one of the principal figures of the English-Speaking Union. Follow the signs for **Walthamstow,** where Penn's family lived, and thence into central London. (The William Morris Gallery, in Lloyd Park on Forest Road, Walthamstow, superbly brings to life the work of the famous designer; his chief furniture designer was an American, George Jack.)

Or you may follow an interesting circuit north and then west. Leave Harlow northwards on the A11, and at Sawbridgeworth turn right on the A414. At Hatfield Heath, turn left on the B183 to **Hatfield Broad Oak,** the village used by the American novelist Marion Crawford for his book *The Tale of a Lonely Parish.* Carry on to the A120. A right turn goes to **Great Dunmow,** site of the ancient ritual of the Dunmow Flitch – the giving of a side of bacon to married couples who swear they have had no quarrel for a year and a day. There is a memorial to American airmen on the Blue Gates of Easton Lodge. To the west the A120 passes the pitiful remnant of Hatfield Forest and through Bishop's Stortford (see the beginning of this tour). Bear left on the B1004 to **Widford,** where John Eliot was baptized in the parish church, which contains a memorial window to him. Eliot emigrated to Boston and became a missionary to the Indians; in 1663 he translated the Bible into Algonquin; his was the first Bible to be printed in America. He also helped compile *The Bay Psalm Book,* the most valuable American publication. (Widford is the village in which lives the lady who makes the attractive miniature mice figures one can purchase in London's Burlington Arcade.) The B1004 goes on to **Ware,** where the parish church contains a memorial to Charles Chauncy, second President of Harvard College. North of Ware on the

A10 is Wadesmill, where a roadside obelisk marks the spot where the Father of English Abolitionism, Thomas Clarkson, resolved in 1785 to spend his life fighting slavery. Beyond Ware on the A414 is **Hertford.** The All Saints Church here is linked to Hartford, Connecticut. Beyond is **Hertingfordbury,** where the church contains a monument to Anne, wife of Lord Baltimore, founder of Maryland. Continue on the A414 past Welwyn (pronounced 'Wellin') Garden City, one of the original (1920) New Towns, to the A1. Just north is **Brocket Hall,** home of Lord Melbourne, Lord Palmerston and Lord Mount Stephen – he who built the Canadian transcontinental railway. Now follow the A1 south into London and take the A41 right-hand fork after Mill Hill for Marble Arch.

WHAT TO READ   E. M. Forster is one of the 20th century writers intimately associated with Cambridge. Longfellow is one American, for he lived in Craigie House in 1829. Looking backward, feast on Erasmus, Christopher Marlowe, Milton – who had rooms in Christ's – Samuel Pepys, Laurence Sterne, Thomas Gray (of both Peterhouse and Pembroke), Wordsworth, Byron, Thomas Babington Macaulay, William Makepeace Thackeray, Coleridge and A. E. Housman – all students at the university. Byron's statue, rejected by Westminster Abbey, is the Thorvaldsen masterpiece in Trinity library. Of course, read T. S. Eliot. By the time you have finished, you will be of like mind with Gray, who thought Cambridge 'a delight of a place when there's nobody in it' – for if you come in the summer, your reading (bought, one hopes, at Bowes or Heffers on the spot), your punting and your walking will be much jostled by the crowds. Let modern Cambridge jostle you by reading of it in J. D. Watson's vivid book, *The Double Helix,* or some of C. P. Snow's 'Lewis Eliot' sequence of novels, especially *The Masters* or *The Affair.* When near Newmarket, read the thrillers of Dick Francis, whose books generally revolve round horse racing.

10 Based on York: Hull Whitby Ripon

Perhaps the Englishman's best-loved city, outside London, is York. It is the focus for a number of tour operators based in London, and if one wants the convenience of a totally organized package, in two-day to five-day segments, one has only to contact one of the companies advertised in the back of *In Britain* magazine. Assuming that one prefers the flexibility of a self-conducted tour, and that one will want to combine cities and scenes in a point-to-point way, the following tour is arranged on the basis of three to six days, and, as with all tours in this book, includes several American-related sites. The region is, with the exception of Wales, one of the least promising in terms of good food, and by English standards the distances to be travelled are relatively great, but the rewards of York, the North York Moors, Rievaulx and Fountains abbeys and the Yorkshire Dales more than compensate for gastronomic inconvenience. You may also intersect with Tour 8, to the Pilgrim Country.

If travelling to York by rail, there to rent a car, as I recommend, one leaves London from King's Cross, one of the city's least interesting stations. You will be travelling on an historic line, however, for the Great Northern started from Doncaster, south of York, and reached London in 1846; further, at Darlington, between York and Durham, one may see Stephenson's original locomotive, the first in Britain, placed within an enclosure on the platform (if travelling by train onward from York to Newcastle or Edinburgh, you will have just enough time to pop out of your carriage, to the right, to see it before the train moves on). For train spotters – a particularly English breed of young children, who collect engine numbers – this is especially rewarding country. But for yourself, you will need only to know that the world's steam traction speed record of 126 mph was set on this route, and that the longest non-stop run in Britain begins at King's Cross four times a day – 268 miles to Newcastle, on the way to Edinburgh, at an average of 60 mph. (High-speed passenger trains running regularly at 125 mph have been used on parts of this route.) Be certain, then, that you are on the right train for York, only 188 miles away. The journey should take about 2 hours and 45 minutes, unless you stray onto a stopping train, and it's worth finding out about any special British Rail excursion tickets as some of these include accommodation in York as well (inquire of Golden Rail Holidays, York).

York, a city of 120,000, is one of the few remaining truly medieval communities in England and one of the most attractive. Although it is a major railway junction, it has also retained an air of relative peacefulness, and is one of the most attractive cities in Britain for the aimless stroll. Once the second largest city in England, York retains 3 miles of medieval city wall, a maze of old streets, many still cobblestoned, including the Shambles, hundreds of ancient buildings, and several good museums. There is a Triennial Festival (there is one in 1984) in midsummer. The highlights, however, are Britain's finest minster, the largest railway museum in the world, an attractive university, and the Yorkshire Dales and North York Moors national parks, both relatively nearby. An Archbishop here, Edwin Sandys, was the father of the **Edwin Sandys** who helped found Virginia, and it was by the chancery court in York that Richard Clyfton, the man who was rector at Babworth and pastor at Scrooby, and thus instrumental in the emigration of the Pilgrims to America (see Tour 8), was excommunicated. The numerous Yorks in the United States are the namesakes of this, the original.

You may begin sightseeing in York immediately upon arrival, for a right turn when leaving the railway station, and a short walk down hill, brings you to the new **National Railway Museum.** It is unique in its varied collection of locomotives, coaches, models, lamps, signalling apparatus and uniforms. Here you may see a Stourbridge locomotive. It was a Stourbridge engine, the *Lion*, exported to America in 1829, that was the first to run on rails in North America. If you are staying the night, you may then want to take a taxi from the station to your hotel. In York there is little choice, and there is nothing that can be thought of as 'quaintly English', whatever that may mean. The best hotel is the Viking, newish (1968) and rather American, with a high-rise over the River Ouse and a central location to recommend it. But since the English 'traveller' (travelling salesman) and businessman think it excellent, a night spent there will provide insights you will miss if you restrict yourself to American Hiltons on the one hand and tastefully converted Georgian mansions on the other. In York you definitely must book in advance.

York was a Roman fortress town from AD 71 and since the Roman occupation lasted 340 years one may expect to find reminders about.

YORK MINSTER

From the 7th century, York was also a major place of learning, with one of the most famous of the early teachers, Alcuin, establishing the equivalent of a university here until Charlemagne called him to Aachen in 782. The Danes captured York in 876, and it was destroyed by fire in 1069, just in time to give the Normans an opportunity to rebuild on the ruins. In due course York grew to prominence on the prosperity of the English wool trade, then declined, only to recover again on the basis of the railway age in the 19th century. It is this layering of differing cultures that gives York its peculiar fascination, as you will discover by wandering about.

Start at **York Minster.** When St Augustine came to convert the English in 597, his group brought instructions to use London and York as their base. The present building dates from the 13th century and is the largest Gothic structure in England; struck seriously by the death-watch beetle, York Minster was the object of a massive campaign to raise funds so that the church might be saved, and for years it was of interest for a most unusual reason: one could watch one of the most difficult repair operations in the world in progress. In 1974, however, the scaffolding was removed and the cathedral stood again in all its medieval glory. Its special attraction, other than sheer size and the intricacy of its Gothic tracery, is in its stained glass, regarded by many as the finest in Britain. Special talks are often given, at other churches as well as the Minster, on the history and art of stained glass, and if the subject is of interest to you, York is the place to begin. The choir screen is the most ornate in England, and an astronomical clock – a memorial to the airmen, British, Commonwealth and American, who died in World War II – and the Grinling Gibbons sculptures are of major importance. There is also a superb undercroft museum. But it is the glass which stuns the visitor: nearly half of all the 12th century glass which has survived in Britain is here, in the Minster's 117 windows. The Five Sisters Window contains the largest expanse of ancient glass in the world. (Incidentally, if terminology confuses you here, you should know that a cathedral is a church which is the headquarters of a bishop; thus, York *is* a cathedral. However, mission buildings established to evangelize Anglo-Saxon England may still be called minsters, as is the case here.) Do not miss the polygonal chapter house, one of the two or three finest in Britain. Behind the Minster is the Treasurer's House, a superb 17th century building (open except Wed., 10–1, 2–4).

Beyond the Minster, on Bootham, is the **City Art Gallery** (open weekdays 10–5) where there is a good collection of Old Masters and a John Singer Sargent. Further on in the park are the ruins of St Mary's Abbey, with a small museum nearby. Here too is the impressive Multangular Tower. The **Guildhall** and Mansion House are on the river's edge on the way back toward the railway station: inside is a memorial tablet from New York City to its namesake (although New York City was, in fact, named after the Duke of York, not the city). The Guildhall was largely destroyed during World War II and was rebuilt in 1960; in it, and in the Mansion House, is one of England's finest collections of old silver, and the Guildhall contains an excellent example of modern stained glass work. Nearby is the Yorkshire Museum, off Museum Street (open weekdays 10–5) where one may learn in particular of the city's Roman past. The maze of streets in this area is quite complex, and it is best to ask your way to the Church of All Saints, Pavement, a 15th century church famed for its pulpits, and for the Church of All Saints, North Street, which is singled out for its medieval glass, especially fifteen panels devoted to the last fifteen days of the world. In the **Friends' Burial Ground,** Cromwell Road beyond Bishophill – from All Saints, walk with the river to your left five long blocks and turn right up Carr Lane – is the tomb of John Woolman, an early leader of the anti-slavery movement and famous American Quaker essayist, who died while visiting England.

The other focus of interest in York is around Clifford's Tower. Walk across the Ouse Bridge onto Nessgate, and if you continue straight on into the Stonebow to Aldwalk, you will find **St Cuthbert's Church,** which has associations with General Wolfe. Here too is St Anthony's Hall and, beyond, the Merchant Taylors' Hall and portions of the old city wall. A right turn, away from the bridge, brings you quickly to the fine Castle Museum, one of the most unusual folk museums in Britain. A series of reconstructed streets reveals much about English life from Tudor to

Victorian times and there is a unique collection of fire insurance marks
and constables' truncheons, a fine collection of Treen, and a gallery devoted to the evolution of the fireplace. Adjacent is the old Debtors'
Prison, now a museum, with a collection of old weapons and toys, and
nearby is Clifford's Tower. Behind the museums is Piccadilly, and parallel
to it is Fossgate. Here is the **Merchant Adventurers' Hall** – the company
which controlled much early colonial trade. Outside the city, off the A1079
in Heslington, is the architecturally attractive new University of York,
easily reached by bus.

Before leaving York, be certain to walk around the inner city on the
ancient wall. You may mount the wall at several points and in spring and
summer, when the gardens are in bloom, the walk is especially attractive.
And do not fail to go shopping in the maze of tiny streets below the
Minster.

York is an excellent base for a number of circle tours. By one, you may
leave York on the A1079, going east toward Kingston upon Hull, crossing
the Humber at Hull and returning to York via Selby. This is route One A.
Second, you may circle north from Hull back toward York. This is route
One B. Third, you may circle through the North York Moors to Whitby
and return via Teesside. This is route Two. Fourth, you may go west, from
York, to Ripon, to explore the Yorkshire Dales – like the Moors a national
park – and by relatively minor roads see Richmond and either carry on to
Durham or return to York. This is route Three. You could also, of course,
move southwest from York, into Leeds and the industrial cities of Yorkshire, but unless factories fascinate, there is little to recommend such a
decision. These options are described separately below.

Option One   Leaving York on the A1079, turn left on the A166 to Stamford Bridge. Here, to the south and on the east bank of the Derwent, was
fought in 1066 the Battle of Stamford Bridge, one of the dramatic moments in Britain's history: for here Harold won, defeating the Earl of
Northumbria, before racing south to suffer final defeat at Hastings at the
hands of William the Conqueror. In general, Britain has done little to
preserve its battle sites – you will find nothing like the carefully groomed
American Civil War parks – and such is the case here, but the land has
changed very little. (Another notable battle site is that of Marston Moor,
associated with the Parliamentarian siege of the Royalist army in York
during the Civil War in 1644; it may be seen 5 miles west of York via
the B1224, and thence on a country road signposted for Tockwith.) There
is an excellent pub in Stamford Bridge, the Corn Mill.

Having done your duty to History, follow the country road south along
the Derwent to its junction with the A1079, turn left, and hurry on
through Yorkshire's East Riding to **Beverley.** There are many connections
between this town and American Free Masonry, but this is not why you
are here: you have come to see Beverley Minster, visible for miles as you

approach, felt by many to be the Gothic masterpiece of the north. It is a truly great church, striking in its elegance and its facade is considered to be the finest of the 14th century in England. The perfection of interior detail is often quite subtle here, and to understand Beverley Minster well you must purchase, even if you generally do not do so, the illustrated guide book available inside. See in particular the tomb of Lady Eleanor Percy, the exceptional east window, the west door, and the fine stone carvings and corbels throughout. Visit also St Mary's Church, to see its 15th century painted chancel roof.

Then on to Hull, as Kingston upon Hull is always called. Halifax, Huddersfield and Hull are a trinity invoked by the British (Hull usually pronounced in this case as Hell) to indicate just how unattractive industrial cities are, and the phrase is not mistaken. One visits Hull partially because it is there, on the edge of the Humber, with a new connection – the world's longest single-span suspension bridge, opened in 1981 – to the south shore; partially because one may want to pay one's respect to the British anti-slavery movement by visiting Wilberforce House; or simply because one may be interested in industry, and especially fishing fleets. If none of these apply, avoid Hull, either returning to York from Beverley or turning north toward Great Driffield.

As for Hull, you will enter from the north. To the right, signposted, is the University, with an interesting collection of Southeast Asian material. In the **Western Cemetery** is a memorial to the 44 American and British members of the crew of Airship R38, which broke in two over Hull in 1921. The A1079 reaches the middle of town; bear left and park near City Hall. Across the road is the **Ferens Art Gallery,** with lesser works by Canaletto and Frans Hals, and sculpture by Moore and Hepworth, as well as representative modern British painters, a good collection of marine paintings, and four works by Benjamin West. Beyond is Trinity House, responsible for pilotage in the Humber, its students in uniforms similar to 18th century midshipmen, and its location a block from the Church of the Holy Trinity, easily seen ahead and to the right and one of the largest parish churches in England. Follow the street down the north side of the church into High Street, turn left, and **Wilberforce House** will be on the right in a quarter-mile. Here William Wilberforce was born, and the house is now a museum to the abolition of slavery, with all the obvious American connections this implies. Going in the opposite direction on High Street brings you to the river's wide edge, where you may look out upon the scene which has made Hull Britain's third largest port, after London and Liverpool. If trawlers, oil tankers, cargo ships, car ferries, and a variety of fishing fleets attract you, the entire area from here east, 21 motor miles to Spurn Head (although it is seldom that the roads are near the water) awaits your exploration. (The village of Paull is a good place for boat watching.)

One A You may wish to take the bridge across the Humber, passing New Holland, and drive on the A15 and the A1077 to the A160, then to B1210, thence east to **Immingham,** and by local road on to Killingholme Creek, where there is a monument commemorating the departure of the Pilgrim Fathers for Holland in 1609. The monument is hard to find, being lost among the great Immingham Dock opened in 1912. You may unite here with Tour 8 of the Pilgrim Country.

Or you may return via the B1210 to its junction with the A18, and bear directly west via Scunthorpe and Doncaster (where there is an interesting museum, given time to spare). Beyond Doncaster on an unmarked country road is **Sprotbrough,** 3 miles, where in the parish church Francis Washington is buried. At Doncaster turn right on the A638 through **Adwick le Street.** Pause here to visit the parish church, where a small chapel contains James Washington's tomb, with the Washington arms. Follow the A638 to the A628, then right into Pontefract for the ruined castle. The B6134 west reaches the outskirts of **Normanton,** where a Pilgrim, the Rev. Richard Clyfton, was born, as was Martin Frobisher, the great 16th century explorer who began the search for the northwest passage. Retreat to Pontefract, follow the A645 to Low Eggborough, thence left on the A19 through **Selby,** where the Stars and Stripes hang within the parish church, and by that route a further 14 miles back to York. A window in Selby Abbey shows the Washington coat of arms.

This circuit is devoid of good eating, but if you seek lunch, take it in Hull or carry some bread, cheese and wine with you.

One B Of course, you may (wisely on the whole) have resisted the Humber bridge and have turned northeast and north from Hull. To the east on the A1033 is Patrington, with one of the loveliest village churches in Yorkshire. The A1033 ends at Withernsea, after which the B1242 makes its meandering way north along the coast toward Bridlington, via **Mappleton,** upon which John Paul Jones once fired (a memorial shows where his cannon balls landed) and Hornsea, an attractive resort town.

While in Bridlington, time permitting, you should drive west on the A166 to Burton Agnes, there to see the Hall, for it is one of the many attractive country houses which is haunted, in this case by the daughter of its first owner. British travel agents in London will be happy to arrange a tour of several days exclusively devoted to haunted houses, if you like, but unless you are a true believer be satisfied with this one, and view the excellent collection of Impressionist paintings while at it.

Also west of Bridlington via the B1253 is **Boynton,** where there is a memorial to William Strickland, who introduced turkeys into Britain from America after his voyage with Cabot. Beyond Bridlington via the B1255, then the B1259, is **Flamborough Head.** To reach it you must walk, to be rewarded with a great chalk cliff, where the Vikings successfully invaded in the 10th century, today offering the only mainland colony of gannets in

Britain. It was off this head that John Paul Jones fought and won his great naval duel in 1779, pitting his flagship *Bonhomme Richard* against the British *Serapis*.

From Flamborough village follow the B1229 north to the A165, through Filey (to the right on the A1039) with a great cliff and a fishing fleet of 'cobbles' (a type of small boat not to be seen elsewhere) thence into Scarborough, with all that goes with a well-organized English holiday town. Anne Brontë is buried in the parish church and there is a 12th century castle ruin. Immediately to the north begin the North York Moors (see the circular route following below). But time will probably now be short and you may return to York on the A64, perhaps diverting to the right beyond Malton for Castle Howard, one of the finest of the great estates, where Holbein's picture of Henry VIII hangs. The avenues here are particularly striking. George William Howard travelled often in America before his death in 1864. Stop also at **Foston** (signposted as for Thornton-le-Clay; open June–Sept., Sun. only, 2.30–6) 2 miles from the main highway, where it seems fitting to visit the Old Rectory and the parish church, a mile apart, in memory of the great British writer and critic, Sydney Smith – he who in 1802 helped found the *Edinburgh Review*, in which he put the question, 'Who reads an American book?', and answered it in the negative. Thus righteously reinforced, continue on country roads posted for Flaxton and **Strensall.** Here is Strensall Camp, base of the King's Regiment, which fought in America during the War of 1812. It was this regiment which set fire to the White House. Continue through Towthorpe and Huntington into York.

Option Two   A second circle tour from York, which you may complete in one busy day, is into the North York Moors. You may also contact circle tour One B, described above, at Scarborough if you wish. Leave York north on the A19 to Easingwold, a town of cobblestones, red brick, and copper beeches (remember your Sherlock Holmes) and then east on a country road signposted for Crayke, a village on a hill from which you may look back 13 miles to see York Minster over the vale. Turn north for Coxwold; here Laurence Sterne, of *Tristram Shandy*, lived at Shandy Hall, just behind the still-active parish church in which he preached. Newburgh Priory is just south, and a mile north are the fine ruins of Byland Abbey. Three miles northwest of Coxwold is Kilburn, an attractive village which is the heart of the woodcarving industry begun by Robert Thompson, whose work is readily recognizable by the figures of mice cut into each object. These carvings are unique, excellent, and fun to take back (a selection may be seen in the Foresters Arms, and in the church, as well as in a display room). Above the village is a good chalk figure, the White Horse.

From Kilburn follow country roads to Sutton under Whitestone Cliff, on the A170. Turn right and you will shortly mount the ridge known as the

SCARBOROUGH

Hambleton Hills, with a superb view. Bear left on country roads marked for Scawton and Rievaulx (pronounced *Reevo*) to reach the most romantic, surely one of the two finest, of England's majestic ruined abbeys. Founded in 1131 by the Cistercians, the abbey roll had dwindled to twenty-two monks by the Dissolution in 1539. Here you may see this history – made visible in buildings – laid out with great care in exceptionally attractive surroundings.

As you left Coxwold, you entered the North York Moors National Park, one of eleven national parks in England and Wales (see section on NATIONAL PARKS) and in its 553 square miles perhaps the most clearly defined. Largely heather-clad, the park contains many dale-nestling villages, historic sites, and views, and since most of it is over a thousand feet above sea level, it can attract sudden and heavy snows in winter, during which the narrow country roads are to be avoided. There is much worth exploring, and if you have the time, do so with National Park Guide No. 4, by Arthur Raistrick (published by Her Majesty's Stationery Office in 1969) in hand. What follows will, however, give you a representative impression of this area of the old North Riding in perhaps three hours of driving (which is too bad, for these are good moors for walking on). If you wish to move north toward Durham, you may also choose to take the B1257 north from Rievaulx, along Bilsdale and across the park via the Cleveland Hills toward Middlesbrough, for this is an attractive drive. Assuming, however, you intend a circle tour to return to York, the following is recommended.

From the Rievaulx terrace, follow the B1257 southeast to Helmsley, where a ruined castle stands in Duncombe Park, and the wisteria and greystone houses combine in the spring with Rye Dale daffodils to be especially beautiful. Follow the A170 east to Kirkby Mills and turn left onto a country road posted for **Hutton-le-Hole.** This is probably the most beautiful of the nestling villages. Quaker Cottage here dates from 1695, and from it came John Richardson, missionary to America and close friend of William Penn. St Chad's Church is small and attractive. (The Crown Inn here provides a satisfactory meal; try beef in wine 'our way'.) From here north via Low Mill and Church Houses in Farndale the road runs up the River Dove, the entire stretch in April famous for its massed wild daffodils. (You may take a riverside path for a mile and a half between Low Mill and Church Houses to see the best of the flowers.) Turn off at Church Houses, then left a mile or so beyond, and you are climbing to Westerdale Moor; follow this road as far as the ancient, but undated, Ralph Cross, and you will sense that you are in some of England's loneliest land. Return then to the last junction and bear left (southeast) for Rosedale Abbey, a ruin, and via Cropton Forest to a junction, right, for Lastingham, with a beautiful church and unusual 11th century crypt. Continue then to Hutton-le-Hole again and thence to Kirkby Mills, bearing left on the A170 to **Pickering.**

This very pretty town offers a ruined 12th century castle and a parish church famous for its medieval frescoes, and modestly interesting for its chancel monument to Nicholas and Robert King, surveyors of Washington, D.C. There are also brasses commemorating the Anglo-American alliance in World War I and the role of Walter Hines Page, the American Ambassador to London during the war. The choir panelling is a memorial to J. H. Choate, also an ambassador. Robert Pickering, assistant to Major L'Enfant in laying out Washington, was born here. Follow the A170 east to Thornton-le-Dale, another lovely village, and turn north on an unmarked country road toward Lockton, to join with the A169, which winds along Thornton Dale through Forestry Commission land. To the right and ahead arise the moonscape globules of an **Anglo-American Distant Early Warning Station,** a reminder that the peace of these dales is fragile indeed. Bear left for Goathland and by marked lane to Beck Hole. Retreat to Goathland, and southwest on a dead-end lane to Hunt House. Here a posted path leads to the most exciting stretch of Roman road in Britain outside Northumberland, upon which one may walk, but not drive, 3 miles across lofty Wheeldale Moor to Stape. Return again to Goathland, continuing through to join the A169 once more, and then very shortly turn left on a country road to Grosmont, to the ruined priory there. If you wish to see the most forbidding and least frequented part of the moors, carry on through Egton to Glaisdale, and then by a single-track paved road, with gates at both ends, and marked with red danger signs, across the height of the moors and down upon Rosedale Abbey once again, returning into Pickering after completing a 35-mile circuit. (Beyond Egton is **Lealholm,** where a brand-new plaque on the war memorial has been placed by the villagers in honor of two U.S. fliers who crashed their jet into a farmyard to avoid hitting the school.) Otherwise, from Grosmont turn right, to the A169 again, and into Whitby.

But you are hungry. Your choice is an early lunch at the Plough Inn, 2 miles from Hutton-le-Hole in Fadmoor, where service starts at 12 (but you must call ahead to book around mid-morning) and children are welcome, or a later lunch at the Huntsman Inn on the A170 above Pickering. Or you may wish an even later lunch, in which case the village pub in Newholm, the Beehive, just outside Whitby off the A171, is sufficient to your needs.

Replenished, you are in Whitby, a cradle of English Christianity, for it was here that the end came to the Celtic influence on the English Church. Easter was settled upon in the Synod of Whitby in 663. Here the poet Caedmon lived, and from here Captain James Cook sailed in the *Endeavour* in 1768 to Tahiti. In Grape Lane, Cook's house is marked with a plaque. The ruined abbey dates from the 13th century; it was further damaged by German shelling in 1914. A 20-foot cross stands to Caedmon, in St Mary's churchyard, and the church has an outstanding 18th century interior, as well as the largest all-lead roof in England. Whitby is not to everyone's taste but it is not to be missed. Just north of Whitby on the A174 is Sandsend, from which the alum industry operated.

You may now return to York southwards, and then west, 61 miles. The A171 passes along the lower fringes of the moors, still in the national park. A diversion left off the A171 on the B1447 south of Whitby brings one to Robin Hood's Bay, where the streets are so steep that flights of steps replace them, and where the view is magnificent. Further along the A171 an unnumbered country road, sharp left, to Ravenscar, provides another fine view. The A171 passes through Scarborough (see circuit One B, above) where a junction with the A64 brings one via Malton into York. If you have not taken circuit One B, you will want to see Castle Howard, an outstanding example of a Vanbrugh-designed 18th century mansion, with an exceptional costume gallery and an avenue of limes. Return to York via the A64.

You may wish to return to York by a northerly route from Whitby – if so, you will need more time, and may want to spend the night on the way – or not return at all, but continue on toward Durham. To do this, leave Whitby northwest on the A174. There are fine views at Runswick, and **Staithes,** also just off the road to the right, is worth visiting. It was here that much of the jet carving was done – jet is wood which, after being washed to sea, was fossilized and then put under pressure by water and silt – and you may be able to buy some, although it is rare. James Cook was a grocer's apprentice here before he began his explorations of the Pacific. Cowber Lane will take you to England's highest cliff 2 miles west: the Boulby, 700 feet high. One may also approach it by lane from the village of Boulby, further on.

• Just off the A174 some distance on is **Redcar,** a drab town, where Nathaniel Hawthorne lived for some time. This town, on the A1042, gives access to Middlesbrough via the A1085. Middlesbrough and Stockton-on-Tees have combined to form the new municipality of Teesside. While scarcely attractive, this large industrial complex provides an insight into Britain's non-quaint side: the docks and wharves go on for miles, and the great iron and steel plants rise up as though from Hades at night. If one is an engineer, the Dorman Museum in Middlesbrough is interesting.

• If you are continuing north toward Durham, follow the A1085 into Middlesbrough, and through to Stockton-on-Tees, thence the A19 north to the B1275, then right to Haverton Hill and the A178, thence north again through much heavy industry – this route is fine on Sunday and hell on a weekday – past Seaton Carew into Hartlepool (pronounced Hart-le-pool) then by the A1086 through Blackhall Colliery to Easington, then the A182 to Hutton-le-Hole, thence left on the A690 into Durham. This is not the most direct route to Teesside, but it adds very few miles, and in passing through colliery towns it will quickly tell you why the Labour Party has been so traditionally strong in this grim, grey northland. If you have no stomach for 20th century realities, however, you may continue from Middlesbrough to Darlington, there to visit the railway station and see Stephenson's original locomotive, then north onto the A1(M) to Durham. In Stockton-on-Tees, you might also turn south 5 miles on the A19 to Yarm, a town sinking under the rising waters of the Tees, where in the George and Dragon Inn in 1820 the first promoters' meeting was held on behalf of the Stockton and Darlington Railway, the world's first public railroad. A gigantic viaduct here still carries a railway line across the Tees as a reminder of the engineering marvels of the 19th century. And at **Long Newton,** just off the main route midway between Middlesbrough and Darlington, was the home of the Vane family; Sir Henry was a colonial governor of Massachusetts.

If, however, you are pursuing a circle back to York from Staithes, you will leave the A174 beyond Boulby, at Brotton, taking the A173 through Guisborough to **Great Ayton.** James Cook went to school in a building now a museum, and an obelisk marks his former house, since sent to Australia. His monument stands above on the Easby Moor skyline. After the A173 has joined the A172, at Stokesley, turn left on a country road posted for **Osmotherley.** Just northwest of this lovely village is Mount Grace Priory, the best-preserved of the Carthusian houses in England.

John Wesley preached by the cross in the middle of the town. Here begins the Lyke Wake Walk, 40 miles east across the moors to Ravenscar; the walk is named after a Cleveland Hills dirge, and you may become a member of the Lyke Wake Club (in the Queen Catherine Hotel in the village) if you walk the 40 miles in 24 hours. Leave Osmotherley for the A19 and the A684, thence to Northallerton, then north on the A167 to the B6271, which carries one to **Kiplin,** where the great hall (open Sun. in Aug., Sept., 3–6.30) was the ancestral home of the Calverts; George Calvert – first Lord Baltimore – was born here. He was converted to Catholicism, given estates in Ireland, established Avalon in Newfoundland in 1621, and was granted a charter for Maryland by Charles I; upon his death the second Lord Baltimore founded the colony.

From Osmotherley, you may follow the A19 into York, 35 miles, via Thirsk and Easingwold, or, if two days have been allowed for this circuit, you may take the A61 from Thirsk to Ripon, there to see one of England's more attractive cathedral towns, Fountains Abbey, and Harrogate, before returning to York. If this circuit is viewed as taking two days, Whitby would be a convenient place to spend the night.

Option Three From York there are yet other circuits one may easily take. One, to Ripon, as described here, provides a leisurely day if one intends to return to York for the night, or may be used as an attractive route to Durham. The various detours described below, on the other hand, will require a day and a half if taken collectively.

Leave York southwest on the A64 to the A1, then briefly south to the road for Aberford. In the village turn right on the road posted for Barwick, and take the first turning to the left, into the grounds of the Parlington Estate. This is private property so ask permission if possible. Follow the lane a mile; in front of you will be the unique **Parlington Arch,** the only triumphal arch erected in Britain in celebration of the victory by the American colonies in the Revolution. Designed by John Carr at the behest of Sir Thomas Gascoigne, a Rockingham Whig who wished for peace with the colonies, the arch bears the inscription, 'Liberty in N. America Triumphant MDCCLXXXIII' (1783).

Return to the A1, going north, to the A659, west. Continue to **Harewood House** (open Easter–Sept., daily, and Oct. Sun., 11–6). A residence of the late Princess Royal (who married the Earl of Harewood), this magnificent house of Adam interiors and Capability Brown gardens has a famous art collection – including John Singer Sargents in the East Dressing Room – Chippendale furniture, Sèvres porcelain, and a bird garden. Jacob Epstein's 'Adam' is in a separate building. Harewood is the single most impressive country house in the vicinity of York.

North on the A61 one passes through Harrogate, a spa town with attractive gardens and Royal Baths. At **Rudding Park,** off the A661 southeast, one may see John Singleton Copley's copy of Benjamin West's

'Death of Wolfe'. The Harlow Car Gardens, west, are 40 acres of flowering shrubs; John of Gaunt's Castle is to the west of Harrogate off the A59 and Ripley Castle is just to the north on the A61. Ripon is 10 miles further north on the same road. Or you may turn west at Harrogate on the A59 for Bolton Abbey and the Yorkshire Dales National Park, for a circuit of 80 miles into Ripon, over one of the most highly recommended drives in England.

• The A59 passes over Forest Moor and through Blubberhouses to Bolton Bridge. Just to the right on the B6160 is Bolton Abbey, a ruin set against the River Wharfe. While relatively small, this is one of the best known of the abbeys, having been made famous by Britain's great romantic painter, Sir Edwin Landseer. (If you want only a taste of the Yorkshire Dales, you may continue north here, diverting to Appletreewick, a singularly attractive tiny village, and then joining the B6265, a striking road, to the east, which cuts across the moors to Ripon passing near Fountains Abbey. This short Harrogate–Bolton Abbey–Ripon circuit is only 40 miles in all.) But if you really want to experience the Dales, you must opt for the much larger circuit which follows, which turns the 10 miles between Harrogate and Ripon into 140 miles.

• From Bolton Abbey continue north on the B6160, bearing right on country roads posted for Appletreewick and Hebden, the last being on the B6265. Just to the west is Grassington, the major village of Upper Wharfedale, after Wensleydale the largest of the Dales; here are narrow cobbled streets, a market square, and an ancient bridge. Remain on the east bank of the stream along a country road to Conistone, and cross here to Kilnsey on the B6160, where there is both a packhorse bridge and a clapper bridge (named for the long flat stones which rattle as one crosses). Abandoned lead mines lie to the right between the two villages. Now turn south on the B6160, to reach Cracoe. Here bear right on country roads posted for Hetton, Airton and Malham, the last a village set against Yorkshire's most rugged scenery. To the east of the village a mile (followed by a half-mile walk) is Gordale Scar, a high cliff marked by waterfalls, and one mile north of Malham is Malham Cove, a huge natural semicircle. Comparisons with the American West are scarcely relevant, but be prepared to find it handsome in the manner of New Hampshire's Franconia Notch, not Utah's Dead Horse Point. You can continue past the Cove, and keeping right, cross over a low summit to Arncliffe, a sycamore-bedecked village of grey stone houses. (All of this is 'pot', or cave country. The 'most severe' pot in England is Langcliffe Pot, near Kettlewell, a lovely village 3 miles to the east.) Turn north from Arncliffe to drive 4 miles to Halton Gill past the stone barns of this remote area, and then left again to Stainforth, on the B6479. Turn right here and follow this lovely road to the B6255, and right again to mount up over the height of the moors on the longest stretch of road without a house in

England. You will come out at Hawes, on the A684, at the head of Wensleydale, from which one of England's finest cheeses once came (alas no more, although you can enjoy Wensleydale produced elsewhere). By these crossings you will have mounted the finest of the Pennines, passed an ancient Roman road, and at Gayle (near Hawes) made contact with the Pennine Way – after Hadrian's Wall the finest walk in the interior of England. The fells march down upon the villages, the becks (or tumbling streams) chatter, and the hills rise back toward the sky in stunning grandeur.

• At Hawes, you must again make a decision. You may take 1 the A684 east down Wensleydale to Ripon via Richmond as a diversion – this being the 140-mile circuit referred to. You may 2 continue north by a country road to Thwaite, then east on the B6270 down Swaledale directly into Richmond. This route is no longer. Or at Thwaite you may 3 continue north via Keld to the A66, and then into Richmond via Bowes, adding another 38 miles to the circuit. The blessings of each are quite different.

• 1 Driving east from Hawes on the A684 you will pass through Bainbridge (where every evening a hunting horn is still blown from the green), Aysgarth (just to the north past the church is Aysgarth Force, a series of low waterfalls) and Bolton Castle (where Mary Queen of Scots was imprisoned), this last by diverting left at the falls on a country road posted for Carperby. Then into Wensley, and at Leyburn turn north on the A6108 to **Richmond.** Francis Johnson, a Pilgrim, was born here; the ruins of the Norman castle should be seen, and also the Theatre Royal, one of the oldest in the country. If military museums hold any interest for you, the **Green Howards Regimental Museum** in the market place (open weekdays 10–5, Sun., 2–5) is an especially good one, commemorating an intriguing and controversial body. This regiment served in South Carolina in the 1770s, as well as in Malaya against the Communist Terrorists of the 1950s. The museum has a number of relics that belonged to Colonel L. D. H. Currie, who was commissioned by Abraham Lincoln to command the 133rd New York Volunteer Infantry in the Civil War. Return to Ripon by main roads.

• 2 At Hawes, continue north from the village on a country road posted for High Shaw and the Butter Tubs. The narrow road passes over Butter Tubs Pass, where one may stop to see typical Pennine potholes close to the road. At Thwaite you may pause to walk the most accessible portion of the Pennine Way. A section of the path leads 3 miles north past falls and limestone cliffs to the post office in Keld; these two villages are also joined by the B6270. At Thwaite you may turn east on the B6270 to Richmond, via Grinton, where the large parish church is called the Cathedral of the Dales, and past the ruins of Marrick Priory, thence by the A6108 into **Richmond** (see above).

- 3 At Thwaite you may carry north to Keld on the B6270, thence right on a country road posted for Tan Hill. This is a difficult route, being only a lane, but it will reward you well, first with Tan Hill, where stands England's highest and loneliest inn. Turn west from Tan Hill; thence right to the A66, then right (east) through Stainmore Forest to Bowes. The original Dotheboys Hall of Dickens' *Nicholas Nickleby* was here (it is now a restaurant of no note). Here bear left on the A67 to Barnard Castle, written of by Dickens and Scott, to see its castle ruins on a cliff above the river, and the Bowes Museum (open weekdays 10–4 or later, Sun. open 2) which features Napoleonic relics and fine china. The ruins of Egglestone Abbey are just south, while **Cockfield,** 7 miles northeast via the A688 and left on a country road, was the home of Jeremiah Dixon, he of the Mason-Dixon Line. Leave Barnard Castle east on the A67, then right on the B6274 to **Richmond.**

- From Richmond, you may take B6271 southeast to **Kiplin** (see page 279) thence to Ripon, or (more directly) take the A6136 via Catterick to the A1, thence south to the A61, and right 4 miles into Ripon. If you have a few extra minutes, leave the A1 earlier, on the A684 right to Bedale, a lovely small town with the old North Riding's finest church, and carry on south on the B6268 to a country road marked for Snape. Here is the castle in which lived Catherine Parr, last of Henry VIII's wives. Bear right (west) to Masham, where at the King's Head Hotel you may try the local brew, Old Peculiar, said to be the strongest draught beer in the country. If able, then continue carefully down the A6108 into Ripon.

Ripon offers an agreeable smaller **cathedral** which, if you are fortunate enough to encounter it arising just beyond the market square in heavy fog, will impress its austere lancet west front upon you. Begun in the 12th century, this cathedral has relatively few monuments, and its interior thus leaves you time to explore the town – the second smallest cathedral city in England (population 10,500) – and the market. However, in the cathedral, the 34 misericords are especially fine, the nave is unusual, and the geometrical tracery in the chancel's east window is regarded as among the best in the land. There is a slab to Robert Porteous, cousin of George Washington. The Cathedral Library also deserves close examination. Ripon is one of the few towns in which, at 9.00 each night, the town Wakeman still sounds his forest horn – from the obelisk in the square.

   To the west of Ripon, 4 miles on the B6265, is Fountains Abbey which, together with Rievaulx, is one of the two most romantic of the fine old English ruins. Cistercian monks came here in 1132 and created perhaps the most beautiful of all the remote abbeys, through the prosperity brought by the wool trade. You may enter via Studley Park drive or by road from near Aldfield; the former is the more striking, but it entails a walk through

RICHMOND CASTLE

the park. The setting on the Skell is handsome, the ruins extensive, and
children will love it. You need at least an hour here and preferably much
more. Thereafter return to Ripon, and then make for Boroughbridge,
south on the A1, where ancient ruins, both Stone Age and Roman, may
be seen. Continue down the A1 and turn east to York on the A59, 22 miles
beyond Ripon.

Where to eat within this series of circuits within circuits? The *Good
Food Guide* reveals a surprising number of more than acceptable places
in the Dales area. From personal experience I can recommend four modest, and two exceptionally fine, places to dine along the routes described
above. The modest ones, in order of your approach, are: the Red Lion
Inn in Burnsall, on the B6160 just beyond Appletreewick (north of
Bolton Abbey), which is old fashioned and on the river (lunch begins at 1
and there is a set menu; children are welcome); the Peacock and Calvert,
actually within Bolton Castle and good fun, especially for the children,
for that reason alone; and the Black Bull Inn in Moulton (which except
on Sunday serves only dinners from 8.30), an unusual place serving up
large portions for a reasonable price. (To reach Moulton, which is 5
miles from Richmond, leave northeastwards on the A6108 toward Scotch
Corner, then follow the posted country road.)

It is the setting of the Wilson Arms Hotel in Grassington, up Wharfedale, that especially pleases, for this is one of the area's most attractive villages. The food is good, although not outstanding, the prices reasonable, and should you be there for breakfast, the servings huge. Service for lunch begins at 12.30, and if you did include Harewood House in your itinerary, you can still arrive for a latish lunch. The two really exceptional places, both deservedly rating a Distinction by the *Good Food Guide*, are slightly off the described routes. The first, the Pool Court Restaurant, is in Pool-in-Wharfedale, 4 miles west of Harewood House (closed for lunch). The imagination exercised here requires you to linger, and your meal very possibly may be the best you will have in the North of England. If not, it is because the Box Tree Cottage in Ilkley has gone one better. Ilkley is an interesting town in itself, 5 miles southeast of Bolton Bridge on the B6160 and the A65, and hard by **Denton,** ancestral home of the Fairfax family of the great Virginia colonial estates. The Fairfaxes were holders of a title which went out of use after the Revolution, only to be revived by an American who, as the twelfth peer, took a seat in the House of Lords in 1908. **Guiseley,** 7 miles beyond Ilkley on the A65, is the ancestral home of the Longfellows, and poet's family name appears on several tombs in the parish church.

WHAT TO READ   Dickens' *Nicholas Nickleby* and Scott's *Ivanhoe*, clearly. Sterne and Caedmon for the North York Moors tour, of course. Robinson Crusoe is said to have been born in York. W. H. Auden, who became an American citizen in 1928, was born in York in 1907. And with luck you may come across some of the many English detective or adventure stories that use either the moors or the Dales for their settings. If not, then content yourself with sampling the many cheeses available in the area, with the unusual local beers, and with reading the clouds in order to test your driving skills on those high, lonely, country roads by which you will penetrate the two remote national parks.

11 Based on Durham: Newcastle The Roman Wall

Durham (population 28,000), is one of the most interesting, and in some ways the most dour, of England's cathedral cities. The cathedral itself is massive, unlike any other in the country, and clearly the outstanding example of Early Norman architecture in England. Nothing compares with it, and if you can see only a handful of England's great cathedrals, Durham should be among them. The city itself also demands attention – for its narrow streets rising sharply from the Wear, for its old university, for one of the finest museums in Britain, for its revelations about Scots–English tensions, and coal mining, and how the cold may enter your bones. You can see the cathedral, rising on its near-island, from the London–Edinburgh railway line, but to know Durham you must park your car and walk (and since the streets are so complex and narrow, your sanity demands that you do so in any case). Durham has been a disaster area in terms of good hotels or restaurants, but you will survive well enough in the Three Tuns Hotel on New Elvet.

The best approach to Durham is from York, either by car or rail. If you leave by train from London, the journey will take roughly four hours. Or go on to Newcastle, hire a car, and double back to Durham. Newcastle is much the larger city but also less interesting – hence the use of Durham as a base.

If entering Durham from the A1(M) from the south, bear left on the A177, and follow the signs for the cathedral, which will be seen rising to the left on the Wear: make for it and surrender to the car park immediately behind it. Begin your walking tour, then, with the cathedral itself, and know that you tread upon the ground of one of the three traditionally most powerful bishoprics in the land. Note the sanctuary knocker on the great north doors, a visible symbol to the invisible past summed up in that word, *sanctuary*. The massive structure before you dates from the year 995. Particularly important are the use of pointed arches in the nave, the tomb of the Venerable Bede in the Galilee Chapel, the high throne built by Bishop Hatfield, the elaborate Cosin Font, the tomb of St Cuthbert, the sumptuous Nevill Screen behind the high altar, the monks' dormitory, and, in the cloisters, a plaque to **John Washington.** There are also two Washington seals in the museum, in the monks' dormitory. Directly opposite the cathedral are parts of the university, the third oldest in England. Durham was the founding university for the first university colleges in West Africa in this century. Here are the Old Shire Hall, the old library, and part of the university, housed within the castle. The castle itself is magnificent; the main entrance hall has been called 'the most extravagant piece of Norman work to survive'. (The public rooms are open July–Sept. weekdays 10–5.30, the remainder of the year Mon., Wed., Sat., 2–4.) Beyond the castle turn right, into Old Elvet Hill, and swing a mile and a half south to St Aidan's, to reach the exceptional Gulbenkian Museum of Oriental Art, the only such museum in Britain. Three colleges of the university share the peninsula with the cathedral, and seven others are dotted about the city. The ideal antique to purchase here is a well-polished miner's lamp, for they are unusual and cost substantially more elsewhere.

Turn north on the A1 to a country road, right, marked for Finchale (pronounced *Finkle*) Priory, a fine small ruin dramatically first seen from a short footpath across the Wear. Here turn left (north) on a country road marked for Great Lumley to the ruins of Lumley Castle, beyond. Join the A1 and turn right, shortly to unite with the A1(M). Take the next exit, marked Washington, and follow the signs to visit **Washington Old Hall** (open 10–1, 2–6, closed Fri.). Here is one of the American-related sites clearly worth a side trip in itself, for the manor has been preserved by the National Trust since 1957, and is a memorial to the Anglo-American colonial connection. The Old Hall consists of a portion of the 12th century ancestral home from which George Washington was descended, and while it is sparsely furnished and bleak in appearance, there is much of historic, as well as filiopietistic, interest here. It is described in detail in a pamphlet which you may purchase inside.

Continue to Usworth and Castletown. Here is **Hylton Castle,** in fact a gatehouse keep; on the front may be seen a stone shield bearing the bars and mullets of the Washington family. (Feeling fey? Carry on to Sunderland, a large industrial city, where in the museum you may see the stuffed walrus head that inspired Lewis Carroll to write 'The Walrus and the Carpenter'.) Thereafter follow the signs via the A108 and the A184 to Gateshead (the **Shipley Art Gallery** here has a bust by W. T. Story) and Newcastle, crossing over the deep cleft of the Tyne on one of England's most dramatic high bridges – the best example of an early cast-iron bridge still used – with unhappily representative views of an auto graveyard and sooty ships below: for this is the land to which the saying 'coals to Newcastle' applies.

Newcastle, a city of 220,000, is one of the best walking cities in England. The local Geordie accent is often quite difficult to grasp, but you will have to ask for directions nonetheless. There are several gracious streets (especially Grey) and the air of a pulsating and growing port city; despite the grime, Newcastle has its charms (and a complex one-way system). Turn left at the first opportunity coming off the bridge and you will pass in front of the fine railway station, at which you may be leaving your car. Just beyond is the Roman Catholic Cathedral, with a car park nearby. Walk back past the station to St Nicholas Cathedral, built as a church in the 14th century and elevated to its present status in 1882. It is best known for its high tower with flying buttresses and, inside, for a superb carved canopy. A right turn on Dean Street brings you to the small castle ruins, where you may visit the old Black Gate. A left turn into Dean Street quickly becomes Grey Street, which ends at a monument to the Earl Grey. Two blocks to the right from the monument is the **Laing Art Gallery and Museum** (open weekdays 10–6, to 8 on Tues., Thurs.; Sun. 2.30–5.30), which is solid and provincial. There are seven American paintings here, including two good John Singer Sargents. You will have crossed Northumberland Street; retreat to it, turn right and you will confront the University of Newcastle upon Tyne and, again to the right, the startling new civic hall with decor in the Viking manner. Probably the handsomest new civic hall in England, it deserves a close inspection, and should you be able to gain access to the Lord Mayor's Gallery to see the display of city plate and regalia, you will be well rewarded. To the north on Town Moor is the Museum of Science and Engineering, the second best in Britain. And if you have the time, and it is Sunday, conclude your visit with the first-rate down-river trip through the shipyards by boat. This takes 3 hours to Tynemouth and to **South Shields,** where Ernest Thompson Seton, nature writer and first Chief Scout of America, was born. If you do wish to eat, it is best to remember that Newcastle has the reputation among English gourmets that Bridgeport has among Americans (try Burbank, then). This is steak and chips land. But you can eat perfectly satisfactorily at the Royal Station Hotel, a landmark, or at Pumphreys in the Cloth Market, which is a genuine coffee shop. If you look hard, you can sample those Northumberland specialties, pickled snails, and perhaps have marrow pudding as well.

• Alternatively, from Durham, drive southwest on the A690 to Willington, thence westwards by the A689 up the Weardale through Crook, Stanhope, and Alston – well up into the Pennines. This is lovely, highly rural country. Between the last two towns the road reaches the highest elevation of any A route in England, 2,056 feet at Killhope Cross. Then follow the A689 to Knarsdale, where an unnumbered country road right via Eals and Park brings you to Greenhead on the A69. It is here that you make contact with Hadrian's Wall, at the end of its most interesting visible stretches (and about two-thirds along its original length) and from here via the B6318 you may drive some 40 miles to Newcastle, paralleling the wall most of the way and stopping frequently. The road from Greenhead to Walwick runs just inside the boundary of Northumberland National Park, although the major part of the park lies to the north.

The Roman Wall was built by the Emperor Hadrian between 121 and 126, to keep out raiders. It runs 73½ miles, from Wallsend, just north of Newcastle, to Bowness-on-Solway, on the coast beyond Carlisle. A milecastle was erected at every Roman mile; the eastern end of the wall was stone, and for the first 20 miles it was 9 feet thick, thereafter 7' 9", as far as the Irthing River, at present-day Gilsand. The section beyond was of clay or turf. Two turrets were erected between each milecastle. To the south of the wall, a Military Way, or road, was built, and further south, there was an earthwork, or flat-bottomed ditch flanked by mounds, called the Vallum. One may see the Wall, the Way, and the Vallum in conjunction at several points. To walk the length of the Wall, often upon it but equally often by its side, is still regarded as one of the most attractive of Britain's Long Walks – the path itself is not difficult, and anyone in good condition and with a good pair of boots may walk the length (and sightsee as well) in three days, spending the two nights at country hotels nearby, or camping out.

Today there are twenty-four specific sites to be visited along the Wall's length, fifteen of them in Northumberland, the remainder on the Cumberland side. The circuit described here (which starts in Newcastle) includes all these sites as well as other ancient monuments, all of which are in the care of the Department of the Environment. Before beginning the drive, you may also wish to see the Roman relics in the Museum of Antiquities at Newcastle University and, if madly keen, the Roman Museum in South Shields. The outstanding remains in the paragraphs that follow are marked with an *.

You may begin in Newcastle with two small sites, Benwell (or Condercum), a causeway across the Vallum to be seen at the bottom of Denhill Park, and the *Shrine of Antenociticus, where casts of the original altars may be seen in place on Broomridge Avenue. Leaving Newcastle on the A69 you will see a section of 70 yards of the Wall on the south side of the road, west of Denton Burn, and another such stretch a further 250 yards along in West Denton. At Heddon-on-the-Wall, just before reaching the village, there is an excellent 280-yard stretch of *Wall and ditch with a medieval kiln. Here bear right on the B6318, paralleling the Wall, which generally runs on the left of the road.

Just beyond Stagshaw Bank there is a fine view of the countryside and you come shortly to the *Planetrees Farm section of the Wall, which is particularly well preserved. At Low Brunton, turn south on the A6079 half a mile to the *Brunton Turret, perhaps the best preserved of the turrets, and then return to the B6318. Just ahead is one of the three finest of the ruins, *Chesters (or Cilurnum) where there is a fort, and Roman baths, a bridge abutment and a museum. Continuing, you will come to the Temple of Mithras at Carrawburgh, followed at Sewingshields by 2 Roman miles of the Wall with the best preserved sections of the *Way and the Vallum. Shortly after comes *Housesteads (Borcovicium) a five-acre fort for 1000 men, well preserved and with a museum. In 3 miles, at the Twice Brewed Inn, take a footpath north to see the *Windshields Mile-castle, on a stretch of 350 yards of Wall at its highest elevation. There is a car park and a fine view here, and the walk back to Housesteads is superb. Not far along the highway is Cawfields Milecastle. Before reaching a junction with the A69 at Greenhead you can see another 400 yards of Wall at Walltown Crags.

Beyond Greenhead, remain on the B6318 to Gilsland. From the railway station take a short footpath south to Poltross Burn Milecastle, then return and take Low Row past the school to the vicarage, where a section of the Wall shows in the garden. From Low Row you can then go on to the longest stretch of Wall, 1000 yards, running to the *Willowford Bridge abutment. On the west side of the River Irthing the turf wall begins, and you can see *Harrow's Scar Milecastle just beyond Birdoswald. Leave the B6318 on a country road left to *Birdoswald (Camboglanna) itself, where another five-acre fort may be seen. The fort is dull, the view superb. The country road carries you past a good example of the turf wall turrets at Piper Sike, and yet another, Leahill, a quarter-mile beyond. Another half-mile yields Banks East turret. Two unrelated sites now intervene: Lanercost Priory, an Augustinian Canon house founded in 1166, which is well worth viewing (and the Bridge Hotel here still does a real afternoon tea) and Naworth Castle. At the priory turn right, then left on a country road posted for Walton. Here is the last of the visible remains of the Wall, 22 yards of it. While the path which follows the military road and ditch continues to the coast, there is nothing else of note that may be seen by automobile, except for the small ruins of a fort at Stanwix, just outside Carlisle. (If you desire to complete the route, drive south from Walton to the A6071, right to Newtown, left to Irthington, on to the B6264, and then west to Carlisle. Leave Carlisle southwest on the A595, bear right on the B5307, and right again on country roads posted to Kirkandrews, Beaumont, Burgh-by-Sands, and Bowness-on-Solway, where the wall ended.)

Otherwise, from Walton, turn left, preferably on the A6071 to Brampton and follow the A69 east through Haltwhistle. Turn left on a country road just beyond Henshaw for *Chesterholm (Vindolanda) the last of the major remains, and the only one not easily accessible from the B6318 on the outward journey. The plan of the headquarters building of the Roman fort is very clear here. Continue on the A69 to Hexham, where the Saxon Priory Church is important, and yet another shambles – actually an old word for slaughterhouse – may be seen. At Corbridge, to the northwest on the river bank, is Corstopitum, a Roman town.

Turn south at Corbridge on the A68, then east on the A695. At the junction with the B6309, a left turn across the river brings you to Bywell, where ironwork used to be made and which is one of the most attractive villages in the area. Continue on the A695 and back to Newcastle.

• One may drive north from Newcastle into the Border Country, staying overnight at the Ednam House Hotel in Kelso (see page 375) and having lunch on the second day at the excellent Wolfelee Hotel at Bonchester Bridge. This route can include Seaton Delaval Hall (Sir John Vanbrugh's masterpiece); **Morpeth,** associated with Sir George Downing, nephew of John Winthrop; the fine Northumberland National Park, perhaps best entered at Alwinton (see page 85); and the Coquet River, considered by some the most beautiful in the Border region. John Paul Jones bombarded **Alnmouth** in 1778. At **Alnwick** there is a dramatic Border castle, seat of the Percy family; Sir Hugh Smithson, whose son founded the Smithsonian in Washington, lived in Alnwick. Nearby is **Embleton.** W. T. Stead was born in the Presbyterian manse here, to die on the *Titanic.* Foe of prostitution and the Boer War, he was the first 'crusading journalist' to have a statue erected to him in America. One should also visit Chillingham, to see the famous herd of wild white cattle, reputed to be pure-bred since the time of the Romans; Lindisfarne (see page 61); Berwick-upon-Tweed, with its ancient walls; the beautiful ruins of Melrose Abbey; and Abbotsford, the home of Sir Walter Scott, with his study as he left it.

WHAT TO READ   While in Newcastle, discover a truly delightful British writer of the 19th century, one possibly little known to you: Robert Surtees, creator of Jorrocks, a sporting Cockney grocer, who devotes his time to fox hunting. The Surtees novels are much admired by those who enjoy close observation of society with a pleasant touch of satire. Surtees lived at Hamsterley Hall, off the A694, 10 miles southwest of Newcastle, and he is buried in Ebchester, a mile beyond. (*Jorrocks' Jaunts and Jollities* suggested to the publishers the idea that Dickens might write a similar series of sketches about a club of amateur sportsmen. Dickens adapted the idea and thus started *The Pickwick Papers.*)

12 The southwest of England: Dorset Devon Cornwall

Probably the single most popular extended trip to England is that which takes one from London through Dorset, Devon and Cornwall, to Land's End and back again. In the tourist season, main roads will be crowded and the most famous of the picturesque coastal villages, like Clovelly and Tintagel, will be thronged. Even so, one can avoid the worst of the crowds most of the time (but not all of the time – Cornwall in particular is like a narrow funnel). Part of the long drive from London can be eliminated by going, at the least, as far as Winchester by train – an hour's trip from Waterloo Station, that most cavernous of British Rail's depots – or to Exeter. Most trains from late May to early September are West Country Holiday Trains, and one must book a seat and confirm a car booking well in advance. The train journey is especially attractive in May or June, when the rhododendrons are out in full glory along the track. One may also drive to Exeter via two motorways, the M4 and the M5.

The West Country is popular for a good reason: much of it is stunningly beautiful, capturing that green and pleasant land that once was England to a superlative degree. Roads are slow and there is much to see. The following tour begins at Winchester, ends at Taunton, and requires seven days. Added time, as in all tours, is required for those places set off from the main text with the symbol • or included in parentheses.

FIRST DAY

The 8.47 is a popular train from Waterloo to Winchester, enabling you to be in your car by 10.00. For a description of what to see in Winchester, consult tour number 4.

Leave Winchester east on the A272 to **Cheesefoot Head,** an amphitheatre made by nature, 3 miles from the city. Here General Eisenhower addressed the massed Allied troops just before D-Day in June 1944. Return towards the city and take the A33 south, then the A333 left into **Twyford.** Benjamin Franklin stayed at Twyford House in 1771 while writing portions of his autobiography. The A333 continues into the A3051 and through **Horton Heath,** birthplace of Samuel Sewall, judge in the Salem witchcraft trial who later repented the executions. At Botley turn west on the A334 into Southampton.

• East on the A334 is **Wickham.** The mill here was made from the timbers of the *Chesapeake.* South on the A32 from Wickham is **Gosport.** In the Rowner parish church there is a memorial to a British sailor killed by John Paul Jones.

Southampton, a city of 210,000, has long been a port of entry to Britain, for it is here that the trans-Atlantic steamers docked. The city was severely damaged by air raids in World War II, and much of it is new. John Alden, he who was asked to 'speak for yourself, John', was a cooper here. Enter over the River Itchen into Northam Road and continue to the **Civic Centre,** which contains plaques explaining the centre's role as the headquarters for the U.S. Army during D-Day in 1944. Just north is the information center, and opposite is the **Polygon Hotel,** which bears a plaque to the Fourteenth Major Port, U.S. Army. Follow above Bar Street south to Bargate – there is a statue to **George III** here – turn left into Fast Street; park and walk. This is the old section of the city. Walk towards the sea to visit the **Wool House Museum,** which is small and quite good (there is a fine painting of the *Trent* affair of Civil War fame). To the right (west) along the Esplanade is the **Mayflower Memorial.** The Pilgrim Fathers sailed from here in *Speedwell* and *Mayflower* on August 15, 1620. Trouble with *Speedwell* forced them to put in at Dartmouth and again at Plymouth, from which *Mayflower* set out alone on September 16 for the sixty-seven-day voyage. There is also a plaque to Alden. Later a tablet was added to honor the two million men and women of the United States armed forces who sailed from the English coast in 1944–5. Adjacent is **Mayflower Park,** and beyond, on the pillar of **no. 8 Gate** to the Western Docks, is another tablet, presented on behalf of the American forces. There are many other interesting memorials to events in the history of the port strung out along the walk along the old wall. At the **Maritime Chambers** on Canute Road is another plaque to those who helped move the United States forces through the port. Running north from Canute Road is Terminus Terrace; a plaque on the **London Hotel** marks where Charles Browne died. Best known as Artemus Ward, he was an American humorist who gave much pleasure to Abraham Lincoln.

• From Southampton one may take a ferry to the Isle of Wight. A circuit drive around the island is 65 miles, and one may return to the mainland on ferries running to either Gosport or Lymington. The Southampton ferry lands at **Cowes,** yachting capital of Britain. The Royal Yacht Squadron is probably the most exclusive in the world. During World War II its clubhouse housed the main operations' center for D-Day. Osborne House, at East Cowes, was Queen Victoria's favorite spot, and it contains more authentic Victoriana than any other of her homes (open Easter–Oct., Mon.–Fri., 11–5, from 10.30, July–Aug.).

• The best circuit of the island is clockwise into Newport, the 'capital city', then east on the A3054 to Hyde, and south on the A3055 through **Shanklin** – Longfellow stayed here in 1868, as the fountain by the Crab Inn attests – and Ventnor (remember your Monopoly set?), and along the south coast. At **Chale** there is a church with several memorials to the Hearn family in America. At the western end is Freshwater Bay. Lord Tennyson lived here for 15 years, wrote 'Idylls of the King' here, and is memorialized on the down to the west, from which one has a fine view of The Needles. Continue on the A3054 to **Yarmouth,** for the ferry to Lymington. The *Arbella* sailed from Yarmouth to Massachusetts in 1630. East is **Shalfleet,** where Longfellow stayed for a time.

Leave Southampton west on the A36 to the A35 left and left again on the A326, then right on the B3054 to Beaulieu. Here is the highly commercialized, yet well-maintained, Beaulieu Abbey and Palace House, with the **National Motor Museum,** owned by Lord Montagu of Beaulieu, probably the most successful of those members of the aristocracy who have turned the burden of a great estate into a tourist attraction. Everything is open every day except Christmas (10–6; Nov.–March closes at 5). The village is pleasant, and the museum of automobiles is perhaps the best in the world; there are ten American cars, including one of the first Ford Model-Ts. Unless you wish to press for Salisbury, drive west on the B3055 to Sway, where there is a delightful seven-room inn with excellent food, the Pine Trees.

The drive west on the B3055 and then north on the A337 through the New Forest is pleasant; this former royal hunting preserve is now largely open to the public. Beyond Lyndhurst bear left on a country road to Minstead, where one may see the Furzey Gardens and the grave of Sir Arthur Conan Doyle. Continue via country roads southwest to Newtown, right to cross the A31, and north to the B3078, thence left, right on a country road for Woodgreen, and left to Braemore, the most beautiful village of the forest. Continue north on the A338 into Salisbury, where a good dinner may be had at Crane's and a pleasant night at the Red Lion Hotel, one of the oldest in England.

SECOND DAY

Continue through Salisbury on the A360, just beyond Stonehenge, watching for a country road right to Wilton. Nathaniel Hawthorne was descended from a Wilton settler. The **Parish Church** on the side of the market square was restored by American Ambassador Robert Bingham just before his death in 1937. The Royal Wilton Carpet Factory may be visited – Wilton carpets began in the 17th century. Do not miss Wilton House, seat of the Pembrokes – allow an hour for the tour (open April–Oct., Tues.–Sat., 11–6, Sun. at 2). Shakespeare's *As You Like It* was first performed here, and Sir Philip Sidney wrote *Arcadia* here. Rebuilt from ruins by Inigo Jones, the house holds an exceptional collection of paintings, furniture, and books, as well as an immense display of model soldiers. The art includes works by van Leyden, Van Dyck, Rubens, Hals, Rembrandt and Hogarth, and a unique set of fifty-five gouaches of the Spanish riding school. The great Double Cube Room is one of the handsomest in England; it served as the Southern Command headquarters for the British Army in World War II. Wilton is just small enough to be grasped in one visit, and of all the great English country houses, those apparent bastions of security and stability, it is my favorite.

Leave Wilton on the A30 west to the B3089, and turn right. This road passes through two of the most attractive villages in the southwest, Teffont Evias and Chilmark. The stone used in Salisbury Cathedral came from the latter. Further west is the ruined Fonthill Abbey, actually a residence built for the reclusive William Beckford, author of *Vathek*. At the A350, turn south through Shaftesbury, set on the edge of Blackmoor Vale. This was the Shaston of Hardy's *Jude the Obscure*. Gold Hill is cobblestoned. West on the A30 is Larry's Wayfarers, a good stop for lunch.

• Further west via the A303 and right on the B3092 is Stourhead House, with fine Chippendale and magnificent gardens laid out in the 1740's. Yet further west, reached by country roads from Stourhead, is **Bruton,** ancestral home of the Berkeleys of Virginia. In the parish church is a stained glass window to John and William Ames, who emigrated in 1635. Bruton Parish Church in Williamsburg, Virginia, took its name from this village.
• East from Shaftesbury off the A30 is **Wardour Castle.** A tree brought from Maryland by Lord Baltimore grows in the grounds. Adjacent is a fine Gothic Roman Catholic chapel. West on the A30 is West Stour, scene of Henry Fielding's *Joseph Andrews*, and **Henstridge,** a town in which Sir Walter Raleigh is said to have had his pipe extinguished by a maid who thought he was on fire.
• **Sherborne,** 16 miles west of Shaftesbury, is the site of Sherborne Castle, built by Raleigh in 1594 (the pipe-smoking story is repeated here). Further on the A30 to Yeovil, and south off the A37, is **East Coker,** where T. S. Eliot is buried. North of Yeovil via the A37 and the A303

east is Yeovilton. The **Fleet Air Arm Museum** contains many old military aircraft, including American aeroplanes, among them a Douglas Sky-raider and a Grumman Hellcat. West is Ilchester, famed for its cheese made with beer.

Southwest of Shaftesbury on the B3091 is Sturminster Newton, a marketing town. Hardy wrote *Return of the Native* while staying in Riverside House here.

Right off the A350 south of Shaftesbury is Iwerne Courtney, a lovely village, and 2 miles west is **Child Okeford,** where General Wolfe prepared his troops for the attack on Quebec City. (At Blandford Forum on the A350, one may drive 2 miles east on the B3082 and by a country road to Blandford Camp. The **Royal Signals Museum** here contains American-related objects, and there is a **Franklin Roosevelt Memorial Park** at the camp.) Continue on the A350 until it joins the A35 just north of Poole.

• East on the A35 7 miles is Bournemouth, the major holiday center of the region, and perhaps the best maintained of England's mass resort towns. A city of 150,000, it has many huge hotels, fine gardens, a seven-mile-long sheltered beach, a good small art gallery – the Russell-Cotes (open daily 10–6), on the cliffs near the sea – and a fine marine collection in the Rothesay Museum in Bath Road. There is a memorial garden on Alum Chine Road marking the site of the house Robert Louis Stevenson lived in when he wrote *Dr. Jekyll and Mr. Hyde* and *Kidnapped.*

The A35 west meets the A351; bear southwest to Wareham. In St Martin's Church there is a fine effigy of Lawrence of Arabia, and there is a Lawrence museum in North Street. Continue on the A351 across the Isle of Purbeck – not an island – famous for its building stone, to Corfe Castle. The romantic ruin on the hill above was the scene of the murder of King Edward in 978. Turn west on a country road just north of the castle to **Steeple** – the parish church has a memorial to George Washington's ancestors – and via the B3070 to Lulworth Cove. Drive north on the B3071 to Wool; The Woolbridge Manor House is here, in which Tess of the d'Urbervilles and Angel Clare passed their wedding night. 2 miles west is Bovington Camp, site of the Royal Armoured Corps and Royal Tank Museum, largest of its kind in the world. Southwest from here sweeps the heath described by Hardy in *Return of the Native.* Continue past the camp to Clouds Hill, the cottage taken by T. E. Lawrence after he had disguised himself as T. E. Shaw and sought escape from the public by joining the tank corps (open April–Sept., Wed., Thurs., Sun., 2–6; Oct.–March, 2–4). He is buried at Moreton, 2 miles southwest. To the south can be seen the radio masts of the U.S. Air Force at **Ringstead Bay.** The country road emerges onto the A35 at Bere Regis; Tess of the d'Urbervilles is buried in the church here. Turn left through Tolpuddle, from which the martyrs – five laborers sent into exile to Australia for trying to form an illegal union – came. Their actions are regarded as the beginning of the trade union movement in England. Just beyond is Athelhampton House (open late March to early Oct., Wed., Thurs., Sun., 2–6); a continuous residence for 500 years, it has a fine Great Hall and wine cellar, and good gardens. Said to be the site of Athelstan's Palace, this was the Athel Hall of Hardy's work. Just ahead is Puddletown; for a picturesque small hotel that serves an excellent dinner, take the A3142 northwest to the B3143, through Piddletrenthide, right on a country road marked Plush, to the Brace of Pheasants Inn (only six rooms, so book early).

THIRD DAY

One is now in the heart of Hardy country, Saxon Wessex. Hardy was born in a cottage in Higher Bockhampton (return to Puddletown and go west on the A35), which one may view from the outside and, by appointment, see inside as well. Continue south on the country road that runs through Bockhampton, and turn right to cross the railway tracks and pass Max Gate (Hardy's former home, in which there is a reconstruction of his study), thus joining the A352 into **Dorchester.** The county town for Dorset, this handsome city was the birthplace of Reverend John White, who helped found the Massachusetts Company and sent 140 Dorset colonists to New England in 1630. He was the rector of Holy Trinity Church and is buried in the porch of **St Peter's.** The Massachusetts state flag hangs inside. The site of his house is directly behind. The **Dorset Military Museum,** in the Keep, includes a display devoted to Major John André, who was hanged as a spy at Tappan, on the Hudson, in 1780.

• North of Dorchester a few miles on the A352 is Cerne Abbas, site of the great testicular figure of the Cerne Abbas Giant cut into the chalky hillside, and of a ruined abbey. South of the A354 2 miles is Maiden Castle, the largest Roman ruin in Britain. 8 miles south is **Weymouth,** a resort town. Opposite the pier is a memorial to John Endicott and Richard Clark, who sailed to join Sir Humphrey Gilbert in 1583 on his voyage of discovery to North America. In 1628 Endicott took sixty settlers to Salem, Massachusetts. There is also a monument to the American assault force that sailed from here on D-Day in 1944, and on the esplanade is a statue of George III. It was he who made Weymouth a popular resort, by venturing out into the sea in 1789 in a bathing machine. The A354 continues past Pennsylvania Castle (now a hotel) – built for John Penn – to the **Isle of Portland,** from which limestone has been quarried for hundreds of years. The United Nations buildings in New York City are built of this stone. Northwest of Weymouth on the

B3157 is Abbotsbury. There is a fine tithe barn, the largest swannery in England (open 10.30–4.30, May–Sept.), and the subtropical Abbotsbury Gardens (open March–Sept., 10–5.30, Sun. 2–7, Oct.–March, close at 5).
• The Channel Islands. Steamers sail from Weymouth to the Channel Islands daily in summer and on a reduced schedule in winter. Guernsey is a four-hour trip; the boats then continue to Jersey, another two hours. One may also fly to either of the islands from Heathrow and Gatwick airports, London, and from Southampton and Bournemouth. An inter-island air service (often delayed by fog) connects Guernsey, Jersey and Alderney with Dinard and Cherbourg in France. There is a hydrofoil service between Jersey, Guernsey and St Malo on the French coast. One must reach Sark and Herm by motor boat only, which leaves from Guernsey every 30 minutes from 10.00 on. In the summer there is a hydrofoil to Sark from Jersey only. The local boat from Guernsey to Sark runs year round. The islands have been part of Britain for over 800 years, despite their location off the French coast. French is the official language, although English is spoken everywhere. One can sample the islands in three days – not less – and fruitfully use much more. The Channel Islands warrant a separate guide, and happily they have it: one of the very fine *Travellers' Guide* series, by R. M. Lockley (published by Jonathan Cape, London). America's common milk cows, the Jersey and Guernsey, came from here, as did the Alderney, which is no longer to be found on the island.
• On Jersey the major points to be seen include the 'capital' of Jersey, St Helier, with its **Museum of the Société Jersiaise,** which includes Ameri-can objects, on Pier Road; the German Military Underground Hospital, a substantial engineering achievement left as a reminder of the German wartime occupation of the islands; and La Hougue Bie, with its German Occupation Museum, Agricultural Museum and two old chapels. The Jersey Potteries are worth a visit. At Gorey is **Mont Orgueil,** a 13th cen-tury castle with a fine view (open weekdays 10–6). Inside is a tableau of Charles II presenting a charter for Virginia property to Sir George Carteret. There is a plaque at **Gorey Harbour** to Wilfred John Bertram, who received the American Medal of Freedom for saving two American officers from drowning in the harbor. The Jersey Zoological Park, main-tained by Gerald Durrell, is fun for children or anyone who admires his work. There is a delightful hotel, Le Couperon de Rozel, at Rozel Bay, to stay in, and both it and La Capannina in St Helier offer excellent meals. The Little Grove Hotel at St Lawrence is also charming.
• On Guernsey, the major sights are the 'capital', St Peter Port, which is particularly pleasant, with Hauteville House, where Victor Hugo lived from 1856 to 1870 (open weekdays except Thurs. afternoons, 10–12.30, 2–4.30), of great interest. It is owned by the City of Paris. The Lukis and Island Museum (open weekdays, 10.30–1, 2–4) is instructive, and **St Peter's Parish Church** is the finest in the islands. There is a memorial

here to Sir Isaac Brock, killed defending Canada against the American invasion in 1812. The rose window was partially destroyed by an American bomber during an attack on a German submarine in the harbor. The panels on the choir stalls are very fine, as is the Liberation Window. The Old Government House Hotel is a good place to stay.

(I have not been to Sark, so I rely on a friend for a report: Sark is a day's outing from Guernsey by steamer from St Peter Port every weekday morning at 10, returning at 5. The scenery is wild, and one must either walk or ride in wagons that meet the steamers. The island is the Dame of Sark's seigneurie, and because of her stern if benevolent rule, the island is free of clutter. The Avaldo Creux attracts many visitors, for both accommodations and meals are very good.)

WHAT TO READ   While on the islands, you may wish to read Victor Hugo's *Les Miserables,* written at Hauteville House in 1862. Hammond Innes' best book, *The Wreck of the Mary Deare,* is set around the Channel Islands and on the Minquiers, French-owned rocks south of Jersey. Elizabeth Goudge's 1944 best-seller, *Green Dolphin Street,* is set on Guernsey.

From Dorchester, drive west on the A35, through **Kingston Russell.** John Lothrop Motley, historian of the Dutch Republic and American Ambassador to Britain, lived in the manor house here. A stone commemorates his death in 1877. Bridport is a handsome town, and Lyme Regis (left on the A3052) is the scene of Jane Austen's *Persuasion,* and (I think an even better book) John Fowles' *The French Lieutenant's Woman.* Beyond and towards the sea is the area of the Dowlands landslip, where on Christmas Day 1839, 800 million tons of cliff collapsed, leaving a scar 6 miles long. This is probably not the place to read Douglas Warner's thriller, *Death on a Warm Wind,* about a southern English seacoast resort wiped out by an earthquake and land slippage, but have it ready for the evening and a more comforting setting. The A3052 continues through **Colyford,** birthplace of Sir Thomas Gates, who governed Virginia 1611–4; he and others were shipwrecked in Bermuda in 1609, and the account of the event written by Samuel Purchas may have inspired Shakespeare's *The Tempest.* (Just north on the B3161 is the charming village of Colyton.) Turn back 2 miles to the B3172 south, to drive through Beer and by a country road to Branscombe, both beautiful villages, and thus via the A3052 into Sidmouth. (Samuel Taylor Coleridge was born in Ottery St Mary, north on the B3176.) 3 miles beyond Sidmouth, turn south on the A376.

To the right are the Bicton Gardens, laid out by the designer of the gardens of Versailles, and ahead is **East Budleigh.** In the church are pew ends carved by the men who sailed with Sir Walter Raleigh, depicting sights they had never seen before. There is also a memorial in the church to the man who laid the first trans-Atlantic cable. The Conant family descends from East Budleigh. Just west is **Hayes Barton,** a thatched farmhouse (open weekdays, mornings), birthplace of Sir Walter. Continue through Budleigh Salterton to Exmouth, and via the A377 to Exeter.

• Alternatively, leave Lyme Regis north on the A3070 to the A35, thence into Axminster. Carpets have been made here since the 18th century, and one may tour the factory. The A35 continues through Honiton, famous for its lace. From Honiton take the A30 to Exeter; just beyond Honiton a country road right goes to **Buckerell.** Here is a memorial to Admiral Samuel Graves, the person charged with closing the port of Boston after the incident of the Tea Party. He is buried at **Hembury Fort,** 3 miles northwest.

Exeter, county town for Devon, is a Cathedral city of 100,000. Much of the city was destroyed in 1942, but the great cathedral – one of the handsomest in Europe – survived even though hit. The West Front is dazzling in its detail, and the minstrels' gallery, elaborate bishop's throne, fine 14th century east window, Speke chantry, and remarkable tombs provide individual details of unusual quality. The wood carving and roof bosses are very good throughout. The Guildhall on the High Street is the oldest municipal building in England, built in 1330. The **Royal Albert Memorial Museum & Art Gallery** on Queen Street (open weekdays 10–5.30) has works by Reynolds, Turner, James McNeill Whistler and Mark Fisher, and a shield reputed to have belonged to the Apache chief Cochise, as part of a gallery devoted to American natural history and ethnography. Exeter University is on the north side of town. Its **Library** has many photographs of American Indians, and the **American Arts Documentation Centre** here publishes handlists and assists research into American music, film, poetry and black and underground literature – a fitting project for the city from which Daniel Boone's grandfather came. In the **Heavitree** parish church, just east of Exeter, is a memorial to Thomas Gorges, who helped found the early settlement of Maine. South off the A377 is a good Maritime Museum with over sixty types of craft. Craftsmen reconstruct extinct forms of vessels here and sail them on the River Exe. And while in Exeter, try to find some Dorset Blue Viny, an unusual cheese.

To see both Dartmoor National Park and the interesting coast between Exeter and Plymouth requires some doubling back. I would recommend driving over Dartmoor to Yelverton, to spend the night at the Moorland Links Hotel, but having dinner at what surely is one of the best restaurants in the far southwest of England, the Horn of Plenty at Gulworthy (closed Thursday), 3 miles west of Tavistock, 8 miles from Yelverton. The drive across the moor is 45 miles, but if you are away from Exeter in summer light by 5.00 p.m., you will have enough time. The Horn of

Plenty features a different, usually French, regional dinner each evening, and serves fish superlatively well. Last orders are taken at 9.30. Book both the hotel and the restaurant, and tell the hotel you will not be having dinner. A few years ago when the *Guide Michelin* people were preparing their guide to dining out in Britain, there was much speculation as to whether any British restaurants would win the coveted stars. In a well-discussed article, British food expert Margaret Costa declared that the one restaurant in England that deserved the designation 'worth a trip' was the Horn of Plenty. As it happened, none in Britain won the 'vant le voyage' (three stars), but of the nineteen single stars awarded in Britain, one went to the Horn.

Leave Exeter west on the A30, then left on the B3212. (The B3193 runs south to **Christow,** where there is a window in the parish church to one of the British who fought with Burgoyne at Saratoga.) Dunsford contains several cob houses. Here one enters the 365-square-mile national park, and crosses the most famous moor in England. Always bleak, even under sun, this high moorland is virtually empty. Often there is rain or fog, and the unexplained prehistoric ruins that dot the moor add to the sense of mystery. It was here that *Hound of the Baskervilles*, Conan Doyle's masterpiece, was set. At Moretonhampstead, divert right to North Bovey, an unspoiled show village, and then back to the B3212, which continues across the moor to Postbridge.

• North on the A382 from Moretonhampstead and left on a country road is Castle Drogo, built by Sir Edwin Lutyens, designer of the imperial city of New Delhi; the setting is more interesting than the contents (open April–Oct., daily 11–1, 2–6). When the A382 meets the A30, turn west. At Sticklepath is the Museum of Rural Industry, built around the Finch Foundry (open summers, 11–6). At Okehampton is a fine ruined castle. The highest point on Dartmoor, High Willhays (2,038 feet), is reached by a narrow road past Okehampton Camp, and a mile of walking. 19 miles further west on the A30 is Launceston, with a commanding though ruined castle.

At Postbridge is an ancient clapper bridge, and one may get directions here to walk to the relatively inaccessible Grey Wethers Stone Circles, the most impressive of the Bronze Age sites on the moor. Continue through Princetown, site of **Dartmoor Prison,** built in 1806 to house French and American prisoners of war; it was used for convicts after 1850. During the War of 1812 over 2000 American seamen who resisted impressment were imprisoned here; 200 died, and there is a memorial window to them in the church. Many are buried in the churchyard. The B3212 continues to Yelverton. (Gulworthy is north on the A386 to **Tavistock,** birthplace of Sir Frances Drake – a tablet and statue mark the site at Crowndale Farm, 1 mile south of town – and west on the A390). North of Gulworthy is **Blanchdown.** Here was the Devon Great Consols Mine, which produced the arsenic used to control the boll weevil on the cotton plantations in the American south. Cotehele House, southwest of Gunnislake (open April–Oct., daily 11–1, 2–6, garden only Nov.–March, to dusk), is the best preserved Tudor house in Cornwall, with fine furniture, tapestries and armor, and a resplendent garden.

FOURTH DAY

Begin the day with a visit to **Buckland Abbey,** now a museum, just west of Yelverton. The abbey was founded in 1278; it was then converted into a mansion which Sir Francis Drake purchased in 1581. Return to Princetown on the B3212 and bear right beyond into the A384, which passes through Dartmeet, often regarded as the prettiest of Dartmoor's villages. Just northwest of Dartmeet is a country road southwest to Huccaby; follow it across Holne Moor to Holne Village. Charles Kingsley lived here as vicar, wrote *The Water Babies* and *Westward Ho!,* and preached Christian socialism. Follow the signs for Scorriton, Combe and Buckfastleigh, on the A38. Just south is Dean Prior; Robert Herrick was the vicar here – the church contains a window to him. Return north on the A38 through Buckfastleigh to Buckfast Abbey, which is modern, and to Ashburton. Follow the country roads left for Buckland-in-the-Moor, Widecombe-in-the-Moor, and right past Hound Tor, Rippon Tor and Hayton Rocks to Hayton Vale, thus to Ilsington. These are very narrow roads and require care. Continue on to Bovey Tracey, where the Coombe Cross Hotel offers a good lunch or, if you are running late, afternoon tea.

Now strike for the sea again, south on the A382 to Newton Abbot. (East on the B3195 and right on a country road is **Stokeinteighnhead;** the parish church contains a monument to a soldier killed in the American Revolution.) The A380 leads to Torquay, center of England's Riviera, a truly handsome coastal city. This is the kind of town where people take their croquet seriously. West off the A3022 is **Compton Castle** (open Mon., Wed., Thurs., 10–12, 2–5), associated with the Gilbert family, and just below it, in **Marldon,** is a parish church with monuments to the Gilberts, including Sir Humphrey, colonizer of Newfoundland. In the center of Paignton, south of Torbay, is **Oldway** (open Mon.–Fri., 9–1, 2.15–5.15; also Sat.–Sun., May–Sept., 2.20–5), used as an American hospital during World War II.

West on the A385 is Totnes, one of Devon's most attractive towns, with a ruined castle, fine parish church (the rood screen is considered one of the best in England), and museum. Two of England's best thriller writers, Desmond Bagley and Edmund Crispin, lived here. (South off the A381 is **Harberton,** from which came Nathaniel Mather.) Northwest is

Dartington Hall, a superb crafts and art school built around a 14th century manor house. In 1925 the main hall and 820 acres were bought by Mr and Mrs Leonard Elmhirst, Americans who were determined to see England's arts and crafts survive. Now Dartington Hall is a fine school which runs its own crafts courses and maintains, in the village nearby, a shop selling its products. The village pub is an attractive place to stop; it has 'scrumpy', the hard cider of Devon, and it does a good pub lunch.

Return along the A385 through Totnes, and beyond take a country road right through Waddeton, and toward the Dittisham ferry. On the left before reaching the ferry is **Greenway House,** birthplace of Sir Humphrey Gilbert. Continue on to **Brixham** via the A3022. This is where William of Orange landed in 1688; the stone on which he is said to have stepped first is on the pier. Once the leading fishing port of England, Brixham is now a holiday center. There is a good replica of Sir Francis Drake's *Golden Hind* in the harbor. Then follow the signs towards Dartmouth, which can be reached by one of three ferry crossings.

Dartmouth is a charming, often very crowded, town near the mouth of the River Dart. The *Mayflower* and *Speedwell* spent a week here undergoing repairs and the site of their anchorage is marked by a plaque at Bayard's Cove. The house in which the crews stayed is now a curio shop. There is also a marker to the American troops who embarked from here in 1944, in a massed invasion of 485 vessels. Thomas Newcomen was born here, and his steam engine is on display. A mile south is Dartmouth Castle, which long overlooked the ships that returned from the Newfoundland fishery, and St Petrock's Church. Continue south on the B3205 from the castle to the A379 through Stoke Fleming (where one may see local Red Ruby cattle on the beach) and along the **Slapton Sands.** An obelisk at the Slapton road junction, put up by the American army, commemorates the use of the South Hams area as a training ground from 1942 to 1944. The villages throughout the district were evacuated in preparation for the battle training that led to D-Day. Continue 30 miles on the A379 to Plymouth.

• Three interesting short diversions from the main road will add two hours to one's driving time. The first is the A381 from Kingsbridge to Salcombe, a lovely town where orange and lemon trees grow. This is 'England's Mediterranean', or what little there is of it. The sand bar that nearly blocks the harbor is the one that led Tennyson to write 'Crossing the Bar', for it is unusually dangerous. From Malborough, on the Salcombe road, one may drive west, then southwest on bad roads to Bolberry Down, an area opened up during the war for training purposes. And for fun and a challenge, turn left at Aveton Gifford, on the A379 west of Kingsbridge, and follow the signs for the tidal road. This route crosses a number of fords and runs over tidal mudflats; at high tide, posts mark the edge of the road so that it may be followed even when under water.

Plymouth, a city of 250,000, has been rebuilt completely since World War II, and it is not easy to imagine now the city from which the Pilgrim Fathers at last successfully sailed in the *Mayflower* in 1620, having decided to leave *Speedwell* behind. Still behind, and restored, it can be visited at Sutton Harbour. From here sailed Captain James Cook on his voyage around the world, Sir Francis Drake to attack the Spanish Armada, Raleigh and Frobisher on their explorations, and Sir Francis Chichester on his one-man circumnavigation of 1966–7. Visit the **City Museum and Art Gallery** (open daily 10–6, Sun. 3–5) on Tavistock Road, which contains several items relating to Drake, including a replica of the plate of brass which he set up on the coast of California in 1579, and a fine Epstein bronze as well as work by other American artists. Follow signs for The Hoe (where Drake finished his game of bowls before sailing against the Armada) on the waterfront; here are a number of memorials, an aquarium, and the old citadel. On a clear day one may see the Eddystone Light, 14 miles south. Along the Barbican one finds the **Mayflower Steps.** There is a memorial to the sailing of the *Mayflower,* and another to the safe arrival of the NC4, an American seaplane which crossed the Atlantic via the Azores in 1919. **St Andrew's Church** dates from the 15th century; it has a window by John Piper, Captain Bligh of the *Bounty* was baptized in the font, and Sir Martin Frobisher is buried here. The doorway to the cemetery is a memorial to two American soldiers killed in the War of 1812. Saltram House, on the eastern edge of the city off the A38, is the largest in Devon (open April–Oct., daily 11–1, 2–6; grounds open Nov.–March). There are two fine Robert Adam rooms, good furniture, and pictures by Sir Joshua Reynolds, and a handsome garden. Just northwest on the A388 is **St Budeaux;** in the parish church is a monument to Sir Ferdinand Gorges. Drake was married here. A tablet under the **Saltash Bridge,** just beyond, marks the embarkation of American troops on D-Day.

There are no hotels in Plymouth that can be recommended with complete confidence. I have stayed happily in the Duke of Cornwall on Melbay Road. For those who are homesick, there is a Holiday Inn.

FIFTH DAY

At last, Cornwall – very crowded in summer, lovely in spring and autumn, attractive even in winter. Cornwall was once quite separate from England, with its own sense of identity and its own language. Cornish is now spoken only in an academic sense, and a large influx of retired people into the coastal villages has tended to homogenize Cornwall with the rest of England.

At the B3249 turn left to St Germans, where the 16th century church is built on the site of an ancient cathedral. The church contains a Burne-Jones window and a fine Rysbrack monument. Continue to the A374, west, into the A387 to Looe, an attractive Cornish fishing village, and Polperro, perhaps the best of the south coast villages. One may continue by unnumbered though well-marked country roads to the Bodinnick–Fowey ferry (long queues at the height of the summer), or turn north via the B3559 to the A390 and southwest through Lostwithiel. The ruined Restormel Castle is just north, and above it is **Lanhydrock House** (open April–Oct., 11–1, 2–6; garden only Nov.–March), with a fine garden. This has been turned into a training center for Americans by the National Trust. Continue south on the B3269 to Fowey. Here is Menabilly (originally Manderley), Daphne du Maurier's home, where she wrote *Rebecca*. West of Fowey at the junction of the A3082 and the B3269 is the reputed Tristan stone, and north of Fowey in Golant, the church marks the scene of Tristan's meeting with Iseult. (Several sites in this area are associated with this famous 12th century romance, and there is a useful guide to them by E.M.R. Ditmas.)

Continue on the A3082 to St Austell. The sand and quartz pyramids of the china clay industry form a lunar landscape to the north. It is interesting to drive a short circuit through the area, leaving St Austell north on the B3374, crossing the Carclaye Downs to Bugle, passing over the A391 to Roche, south on the B3274, and diverting right on a country road just past Tresayes, to St Austell again. The British historian A. L. Rowse, who grew up here, writes affectionately of St Austell, as does Silas Hocking, now forgotten, who wrote dozens of novels and was the first author to sell a million copies in his lifetime. Hocking was born in St Stephen, west of St Austell.

Follow the B3278 south from St Austell to Mevagissey (a shark fishing center) and by country roads to the A3078 above St Mawes. This handsome resort and retirement town is attractive for walking, and the Rising Sun Hotel offers a good lunch until 1.45. Drive north through St Just to the B3289 and the King Harry Ferry to Trelissick. At **Tolverne,** just north of the ferry slip, is a concrete landing platform used by the Americans for loading tanks on barges for D-Day. Cross via the ferry and follow the B3289 into the A39, to Truro.

County town for Cornwall, Truro has a handsome Cathedral, completed in 1910. Its bishop's throne, baptistry, and windows are good, and there are memorials to Sir Arthur Quiller-Couch ('Q') and Samuel Wallis. South on the A39 is Falmouth; just before reaching it a side road left runs to **Mylor,** from which Thomas Peter, one of the founders of New London, Connecticut, came. Falmouth was once the second busiest port in England. Developed by Raleigh, it was the first or last port of call on the trans-Atlantic voyage; here the North American and West Indian mail packets put in. Bartholomew Gosnold sailed from here in 1602, to explore the coasts of Maine and Cape Cod. Pendennis Castle offers a fine view of the sea.

Follow now the coastal roads, unnumbered country lanes via Penjerrick and Glendurgan gardens, Constantine, the B3291 to Mawgan, and south on the A3083 toward the Lizard. In so doing, one skirts around the Helford River. An inlet off its south shore is the Frenchman's Creek of Daphne du Maurier's novel. One passes the Culdrose Air Force Base at the junction with the A3083. The Goonhilly Downs, south on the peninsula, are used for satellite communications. A country road right goes to **Poldhu Cove:** there is a marker on the spot where Marconi received the first trans-Atlantic radio message in 1901. Continue to Mullion, a smuggling center until 1840, and join the B3296, thence via the A3083 on to the Lizard. The point is the most southerly in Britain (no, Land's End is not). A toll road runs to Kynance Cove, the most dramatic on the south coast. Return north on the A3083 to Helston, a former center of the tin trade. The area north of here, through Camborne and Redruth to St Agnes, is covered with abandoned mine shafts, engine houses and other objects of industrial archaeology, and one can spend days exploring the great ruins that loom up against the sky like medieval fallen castles. (If this subject is of interest, obtain from Tor Mark Press in Truro its excellent pamphlets on industrial archaeology in Cornwall.)

From Helston follow the A394 to Marazion. Offshore is St Michael's Mount, with a castle on top. A causeway is uncovered for three hours at low tide; at other times, take a boat from Marazion. Edward the Confessor opened a chapel here, placing it under the control of Mont St Michel in Normandy. It is still the home of the St Aubyn family (open Wed., Fri., 10.30–4.30, also Mon., June–Sept.). Legend says that the island is a remnant of the land of Lyonesse, which lay between Land's End and the Scilly Isles; it is said to have subsided in a single night, leaving 140 churches under water and drowning every living human being save for one man who escaped to tell the tale. The A394 joins the A30 outside Penzance.

Center of the Cornish Riviera, **Penzance** was also made notable by Gilbert and Sullivan in their famous operetta. South is Mousehole (pronounced Moozel), a fishing village. The Lobster Pot there is a good restaurant. At Paul, on the hill above the village, is buried Dolly Pentreath, last person to use Cornish as her native tongue (she died in 1777). Follow the B3315, diverting to see Porthcurno, and on to Land's End. This is the westernmost point in England, although it is usually contrasted with John o'Groats in Scotland (which, contrary to popular belief, is not the northernmost point) as the southern tip of the land, and to have travelled Britain from Land's End to John o'Groats is to have 'seen it all'. One may look west to the Scilly Isles, and will wish to, for the immediate environs are a mess of candy wrappers and soft ice cream cones.

• The Scilly Isles, sometimes called the Flower Islands, can be reached by helicopter in 20 minutes from Penzance. There is also a daily ferry each way from mid-April to mid-September, Monday to Saturday, and on alternate days the rest of the year. The islands are crowded in summer, and the best month to see the flowers and avoid the mobs is March. St Mary's is the largest island, and Hugh Town is the seat. Launches serve the other islands from it. Bryher, the author, lived on the island of that name.

• The most interesting island is Tresco, where there are fine botanical gardens with rare plants from around the world. In the gardens is **Valhalla Maritime Museum,** with figureheads from vessels wrecked in the Scillonian area. Included are American ships. The Bell Rock Hotel on St Mary's is a good place to stay.

From Land's End, drive north and east along the coastal road, through St Just on the B3306. North along the coast are the ruins of the Botallack mines; the Levant Mine had a shaft that worked out under the Atlantic for a mile, 2100 feet below the sea. In Botallack the Count House offers an excellent lunch or dinner. A lane to Pendeen Watch makes it possible to look back down the cliffs, which are spectacular in a storm. (Right on a country road from Morvah 3 miles towards Madron, on the left side of the road, is the Lanyon Quoit, a fine dolmen, perhaps the best of the thirty Bronze Age sites in Cornwall.) The road passes through Zennor. D. H. and Frieda Lawrence lived here at Higher Tregerthen during World War I while he wrote *Women in Love* and *The Rainbow*; they were driven away when the locals decided that they were German spies. **St Ives** became an artists' colony when James McNeill Whistler and Walter Sickert went there, and after them came Barbara Hepworth, Ben Nicholson and Bernard Leach. Follow the A3074 into the A30 to Hayle, where Virginia Woolf passed her summers at Talland House. *To the Lighthouse* invokes Godrevy Light, northeast off the B3301, a road that passes above the startling cliffs of Hell's Mouth.

St Ives is the best place to spend the night on the north Cornish coast, and the Tregenna Castle or Garrack Hotels are dependable. The Sloop Inn is a pleasant pub with fine views and cartoons by artists who have lived in St Ives; it is on The Wharfe.

SIXTH DAY

Follow the B3301 to Portreath and continue east on the B3300, to the Tolgus Tin Company. This historic works is now a museum (open daily, 10–4, May–Sept.), where one may see water-powered machinery operating.

• Make a small circuit from Redruth to see the most imposing of the abandoned mine shafts and engine houses, and visit two steam whims that are preserved by the National Trust: leave Redruth south on the A393, right on the B3297, and right for Carnkie; a sharp right again takes one to Carn Brea. Return south past Carnkie, Medlyn Moor, and southwest to the B3297 again, then south a mile, and right on the B3280 and right again for Bolenowe and Troon, thus into Camborne, over a ruin-cluttered landscape. The Holman Museum here (open Mon.–Fri., 10–12, summers only) explains tin mining well. Right on the A30, past Dolcoath Mine (closed), the deepest – 3500 feet – in Britain, and left on a country road posted for Pool, brings one to the National Trust property where, in summer 11–1 and 2–6 daily, one may inspect the historic engine of the East Pool Mine. Continue on the A30 to Redruth. This is all *Poldark* country.

Leave Redruth on the A393, continuing southeast to Gwennap, where one finds a pit, a natural amphitheatre caused by a subsiding mine, which John Wesley turned into the Cathedral of the Mines. Turn north on the B3298 through St Day and follow country roads to Chacewater and the A390, then left to the B3277 to St Agnes. In these brief circuits one will have reconstructed the rise and fall of the Cornish mining economy, a decline that began in the 1870's and was completed with the full introduction of cheap Malayan tin in the 20th century.

Adhere to the coast as much as possible from St Agnes (leaving on the B3285) to Bude, 85 miles northeast. Pass through Perranporth to the A3075, north to Newquay, an attractive resort town with magnificent beaches – the best place for a swim. Continue north on the B3276, across the Vale of Mawgan, to the Bedruthen Steps. These great jagged rocks, with surf rushing to the sands around them, are the most dramatic sight on a coast of many such sights. Steps down the cliff have recently been restored. At **Padstow** is a fine parish church, Prideaux Place (with John Opie paintings), and the court house where Sir Walter Raleigh presided as Warden of Cornwall. The seafood, on the quay, provides a good lunch.

Circle around the Camel River via the A389 to the A39 through Wadebridge – which has the largest medieval bridge in England – and take the B3314 back towards the coast through St Minver. A road to the left takes one to Port Isaac, an attractive fishing village. From Delabole, where there is the largest quarry in Britain, continue to the junction of the B3314 and the B3266. Here at Slaughter Bridge is the legendary scene of King Arthur's last battle with Mordred.

• At Wadebridge, the A389 inland leads to Bodmin, the historic county town of Cornwall (despite Truro's claim). From here the A30 crosses lonely Bodmin Moor. Northeast at Bolventor is the Jamaica Inn used by Daphne du Maurier in her book. South on the St Neot road is Dozmary Pool; when Arthur was gravely wounded in his last battle, it is said that he told Sir Bedivere to throw the great sword of Excalibur into this pool, where the Lady of the Lake grasped it. One may continue to Altarnun, and left on country roads to reach the A39 above Camelford (another location legend credits as Camelot), and thus to Tintagel.

Any pilgrimage to Arthurian sights must include at least Tintagel and Glastonbury (for the latter, see tour number 7). A compelling book on the Arthurian legend, covering Britain from 367 to 634, is Leslie Alcock's *Arthur's Britain*. Nowhere can one find a fuller, better statement on all that is known and deduced about Britain's legendary hero, and Tintagel is the place (along with Camelford and Bodmin Moor, above) to make this sensible book a constant companion. The castle is jaggedly romantic (open May–Sept., weekdays 9.30–7, Sun. at 2, earlier closing other months). In truth, no evidence at all has been found to support the legendary connection between castle (which dates from the 12th century) and king, but most of us know Tennyson better than we know history, and the place is too romantic to let legend slip. Sometimes, as the historian knows, what people believe to be true is more important than what an historian's grey research may reveal. Also in Tintagel is the Old Post Office, a 14th century stone house (open April–Oct., weekdays 11–1, 2–6, Sun. 2–6), and **King Arthur's Hall,** with exhibitions on the legend, and windows provided by American admirers. This, like Old Sarum, is rotten borough country, and Bossiney, just north of Tintagel, where one vote once sent two members to Parliament, was among the constituencies eliminated by the Great Reform Bill of 1832.

Continue northeast through Boscastle (right off the main road is St Juliot, where Thomas Hardy restored the church while working as an architect), and divert left on a country road with a sign for St Gennys, holding to the coast beyond it via Whitemore, Widemouth and Bude. The sands here northwards offer the best surfing beaches in Britain. At Bude join the A39 north 15 miles to country roads, left, marked for Hartland and then Hartland Point. The great headland here presents the roughest sea in Britain; it was the Promontory of Hercules written of in Ptolemy's geography, and guidebooks tell us that the force of a winter wave on the rock averages 2000 pounds per square foot. Spray reaches to car windshields high above. The Isle of Lundy is 12 miles northwest – it can be reached from Northam, near Bideford.

Return then to the A39, and turn left almost immediately on the B3237 to Clovelly. One leaves the car at the top of the hill and walks down a cobblestoned lane; there is a Land Rover service back to the top. A portion of **Mount Pleasant Park** was provided by Americans. From the parking lot Hobby Drive (open 10–7) runs east; a small toll is charged, but the woodland road is worth it. It comes out on the A39, to Bideford. Between Clovelly and Westward Ho! on the coast is the land associated with Charles Kingsley – Westward Ho! was named after the novel, not the reverse. Rudyard Kipling went to the United Services College (now houses on Kipling Terrace) in Westward Ho! and his *Stalky & Co.* is based on his experiences. Appledore is a charming town north of **Bideford,** while the latter has many interesting old streets. Sir Richard Grenville was born here: claims are made for three different houses, at 3 Church Walk, the Castle Inn and Ford Farm. Grenville commanded the vessels that went to Roanoke, and he brought back with him an Indian named Christian Rawley, who is buried in Bideford churchyard. Grenville died as captain of the *Revenge*, immortalized in Tennyson's poem. The town became rich on the tobacco trade with America and Biddeford, Maine, bears its name. The **Burton Art Gallery** on Kingsley Road is quite good; it contains eight works by Mark Fisher and fourteen by E. Aubrey Hunt, American artists.

This has been a long day of twisting roads, and a particularly good meal and hotel are deserved. 18 miles away is one of the finest in England, where I have had one of my four or five most memorable meals: Highbullen Hotel in Chittlehamholt. Dinner is served until 9. Take the A386 south from Bideford to **Great Torrington,** where Increase Mather lived, then left on the B3227 at Atherington, then right on the B3217 and after High Bickington left on a country road posted for Chittlehamholt. (Do not confuse the towns of High Bullen or Chittlehampton with your destination.)

SEVENTH DAY

This can be an easy day, for the Highbullen's breakfasts are both famous and late. When ready, drive back to the A377 and north to **Barnstable.** Long a staple for the wool trade, this old town is essentially Georgian. St Anne's Chapel was once a school where John Gay was a pupil; it is now a museum. Nathaniel Mather was a vicar here as well. Follow the A361 north to Ilfracombe, a popular resort with several fine beaches, some reached through tunnels. Kaiser Wilhelm II was educated here. The coastal road east (the A399) is attractive; it rejoins the A39 at Blackmoor Gate.

Rising above are the heights of Exmoor National Park, a heather and bracken plateau broken by many river valleys. Wild red deer and wild ponies may be seen near dawn or at twilight, especially in the western part of the park. While it is crossed by a major road (the B3223), this national park more than any other requires walking to see. There are a number of 'waymarked walks' for this purpose, and one may purchase booklets on them, or on the park, at the information office in Combe Martin (which was, incidentally, the scene of Marie Corelli's best-seller,

The Mighty Atom) on the A399 east of Ilfracombe. One may also hire horses, for example at Malmsmead, to ride up the narrow valleys.

Divert left from the A39 for Hunter's Inn and Martinhoe, to reattain the cliffs above the sea. A toll road passes through the Valley of Rocks into Lynton, on a cliff above Lynmouth (the towns are connected by a cliff railway). Shelley, Wordsworth and Coleridge popularized Lynton, and it has been a favorite holiday resort ever since. There is an informative museum. The road from Lynton to Porlock has the steepest continuous gradients in England, and one sustained stretch just outside Porlock (you will be going downhill) is the steepest mile on any main road. After passing Countisbury Church, watch for a side road right to Brandon, thence to Malmsmead. This was the setting for R. D. Blackmore's *Lorna Doone*. From here one may walk up Badgworthy Water 2 miles to Doone Valley, no longer a secret valley (the path is likely to be crowded) but still attractive. At Oare, a mile east of Malmsmead, is the church where Carver Doone shot Lorna Doone at the altar as she was being married to John Ridd. (The book was very successful in America under its title *Slain by the Doones*, which suggests that the American penchant for violent books was already at work.) One may continue on a narrow road east to the A39 into Porlock. The villages can usually be counted on to provide a good Devonshire tea.

• Drive west on the B3225 to Porlock Weir, a quaint seaside town, and continue to the toll barrier. A mile west by path is the tiny Culbone Church, the smallest parish church in England, on the site of a former leper colony. At Ash Farm here in the fall of 1797 Samuel Taylor Coleridge took two grains of opium 'to check a dysentry', fell asleep while reading *Purchas his Pilgrims* at the line, 'In Xamdu did Cublai Can build a stately Palace', dreamed his poem, and upon awakening wrote out fifty-two lines of *Kubla Khan* before being interrupted by a 'person from Porlock', no more to be able to write of his dream, later lamely concluding the whole with two final lines.

Beyond Porlock turn right on country roads posted for Luccombe, Dunkery Hill and Luckwell Bridge on the B3224. This road passes within a quarter mile of the summit of Dunkery Beacon, at 1705 feet the highest point on the moor. At an AA call box, turn left toward Winsford, and in that pleasant village – where one may have an excellent lunch at the Royal Oak Inn – turn right across Winsford Hill and on to the Tarr Steps at Ashway Farm, birthplace of George Williams, founder of the YMCA. Continue to Hawkridge and by country roads to Dulverton on the B3222. Turn north on the A396 to **Dunster,** where there is a fine medieval dovecot, a castle with a striking carved staircase (open July–Sept., Tues.– Thurs., and Wed. in June) and an eight-sided yarn market. The chimes of the church play daily at 1, 5 and 9, a different tune each day of the week: Monday provides the most interesting contrast, with 'Drink to Me Only' ringing from the church tower. One of Harvard's best known Houses bears Dunster's name. At Hathaway's one may have an exceptionally good cream tea (open 3 to 5). In Minehead the old street known as the Quay is attractive.

East via the A39 and the B3191 is Watchet, where Coleridge was moved to write 'The Ancient Mariner'. A country road east leads to the A39, and 2 miles beyond and to the left is East Quantoxhead, an attractive hamlet. Here one rounds the Quontox Hills to pass through Nether Stowey, where one may visit the cottage Coleridge lived in from 1796–8. The Wordsworths rented the Alfoxden manor house, 3 miles west, and walked the Quantock Hills with Coleridge, talking out the theories that were given expression in the *Lyrical Ballads*. Continue on the A39 to Bridgwater; here is the site of the Battle of Sedgemoor in 1685, the last battle fought in England. At Bridgwater one can join with tour number 7 and go north to Bristol, east to Glastonbury, or south on the new M5 motorway to run 11 miles to Taunton, there to board a train back to London (last train, except Sun., 7.35, reaching London at 10.20). The train has a restaurant car, and one may have a leisurely dinner while travelling through the Somerset countryside.

WHAT TO READ   Surely no journey in the whole of Britain could be richer in its literary associations, for this has been the land of The Matter of Britain (the Arthurian cycle), and especially Geoffrey of Monmouth and Thomas Malory's *Mort d'Arthur*, Jane Austen, Henry Fielding, Anthony Trollope, Thomas Hardy, William Thackeray, Charles Kingsley, Rudyard Kipling, Tennyson, Conan Doyle, R. D. Blackmore, Coleridge, Wordsworth, D. H. Lawrence, Shelley, Virginia Woolf, Daphne du Maurier (*Rebecca*, with its surfeit of rhododendrons, is set here), Arthur Quiller-Couch, William Golding and a host of others. Even Dickens, whose haunts were elsewhere, let Nicholas Nickleby be born here, and his short story, 'A Message from the Sea', is set in Clovelly. A host of detective stories and a variety of thrillers are set on the moors or in the coastal villages. Agatha Christie's classic *Ten Little Indians* starts, as one might expect, in a first-class smoking carriage with Mr. Justice Wargrave reading *The Times* on his way to an island owned by an American millionaire off the Devon coast (close reading suggests St George's near Looe). *Peril at End House* is set in Cornwall. This is the West Country, described so often in Eric Delderfield's historical romances, invoked frequently by Georgette Heyer. The range of reading is enormous, the countryside always compelling; whether for scenery, for literary pilgrimage or merely to see the coziest corners of England, this journey remains a favorite for all who take it.

13   To the Lake District

The Lake District is Britain's most popular holiday center, and with good reason. It is exceptionally beautiful, provides both rugged and pastoral landscapes, and can be reached in a comfortable day from London via the MI and the M6. The other side of the coin is that if one goes during the Easter holiday, or at the height of the summer season, one finds the roads impossibly crowded. The British seem content to sit in orderly motor queues, whether in the midst of the Cumbrian Mountains or waiting for a cross-channel ferry, for lengths of time that would drive Americans to riot. Still, one can enjoy the Lake District even in mid-season, if lesser roads are used when they are available, and if one leaves the motorway from London at some point reasonably near Preston.

Most of the Lake District requires a car, although buses ply the major roads. If the long drive from London does not appeal, fly to either Liverpool or Blackpool, or take the train to Liverpool or Preston from Euston Station. Car rental agencies are available at both locations. For the journey, take the excellent guide book to the Lake District National Park issued by Her Majesty's Stationery Office, plus (at the least) a selection of Wordsworth's poems, perhaps the fine and short collection by Roger Sharrock. Be certain to have booked accommodations, preferably a month or so in advance. As the standard guides show, there are many good hotels and inns in the district. A favorite country hotel is the Leeming Country-House, in Watermillock, a Georgian house on its own handsome grounds. More expensive, and of the highest quality, is the Sharrow Bay Country House in Ullswater, the hotel that consistently wins the *Good*

Food Guide's plaudits as perhaps the very best in England. In Grasmere there is the fine Michael's Nook and in Windermere the Miller Howe, which is expensive. In Ambleside is the Rothay Manor, a small hotel which specializes in a morning Cumberland platter for breakfast, and which won the (perhaps slightly facetious) English Tourist Board's contest for the best set tea in England – scones, Cumberland rum nicky with rum butter, homemade marmalades, and damson cheese (which is actually a jam).

If driving from Liverpool, take the A565 north through Bootle and Formby (where the sand dunes are attractive, and one can walk out on them to watch sea traffic entering the Mersey), to Southport, a splendid and quiet resort town. The A565 meets the A59, and one continues on to Preston. Home for 102,000 people, Preston is a cotton-weaving town and the center of northern Catholicism. Sir Richard Arkwright and Robert Service, the Canadian poet of far north adventure, were born here, as was Francis Thompson (at 7 Winckley Street), author of 'The Hound of Heaven'. The Harris Museum and Art Gallery (open weekdays 10–5), Market Square, has a fine collection of modern British paintings. The **Museum of the Queen's Lancashire Regiment,** at Fulwood Barracks (north edge of the city), contains American-related objects, including an unusual casket of solid silver. At Cooper Hall in **Walton-le-Dale,** on the A6 just south of town, Benjamin Franklin set up his famous lightning rods. 5 miles southeast on the A675 is Hoghton Tower, where James I allegedly knighted his loin of beef 'sir loin'. (A mile and a half below **Chorley,** 8 miles south of Preston on the A6, Miles Standish was born. The site, Duxbury Hall, has been torn down.)

Just north of Preston one may pick up the M6 to Lancaster. Alternatively, two interesting side excursions beckon:

• East of Preston is Blackburn (via the A59 and the A677), 10 miles. The descent into this city of 100,000 offers excellent views of its row houses. The Cathedral, although relatively small, is one of the most interesting in the north. Built as a parish church in 1826, it became a cathedral a century later. Its nave roof is a fine example of 19th century Gothic revival, and the modern corbels and invocations to the loom are attractive. As befits the former largest cotton-weaving center in the world, the Lewis Textile Museum on Exchange Street (open weekdays 10–5, Wed. and Fri., to 7.30) contains full-scale models of Hargreave's spinning jenny, Crompton's spinning mule, and other developments in the technology of weaving.
• From Blackburn the A679 runs to **Accrington,** 5 miles. The Haworth Art Gallery (open daily 2–5) contains the most extensive collection of Tiffany glass in Europe. Return to Blackburn and go north on the B6245 to Ribchester, on the Ribble. Here is the largest Roman fort in Britain. Return to the A59, and drive west to join the motorway.

• The alternative drive from Preston is west, on the A583 to Blackpool, a bustling resort city of 150,000. Almost always crowded – it receives eight million visitors in the summer – the city offers the best opportunity to see much of Britain at play. While the town is enveloped in carnival atmosphere, it is far less sleazy than its American counterparts. In this Atlantic City of England, one can find every type of entertainment for adult or child, as well as a very good art gallery featuring modern British painters. Drive as far as Cleveleys, then follow the A585 and the A588 to Lancaster.

• From Blackpool Airport one may fly to the Isle of Man, pick up a hire car at Ronaldsway Airport, near Castletown, circuit the island's 85 miles and (if mad) return the same day. The isle is self-governing, has its own parliament (the Tynwald), and is a popular resort. Be certain to see Douglas, with its House of Keys, where the parliament meets. The Manx Museum will help orient you to the island. Laxey, where the largest waterwheel in the world still turns away, and from which one may take a branch of the Manx Electric Railway to the top of Snaefell (2034 feet) to view the island, is often very crowded. See also **Ballaugh,** where the old church has a tablet on the Veale family connection with America; Peel, where the walls of the castle enclose ruined St Germain's Cathedral (open May–Sept.), and where one may have a meal of local scallops at the Lively Lobster on East Quay; and the Manx Folk Museum (open May–Sept., Mon.–Sat., 10–1, 2–5) in Cregneash.

Lancaster is set in a commanding position to view both the sea and the countryside. County town for Lancashire, it is dwarfed by both Manchester and Liverpool, now in new counties to themselves but irredeemably associated with the idea of Lancashire. Once the center of the West Indian trade, Lancaster is now a linoleum manufacturing city. The Roman Catholic cathedral is modest; the old castle (open Easter–Oct., weekdays 10.30–12, 2–3.30) contains the law courts and is worth visiting; Priory Church of St Mary has handsome stalls. The Museum of the King's Own Royal Regiment, which was involved in the Revolution and the War of 1812, and the city museum are in the **Old Town Hall.** George Whitfield preached in the Friends' Meeting House in Meeting House Lane, and the old Custom House saw many receipts from America come and go. Northwest at Halton, E. C. Lorac (the thriller writer) lived. South of the city on the A6 is the handsome new University of Lancaster. Southwest by country roads (after leaving on the B5321, then the B5273 for Morecambe) in the direction of Overton is **Sunderland Point.** The first bale of cotton delivered to Britain was unloaded there, thus starting the close tie between the textile district and the American South, leading to the Confederacy's attempt to exploit King Cotton during the Civil War.

Divert west to Morecambe, a seaside resort, and drive northeast along the shores of Morecambe Bay via the A5105. At low tide the entire 150 square miles of the bay are reduced to sand, as one looks across to the mountains in Furness. Rejoining the A6 north of Lancaster, follow the signs, left, for **Warton.** George Washington's ancestors came from here – and the tomb of the last may be seen – and the Washington coat of arms is set into the church, which also flies the American flag on July 4. Continue on the A6 to Levens Hall, well known for its topiary garden, and **Sizergh Castle,** associated with Washington, with a fine tower (open April–Sept., Wed. 2–5.45; gardens Tues.–Thurs.). Beyond is Kendal, largest town of the former Westmorland (now absorbed into Cumbria). Trinity Church is interesting, and **Abbot Hall Art Gallery** contains two American works. The Woolpack Hotel is acceptable, and 4 miles beyond at Underbarrow the small (twelve rooms) Greenriggs County House is very fine. A ritual in Kendal is to buy a Kendal mint cake – a slab of sugar covered with mint – and one will want to watch out for char, preferably broiled, and bilberry (whortleberry) pie on menus.

Lake District National Park begins just beyond Kendal. It is the largest national park in Britain – 855 square miles – and the most romantic, filled with 'wild rocks, dark chasms, mysterious ruins, stone circles on the moors, old churches in the dales', so precisely calculated to stir Thomas Gray (of the 'Elegy') when he visited in 1769. Since then, the fells and lakes have attracted poets, travellers and hikers in ever greater numbers.

I recommend the following highly zigzag route. One can pass over it in a day, although surely at least two days are wanted (and more for any walking). The route touches all of the major lakes, makes maximum use of byways to avoid the heaviest traffic, and is exceptionally beautiful. Hotels are recommended above.

From Kendal follow the A591 to the B5284, thence left to Crook, and there left on a country road through Underbarrow, right to the A5074, crossing it for Cartmel Fell and thence south across the A590 to Cartmel to see the ruined priory. Continue on to Cark, then north on the B5278 to the A590, right to the A592, and north along the shores of Lake Windermere, England's largest. In the parish church of **St Martin,** in Bowness-on-Windermere, is a window with the arms of John Washington. Return south a mile to the ferry that crosses the lake, thus to Far Sawrey. Here is Hill Top Farm, where Beatrix Potter lived from the early 1900's until her death in 1943. After she wrote the *Tale of Peter Rabbit* in 1902, her fame grew, and the National Trust property is now a museum and a place of pilgrimage for young and old.

Continue on the B5285 to Hawkshead, then south on a country road through the Grizedale Forest via Satterthwaite to Greenodd and via the A590 to **Ulverston.** Swarthmoor Hall, a mile southeast on the A590, gave its name to Swarthmore College, in Pennsylvania; George Fox's meeting house is hard by. Return to Ulverston and take the B5281 north to the

A5092, then east to the A5084, north. At Lowick Bridge cross to the east side of the river and follow the country road up the shore of Coniston Water, with good views of the Old Man of Coniston across the lake. At Brantwood House, one may see exhibits relating to John Ruskin, who lived there for twenty-nine years, and is buried at Coniston Church. There is also a Ruskin Museum in Coniston, at the head of the lake on the A593.

Leave Coniston on the B5285, back the way you came, and shortly left to The Tarns, perhaps the loveliest of the lakes, and thence to Hawkshead again. Wordsworth was a pupil here, and in summer both his school and Tyson Cottage, where he stayed, are open. Drive north on the B5286 to the A593, left, and then a right onto the B5343 (in the worst of traffic, the road is turned into a one-way circuit). This loop road into Langdale Fell is narrow and often crowded but also quite beautiful. Scafell Pike, the highest peak in England (3210 feet), lies directly ahead. The British historian George Trevelyan gave most of his patrimony to buy the land here for the National Trust. The loop comes out on the narrow and difficult Hard Knott Pass Road, west – follow it over the pass (with 1 in 3 gradients) to the River Esk, then turn around and come back to Ambleside.

This is the most congested part of the Lake District. It is also the center of literary associations with Wordsworth, Coleridge, Arthur Hugh Clough and Thomas De Quincey. In **St Mary's Church,** Ambleside, there is a window to Wordsworth placed there by his American admirers. Harriet Martineau lived at The Knoll in Ambleside, and Matthew Arnold lived in the house his father built, Fox How, as a child. Just north on the A591 is Rydal Mount, former home of Wordsworth, above Rydal Water (open in summer). Another mile brings one to Grasmere. Here is Dove Cottage, where Wordsworth lived from 1799 to 1808 (writing 'The Prelude'), to be followed into the house by De Quincey, who stayed on to 1830. There is a Wordsworth museum, and he and his wife and sister Dorothy are buried in the Grasmere churchyard, where there also is a memorial to Clough. This area is featured in the novels of Hugh Walpole and Mrs Humphrey Ward, and Robert Southey set *Goldilocks and the Three Bears* nearby.

Continue on the A591 along the shore of Thirlmere into Keswick. Southey lived in Greta Hall from 1803–43, and Scott wrote in the Royal Oak Hotel. The **Keswick Museum** contains objects relating to Wordsworth and an Epstein head of Hugh Walpole, who is buried in the churchyard of Great Crosthwaite. Near the bridge is an exhibition room devoted to ways in which lead pencils were made in Keswick from 1558; it is more interesting than it sounds (though not much). Leave town south on the B5289 along Derwent Water, over Honister Pass and into Buttermere; this is an especially attractive drive. Continue to Cockermouth, where Wordsworth's birthplace is now a museum. (14 miles southwest on the

A66 and A595 is **Whitehaven.** John Paul Jones was apprenticed here; in the Revolution, he anchored off St Bees Head, captured the harbor's fort and burned a ship. The public library has materials relating to Jones. George Washington's grandmother is buried in St Nicholas churchyard. Stone from Whitehaven, shipped in 1783 at Washington's request, was used in the porch at Mount Vernon. The American marine artist Robert Salmon was born here.)

Return from Cockermouth on the B5292, over Whinlatter Pass, into Keswick on the A66, continuing towards Penrith to the A5091 south, which connects with Ullswater. (Northeast via the A66 and the B5288 is Greystoke – do you remember your Tarzan?) Drive south on the A592 at least to the head of the Ullswater and preferably to the summit of Kirkstone Pass, the highest road in the park; then return along the lake, via Watermillock, to Pooley Bridge. The Sharrow Bay Hotel is back up the east side of Ullswater on a country road, which should be driven even if one is not staying at the hotel. Then continue towards Penrith on the B5320 to a country road right with a sign for Askham. Here is the imposing ruin of Lowther Castle. Return north into Penrith.

From here one may turn east into the Vale of Eden – Appleby, county town of Westmorland, is 13 miles; or south, toward Haweswater and Shap (where there is a ruined abbey). Just outside Penrith off the A686 going northeast is Edenhall, of the Musgraves (remember your Holmes and your Longfellow); the church contains relics. But the main route lies north, either on the M6, the A6 or the more leisurely wandering path of the A686, the B6412 and the B6413. The first two are both 18 miles to Carlisle. The last winds through the lovely village of Kirkoswald, to Brampton (the ruined Lanercost Abbey is just northeast), and into Carlisle on the A69 in 30 miles.

Carlisle is the gateway to the north, virtually the terminus of the Roman Wall, and is the place to connect with either tour number 11 from Newcastle (which takes in the whole of the Roman Wall) or with the Scottish tour (see Twelfth Day). The border of Scotland is only 9 miles north. A city of 72,000, Carlisle was the county town of Cumberland (now Cumbria). Woodrow Wilson's mother came from here, and his grandfather was pastor in the **Lowther Street Congregational Church** (there is a tablet inside). Wilson made his pilgrimage to the town in 1918. Though the Cathedral is one of the smallest in England, it is very good. Completed in 1123, it contains much of interest, including a superb East Window – which exceeds even the stained glass of York Minster – decorated piers, a fine old undercroft, a Renaissance screen and excellent choir stalls. The old castle, begun in 1092, includes a massive keep, one of the best in England. The **Carlisle Public Library, Museum & Art Gallery,** in Tullie House (open weekdays 9–5, Sun. in June–Aug. 2.30–5), contains several American-related objects, and the unique William Rothenstein Collection. (11 miles southwest via the A595 and the A596 is **Wigton.** Several Quaker families from here settled in Pennsylvania.) One may drop a rented car at the Carlisle railway station.

WHAT TO READ   Clearly one must read Wordsworth, Coleridge, Ruskin, De Quincey, Hough, Lamb (who visited Wordsworth), Walpole, Beatrix Potter, Southey and the other Lake Poets while in a region such as this. Surely one begins with Wordsworth's 'Prelude' and 'Home at Grasmere'.

14 The bit in the middle: Three short trips in the Midlands

The Midlands are little visited by overseas tourists, and they tend to get bad press from American travel writers. To argue, correctly, that one does not know the 'real England' without knowing the Midlands seems to some to damn with faint praise, for Americans fear that the Midlands are nothing but slums, coal faces and rain, and that while all of this is real enough, there is no reason to inflict it upon oneself. Yet this is to miss the point, or, rather, the several points. The dismal picture of the Midlands is no longer true (although one may still find some slums, especially in non-white areas in cities like Manchester, Bradford, Liverpool and Wolverhampton). Further, the great cities of the Midlands have good art galleries and museums, and the countryside – especially near Sheffield, itself a handsomely rebuilt city – is dotted with fine country estates. The Peak District National Park, while not one of the major parks, affords many handsome scenes. And the literary and American-related sites are many. In short, while the Midlands may not be a prime target for one's first visit to Britain, it might well be the focus of a second or third trip. To claim to know Britain without having been to the area roughly bounded by Northampton, Birmingham, Manchester and Sheffield is rather like claiming to know the United States without having been west of Pennsylvania or east of Kansas.

The Midlands are crisscrossed with rail lines, so that one may visit all of the major centers without a car. On the other hand, the country estates and the national park require wheels. Accordingly, I have compromised and outlined three trips below, each of approximately two days' duration, so that in a week one may come to know the area well. The assumption is that one travels out from London to Northampton by rail and there rents a car and tours the areas to the west as far as Birmingham; or that one travels to Birmingham by car and uses it as a base for moving north through Stoke-on-Trent, Cheshire and Liverpool to Manchester; or that one comes by rail to Manchester, and drives to Sheffield and Leeds.

Midlands Tour One, Northampton to Birmingham Northampton is well served by frequent trains from Euston Station. Euston is the most modern of London's great terminals, and in many ways it is the least interesting despite its chrome, marble and glass. As an alternative, consider driving, for several American-related sites stand between London and Northampton. And if you have not seen **Sulgrave Manor,** described in tour number 1, you may do so from Northampton, as this ancestral home of George Washington is only 11 miles southwest on the A45 and the B4525.

Northampton, a city of 125,000, is the county town of Northamptonshire (Northants.). It is a lively place, the center of Britain's shoe industry (so it is no surprise that the Central Museum and Art Gallery, on Guildhall Road, features a display on the evolution of the shoe and contains a full cobbler's shop), and the metropolis of the River Nene. The major attraction is St Matthew's Church, in the northeast part of the city on the A43, for this Gothic revival structure contains a crucifixion painted by Graham Sutherland and a fine Madonna and Child by Henry Moore. The church is historically famous for the role it played in relation to the evangelical Oxford Movement, a High Church renaissance of the 19th century. The **Northampton Library** has busts of George Washington (because of the proximity of Sulgrave Manor) and Andrew Carnegie (who was a prime benefactor). Anne Dudley, from whom Oliver Wendell Holmes descended, was born in Northampton.

The best direct route from Northampton to Birmingham via Coventry is west on the A45. However, you may wish to take two excursions from Northampton first:

Option One Leave Northampton eastwards on the A45 towards Wellingborough. 4 miles from Northampton is the village of **Ecton** (the home for generations of the Franklin family) from which Benjamin Franklin's father emigrated in 1685. His uncle is buried in the parish churchyard, and a portion of the ancestral home has survived in the old forge barn. Beyond Ecton turn right on the B573 to Earls Barton and continue straight on country roads to **Castle Ashby.** Bret Harte wrote much of his best work while staying here as a guest of the Marquis of Northampton. The Castle (open Sun., Easter to Sept., also Thurs., Sat., June–Aug., 2–5.30) is in fact an Elizabethan mansion; it contains a fine collection of Italian paintings. The grounds are by Capability Brown, and the avenue beyond is quite handsome. Return to Earls Barton and follow the B573 east to join with the B571, bypassing Wellingborough. At Irthlingborough cross over the A6 and follow country roads via Great Addington and Woodford to the A510, then right to **Islip.** This village has ties with George Washington, and Mathias Nicholl, who prepared the first code of laws for New York, was born here. Just beyond, on the A510, is **Thrapston.** The parish church contains a memorial to the Washington family which shows the stars and stripes. A mile northeast off the A605 is Titchmarsh; in the church is a bust of the poet John Dryden, who spent his childhood in this village. Dryden was born in the rectory of All Saints in Aldwinkle, a mile northwest. Another mile to the left off the A605 is **Achurch,** the birthplace of Edmund Quincy, who emigrated to New England in 1633. The father of the founder of Maryland, Robert Browne, was rector here for forty years. At Oundle, beyond, is one of England's best known public schools. You may return to Northampton or go by country roads southeast to Great Gidding.

Option Two Leave Northampton to the southeast on the A428. At **Little Houghton,** 3 miles from the city, one finds the origins of the Randolph family of Virginia. William Randolph emigrated in 1674; in 1774 Peyton Randolph would become the President of the First Continental Congress. Just beyond, a country road right runs to **Horton,** where the first governor of Virginia, Sir Ralph Lane, was born. Carry on via the A428 to Yardley Hastings, then north by a country road to **Castle Ashby** (see description above). Return to the A428 and just beyond Yardley Hastings bear right into the B5388 to Olney, on the A509. Here is the Memorial Museum to William Cowper, the poet. His former home is a faithful literary re-creation. Rejoin the A428 via the B565 north of Olney. At Turvey turn left on country roads posted for Carlton, Harrold and **Odell.** Reverend Peter Bulkley was rector here from 1620 to 1635; he emigrated to Massachusetts and there founded Concord. Carry on to Sharnbrook and the A6, thence into Bedford.

Bedford is the county town of Bedfordshire, a pleasant city of 65,000 on the Ouse. The A6 brings you past the statue of John Bunyan, the most famous of Bedford's citizens. It was while in the old town gaol (jail) that Bunyan wrote the first part of *Pilgrim's Progress.* The Bunyan Meeting House and Museum, in Mill Street to the left from High Street as you enter from the north, is on the site of the barn where Bunyan preached (open Tues.–Fri., 10–12, 2–4.30). In the next street towards the river, in Castle Close, is the **Cecil Higgins Art Gallery** (open 11–6 daily, Sun. 2.30–5), which contains excellent porcelain, a bust of Ralph Vaughan Williams by the American-born sculptor Jacob Epstein, two Benjamin West and three James McNeill Whistler pictures, and some good work by Louis Comfort Tiffany. A mile south of Bedford, on the A6, at Elstow, is the Moot Hall associated with Bunyan; it is on the site of his conversion.

Leave Bedford on the A5140 southwest to **Kempston.** The parish church contains a memorial to Henry Stuart, an early ancestor of William Penn. Turn left on the A5134 to the A418, then south to **Ampthill.** There is a church memorial here to Robert Nicholls, the first Governor of New York; it was he who renamed the settlement on the Hudson in honor of the Duke of York (who became King James II). Follow the A418 to Woburn, here to see **Woburn Abbey,** the seat of the Duke of Bedford rebuilt on ruined abbey walls. The great house (open daily 12.30–5.30) contains twenty-four fine Canalettos and other paintings, and the handsome park (in which you may drive a 12-mile circuit) holds American bison, 2000 deer, and Chartley wild white cattle. Continue on the A418 to the A5.

Return now to Northampton via the A5. The road passes through Bletchley, original home of Britain's Open University (or university of the air). Very near here was the location of British Intelligence during World War II. Milton Keynes, one of Britain's New Towns, is to the right. Next is **Stony Stratford,** birthplace of Theophilus Eaton, one of the founders of New Haven, Connecticut. It is said that the phrase 'cock and bull story' arose from tales told at two famous inns here. (Just beyond town turn left on the A422, and take the second country road right to **Wicken.** Robert Washington lived here from 1610 to 1616.) The A5 continues to Towcester (pronounced *toaster*). The Saracen's Head Inn was one of Mr. Pickwick's stopping places, and the 13th century church contains chained books. Turn right on the A43 toward Northampton, then right on a country road to Stoke Bruerne. Here is a unique and fascinating museum, The Waterways, directly on the towpath of the old Grand Union Canal just before it plunges into a mile-long tunnel; you may learn more about canal life in an hour here than anywhere else in Britain. Just beyond are the colonnades built by Inigo Jones, known as the Stoke Park Pavilions (open Sat., Sun., afternoons, July and Aug.). One joins the A508, and Northampton is 7 miles to the north.

Shortly beyond Northampton on the A45, turn right on a country road to **Harpole.** Sir Ralph Lane, first Governor of Virginia, lived here. The A45 junctions with the M1; continue on to **Flore.** Adams Cottage is ancestrally linked with both John Adams and John Quincy Adams. Turn north on the A5, then right on a country road to Brockhall, a good Elizabethan mansion with a portrait collection (open Easter–Aug., Sun., 2–6). By country roads continue to **Little Brington.** In the street here is a stone house in which Lawrence Washington lived after selling Sulgrave Manor; he obtained it with the help of his cousin, the first Lord Spencer, who lived at Althorp house nearby. A mile north is **Great Brington,** where Lawrence Washington's younger brother, Robert, lived (the house is on the Whilton Road). The parish church contains Spencer tombs, as well as that of Lawrence Washington, great-great-great-grandfather of George and Robert. Facsimiles of the brasses on both tombs were given to Charles Sumner by Earl Spencer in 1860. The Washington pews are also marked, and there is an engraving of a Gilbert Stuart portrait in the vestry. Just beyond is **Althorp House,** family home of the Princess of Wales, with its many associations and a famous collection of paintings (open June–Sept., Tues., Thurs., Sun., 2.30–6), highlighted by Van Dyck, Reynolds, Gainsborough, Raphael, Rubens and Murillo. North of Great Brington by country roads is **East Haddon,** where Anne, widow of Robert Washington, lived. East Haddon is just off the A428, which you may follow northwest to Rugby.

This unattractive town is famous mainly for Rugby School, described in Thomas Hughes' *Tom Brown's School Days*; Hughes also founded a utopian community in Rugby, Tennessee. The school is the site of the first rugby game, that fascinatingly complex chess for the muscular which evolved, among other directions, into the American game of football. By appointment with the school porter you may see the tablet inside the grounds which tells how in 1823 one William Webb Ellis 'with a fine disregard for the rules of football as played in his time, first took the ball in his arms and ran with it. . . .' Then continue via the A428 to the B4029, then north to Brinklow. Sir Thomas Malory, author of *Morte d'Arthur*, lived here. The A427 west carries one to Coventry.

Before World War II there may have been a variety of reasons to go to Coventry. But after the German bombers' systematic levelling of 40 acres of buildings in the center of the city on the night of November 14, 1940, there has been one main reason: to see the city that is, along with Rotterdam, Dresden and Hiroshima, a living memorial to man's capacity for mass destruction. A new city has risen out of the ruins, and the new Coventry Cathedral is its symbol. The ruins of the old cathedral are a backdrop to the new, and a wooden cross, made from the charred timbers of the old, and now simply inscribed 'Father Forgive', is the only explicit reminder of the cause of the destruction. Sir Basil Spence designed the new cathedral, and if emotion did not intervene, one suspects that many would admit that it is not to everyone's liking, for it is highly modern in every respect, and even its pink sandstone exterior speaks to the future as though the past were not to be remembered. Recent research has shown that Churchill was forewarned of the German raid, for the British had broken the German codes, and he made the agonizing decision to let a defenseless Coventry burn rather than reveal to the enemy that its most precious secret was known. Germans by the thousands come in penance here, but Coventry is not for Germans alone.

You will enter **Coventry** on the A428 from the east. In medieval times this was the city of Lady Godiva, who rode naked through the streets; in modern times, it is the industrial city of the phrase 'sent to Coventry', by which a fellow worker is cut off from all conversation for an offense against union solidarity. Here is the only John F. Kennedy House (a residential center for the young) in Britain; it was opened by the chief burgomaster of Berlin, Willy Brandt, in 1965. John Davenport, a founder and first minister of New Haven, Connecticut, was born here; his ancestral home fell under the bombing. Here, too, in the 17th century, lived Peeping Tom, who came out to look upon Lady Godiva as others averted their gaze; since she made her ride in the 11th century, Tom is clearly a much later addition to the mythology. One will find him on the clock at Broadgate, in the city center: as Lady Godiva rides across the clock, his head pops up. Her statue also stands in Broadgate, into which you will have run directly from the A46 (into which the A428 emptied). There are car parks here.

The Cathedral, consecrated in 1962, is a block east. Begin with the ruins of the old and proceed into the new. Do not miss the Bethlehem Font and save time for John Piper's baptistry window and for Graham Sutherland's massive tapestry, the largest in the world. The furnishings consist of gifts from many countries, including the United States (a 'Christ Crucified'). Afterwards, go down the broad steps to Priory Street, and with the ruins to your back, turn right and then left to the **Herbert Art Gallery and Museum** (open 10–6, Sun. 2–5, until 8 Tues., Wed.). There is a fine Epstein bust of Rabindranath Tagore. Coventry is Treby Magna in George Eliot's *Felix Holt,* and it and Nuneaton (9 miles north on the A444) are closely associated with *Middlemarch.* The exact center of England is said to be 8 miles west of Coventry off the A45, at the medieval town cross in Meriden.

Kenilworth is 6 miles southwest of Coventry on the A46. Do not miss it, for here is Kenilworth Castle, a striking and romantic ruin. Built in the 11th century and remodelled by John of Gaunt in the 14th century, it was the seat of the Earls of Leicester. Not lived in since the Restoration, the castle was used as the setting for Sir Walter Scott's *Kenilworth.* A massive gatehouse and the banqueting hall have survived (open all year at least 9.30–4, Sun. 2–4).

Continue from Kenilworth south on the A452 to pass through Royal Leamington Spa, a handsome late Georgian health resort, and south on the A445 to Warwick. Here is the massive Warwick Castle, one of the most imposing inhabited medieval castles of Europe. The State Apartments (open Easter–Sept., 10–5.30, shorter hours other months, closed Nov.–Feb.) contain works by Rubens, Reynolds and Van Dyke, and the grounds were landscaped by Capability Brown. The armory is one of the best private collections in the country. Warwick is well worth walking about in, and the Joy Robinson Doll Museum, in Oken's House, is fun.

You may now continue 8 miles on to Stratford-upon-Avon, there to connect with tour number 1, or turn northwest on the A41 towards Birmingham. Bear left on the B4439 and then right to Packwood House. Here is one of the most famous gardens in Britain, with a symbolic sermon laid out in yew trees. The house itself (open April–Sept., daily except Mon., Fri., 2–7) is a 16th century timber-framed Tudor building owned by the National Trust. The B4439 junctions with the A4023 beyond the house, near Dorridge; turn left and carry on to the A448 beyond Redditch. Southwest of Tardebigge are the Tardebigge Locks, the most impressive flight in Britain, where thirty consecutive locks on the Worcester & Birmingham Canal raise the water level 217 feet in 2½ miles. You can get an especially good view of the flight by turning left just before Tardebigge center on a country road, and then right. This road brings you back onto the A448 just below Bromsgrove. From here south one is in A. E. Housman land, for he was born at Valley House (now called 'Housmans') in nearby Fockbury. At Bromsgrove one may turn south on the A38 to Worcester, or north on the A38 into the center of Birmingham. In Worcester there is a fine cathedral and the Dyson Perrins Museum of Worcester Porcelain. (Northwest of Bromsgrove 18 miles on the A448 and the A442 is Birdsgreen. 1 mile east on a country road is **Coton Hall** [open May–Sept., Sat. only, 2–5], the ancestral home of the Lee family of Virginia, including, of course, Robert E. Lee. Glass from the hall's ruined chapel has been used in **Alveley Church,** 1 mile west of Birdsgreen.)

The main road approaches through the suburbs of Bournville and Edgbaston. The first is a garden suburb laid out in 1879 by the Quaker chocolate manufacturer, George Cadbury, while the second is an upper middle class area in which Birmingham shows a pleasant face. Here is the truly red-brick University of Birmingham. It is well worth visiting, and immediately adjacent is **The Barber Institute of Fine Arts,** a fine smaller gallery with single examples of the best work of a number of artists, including della Robbia, Rodin, Degas, Botticelli, Tintoretto, Rubens, Gauguin and Toulouse-Lautrec. I would consider this to be the museum gem of the Midlands, and it should not be missed. There is a good James McNeill Whistler as well.

Birmingham is the second largest city in Britain. With a population of 1,200,000, and with suburbs like Wolverhampton (150,000) and Solihull (100,000), it comprises an extensive, time-consuming urban mass. One of the great industrial cities of the world, a center of the Industrial Revolution – during the American Civil War it sent 800,000 guns to the United States – Birmingham was once ugly, shoddy and squalid. Elihu Burritt, the 'learned blacksmith' and early American socialist, also saw it 'as a place American as Chicago'. Building upon the misfortune of heavy bombing during the war, the city has become a dynamic, even bright, place, and if one concentrates upon the area around the Bull Ring, the impression will be very much of a city of the late 20th century. Birmingham is reached from Euston Station by thirty trains every weekday, and an express covers the distance in less than 90 minutes. You can, therefore, take the tour described above backwards by coming into Birmingham first, or use it as the starting point for the next tour.

But see Birmingham first. The A38 comes into the center of the city quite near the gleaming New Street Station; leave your car in the car park near here. The one-way streets are complex and you are well advised to walk. The Bull Ring (posted from the station by pedestrian walkways) is southeast of New Street; St Martin's Church here has many fine monuments. North of the station Temple Street leads to the Cathedral of St Philip, a Palladian building with stained glass windows by Sir Edward Burne-Jones, who was born nearby. Just beyond is Snow Hill; St Chad's Roman Cathedral is behind the bus station: it was the work of Augustus W. Pugin and was the first Catholic cathedral built in Britain since the Reformation. Walk along Edmund Street past the handsome public buildings of the city. On the left is the **Corporation Art Gallery and Museum** (open 10–6, Sun. 2–5.30), one of the most important collections outside London. It offers extensive insights into the work of Burne-Jones and David Cox, into the pre-Raphaelites in general, and into the oeuvre of such artists as Gainsborough, Reynolds, Rubens, Rembrandt, Hogarth, Botticelli, Turner, Constable, Degas and Courbet. There are eight John Singer Sargents, a good Benjamin West, a Mary Cassatt and a Copley.

The street empties into the former **Easy Row.** Here stood the house where Washington Irving wrote 'Rip van Winkle' in 1818. Four roads on, to the right side of Broad Street, is the Church of the Messiah, Unitarian, with a monument to Dr **Joseph Priestley,** the discoverer of oxygen, who lived in Pennsylvania for a time. His house near here was destroyed by rioters in 1791. A mile further, past Five Ways and into Hagley Road, is the Oratory of St Philip Neri, established by Cardinal Newman in 1847, the English home of the Congregation of the Oratory, and a site second only to Brompton Oratory in London in modern English Catholic significance. (Newman is buried next to the house of the Oratory Fathers at Rednal Hill, on the Bristol Road, which opens up to the south of New Street Station.)

To the north of the central part of the city is Aston (follow the A34 from the Bull Ring). Here is the new University of Aston, representative of the upgraded technological institutes, and **Aston Hall.** A fine Jacobean house, the hall contains a good picture collection and superb period furniture. It was the original Bracebridge Hall of Washington Irving's tale of that name (open 10–5, Sun. 2–5). There is also a children's museum, and opposite, a very nice old church. Just to the west is Handsworth. Here is the Avery Historical Museum, housed in the old Soho Foundry where James Watt and Matthew Boulton worked on the steam engine (both are buried in St Mary's Church). The museum is unique in being devoted solely to the history of weighing.

Beyond Aston Hall continue on the A34 to the M6, follow it briefly to the A454, and enter Wolverhampton. Button Gwinnett, a signer of the Declaration of Independence for Georgia, lived here from 1755–65; he was married in **St Peter's Collegiate Church,** on Queen Square. Wolverhampton is a substantial city in its own right and does not care to be thought of as a suburb of Birmingham, 12 miles away. It is the 'capital' of the Black Country, which runs north from here, and is noted for ironworks. The Art Gallery and Museum (open 10–6 weekdays), next to the church, contains an excellent collection of Bilston enamels.

5 miles to the southeast of Birmingham, on the A45 to Coventry, is the suburb of **Sheldon,** where in the church is a memorial to Thomas Bray. Bray founded a mission to Maryland in 1699, and the following year he organized the Society for the Propagation of the Gospel in Foreign Parts, the first of the major missionary societies, with particular interest in North America. Later a second society, Dr Bray's Associates, was set up to provide Christian education to indigent black North Americans and West Indians.

WHERE TO EAT This is not good eating country, although you may be able to have some truffles around Northampton, and Coventry is known for its godcakes and treacle tarts. From my experience you are on your own in this land, with two exceptions. There is a good Spanish (!) restaurant in Rugby, the Andalucia at 10 Henry Road, which serves both lunch and dinner. Jonathan's at 16 Wolverhampton Street, which is also open for both meals, is also good. As to hotels, spend the night in the new and rather featureless, if comfortable, De Montfort in Kenilworth, or the very central and new Albany Hotel in Birmingham, on the Ringway.

WHAT TO READ Make up for the lack of good food with the plethora of good reading for the area. Thomas Hughes for Rugby (*Tom Brown's School Days*), Sir Walter Scott's *Kenilworth*, Jane Austen's *Middlemarch*, John Bunyan's *Pilgrim's Progress*, A. E. Housman, Washington Irving and Dickens are called for in this area. Do not neglect Francis Brett Young's novels of the land west of Birmingham, and sample the detective fiction of Maurice Proctor, several of whose thrillers are based in the city of the Big Brum (the clock tower in the city center), as well as in Manchester and London. Elihu Burritt, American Consul in Birmingham under Abraham Lincoln, wrote a fascinating and shrewd book in 1868, *Walks in the Black Country*.

Midlands Tour Two, Birmingham to Manchester via Liverpool (See Midlands Tour One, above, for information on trains to Birmingham, and for a description of that city and its environs.) This tour may be taken independently of other tours, of course, or can form part of a week devoted to the Midlands, in combination with Midlands Tours One and Three.

If pressed for time take the M6 from Birmingham to Stoke-on-Trent, less than an hour's drive away. If you have allowed yourself a full two days for this tour, I strongly recommend the following option:

• Leave Birmingham on the A38 to **Lichfield,** a cathedral city noted for its associations with Samuel Johnson and with Major John André, the soldier put to death on George Washington's orders during the American Revolution. There are paintings of André, early editions (1781) of Anna Seward's *Monody* on his death, and in the Johnson Birthplace Museum on Breadmarket Street, several other relics relating to him. During World War II the **Whittington Barracks** (follow the A51 southeast from Lichfield and turn left on a country road) were the headquarters of the Tenth Replacement Depot of the American Army, and the west window of the garrison church was presented by them; an American flag always flies by the window. The church also contains a portion of the Regimental Colour carried by the Sixty-fourth Foot during the American Revolution, and the Staffordshire Regimental Museum contains a few relics relating to the war, and especially to Bunker Hill and Yorktown.

From Lichfield, run northwest on the A51 through Rugeley to **Colwich;** in the parish church here is buried Admiral Lord George Anson, of Carolina fame. Retreat a half mile to the A513 and go west, to **Shugborough Park,** a fine white colonnaded mansion, the seat of the Earls of Lichfield. The grounds are especially attractive (open March–Oct., daily except Mon., 11–5.30, Sun. open 2). George Anson lived at Shugborough for a time and there are several relics relating to his nine years in Charleston. As three sons of the second Earl of Lichfield emigrated to Texas, there are also Lone Star mementoes. Continue to Stafford, birthplace of Isaac Walton (at 92 Eastgate Street); his bust is in St Mary's Church. To the right on the A518 14 miles is **Uttoxeter,** where there is a lively cattle market every Wednesday, and to which Nathaniel Hawthorne made a pilgrimage (described in his *English Notebooks*) to see the spot in the market place where Dr Johnson stood in the rain for several hours as a penance. To the northwest of Stafford on the A5013, and right on country roads to Norton Bridge, is Shallowford. Given by Isaak Walton to Stafford, his fishing cottage here is a memorial to him and to the patient fishermen for whom the *Compleat Angler* became a Bible. At Stafford, one joins the M6 for a fast 11 miles north to Stoke-on-Trent.

Stoke-on-Trent, an industrial city of 265,000, is in the center of the Staffordshire potteries. Arnold Bennett made these towns famous in a series of novels, including *The Old Wives' Tale, Clayhanger* and *The Card*, set in the Potteries; he was born in Hanley, the largest of the 'Five Towns' (there are actually six), and his home at 205 Waterloo Road, in the Cobridge section on the edge of Burslem, is open Mon., Wed., Thurs., Sat., 2–5. The other pottery towns are Burslem, Fenton, Longton and Tunstall, and all radiate out from the center of Stoke, which was Bennett's 'Knype'. If you are interested in pottery, there are several major attractions here. Enter Stoke off the M6 on the A5006. The Minton Pottery

Works is on your right on London Road, and the road runs directly into the Spode Works. The Spode pottery provides an excellent tour, which you must have booked in advance, illustrating how high quality work is made, and one may see an old oven as well. Adjacent is a good shop in which one may buy Spode seconds at very reduced prices, and just beyond is the Spode–Copeland Museum, which you may visit by previous appointment.

At Barlaston, 4 miles south off the A34, is the Wedgwood Museum, showing the many experimental efforts of Josiah Wedgwood. The museum here is very good, and it is open by appointment for guided visits four times daily Monday to Friday. South of Stoke off the A50 is **Caverswall,** where Matthew Cradock, a founder of Massachusetts, lived. Do not miss the Hanley Museum and Art Gallery (open 10–6, Sun. 2.30–5), north off the A5009, for here is the world's largest collection of Staffordshire figures. And west on the A525 beyond Newcastle-under-Lyme is Keele, where one may see the handsome new university, the only one in England offering a four-year B.A. degree, as in the United States (B.A. degree courses run for three years at other English universities, and for four years only in Scotland). The **David Bruce Centre of American Studies** at the University of Keele is the largest such program in Britain, especially at the M.A. level. Leave Stoke-on-Trent on the A52 northwest. Chester is 35 miles. At Nantwich take the A51 northwest into Chester.

If pottery is of little interest, there is an attractive country route from Birmingham to Liverpool. It carries one through Shropshire, the land of A. E. Housman's poetry, and it includes Shrewsbury and Coton Hall. It unites with the route described above at Chester.

Leave Birmingham on the M6, to exit no. 12; turn west on the A5. The road passes Weston Park, a fine post-Restoration estate owned by the Earls of Bradford. The gardens and parklands were designed by Capability Brown, and there is an excellent picture collection, including Holbein, Reynolds and Van Dyck (open April–Sept., daily except Mon., Fri., 12–7.30, Sun. open 11). At the A41 turn south to the lovely village of Tong; it, and Shifnel, reached by country roads to the west from Tong, are described in Dickens' *Old Curiosity Shop*. At Shifnel take the A4169 to Ironbridge. This is often called the birthplace of the Industrial Revolution, for an extensive coal, iron and pottery industry was built up in the region, and the old iron bridge across the Severn here was the world's first. It still stands and is part of the very fine Ironbridge Gorge Museum, actually seven museums which, in Coalbrookdale, just north, include the first furnace to use coke for smelting (open April–Oct., 10–6). To the southeast 2 miles is Coalport, famous for the china of that name.

Follow the B4380 to Buildwas Abbey, in ruins, and the B4378 to Much Wenlock, where the remains of the Wenlock Abbey may be visited. Turn north on the A458, then left on the B4371 to Presthope, and there right on country roads via Hughley, Church Preen and Ruckley to **Acton**

Burnell. The parish church here contains some of the finest 14th century brasses in England, including monuments to the ancestors of Robert E. Lee. Here one may continue north to Shrewsbury on country roads.

• Alternatively, if a very attractive hill country drive through Wenlock Edge, over the Long Mynds, and via the rocky Stiperstones ridge to 1700 feet is alluring, take the following route (allow two hours, for the roads are narrow and often only lanes): Turn south from Acton Burnell on country roads and follow the signs for Ruckley, Plaish, Longville-on-the-Dale, Wall-under-Heywood, Ticklerton, Harton, Westhope and Craven Arms, to emerge on the A49. A long mile north, turn west on the A489 to Bishop's Castle. Return to Eaton on the A489 and turn north on country roads marked for Wentner, Stiperstones and Pennerley, to Plaxgreen on the A488, and thence into Shrewsbury.

Shrewsbury, an attractive city of 55,000, sets astride the Severn, England's second longest river, which winds its way south to Bristol. Pronounced 'Shrowsbury' by the people of Shropshire (known as Salopians), the town is famous for its school, its cakes, Charles Darwin and its setting. There are many black-and-white timber and plaster buildings, and the 12th century St Mary's Church is very much worth seeing. Darwin's statue stands outside the public library. A Roman Catholic Cathedral here, by Augustin Pugin and begun in 1856, is not yet completed. The Shrewsbury School is across the river; among its pupils were Sir Philip Sidney and Samuel Butler. In the Sir John Moore Barracks on the Copthorne Road, the B4386, is the **Shropshire and Herefordshire Regimental Museum,** with two captured American flags, and the King's and Regimental Colours carried by the Fifty-third Shropshire Regiment in the American Revolution.

Leave Shrewsbury on the A49, north. 3 miles out is Battlefield, site of the battle in 1403 in which Henry IV defeated the Earls of Northumberland and Worcester and Northumberland's son, Hotspur – whom Falstaff claimed to have slain. The church here was erected as a memorial in 1408. Return a few hundred yards to the A528 and go west and north to **Hammerhill.** Just before reaching it you will pass Lea Hall, on the site of the earliest home of the Lee family (not open to the public). Here take the B5476 north. A country road right goes to Clive; William Wycherley, the first Restoration writer of comedy, was born in the hall here. Further on the B5476 is Wem, which was the home of William Hazlitt. (About 4 miles north beyond Edgbaston is **Coton Hall,** the ancestral home of Robert E. Lee.) The B5476 ends at Whitchurch. From here take the A41 20 miles to Chester.

Chester, a city of 60,000, has – together with York and Berwick-upon-Tweed – retained its medieval city walls, and one can gain an excellent impression by walking the 2-mile circumference. Famous for its mystery plays from the 13th to the 17th centuries, Chester was a Roman camp before then. Shopping in The Rows is fun, for the timbered shops are on two levels. The Grosvenor Park Museum contains a unique collection of locally minted Saxon and Norman coins (open 10–5, Sun. 2.30–5.30). But the main attraction is the Cathedral, especially its interiors. The nave is beautiful and quite simple. Especially important are the only old consistory court in England, the organ loft and case by Gilbert Scott, exceptional choir stalls with perhaps the best misericord carvings in the country, and fine cloisters. In the **South Transept** are the flags of the Cheshire Regiment; two of them flew at Bunker Hill in 1775, and one was used to wrap Wolfe's body after his victory and death at the Plains of Abraham. There is also a memorial to an exiled Loyalist from the Revolution who died in Chester. And if 19th century English history interests you, drive 6 miles west on the A55 to Hawarden (pronounced 'Harden') to see the castle in which William E. Gladstone lived for 60 years. The house is not open but the old castle ruins may be visited (open Easter–Oct., Fri., Sat., Sun., 2–6). Here you may connect with the tour of Wales.

Carry on now to Liverpool. Leave Chester north to pick up the A41, which runs into the M53. (Alternatively continue on the A41 via Port Sunlight, where the Lady Lever Art Gallery, open 10–5, Sun. open at 2, contains a surprising collection of the work of Turner, Gainsborough, Reynolds, Raeburn and Millais.) **Birkenhead,** a city of 142,000 on the River Mersey, is known for the works in which the C.S.S. *Alabama* was launched in 1862, and where the Laird Rams were constructed, those ships which nearly led to an outbreak of war between the government of Abraham Lincoln and that of Britain. John Laird's statue is in Hamilton Square. Ultimately the British government paid the United States over three million pounds in damages for the depredations of the *Alabama*. For a model of the *Alabama* (as well as good paintings) visit the Williamson Art Gallery and Museum on Slatey Road (open 10–5, Sun. 2). Nathaniel Hawthorne lived here for a time when he was American Consul at Liverpool. Either the M53 or the A41 carries one by tunnel under the Mersey and into the center of Liverpool. The great Mersey Tunnel is the largest underwater highway in the world.

Liverpool is a bleak, often dirty city of 750,000 people. Its early fortune was built on the slave trade. Thousands of emigrants sailed from Liverpool to the United States, and more recently the Merseyside beat of the Beatles came from there to revolutionize popular music. Distances are considerable, and it is not a good walking city, so keep your car. If you enter via the A41, the tunnel will bring you directly to the city center; if via the M53 bear right on the first major road. In either case, drive first to the docks, a bustling center of activity, where from George's Pierhead you may get an impression of both the city and the Mersey. From the docks proceed directly up Water Street past the Cunard Building, the

Town Hall, and other trading and municipal structures, to the Kingsway. Brunswick Street parallels Water to the right; the American Consulate was here during the time Hawthorne was in office. Just ahead in William Brown Street is the city museum and library. The **Liverpool Museum** (open 10–5, Sun. 2) contains numerous interesting exhibits relating to the ancient history of the area, a fine shipping gallery, and a unique collection of animal and insect stowaways, especially fascinating creepy crawlies. (At one time the collection included the tunic of Osceola, the Seminole chief, but this was destroyed in the bombing of 1941.) Colonel Boniface Tarleton, of Carolina fame, came from Liverpool, and there are related relics, as well as numerous items produced specifically for the American trade. In the regimental museum there are several objects collected by Colonel A. S. DePeyster in the Great Lakes area in 1775–85, including Indian materials.

Just beyond is the **Walker Art Gallery** (open 10–5, Sun. 2, in April–Sept. Thurs. until 9), which has an exceptionally strong provincial collection including work by Rembrandt, Rubens, Murillo, Monet, Cezanne, Seurat, Renoir, Epstein and six American artists, among them Benjamin West. The work of the British School, in galleries 6 through 9, is quite strong. Just across the way is the famous Lime Street railway station and beyond William Brown Street is London Road. In Monument Square on the road is one of the few statues of **King George III,** against whom the colonies revolted. This is the work of Sir Richard Westmacott. Drive past the front of the station and straight on to Renshaw Street, bearing right into Berry Street, which runs into **Duke Street.** Hawthorne lived at 153 Duke Street in 1853 when he was the American Consul. Turn left into Upper Duke Street. The Anglican Cathedral is directly ahead, while to the left is **Rodney Street.** Here at no. 9 lived Arthur Hugh Clough, English poet who resided for a time in South Carolina and lectured at Harvard. It was his line that Winston Churchill quoted in his broadcast to America upon the fall of France in 1940 – 'westward, look, the land is bright'.

The principal attraction of Liverpool is its two great cathedrals, one Anglican and the other Roman Catholic. The Church of England Cathedral on St James' Road is the largest in Britain; work went on continuously from 1904 to 1981 and Gilbert Scott, the architect, won a competition while in his twenties and launched his career with this work. What impresses most is the sheer size – be certain to go up into the Under-Tower, where one may look down a distance equal to the greatest of any cathedral in Europe. Larger than St Paul's, rivaled only by St Peter's, Milan and Seville, the cathedral can seat over 4000. Examine, in particular, the stone carvings, the fine Bishops' Window in the nave, the ornate reredos and the exceptional Lady Chapel. In the tower hangs the heaviest and highest ringing peal of bells in the world. Save time for St James's Cemetery, immediately outside, and the mausoleum of William Huskisson, a statesman who had the distinction of being the first person in the world to be killed by a moving railway train.

Now compare Scott's vision (which has been much altered) with the most striking Roman Catholic Cathedral in Britain – and after Coventry Cathedral, perhaps the most dramatic example of modern ecclesiastical architecture in the country – by pursuing Hope Street, which runs along the far side of the cemetery, north to where the Cathedral of Christ the King rises dramatically above the road. Consecrated in 1967, this stunning structure is equally impressive inside and out. The serene baptistry, the enormous lantern tower with its colored glass, and the older Lutyens Crypt are all fascinating. For myself, I prefer Sir Frederick Gibberd's circular creation in concrete in Liverpool to that of Sir Basil Spence in Coventry.

Liverpool has absorbed all of its former suburbs save for Bootle, and the more attractive ones are to the south. Beyond the cathedral turn right into Bronlow Hill and right into Crown Street; follow this into the A562 at Upper Parliament Street and turn right to the A561 and left into Park Road. Watch for signs for **Toxteth** and the Unitarian 'Ancient Church' on Park Road. Richard Mather, father of Increase Mather, was minister of this church when it was a nonconformist chapel; there is a relief on the church door of the ship in which he sailed for America. Further on is Mossley Hill, where the Sudley Art Gallery (open 10–5, Sun. 2) has a collection of British paintings, including good works by Turner and Gainsborough. Continue on to the A561 signposted for Liverpool Airport. Just beyond the airport is **Speke Hall** (see section on the Country Houses of Britain), possibly the finest timbered manor house in England, built in 1598 (open weekdays 10–5, Sun. 2).

The best short route from Liverpool to Manchester is on the A580, 34 miles. Pause at Knowsley, just after going past the M57, to see Knowsley Hall (open Tues.–Thurs., summers), where Edward Lear was asked by the Earl of Derby to make drawings of the rare animals in his menagerie, inspiring Lear to compose his nonsense verse for the Earl's children. Beyond and just to the south of the highway is St Helens, an industrial city of 100,000, where by prior appointment one may visit the **Pilkington Glass Museum** on Prescot Road (it is also open Sat. without appointment, 2–4.30). The museum has some American work as well. St Helens was one of the world's major glass-making centers. At the junction with the A49, beyond St Helens, you may wish to divert north 6 miles to Wigan, center of the cannel coal industry, with a population of 80,000. Wigan appears in Sir Walter Scott's *Betrothed*, and is invoked in George Orwell's *The Road to Wigan Pier* (being on the Leeds & Liverpool Canal). Or turn south at the same junction on the M6, then east on the M62, for the fastest route into Manchester. Alternatively continue on the A580, past **Lowton** (left on the B5207), birthplace of the Reverend Richard Mather, father of Increase, minister of Toxteth Park, and co-

compiler of the *Bay Psalm Book*. Both M62 and B580 meet well into Manchester at the A6.

• You may prefer to approach Manchester from the south, by a slower but substantially more attractive route. If so, continue on the A561 from Speke Hall, Liverpool, into the A562 and Widnes, across the Mersey into the A533, and turn left on the A56, ignoring the motorway here. Just north at Daresbury is the site of the birthplace of Lewis Carroll; a window in the parish church shows the Cheshire Cat and the Mad Hatter. (Warrington, straight ahead, is an old industrial city known for its soap works. A plaque marks the spot where Dr. **Joseph Priestley** lived from 1761 to 1767. Warrington Academy, founded in 1757, and now a school, had Priestley as one of its teachers and Richard Malthus as a pupil. The home of the first total abstinence society, and the birthplace of both independent and primitive Methodism, Warrington was a center of dissent in the late 18th and early 19th centuries.)

• From Daresbury turn right on the B5356 and soon right into the A559 to **Northwich,** where William Hilton, a Pilgrim, was born. This is in the center of the salt mines. Turn south on the A533, then left into the A556, to Knutsford. This was the *Cranford* of Mrs. Gaskell's novel, and she is buried in the Unitarian cemetery near the railroad station. Just to the north of Knutsford is **Tatton Park** (open Easter–Oct., daily except Mon., 2–5.30), seat of Lord Egerton. There are fine gardens and walks, and the collection of furniture is very good; among the paintings are two Canalettos and twelve Frederic Remington lithographs of the American West. Turn south on the A50, then left on country roads to **Peover Hall.** The 16th century hall was the headquarters for the American Third Army under General George Patton during invasion preparations in 1944. 2 miles west on country roads is Lower Peover, where there is a most unusual timbered church.

• From Peover Hall follow country roads to Chelford on the A537, then right and right again on the A34 to **Capesthorne.** The house here contains paintings and pottery and an Americana collection (open Easter–Sept., Sun., and from mid-May also Wed., Sat., 2–4 or later). Beyond on the A537 is Macclesfield, famous for its silk. Southwest 4 miles on the A536 is Gawsworth Hall, a 16th century half-timbered manor house associated with Mary Fitton, thought by some to be the 'dark lady' of Shakespeare's sonnets (open late March–Oct., daily 2–6). 2 miles further, and to the west, is the ravine of Lud's Church, associated with *Sir Gawaine and the Green Knight*. Turning north at Macclesfield follow the A523 past Adlington Hall, another fine half-timbered manor house (open Easter–Sept., Sun., also Sat. in July–Aug., 2.30–6), to the B5092 at Poynton. Turn left here to the A5102 and north to Bramhall. Bramall Hall (open daily except Thurs. 11–4) is the other major contender for the finest black-and-white half-timbered house in England; there is a handsome park and a good collection. The A5102 leads into Stockport, an industrial city of 150,000. The **War Memorial Art Gallery** is worth a pause (open 1–7, Sun. 2–5), especially to see Jacob Epstein's bust of Yehudi Menuhin. From here follow the A6 7 miles to Manchester, which is described in Midlands Tour Three, below.

WHERE TO EAT   This is not land noted for gourmet restaurants, for by and large the Midlands people like their steak and chips. In Stoke-on-Trent try the North Stafford Hotel, opposite the railroad station (this is also a good place to stay overnight); in Shrewsbury the Penny Farthing, at 23 Abbey Foregate, provides excellent meals at lunch and dinner if you can be early, and the Prince Rupert Hotel, in the center of town, is also good for meals or a bed. In Chester, the **Grosvenor Hotel** on Foregate Street is dependable and welcomes you by flying the American flag. Liverpool has a fair number of good restaurants and hotels, although the Oriel is the only one I can attest to personally. Churche's Mansion in Nantwich is interesting. The Bells of Peover, in Lower Peover, is a 13th century pub which provides well for the visitor.

WHAT TO READ   This is Arnold Bennett country par excellence. It is pleasant to read Mary Webb's *Precious Bane* while in Shrewsbury, and George Orwell at Wigan. If you care for detective fiction, there is a fine story set in the potteries, *The Spoilt Kill* (a pun on kiln, which is pronounced 'kill,' of course) by Mary Kelly.

Midlands Tour Three, Manchester to Leeds via Sheffield (This tour requires three days for comfort. See Midlands Tour Two, above, for information on routes to Manchester. If coming directly by train from London, you may leave from Euston Station. The trip takes about two and a half hours. Manchester is not a difficult city to drive in, so pick up your rental car immediately at the station. If driving from Liverpool, you will enter Manchester center on the A6.)

Manchester is Britain's fifth largest city, with a population of 600,000. However, if Salford is included – actually an integral part of Manchester although still administered as a separate city of 160,000 – Manchester is then what it always claimed to be, the fourth city of Britain. It has been the center of the Lancashire cotton manufacturing district for over a century and was one focus of the Southern Confederacy's hope that King Cotton might win the American Civil War for the South. It is also one of the world's most densely inhabited areas, exceeded only by certain cities in Asia. Having been heavily bombed in World War II, the city now shows extensive redevelopment, and it is more dependent today on heavy engineering than on cotton goods. Manchester was the home for a time of Anna Lee, who came to America in 1774 and founded the Society of Shakers, a breakaway group from the Society of Friends.

The route enters through Salford, where there is a new technological university and an art gallery (in Peel Park; it includes an **Epstein head**); Frances Hodgson Burnett's home was at 19 Islington Square (the house is gone). *The Secret Garden,* of which she wrote her memorable children's book, may have been next door to her house, though there is another contender for the honor in Kent. She also wrote *Little Lord Fauntleroy.* A Roman Catholic Cathedral, dating from 1848, stands in Chapel Street, into which the A6 runs.

Chapel Street ends at Chetham's Hospital, in Manchester. Originally built in 1422, the Hospital is a grammar school; it contains the oldest free library in England. Just to the south is the Anglican Cathedral, a parish church raised to its present status in 1847. While the exterior is of little interest, the stalls inside are regarded as the finest in Europe, and the Lady Chapel and Chapter House are very good. Between Chetham Hospital and the Cathedral is Fennel Street. Drive to its end, turn left, and the third street on the right is Hanover. Here is **Holyoake House,** Library for the Co-operative Union, proprietors of the Rochdale Co-operative Museum (see below). The library here contains a unique collection of original documents and correspondence relating to Robert Owen, the 19th century Utopian socialist and philanthropist responsible for co-operative communities in the United States. Victoria Street, in front of the Cathedral, runs south into Deansgate. To the left is the Royal Exchange, famed for its Tuesday and Friday cotton-market days. (South of it one block is St Ann's Church; Carracci's 'Descent from the Cross' hangs inside and the writer Thomas De Quincey was baptized here.) On the right of Deansgate is the John Rylands Library (open Mon.–Fri., 10–6, Sat. 10–2), one of the most famous in Europe, containing 700,000 volumes, including thousands of very old books. On display is the earliest securely dated piece of European printing to have survived and the earliest known fragment of New Testament writing.

Beyond the Library turn left into Brasenose Street. Across Albert Square directly ahead is the Victorian Town Hall, possibly the most handsome in England. Left again, then right, brings one to Mosley Street and the **City Art Gallery** (open 10–6, Sun. 2.30–5). It includes work by Hogarth, Reynolds, Gainsborough, Constable, Blake, Gauguin, Pisarro, Rodin, and Epstein's 'Joseph Conrad', as well as fine porcelain, and a superb collection of pre-Raphaelites. The art gallery is richer in American-related items than any other outside London, for it includes John Singer Sargents, James McNeill Whistlers, a good Robert Motherwell and other contemporary American items, as well as seven lithographs and etchings by Joseph Pennell. There is an unusual watercolor by John Piper of American locomotives in Wales, and a fine portrait of John Lathrop Motley, who was the American historian of the Dutch Republic and an Ambassador to Britain. To the south on Mosley Street is the central railway station; on Peter Street, to the right, is the Free Trade Hall.

Running along the side of the art gallery is Princess Street. Follow this to Whitworth Street, turn right to Oxford Road, and then left to the Victoria University of Manchester. Founded in 1880, and one of the largest universities in England, Manchester is especially known for the work of its scientists – Rutherford, who disintegrated the atom; Chadwick, who discovered the neutron; and Cockcroft, who worked on the machine for splitting the atom. Here is the **Whitworth Art Gallery** (open weekdays 10–5), one of the most pleasant in Britain. The modern work, which includes Americana, and the textiles are especially interesting, and the collection of English watercolors is outstanding.

Continue out Oxford Road into Wilmslow Road, to **Platt Fields Park.** Here is a statue of Abraham Lincoln to commemorate the sympathy said to have been shown by English cotton workers for the Union cause during the American Civil War. Here, too, is Platt Hall, a good museum of English costumes (open daily 10–dusk, Sun. from 2). Wilmslow Road continues to Disbury. Here is the Fletcher Moss Museum, with a pleasant garden and a good collection of English watercolors and work by Turner and Cox (open 10–6).

One should not leave Manchester without seeing the docks and paying homage to soccer. For the docks, continue to the bottom of Deansgate (see above) and into Chester Road (the A56), then back into Salford. Trafford Road, right, leads to the dock area, 700 acres on the Manchester Ship Canal, a 36-mile waterway completed in 1895. Chester Road runs on to Old Trafford, home of the Manchester United, together with Arsenal (London) perhaps the most famous professional soccer teams in England. And to the west of Manchester on the A57 (which one picks up with a left turn just below the Cathedral) 7 miles is **Denton,** birthplace of Ralph Smith, Pilgrim. 2 miles further is **Hyde,** home of the Hyde family. Edward Hyde was Governor of North Carolina in the 17th century, and George Hyde was Governor of New York in the 18th.

• To the north of Manchester are a number of substantial industrial cities, running 11 miles up the A666 (off the A6) to Bolton, a city of 165,000. This is now the principal cotton-spinning center. It was here that Richard Arkwright invented the water frame and Samuel Crompton made his spinning mule. These machines, together with Hargraves' spinning jenny, were the three breakthrough inventions of the spinning industry, itself the first industry to be transformed by the Industrial Revolution, and the originals of all three may be examined in the Bolton Textile Machinery Museum in Tonge Moore Road, the A676 (open 9.30–7.30, closed Wed. 1.30, Sat. 5.30, Sun.). Crompton's home is another mile; called Hall-i'-th'-Wood, it is a folk museum (open 10–dusk, Sun. 2–6, closed Thurs.). In Bolton itself, the **City Museum and Art Gallery** at the Civic Centre (open weekdays, 10–5.30) holds a Benjamin West and two very good paintings by Thomas Moran – he was born in Bolton and died in Santa

Barbara, California, and most of his work consists of romantic American landscapes – given to the gallery by Lord Leverhulme. Thomas Cole, who painted the most romantic portrait of the 'Last of the Mohicans', was born nearby; he died at Catskill, New York, in 1848.

The A58 leads east 6 miles to Bury. The surprising **Bury Art Gallery and Museum** (open weekdays 10.30–5) on Manchester Road (the A56) contains the Wrigley Collection, and works by Anna Lee Merritt, Benjamin West and James McNeill Whistler. 6 miles further on the A58 is Rochdale, site of the founding of the world's first cooperative, home of the Rochdale Pioneers, and both birth and burial place of John Bright (who is buried in the Friends graveyard). There is a small museum to the cooperative movement in Toad Lane. One may then drive south on the A627 6 miles to Oldham, a city of 120,000, where the **City Art Gallery & Museum** on Union Street holds a good Paul Jenkins. Complete the circuit back to Manchester, 7 miles, on the A62. Or you may continue north of Bolton via a moorland road, the A675, or by the faster A673 and M61, to Preston, there to join with the Lake District tour.

The most direct route between Manchester and Sheffield is via the A57, the A628 and the A616, 39 miles up Longdendale and through the northern edge of the Peak District National Park. It is a heavily travelled road and not the most attractive route. I strongly recommend the alternative tour outlined here, although the total distance is over 100 miles. It includes the heart of the national park, at least two of the great country houses of England, and Peveril Castle.

Leave Manchester on the A57 via Denton and Hyde (see above) to Glossop, a cotton mill town. The A57 continues through the loneliest part of the Peak District National Park, making contact with the Pennine Way (by which you may hike to the top of Kinder Scout, 2088 feet, the highest point in the area, and on to Edale, where the car may be brought to meet you) and across Snake Pass to Sheffield, some 38 miles. At the A6013, turn right to the A625 and right again to Castleton, a lovely village in the center of the national park. (A left turn on the A625 produces Hathersage, where Robin Hood's 'Little John' is buried.) Above, a short but strenuous climb, is Peveril Castle, founded in 1068 and now in ruins. Sir Walter Scott's *Peveril of the Peak* describes it, although little of the book is set here. Perhaps the most impressive cave in Britain is here too: Peak Cavern (open daily 10–9). It does not compare well with the major caverns in the United States but its mouth is nonetheless striking. A mile west is the Speedwell Mine (open 10–7, April–Oct.), which is fun for children, since one descends some distance and then rides by boat through a gallery half a mile long – originally driven in search of lead – to one of the largest subterranean potholes in Britain. Just past the entrance to the mine the road rises steeply, with fine views down the gorge. Here is the Blue John Mine (open daily 10–6), from which comes the amethystine spar, or bleu-jaune, from which the rare Blue John vases are made. One may buy small objects here (to see the best collection of the ware, visit Lauriston Castle in Edinburgh). Each cave requires about 45 minutes to visit; if your time is limited and your interests general, choose the Speedwell Mine.

The A625 continues to Chapel-en-le-Frith. Turn left and follow the A6 to Buxton, a resort town. The highest town of any size in England, Buxton is an attractive stop. The Crescent, opposite the hot springs, is handsomely Georgian, and for those who enjoy the *Guinness Book of World Records*, see the dome of the Devonshire Royal Hospital, the widest in the world. Follow the A6 through the Peaks to Bakewell – home of the tart of that name. (The Lathkill Cottage Tea Room in Over Haddon, south of Bakewell, serves the best afternoon tea in the Midlands and features the tarts.) There is a fine church in Bakewell with an outstanding chapel. Haddon Hall is just beyond Bakewell (open Tues.–Sat., April–Sept., 11–6). One of the best examples of a medieval manorial home in England, the hall has a fine terraced garden and good furniture.

Turn right on the A524 to Youlgraves. This is one of the fourteen or so Derbyshire villages in which the custom of well-dressing continues. From the 14th century villages have revived the pagan custom, decorating wells once thought to have curative powers; the villages create often quite elaborate pictures by pressing fresh flowers into clay. A visit to one of the villages between Easter and late June (for each chooses its own date, and they fluctuate with the religious feast days) may reveal one of the decorated wells. Although not to everyone's taste, they are interesting as folk art. Perhaps the three best villages for well-dressing are Youlgraves, Tissington (follow the A524 into the A515 and then south) and Wirksworth (follow the A6 south to the B5023). The other villages include Ashford (through which the A6 passes between Buston and Bakewell), Bonsal and Belper (on the A6 below Matlock), Warmhill and Tideswell (reached by the B6049 from the A6 to the east of Buston), Eyam and Stoney Middleton (on the A623 – see below), Hope (between Castleton and Hathersage), Bradwell (on the B6049 off the A625), Dore (a suburb of Sheffield) and Barlow (on the B6051 northwest of Chesterfield).

Beyond Haddon Hall turn left on the B6012, to Chatsworth House (see section on the Country Houses of Britain).

• If you continue on the A6, you will come to **Matlock Bath,** which Nathaniel Hawthorne pronounced among the most 'exquisite scenery' he had seen. To the west 14 miles is Dove Dale – follow the A5012 west below Matlock Bath to the A515, then left to a country road right for Thorpe. Continue towards Ilam and turn north at the Isaac Walton Hotel to a car park. There is a lovely hiking path through the glen, carrying one into the portion which was the 'Eagle Dale' of *Adam Bede* and the 'Happy Valley' of *Rasselas*. Further north the Dove enters Beresford Dale, from Milldale to Hartington; this was Walton's favorite fishing area.

Chatsworth is one of the finest stately homes in Britain. Its collection of tapestries, paintings (including Rembrandt) and sculpture, its valuable manuscripts and books, and its extensive garden, with a world-famous cascade, rightly make it the 'palace of the peak'. There is a fine deer park and a separate Theatre Gallery of Old Master drawings (open April–Oct. daily except Mon., Tues., 11.30–4, later on weekends). Continue north to Baslow and left on the A623, via Stoney Middleton, and right into Eyam. This village is a memorial to the Great Plague of 1665–6, for it deliberately cut itself off from the world when it discovered that the plague had been introduced into the village by a box of infected clothing; this heroic effort to prevent the plague from spreading cost the lives of five out of six inhabitants.

The short route into Sheffield from here is via the B6521 and the B6054 into the A625, thence via Dere into the city center. A long route of considerable interest is to return to Baslow on the A623 and continue east on the A619 to Chesterfield. There is a fascinating church, St Mary and All Saints, in the center of town.

• South on the A61 to the A615 right, then left on the B5035, is Crich, where England's largest **Tramway Museum** takes up the floor of a quarry. American trams are included.

Continue on the A617 from Chesterfield town center to the M1 roundabout and exit on the country road marked for Palterton and Bolsover. A mile beyond is **Sutton Hall,** a classical mansion built in 1724 and largely dismantled in 1920. The fittings were then incorporated into the Philadelphia Museum of Art. Bolsover Castle, beyond, is a grand ruin. 2 miles past the roundabout, off the A617 to the right, is **Hardwick Hall** (see page 230), owned by the National Trust, and perhaps the finest Elizabethan mansion in England (open April–Oct., Wed., Thurs., Sat., Sun., 2–6). Built by Bess of Hardwick in 1591–7, the hall is famous for its windows, picture gallery and needlework. Nearby is Ault Hucknall. Thomas Hobbes, author of *Leviathan*, is buried in the church here.

The area between Sheffield and Derby is sometimes called the Dukeries, for there are more surviving great houses in this 36-mile stretch than anywhere else in England. Haddon, Chatsworth and Hardwick, together with Kedleston Hall (just outside Derby) and Melbourne Hall, south of Derby, are outstanding. For the last two, drive south on the M1 to the A52 exit, then west to Derby, where one connects with tour number 8 in 20 miles.

For Sheffield, return to the roundabout on the M1, and go north to exit 34 and west. Alternatively, exit on 34 and go east to Rotherham, 2 miles, to visit the Museum and Art Gallery (open weekdays 10–5, Sun. from 2.30, closed Fri.) for its outstanding collection of Rockingham china, and then drive north on the B6089 into the B6090, 4 miles to **Wentworth Woodhouse** (not open to the public), a handsome mansion built for the Marquis of Rockingham, in which the pro-American Rockingham Whigs met during the American Revolution. One can then circle back to Sheffield by continuing to the A6135 and turning south past **Ecclesfield**. Joseph Hunter, the first researcher to establish the names of the Pilgrim Fathers, is buried here.

Sheffield, a city of 550,000, manufactures steel. It has long been famous for its cutlery industry, which developed on the basis of the system of mercantilism. More than most English cities, it had reason to advocate continued restrictions on the development of competing industries in the colonies, and the city became a symbol for the ultimate incompatibility of colonial development and metropolitan industrial supremacy. Sheffield has made a dramatic comeback from the devastation of World War II, and it is perhaps the most modern of the Midlands and northern English cities. The train that runs from London's St Pancras Station to Sheffield in a bit under three hours is called the Master Cutler.

The city is laid out in one-way-street patterns, and it is best to follow the signs to the Town Hall and a car park. Walk to the Town Hall on the corner of Fairgate and Surrey streets, then east to the **Graves Art Gallery** (open 10–8, Sun. 2–5). Each room is rehung frequently, since the gallery has too little space, and you may not be able to see all of the da Vinci, Rubens, Gainsborough, Turner, Constable or American paintings. The last include Whistlers, and there is a good Epstein bust. Retrace your steps to the Town Hall, angle left into Barkers Pool and past the Corinthian City Hall, then right two roads into West Street. Turn left and then right into Mappin Street, the fourth road on the right. Here is the central portion of the University of Sheffield. On Broad Street turn left to Weston Park, where the City Museum (open 10–5, Sun. 1–4) contains an outstanding display on Sheffield plate and the development of cutlery. The **Mappin Art Gallery,** adjacent, shows collections from the Graves Gallery, including American work. Then return along Broad into Towhead Street and right into Church Street. Ahead and to the right is Cutlers' Hall and opposite is the Cathedral.

Sheffield Cathedral is a parish church elevated to its present status in 1914. It is possibly the most interesting of the late 19th and early 20th century cathedrals created in this way, and it deserves a careful visit. The Shrewsbury Chapel, dating from the 16th century, contains good monuments, and the details are particularly pleasing. Just beyond the Cathedral is the top of Fairgate, by which you return to the car park.

Follow the signs to the M1, and from there north to exit 39 for Wake-field, 18 miles. The attraction here is a handsome Cathedral, most of which dates from 1470. Its spire is the tallest in Yorkshire, and it has several interior features of interest. On the Calder River bridge is the best surviving bridge chapel in England. 6 miles southeast on the A638 is Nostell Priory (open Easter–Oct., Wed., Sat., Sun., 2–6), a Georgian mansion completed by Robert Adam, which contains excellent furniture, including a magnificent range of Chippendale; a fine collection of Etruscan pottery; and Holbein's painting of Sir Thomas More. The old church at Wragby, within the park grounds of the mansion, is famed for its Swiss glass. 5 miles further, and to the north on the A628, is Pontefract, where one may join tour number 10.

Leave Wakefield northwest on the A61 to join the M1 into Leeds, 7 miles. This industrial city of 520,000 is the center of the English cloth industry. It is relatively modern and comparatively unattractive, although there are several sites of interest in the environs. The city center is compact and may be seen by walking. You will enter via the A61; continue straight on into Birdgate and left on Headrow until you cross Park Row and Cookridge; park the car. The Roman Catholic Cathedral, built in 1904, is just north on Cookridge, while the **Leeds City Art Gallery** (open 10.30–6.30, Sun. 2.30–5) is opposite the town hall. Its holdings include works by Corot, Courbet, Rembrandt, Constable and several Americans, in-cluding Sargent, West and thirteen Whistlers (these last may be on display in **Temple Newsamhouse,** 5 miles east of Leeds off the A64, which is open daily 11.30–6.15, and which was the original 'Templestowe' of *Ivanhoe*. It contains an exceptional collection of furniture as well).

Leave Leeds north on Cookridge, bearing left into Woodhouse Lane. First comes the university, famous for its scientific work, for its round Brotherton Library, and for the massiveness of its new buildings. At Adel is one of the most interesting Norman churches in England, unaltered since the 12th century. Circling back left is Kirkstall Abbey (open 11–4, Sun. 2.30–5), the most nearly complete such ruin in England save for Fountains Abbey. The ruin is just off the A65; continue on northwest to **Guiseley,** where Henry Wadsworth Longfellows' ancestors lie in the parish churchyard. Turn left on the A6038 and left again into Bradford. Before reaching the center, stop at Lister Park to visit the **Bradford City Art Gallery & Museum** in Cartwright Hall (open weekdays 10–5), which houses many interesting model engines and a representative collection of British paintings, as well as two John Singer Sargents and an oil by Mark Fisher.

Bradford, a city of 200,000, is the center of the worsted trade. Keep the central railway station to your left as you come into the city; just beyond the roundabout is the Cathedral, formerly a parish church. The stained glass inside, though modern, is good. Continue through the city on the

A650, and 1 mile south is **Bolling Hall** (open weekdays 10–5), a manor house which was the ancestral home of Edith Bolling, Woodrow Wilson's wife. Beyond bear right for the A6036, and follow it to the A644, right through Queensbury into the A629, and a mile later left on the B6141 to the A6033, thence right to Haworth.

Here is perhaps the most interesting (and the most popular) literary pilgrimage site in Britain: the **Brontë Parsonage and Museum,** and the original Wuthering Heights. The town is interesting despite its grubbiness. (The **Worth Valley Railroad,** at the old railroad station below, has an American steam locomotive.) The parsonage is on the hillside to the west; it was here that the Reverend Patrick Brontë brought his family in 1820. The building is much as it was when Charlotte, Emily and Branwell lived in it. Attached to the rear is a museum (open daily 11–5, Sun. 2) of great interest. See pages 103 and 346. Adjacent is the **Haworth Parish Church,** containing the tomb of Charlotte and Emily. On the cobblestoned village street is the Black Bull Inn, where Branwell fell into dissolute ways.

To see the lonely moor made so famous by the Brontës, take the Stanbury road west and bear right at the sign for Brontë Falls. Though this road deteriorates into a rocky lane you can continue some distance. Park at the end and walk straight ahead parallel to the fence and uphill; in a mile you will reach Top Withens (its ruin visible for some distance as you approach), and the site of Wuthering Heights. A circular path leads back toward the right and downhill to the Brontë bridge and falls, and thence back to your car. Return down the lane and take the first turn to the left, and then left again as far as the road goes. Here is Ponden House, probably the 'Thrushcross Grange' of *Wuthering Heights*. Retreat again, once more take the first left, and left again, into the road to Wycoller, where the ruined hall, 4 miles ahead, was the 'Ferndean Manor' of *Jane Eyre*. This moor road continues at an impressive height on to Colne.

From Haworth turn south on the A6033 to Hebden Bridge. From the bridge go left on the A646 to Halifax. A mile northwest up a steep country road is Heptonstall, an attractive village of weavers' cottages. (A right turn at Hebden Bridge will bring you in 23 miles on the A646 and the A679 to Accrington, to join the Lake District tour.) Although this city of 100,000 is often linked with Huddersfield and Hull as synonyms for the undesirable, it is not that unattractive. Laurence Sterne went to school here, and the Saltonstall family of Massachusetts originated here (Sir Richard Saltonstall helped found Watertown). Just east on the A58 is Shibden Hall (open weekdays 11–7, Sun. 2–5, closed Jan., Feb.), which houses the excellent West Yorkshire Folk Museum, including a brewhouse and craft workshops. Beyond turn right on the A641 to Huddersfield, a city of 130,000. A mile east from the city center on the A642 is Tolson Memorial Museum (open 10.30–5, Sun. 2–5), with an excellent exhibit on the development of the cloth industry.

From Huddersfield center drive northeast on the A62 to Heckmond-wike. This was the home of G. K. Chesterton and of his priestly detective Father Brown. Just beyond is Birstall, associated with Charlotte Brontë's *Shirley*. Off the A62 ahead is **Gildersome,** in which John Reyner, a Pilgrim, was born. The A62 continues into central Leeds, where one may drop a rental car at the railway station and return to London, or continue on the A64 to York, there to join the various options of tour number 10.

WHERE TO EAT   There is a good Mancunian hotel, the Midland, on Peter Street, and its French restaurant is excellent. The Grosvenor House hotel in Sheffield is large and dependable. North of Leeds are three highly recommended restaurants, in the Pool Court at Pool-in-Wharfedale, the Studley Hotel in Harrogate and The Box Tree in Ilkley. And at Kildwick, off the A629 northwest of Haworth 9 miles, is Kildwick Hall. In Leeds both the Queen's Hotel on City Square and the Metropole on King Street are dependable.

WHAT TO READ   This is Brontë country, of course, and the land of G. K. Chesterton, Laurence Sterne, Walter Scott, Frances Hodgson Burnett and Thomas De Quincey. In Manchester read George Gissing and Francis Thompson – both went to school there – and Mrs. Gaskell's *Mary Barton*, which is about the city. Dickens' *Hard Times* is set in Manchester, as is Louis Golding's *Magnolia Street*, which is about the Jewish community. As tradition places Robin Hood's grave at Kirklees Park, southwest of Leeds, a revisit with that fine old legend would seem good company for the end of the journey.

15   Wales

In many ways Wales is a land unto itself. A look at the map shows it to have a geographical coherence that sets it apart from England. Administratively, Wales has so far merged more closely with England than Scotland has; yet in other ways, the Welsh are at least as distinctive as the Scots. Increasingly one sees bilingual highway signs in Wales, which one does not in Scotland, and there are large portions of what used to be called Merionethshire and Caernarvonshire where one hears townspeople and children speaking in Welsh rather than English; a quarter of the population can speak the language, and some 6000 speak no other. Still, the ancient antipathies between Wales and England seem to have withered more than those across the northern border, and Welshmen have risen to so many positions of prominence in Britain, and are so proud a people, that they have little need of the professional patriot.

Rather, the Welsh sense of identity appears to come from the isolated, often bleak landscape that has nurtured them, and to come so clearly that they know themselves well. Famed for song (who can forget 'Men of Harlech'?), for the gift of poetry (Dylan Thomas is only one of the most recent), and for the tongue of orators – expressed in religion, most often Baptist or Methodist, or in politics, most often Labour – the Welsh have a great deal to offer the tourist. There is much that is historical and literary, crafts abound in Wales and outdoor sports are excellent. It is said that there are a hundred castles and a hundred golf courses. Uniquely, the Welsh also offer eight still operating, miniature, narrow gauge railways, so that anyone interested in steam travel should head immediately for central and north Wales. There are six cathedrals, four universities, and three national parks. Bird watching is excellent and the roads good and generally less crowded than in England. Only the *Good Food Guide* has reservations about Wales, giving but one restaurant in the entirety of the country its rating of Distinction. Happily, the unpronounceable names seem not to have been eroded from the map, even though Wales lost its independence in 1282. Much later came the Industrial Revolution, more slowly to Wales than to England, but, when it came, it came with a vengeance, and the area between and to the north of Cardiff and Swansea is among the least attractive in the whole of Britain. For that reason it has a perverse attraction of its own, in its mile upon mile of slag heap, pit head, and row house.

Precisely because Wales forms a convenient unit it is presented here as a single, continuous tour, in a large circuit (with various side excursions) beginning in Monmouthshire and ending at Chester, just south of Liverpool. Wales is difficult to see except by car, for the railway does not penetrate many of the mountain valleys, air service is minimal except to Cardiff and Swansea, and most buses provide so local a service as to require an exceedingly generous allowance of time if one wishes to see much. Hotel costs in Wales tend to be slightly lower than in England (and the hotels themselves more modest) so that you may compensate for the expense of a sustained car-hire by saving on room and board. And while Wales has many intimate connections with the United States, and especially with Pennsylvania, the number of specific and recognizable American-related sites in Wales is small, which leads to a more compact tour description. Monmouth, incidentally, is treated as part of Wales, as it has been administratively, but if you wish to be entirely accurate you should realize that culturally it is as much part of England, and that it was not uncommon to refer to 'Wales and Monmouth' as the actual political unit.

Finally, while you need know no Welsh in Wales, you will find a map far easier to use if you understand that *llyn* means lake, *mynydd* is mountain, *llan* (the commonest prefix in Welsh placenames) is church, *aber* is river mouth, and *bont* is bridge. You will also find *The Shell Guide to Wales*, by Wynford Vaughan-Thomas and Alun Llewellyn, useful and relatively light-weight to carry.

How long do you need? If you are tracing your roots back to Wales, you may want to linger a summer. Few will be able to do so. You can see all that follows comfortably in a week to ten days, including all of the side trips. If you are hard pressed, out to see something of the whole of Britain and wise enough not to want to miss at least a taste of Wales, you may visit the major highlights in four days. In the tour below, material set off with the symbol • relates to a time frame of a week or more, that marked * is to be seen if at all possible. The tour assumes that you have come by train to Bristol, where there are car rental kiosks at Temple Meads Station, as there are also in Chester or Liverpool, the suggested ends of this

CHEPSTOW CASTLE

tour. If you prefer to see only a portion of Wales, concentrating upon a particular national park or area, there are frequent fast trains from London to Cardiff. Should you wish to see only northern Wales, you may go by train to Aberystwyth, 235 miles from Euston Station.

If you have only four days, your stops for the night might best be in Swansea (the Dragon, on Kingsway Circle, is good and has fine views); Ynyshir Hall in Eglwysfach, above Aberystwyth; the Bulkeley Arms in Beaumaris; and the Grosvenor Hotel in Chester or the Adelphi Hotel in Liverpool. For Wales, one may purchase inexpensive booklets, divided by regions, which outline in detail short motor trips of a hundred miles or so. If you have two or three weeks for Wales, do purchase these through the Wales Tourist Board, 7 Park Place, Cardiff.

FIRST DAY

Leave Bristol on roads posted for the M4, which sweeps across the Severn into Monmouth. Exit at the first opportunity (number 22) for Chepstow, an ancient fortress town at the low crossing point on the River Wye. There is a handsome Norman castle here. Just before entering the town, the A466 turns north; follow this road to *Tintern Abbey, a moving Cistercian ruin (dating from 1131) in a ruggedly romantic setting. Suppressed by Henry VIII in 1536, this abbey has been the subject of more picturesque

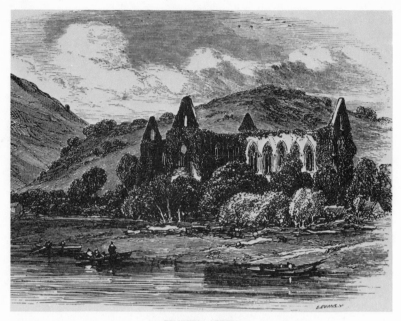

TINTERN ABBEY

and dramatic landscape paintings than any other in Britain. It is perhaps best known to us through the 'Lines composed a few miles above Tintern Abbey' by William Wordsworth, for he visited it with his sister Dorothy in 1798. Here 'these steep and lofty cliffs, / . . . on a wild secluded scene impress / Thoughts of more deep seclusion'. The view from across the river is also superb.

Continue north to Monmouth, the county town. The 11th century castle is worth seeing, and there is a fine museum to Admiral Nelson, and the only surviving Norman fortified bridge in Britain – the Monnow Bridge. From this town came the great chronicler, Geoffrey of Monmouth, who wrote *Historia Regum Britanniae* in *c* 1136. It was in this that 'The Matter of Britain' was first written down, including the legends of King Arthur, the once and future king. And it is, therefore, here that a pilgrimage to Arthurian sites might best begin. It is probably too early to eat, but if not, and if a detour does not bother you, drive 10 miles north on the A40 to Ross-on-Wye, across the border in Herefordshire, and thence 4 miles west on the A49 to Harewood End and the Pengethley Hotel. The Crown Inn, in Whitebrook, off the A466 south of Monmouth, is nearer and also very good.

Leave Monmouth west on the A40, to Raglan Castle, a fine 15th century fortified house. There is a good crafts shop in the village, and another further on in Abergavenny, a market town in a beautiful setting. From here you may continue into the Brecon Beacons National Park, or turn south in order to see Newport. You are in Abergavenny to shop and to eat. The leather and soft goods shops are excellent. If you have booked ahead, you can enjoy the best meal in Wales at the Walnut Tree Inn, 3 miles northeast on the B4521, in the village of Llandewi Skirrid. Lunch is served 12.30 to 2.30 (and dinner 7.30 to 10.30). If the weather is good, ask for a table outside. The menu is basically French and Italian, and nearly as good as anything you will find in London. In particular, if local game is available, have it. (8 miles west of Abergavenny, on the A40, is **Crickhowell.** Here is the Welsh Brigade Museum, which holds the Colour of the Fourth United States Infantry Regiment, which was surrendered to the British at the capture of Fort Detroit in 1812.)

Leave Abergavenny going south on the A4042 to Newport, 17 miles, via Pontypool. Bear left on the B4236 before reaching Newport, to *Caerleon, where one may see a fine ruined Roman amphitheatre and barracks. It was after a visit to this site that Alfred Lord Tennyson wrote *Idylls of the King,* which associates King Arthur with Caerleon, one alleged site of Camelot. Geoffrey of Monmouth asserts that Arthur was crowned here. The B4236 then continues into Newport. Pause to see St Woolas Cathedral, a parish church elevated to this status in 1949, and note particularly the Norman arch leading to the nave, and the rose window by John Piper. Do see the **Newport Museum and Art Gallery,** on John Frost Square (open daily except Sun., 10–5.30) especially for its Epstein bust of the 'tramp poet' W. H. Davies, author of those immortal lines, 'What is this life, if full of care, we have no time to stand and stare'. Also worthwhile is the unusual *Transporter Bridge, which carries six cars and many passengers across the River Usk in an underslung carriage. The view from the catwalk of the Bridge is an excellent one.

Rather than driving directly on to Cardiff, you may wish to leave Newport on the A468 to Caerphilly, from which the fine white Welsh cheese of that name used to come, although it is no longer made there. This is one of the lower valley cities, and, while it is less grim than most, it provides a taste which you otherwise will get only by taking the optional tour described below. *Caerphilly Castle is the second largest in Europe (Windsor being the first); were it not so ugly it would be memorable for nothing save sheer size. But for its bulk alone, it is worth viewing; the interior tour is not particularly good. Rather, continue down off the mountain to Cardiff, via the A469.

By now it is late afternoon, and you may wish to stay overnight in order to do the capital of Wales justice. There is a good castle, a university, major docks, and all that goes with an industrial city of 275,000. Yet, if faced with a choice, I would see three sights in Cardiff and press on for a late-dinner arrival in Swansea. One must not fail to visit the ***National Museum**

of Wales (open Mon.–Sat. 10–5 or later, Sun. from 2). There is an outstanding collection of French Impressionists, and in the science section one may walk into a Welsh mine. The gallery owns a number of American works, including a Benjamin West, James McNeill Whistlers and several Mark Fishers. Then continue northwest from the middle of the city via the A470 and the A48 into **Llandaff,** now a part of Cardiff, where on Cathedral Road one will find *Llandaff Cathedral, much reconstructed after sustaining war damage second only to Coventry. Begun in 1120, the cathedral is the most imposing in Wales. Be certain to note **Epstein's** masterwork, 'Christ in Majesty', and to visit the Welsh Regiment Memorial Chapel. Francis Lewis, a signer of the Declaration of Independence, was born in Llandaff in 1713. Carry on then to the *St Fagans National Welsh Folk Museum, further on the A48 and to the right on a posted road (as it closes at the same time as the National Museum of Wales drive on to see it and then return to see the cathedral afterwards if closing hour is near). Here there is an interesting exhibit of farm implements, crafts, the superb Denbigh cockpit and old Welsh cottages. Swansea, and your bed, is now 40 miles, or an hour's drive, west on the A48.

(If dark has not overtaken you, turn left at Cowbridge on the B4270 to Llantwit Major, to see the fine 8th century church, which contains painted wall frescoes and a stone font over a thousand years old. A mile beyond, on a country road, is **St Donat's,** an attractive old castle which was once the home of William Randolph Hearst. It now houses the Atlantic College, an advanced high school which draws many Americans.)

• If you are taking a slower journey through Wales, one of the more interesting resting places to swim lies along the Glamorgan coast between Bridgend and Port Talbot. Most of the Welsh beaches are either shingly and muddy, or crowded in summer by being close to large-size towns, or dangerous, given that the tides of the Bristol Channel are the second highest in the world. Where sandy beaches offer themselves, shale and limestone cliffs cut them off, or create a hazard below with their frequent small avalanches. And once in the water, it is cold by North American expectations (the average hottest August temperature along the coast is 65°) and there is an average of 18 days with rain in August – all in all, an 'invigorating climate'. But the sun is warming, even hot on occasion, and if time permits one ought to have at least one swim along this open Atlantic shore.

• For this swim, I recommend either Margam or Kenfig Sands, or Ogmore-by-Sea. To reach the last, turn left off the A48 just before Bridgend, onto the B4524, passing a ruined priory, and stopping to view Ogmore Castle before reaching the foreshore. This is a patrolled beach, with lifeguards on duty in midsummer. One must not swim near the mouth of the river and the beach is overhung with lowering cliffs, but the swimming is good and representative of the area. On returning to the A48, divert left on a country road posted for Merthyrmawr to view this unusually attractive village of thatched cottages and to see the fortified manor house of Candleston Castle.

• Rather better swimming, at greater cost of time and exertion, is to be found at Margam or Kenfig Sands. Consider them only if you are prepared to spend half a day. To reach either, turn left on an unmarked lane off the A48 directly opposite the ruins of Margam Abbey. The lane ends at Margam Sands, a secluded and never-crowded beach, which is good both for swimming and surfing. Kenfig Sands is reached by walking south from Margam Sands nearly 3 miles along the foreshore. One comes at the end to Sker House, setting for R. D. Blackmore's lesser-known novel, *The Maid of Sker.* Inland lay the town of Kenfig, which was at its height in the 12th century, and which by the 16th century was nearly covered by the shifting sands. The British government did not get around to dissolving the town officially until five hundred years after it disappeared beneath the sand. Today only the ruined castle can be seen.

• As another alternative expedition (if you have the time), rather than driving from Abergavenny to Cardiff by way of Newport, you may choose to explore the Brecon Beacons National Park. This will take longer but may well be very rewarding. Leave Abergavenny on the A465 west, to **Brynmawr,** founded as a social experiment by Quakers, from which the American town and college take their name. Continue on some 10 miles to a country road posted to Vaynor and Pontsticill, to the right. This narrow and winding road takes you north through the most outstanding of Brecon's views, over the *Torpantau Pass, and down into Talybont, where you bear left on the B4558 to **Brecon.** Here was born Dr Thomas Coke, who founded the American Methodist Episcopal Church.

• Brecon is the base for touring the *Brecon Beacons National Park, an area of some 520 square miles of, largely, red sandstone uplands. The park is 50 miles long, and only 8 to 12 miles wide. While less imposing than the Yorkshire Dales or North York Moors, it has a loneliness and attraction of its own. Before setting out to explore more of it, visit two sites in Brecon: the Cathedral, which serves Swansea as well, and which is small and attractive; and the **Regimental Museum of the South Wales Borderers and Monmouthshire Regiment,** at the barracks in town, where one may view items relating to the Battle of Bemis Heights (Saratoga) during the American Revolution, in 1777.

• Continue west of Brecon on the A40 to Llandovery, thence left on the A4069 to Llangadog, running along the edge of the mountains the while, and then mount up over the Black Mountain on the A4069 to the highest major road point in the national park (1,700 feet, with fine views over Wales) to descend to Brynamman. Here turn east on the A4068 to its junction with the A4067, then left and back into the hills to Craig-y-Nos, the former home of the singer Adelina Patti. Just beyond is the Dan-yr-Ogof, a well-lit limestone cave which, while small, is unusual. Then reverse yourself, to run down the A4067 back to Abercrave. From here drive east on a country road via Henrhyd Falls to the A4109, to Glyn-Neath, and turn left on a country road marked for Ystradfellte. A right turn at the village brings you to a bridge across the Mellte River. This is a remarkable river valley, with many waterfalls (the best a mile south by path) and caves, including the Porth-yr-Ogof, where the river disappears underground (take a flashlight). Then return to Glyn-Neath for a quick 30-mile run down the Vale of Neath on the A465 to Swansea.

• Alternatively, again, at Glyn-Neath you may turn east on the A465 to the A470, and there south through Merthyr Tydfil, a large and unattractive industrial town, thus to Pontypridd, at the base of the Rhondda Valley, and into Cardiff. (A drive up the Rhondda as far as Ystrad Rhondda is useful, if you want to get a sense of the bleak mining towns which produced so much Methodism, so much Labour agitation, and books like *How Green Was My Valley*.) At Cardiff, you will connect with the basic tour for the First Day, as outlined above.

SECOND DAY

Swansea, Wales' second city, with a population of 170,000, offers relatively little to hold you, despite having a good university, a large dock area, and the pleasant Glynn Vivian Art Gallery on Alexandra Road (open weekdays 10.30–5.30), which has lesser Old Masters and excellent Welsh pottery and porcelain. The Museum of the Royal Institution of South Wales, on Victoria Road near the railway station (open weekdays 10–5) is worth a moment, less for its Welsh folk art than for the best display of Swansea porcelain you will find. Otherwise, you are here to pay homage to Dylan Thomas, who was born at 5 Cwmdonkin Drive (reached off Terrace Road, which runs from the police station) and who spent much of his time at 10 Union Street (near the central market). No. 10 is now an Astey's house, and, while not especially good, it provides an adequate meal, a steak bar, and a beer cellar with mementoes of Thomas. If it is evening, you may also visit the Cross Keys Inn, on Princess Way, the oldest pub in Wales.

You must not miss St David's and the Pembrokeshire Coast, so you should be on the road as early as reasonably possible. St David's is 72 miles by the most direct route – the M4 and the A48 to Carmarthen, the A40 to Haverfordwest and the A487 to St David's. For the most part this route misses the coastline, although it is possible to touch upon it by taking the A484 from Swansea through Kidwelly to Carmarthen (only slightly longer if a bit slower) and there is a charming coastal stretch as one approaches St David's.

• If time permits, the Gower Peninsula, at Swansea's doorstep, is attractive, although rather crowded in summer. Leave Swansea on the A4067 to The Mumbles, a pleasant holiday resort which offers protected swimming and good water skiing. Oystermouth Castle, dating from the 12th century, is passed on your right. The B4433 leads to Mumbles Head, where a country road runs around the point to link up with the B4593. Much of the southern Gower coast is in the possession of either the Nature Conservancy or the National Trust, and it offers appealing views and small beaches. Follow postings for Bishopston, where one joins the B4436; turn left and join the A4118. (On a country road, left, is Oxwich, headquarters of the Gower Nature Conservancy office.) The A4118 ends at Port Eynon, on a high cliff above the sea. Descend by footpath across the headland to see Culver Hole, a wall 60 feet high. Retrace your road to the B4247 and turn west to Rhossilli, where, if you have not otherwise taken an opportunity to swim, you might best do so. The beach is romantic and well kept, excellent for surfing and safe for bathing. Return on the B4247 to the A4118, then left to a country road at Llanddewi, and by it north through Burry to Weobley Castle (where there are excellent views across the bay to Llanelli) and then by a country lane parallel to the B4295 (which begins at Llanrhidian) to Crofty. At low tide one may look out to the sands and see the cockle industry at work, as cocklers drive their horsedrawn carts onto the mud. At Gowerton, turn left on the B4296, and either continue to join the A48 at Pontardulais, thence to Carmarthen, or turn left earlier on the A4070, to pass Loughor, through Llanelli and Kidwelly (a good castle here) on the A484, to Carmarthen. The distances are roughly the same, although the latter is slower.

Carmarthen is a market town on the River Tywi. Merlin is said to have been born here, and his oak tree is preserved on Priory Street. Since this was the westernmost Roman military camp, the Carmarthen Museum holds good Roman relics. Leave westwards on the A40 to St Clears, and turn south on the A4066 to *Laugharne (pronounced 'larn'), known for its associations with Richard Hughes, author of *In Hazard* (to my mind the best sea story ever written) which he wrote while living in Laugharne Castle House, and *A High Wind in Jamaica*. There are also links with Dylan Thomas. The poet's former home, The Boathouse, now a museum, can be reached along Cliff Walk (now called Dylan's Walk). Here he was inspired to write *Under Milk Wood*, here at Brown's Hotel he drank more than he should, and although he died in New York City, he is buried in the parish churchyard. If then driving directly on to St David's, return to the A40 at St Clears.

• If time permits, a far more attractive route along portions of the coast begins at Laugharne. Continue southwest on the A4066 to Pendine (on the sands here Malcolm Campbell broke the world's land speed record in 1927, in the *Bluebird*), then by the B4314 to the A477, then left. (On a country road, left, is Amroth, one end of the Pembrokeshire Long Distance Coastal Path, which is a unique and rugged walk that will carry you to St Dogmaels, near Cardigan, in 170 miles. The sections of the path around the Dale Peninsula, and from St David's to the Head, are especially attractive and easily reached, if you prefer a shorter walk.)

• Two turnings beyond the Amroth road, bear left to **Wiseman's Bridge.** Here Churchill, Montgomery and Eisenhower came to watch rehearsals in 1943 for the D-Day landings in Normandy. One may also walk, in a mile and via a tunnel, to the seafront village of Saundersfoot, one of the most attractive in Wales. Or one may drive, joining the B4316, to the A478, and thence to *Tenby, which is an attractive town with many ancient buildings, a good Merchant's House from Tudor times, and a maze of lanes and narrow streets. Caldy Island, and its still active Cistercian monastery, can be reached by boat from Tenby. Only men may visit the monastery. The area between Tenby and St David's is rich in pottery studios, and at least ten are open in summer. Leave Tenby on the A4139 and divert left on the B4585 to Manorbier, where there is an excellent castle, open daily April to September. Here was born Giraldus Cambrensis, whose famous *Itinerary through Wales* is the source of most of what we know of Wales in the 12th century. Rejoin the A4139 and continue to Pembroke.

• Pembroke is known as 'Little England beyond Wales'. Here is a powerful 12th century *Castle, in which Henry VII was born. Its moat and its towering round keep are interesting and impressive. To the south and west is an attractive portion of the Pembrokeshire Coast National Park, a reserve of 225 square miles divided into four major sections. Particularly pleasant are the Bosherston Lily Ponds, reached south from Pembroke on the B4319 and by country road. Here a path leads to three wooded ponds crossed by footbridges. Another section of the park follows the Cleddau River, inland from Pembroke and best explored by small boats which can be rented at Haverfordwest, where the information office of the park is located. From land, one of the most interesting sites in this portion of the park is the Slebech Forest Walk, a lovely 2 mile path through Minwear Wood, looking out upon the Eastern Cleddau. To reach it, follow the A4075 east from Pembroke, to just before its junction with the A40, and then drive by country road to the forest car park. On the walk one may see a handsome stand of **Douglas Fir,** introduced into Britain by the Scottish botanist David Douglas in 1827, after a trip to the western United States. The walk is also excellent for bird watching. Another interesting site is the ruined Picton Castle, which has been in the same family for five centuries. It can be reached by going to the junction with the A40, turning west to the first substantial country road to the left, and proceeding 2 miles. One may then drive on to Haverfordwest. Indeed, unless there is reason to hurry, this Minwear-Picton excursion is much the best route from

Pembroke to Haverfordwest. The short route is only 11 miles, however, as opposed to 24.

• From Haverfordwest, one may drive directly to St David's (16 miles on the A487) or into a third detached portion of the Pembrokeshire Coast National Park, via the B4327 past Walwyn's Castle to the Dale Peninsula and Marloes. Particularly attractive is the village of Little Haven, to the right from the B4327, which is a picturesque settlement at the head of a rocky bay. Bird watchers will be interested in Skomer and Grassholm islands, the last 12 miles offshore, where there are gannets, ravens, vultures and other sea birds (and perhaps Atlantic Grey Seal). Arrangements to visit either island have to be made at the Dale Fort Field Centre, just beyond the village of Dale, at the end of the B4727.

Haverfordwest is on the short route between Swansea and St David's. At Newgale on the A487 one touches the coast and is in the Pembrokeshire Coast National Park again. There are several excellent views to the south. Solva is an attractive village, and beyond is *St David's, where one may visit the most isolated and smallest ancient cathedral in Britain. The town is named for the patron saint of Wales, and although officially a city, it numbers fewer than 2000 people. The cathedral is especially fine, and demonstrates that size does not matter. Its 12th century magnificence has a number of unique elements. Do not fail to notice the misericords, St David's shrine, the 11th century Abraham Stone, the nave ceiling and the fine vaulted ceiling of the Chapel of the Holy Trinity. If crafts interest you, there are two woodworking shops northwest of town. In a shop in town you may find a copy of one of Leonard A. Knight's somewhat dated mystery novels, set in the area; *Deadman's Bay* (actually St Bride's Bay) is the most readable. And for surfing, drive via the B4583 to Whitesands Bay, where the long rollers are considered to be the best in Wales. A plaque by the car park marks the site of St Patrick's Chapel, from which the saint is said to have sailed for Ireland in the 5th century.

If one has driven directly from Swansea, it is lunch time (and, if many of the diversions have been taken, no doubt dinner time). The Whitesands Bay Hotel (open April to October) is nicely located, with annexes that look from the cliff's edge, and you can take either meal dependably if simply here. Should you plan to stay the night, you must book. However, if you plan to reach Aberystwyth by nightfall, it may be best to purchase bread and cheese in a shop in St David's and press on.

The north Pembrokeshire coast is very attractive, and far less well known or frequented than the south coast. The National Park continues to run along the coast as far as Fishguard, and while the main road – the A487 – is a good one, one should take time, even if on a rapid tour, to follow unnumbered country roads closer to the sea via Abereiddy, Porthgain, Trevine, Abercastle, Mathry, St Nicholas, Strumble Head, and into

Fishguard. Each offers its own striking view, and at the Head there is a lighthouse on a high cliff that is open Monday to Saturday afternoons. At **Carregwastad Point,** reached by walking from the village of Llanwnda, there is a small stone memorial to the last invasion of Britain, attempted in February 1797 by 1,200 Napoleonic troops, and led by an American, William Tate. Having meant to sack Bristol, but faced with contrary winds, the invaders landed without opposition. Clearly Tate's heart wasn't in it, for he mistook red-coated ladies for British soldiers, and he surrendered at **Goodwick.** The table on which he did so is in a pub in Fishguard – the Royal Oak.

Just beyond Fishguard is another detached portion of the *Pembrokeshire Coast National Park; one which includes a substantial inland area as well as coastline. The cliffs from Fishguard to Cardigan are massive, but not easily reached, and the best access to them is at Cwm-yr-Eglwys: turn left for Brynhenllan off the A487, and walk on to the beach where a wall marks the remains of St Brynach's Church, which is all that survived of the village after the great storm of October 1859 in which 114 ships were wrecked. At St Dogmaels, just before reaching Cardigan, one may review a ruined abbey, see in the parish church a stone pillar that helped lead to the deciphering of Ogham in 1848, or fish for salmon and sea trout. Cardigan itself is a prosperous county town on the River Teifi, and you can see modern forms of the ancient coracle in use on the water.

At Cardigan our route turns inland, via the A484, up through Tivyside. The drive is pleasant, as it passes by Cenarth, where there is a spectacular bridge and salmon leap, and through Newcastle Emlyn, known for its woollen mill. From here, follow the A475 northeast to Lampeter, site of St David's College founded in 1822, and a branch of the University of Wales. Leave town on the A485 north to Tregaron. A mile north, off the B4343, begins the *Bog of Tregaron, unique in either England or Wales. The bog is 4 miles long, and is rusty red, except in late spring and summer when it is covered with cotton flowers. It is still expanding, and you may see many wild animals, birds and rare plants by walking into the bog on the several isolated footbridges. Unless you are going to Scotland, this is the best place to see the work of the turf cutter.

• Given time and patience, you will find the narrow, winding mountain road east from Tregaron over the Cambrians to Llanwrtyd Wells quite worth driving. This is probably the wildest road in Wales, and while George Borrow did not have this area in mind when he wrote *Wild Wales*, the title is fitting. The road will carry you through the heart of the once proposed (1972) Cambrian Mountains national park. You can then carry on to Builth Wells, on the Upper Wye. (17 miles southeast is **Hay-on-Wye.** Here is the ancestral home of William Dean Howells, the Ohio and Boston writer, and also of the largest used book store in Britain.)

• From Builth Wells, continue on the A483 north to Llandrindod Wells, an Edwardian spa with lovely parks and wide streets. The 18-hole golf course here is one of the highest in Britain, and the Welsh Craft Centre is good. (**Newtown,** a long 27 miles north on the winding A483, was the birthplace of Robert Owen, father of the co-operative movement, whose influence in America was so great. Here is the Owen Memorial Museum, open weekdays 2–4. North of Newtown on the B4568 and the B4389 is Gregynog Hall, now used for conferences, which houses an early printing press and many fine English and French paintings. Northeast of Newtown, via the A483 and the B4386, you cross a clearly visible portion of *Offa's Dyke just beyond Montgomery, as you re-enter England. The dyke, built in 784 by King Offa, leader of the Mercians, to demark the Welsh from the Anglo-Saxons, runs south to Chepstow and north to the sea at Prestatyn, although in few places is it so visible, being 15 feet high at this point. To return to the main route at Devil's Bridge, you must now return to Newtown and continue on the A492 to Llangurig, where the traditional Welsh love spoons are still carved. Then follow the A44 and the A4120. This long circuit of 96 miles, largely to see an archaeological ruin, should not be taken unless this is definitely your bag.)
• From Llandrindod turn west on the A4081 to the A479, and thence north to Rhayader. Craft shops are good here as well. To the southwest on the B4518 is Caban-coch Reservoir. The road to it is attractive, and the waters cover Nantgwyllt, where Percy Bysshe Shelley lived with his Harriet. Francis Brett Young has written of the old village, which was re-exposed by a drought in 1947, in *The House Under the Water*. From the reservoir you can continue by country road to Hirnant, and along another wild and quite beautiful country road to Bryn and Devil's Bridge.

If, however, your time is too limited to follow this alternative excursion, continue beyond Tregaron on the B4343 and turn right to the ruins of *Strata Florida, second only to Tintern as an ancient ecclesiastical structure in Wales. The great Welsh medieval poet Dafydd ap Gwilym is buried here with Wales' medieval princes. Then follow the B4343 to Devil's Bridge.

At *Devil's Bridge one is in the finest hill country of Wales. There are, in fact, three bridges, one above the other – the Devil's is the lowest – and in the spring the falls are spectacular, one leaping 300 feet. One can view them from the grounds of the Hafod Arms Hotel. Climb down to the gorge, or enjoy the only steam-operated narrow gauge railway in Britain, the *Vale of Rheidol Railway, which terminates here. If you have someone to drive your car on to Aberystwyth for you, take the train down the winding forest track. The journey takes an hour. (Of course, you may wish to ride both ways, in which case begin in Aberystwyth. Running between May and September, the round-trip journey takes three hours,

ABERYSTWYTH

covers 24 miles, and is exceedingly crowded in high summer. Indeed, Devil's Bridge is the single most popular tourist town in Wales.) George Borrow stayed in the inn that bears his name, in Ponterwyd, 4 miles north on the A4120. His famous journey, to describe *Wild Wales*, was taken in 1854 and ran from Llangollen to Chepstow.

You can run down the Rheidol Valley from Ponterwyd on the A44, or somewhat more attractively, on the A4120. This route passes Nanteos Hall (open June–Sept., daily 1–5.30), a mansion from 1739 containing good paintings and furniture, and – if you are a believer – the blackwood Holy Grail. You then enter Aberystwyth, a stately yet rather ugly resort town of 11,000, with a stark promenade, interesting university buildings and many good craft shops. Spare a moment for the old university building near the pier, and see the Library, fitted up by Welshmen in America. Drive up-hill on the A44 to visit the *National Library of Wales* on Penglais Road. Here you may see the manuscript of the Black Book of Carmarthen, perhaps the earliest in Welsh, and the Book of Taliesin, as well as an excellent collection on the Welsh in the United States. If you have the time, and did not do so from Devil's Bridge, ride on the Vale of Rheidol Railway.

Now turn north on the A487, to drive 13 miles to Eglwysfach, where you wisely booked a room at Ynshir Hall, a small hotel with ten rooms and good food. (First you pass through Talybont, where the Leri Mills display good hand-woven tweeds.) If the light is still with you, as it will be in summer, you will have time to seek out directions for Bedd Taliesin, a 3 mile drive and 1 mile walk, which is the traditional site of the grave of Taliesin, the Welsh Homer.

THIRD DAY

On this day the temptations to divert on side trips will be great, for North Wales abounds in dramatic castles, isolated valleys and, of course, Snowdonia National Park. If crafts interest you, there are many, and if you enjoy the 'Great Little Trains of Wales' you will find eight cut across or near your path. If you can stretch your time in Wales, therefore, this is the sector in which to do it.

The A487 north soon strikes the Dovey Valley and **Machynlleth** (pronounced Ma-cun-leth). In Plas Machynlleth, a residence of Lord Londonderry, there is an excellent exhibition of Welsh textiles, furniture, glass and pottery. In the Town Hall are the crossed flags of Britain and the United States, testimony to the twinning of the town with Belleville, Michigan, in 1967. Just beyond begins *Snowdonia National Park. Perhaps the most famous of Britain's national parks, and the second largest, Snowdonia covers 845 square miles but focuses on the massive peak of Snowdon, that frequently climbed but still strenuous height of 3,560 feet. There is much to see in the park, and the highlights are described in their proper place.

Avoid continuing on the A487, often congested in summer, and turn west beyond Machynlleth on the A493 through Aberdovey, an attractive village, to Towyn. Here you may ride on the Talyllyn Railway, the first to have been saved from extinction by volunteers, for a round trip of 13 miles from Towyn to Abergynolwyn. At the height of the season there are as many as eleven trains a day, and the trip takes two hours. Even if you do not ride, visit the Narrow Gauge Railway Museum at the wharf in Towyn. See too the Celtic Church in Towyn, which contains the oldest known inscription in Welsh. Then proceed on the A493 to a country road at Llanegryn; turn right, and follow the postings up the Dysynni past Bird Rock (where in spring you may see cormorants) to *Castell-y-Bere, a small but fine ruin which combines Welsh and English architectural features. Here one looks up the Pennant Valley to Cader Idris, an impressive mountain, and just beyond is the simple memorial to Mary Jones, a sixteen-year-old girl who, in 1800, having saved pennies for years to buy a Welsh Bible, walked barefoot to Bala to buy one, only to find all were sold and no more were to be printed. The minister there, Thomas Charles, was so moved that he gave her his Bible and then helped found the British and Foreign Bible Society, to put the Bible into the hands of the needy.

From just below Castell-y-Bere turn right to reach the B4405 at the head of the Talyllyn Railway, by which you can ride back to Towyn. Otherwise, continue to the A487, flanking Cader Idris, into Dolgellau.

• From Dolgellau, turn right on the A494 to parallel the ancient Roman road through wild country to Bala Lake, the largest in Wales. This is the land of the *Mabinogion*, the great Welsh national epic, and of portions of Spenser's *Faerie Queene*. The Bala Lake Railway runs from Bala to Llanuwchllyn, 2 miles, every thirty minutes. George Borrow stayed at the White Lion Royal in Bala, and there is a statue of Thomas Charles here. Bala is regarded as one of the cradles of Welsh culture, and also especially of Methodism. If you wish, you may then turn up the A4212 to the A470, through the Aran Mountains, and then south to Dolgellau again, having made a circuit around the great beacon of Arenig Fawr in 50 miles.

• Alternatively, as you reach the B4405 from Castell-y-Bere, you can turn right back to the A493, then north to Cae-du Farm. Here a lane turns left and leads to the beach; walk left along the beach to Owain Glyndwr's (Owen Glendower's) Cave, where Glyndwr hid while escaping from the English during the great rebellion of 1401–8. The cave is cut off at high tide. Further on the A493 at Fairbourne is the smallest of Wales' railways, with a gauge 15 inches wide, which runs 2 miles along an attractive beach. At the height of the season there are sixteen trains a day, and the round trip takes an hour. Then continue to Dolgellau.

Dolgellau is a handsome market town of grey stone. Beyond, on the A470 at Llanelltyd, is the ruined Cistercian Cymmer Abbey. Here you can begin the Precipice Walk, a famous footpath that leads briskly north with fine views to Tyn-y-groes, some 2 miles away. Just beyond is Dolmelynllyn Hall, a National Trust property which includes a fine waterfall in the grounds linked with the poet Thomas Gray by a stone carved with lines from his Latin ode to the Deity of the Grand Chartreuse. (If time does not permit the walk, you may also reach Dolmelynllyn by driving from Llanelltyd north on the A470.)

From Llanelltyd, drive west on the A496 to Barmouth, at the head of the Mawddach estuary. The hill above this resort village was the first land to be acquired by the National Trust, in 1895, so beginning Britain's most significant conservation movement. Just beyond is Llanaber, where the parish church is the best Early English structure in North Wales. Continue to Llanbedr, where you bear right on a country road into the best of The Rhinogs section of Snowdonia National Park. (If time permits, drive up the Artro Valley, keeping it to your right, to the end of the road just beyond a small lake. Here a mountain path leads in a strenuous mile to the Roman Steps – perhaps not Roman at all, but a stairway built in the 17th century to aid pack horses up the mountain. If a longer hike appeals, bear right out of Llanbedr, up-hill after crossing the Artro, to Maes-y-Garnedd, a house from where you may take the Pass of Drws Ardudwy through the narrowest cleft in Snowdonia to join the A470 in 4 miles.)

Beyond Lanbedr, on the A496, is *Harlech, perhaps the most resounding name in all Wales. The view of Snowdon from here is especially fine, as is the sweep out to the Lleyn Peninsula. The famous castle (open generously, and from 9.30 on Sun. in summer) overwhelms the city, and while it is not quite so jaggedly romantic as paintings have led one to believe, its site on a rocky promontory and its unfenced cliff-top walks (take care with children) make it justifiably the most thrilling of any of the Welsh castles. The memory of the stirring march, 'Men of Harlech', which commemorates the siege of the castle in the Wars of the Roses, adds to the distinction of the visit.

If you have not tarried along the way and have taken none of the diversions, lunch in the Portmeirion Hotel in Penrhyndeudraeth, just off the A487, should be possible. It will be crowded, for *Portmeirion is a major tourist attraction, so book at least the day before. Portmeirion itself is the personal creation of an architect, Clough Williams-Ellis, and while the entire village is technically a hotel, one may visit it for a fee. The juxtaposition of Italian Mediterranean, Welsh and Unidentifiable Luxuriant is not to the taste of all, but no one can deny the interest of the hamlet, which is open Easter to October, 10-7.

Having lunched, drive on via the A487 to Portmadoc. Here you may board the *Ffestiniog Railway, a superb round trip journey of two hours from the Vale of Ffestiniog to Ddualt. At the height of the season there are thirteen trains daily on this oldest narrow gauge track in Britain. At Tremadoc, a mile north of Portmadoc on the A487, T. E. Lawrence of Arabia was born; a plaque on the house named Gorphwysfa, at the edge of the village, commemorates the author of *The Seven Pillars of Wisdom*. Beyond Portmadoc via the A487 is Criccieth, with an interesting castle. For several years this small town was the home of James (now Jan) Morris, probably the finest living British travel writer. Just beyond is *Llanystumdwy, where David Lloyd George, the great World War I Prime Minister, lived as a child. The excellent Lloyd George Museum is here – it includes his copy of the Treaty of Versailles and you can visit his grave on the banks of the River Dwyfor. Now turn back to Penrhyndeudraeth.

• Alternatively, you can continue on along the Lleyn Peninsula, an area of great natural beauty. Pwllheli is its market town. Its principal attractions include Hell's Mouth, a long beach with spectacular waves, which is reached by taking the A499 beyond Pwllheli to Abersoch and then country roads for Llanengan, beyond which a lane gives access. You can also view the beach from near Plas-yn-rhiw, by country road off the B4413 which, in turn, diverges from the A499. Continue on to Aberdaron, where you rejoin the B4413, and to Myndd Mawr, a great cliff 500 feet high, from which there are spectacular views. Beyond is Bardsey Island, long a refuge for religious pilgrims, and said to be the home of Merlin. Boats run to it from Aberdaron in summer. Follow the B4413 back to its junction with the B4417, and thus to the A499 and to its junction with the A487 just below Caernarvon.

If time is especially pressing, you can drive from Portmadoc to Caernarvon via the A487 in 23 miles. The main route outlined here, however, is designed to take you into the heart of Snowdonia. It runs 49 miles. Continue east from Portmadoc on the A487 to the A496, then into the B4391 to Ffestiniog. There is an interesting candle factory here. Turn north on the A470 to Blaenau Ffestiniog, where you may have the unusual experience of riding into the *Llechwedd Slate Caverns in an electric train to learn about underground slate workings. The tour is a unique one, and children will especially enjoy it. Continue on past Dolwyddelan Castle to Betws-y-coed, a pleasant town with craft shops and mountain walks. Turn left on the A5 past the famous Swallow Falls to Capel Curig, a tiny resort village surrounded by mountains. This is the heart of the mountain climbing region. Turn here on the A4086 to Pen-y-Gwryd and the Gorphwysfa Hotel, where you may pause for a drink and notice the memorabilia relating to many famous climbers. The junction is on the site of a Roman marching camp, and many good tracks begin here. One, the Pig Track, leads most directly and dramatically to the summit of Snowdon. At the hotel, turn northwest into the bleak Pass of Llanberis, the most impressive crossing of the range.

• Alternatively, you can drive southwest on the A498, through the Nant Gwynant Pass, to Beddgelert. Many tourists come here to see the grave of Gelert, the dog made famous by the well-known tale: having saved Prince Llywelyn's baby son from attack by a wolf, Gelert was seen with blood upon his jaws and was slain by mistake. Then follow the A4085 into Caernarvon, passing the Beddgelert Path, which lies opposite Pitt's Head and which is the most dramatic ascent of Snowdon. The climb is completed over a knife-edged ridge with sharp drops on both sides.

At Llanberis, on the A4086, are the ruins of Dolbadarn Castle, and the beginning of two narrow gauge railways. The best known, the *Snowdon Mountain Railway, goes to the summit at 3560 feet. The 5-mile journey requires an hour each way and operates from mid-March to the end of October. (Monday to Friday 9.30 at half-hour intervals until 4.30, less frequently on Saturday and Sunday.) The train does not depart until it has the equivalent of 25 adult fares. And across the lake is the Llanberis Lake Railway, which runs from near the largest slate quarry in the world, at Dinorwic, to Penllyn, 2 miles away. The round trip takes 45 minutes. Visit the old quarry workshops as well, for they are now a quarrying museum.

Then continue on the A4086 into Caernarvon. Here you will wish to spend the night. But in summer the city is crowded and very noisy, and at the expense of driving on 12 miles, and having to retrace your steps the next day, I would strongly recommend going on to Beaumaris (on the A487 to Menai Bridge, across to Anglesey, and immediately right on the A545). The Bulkeley Arms, while not exceptional, has always proved quiet and satisfying. While here, be certain to view *Beaumaris Castle, one of my personal choices in Wales, built by Edward I in 1295 (open, in summer, 9.30–7). It is regarded as the finest concentrically designed fortress in Britain. In August, the Menai Strait is filled with yachts for a regatta fortnight, accommodations will be very difficult to obtain, and it will be noisy. In such desperate straits, call ahead to the Tre-Arddur Bay Hotel 21 miles further out on Anglesey, and hope for the best.

FOURTH DAY

Before driving back to Caernarvon, it is best to see Anglesey, which is an area of Welsh culture, with many Welsh-speaking communities. First, drive north on the B5109 from Beaumaris to Llangoed, and follow the postings for Penmon. A narrow toll road goes to Black Point, where there is a fine Tudor dovecot that is open to the public, a ruined priory where you may visit the most famous wishing well in Britain, and views across Conway Bay to Great Ormes Head, and out to Puffin Island, where puffins breed. Then return to Beaumaris and turn west on the B5109 to Pentraeth, thence north on the A5025 to **Moelfre.** Near here was born Goronwy Owen, famous for adapting the themes of English poetry into Welsh and for his work in St Andrew's Church, in Brunswick County, Virginia, where he is buried. The village was the site of the wreck of the *Royal Charter* in 1859, in which – despite a desperate and courageous rescue attempt – 459 lives were lost, in a storm that claimed 114 ships. Charles Dickens was to write *The Uncommercial Traveller*, in part, on this event, which is commemorated by a memorial on the cliff.

Continue on to Amlwch, site of the Parys Mountain copper mine – 2 miles inland off the B5111 – which in 1800 was the world's largest. The village even minted its own coinage and the copper sheathing of boats began here. The mountain is interesting to walk on, being perhaps the least disturbed remnant of industrial archaeology in Britain, with its nightmarish copper-stained pools, many tunnels and shafts, ruined cottages and wind-mill, and engine houses. Exercise extreme caution if you do decide to hike up the slope (actually only 600 feet high).

The A5025 then continues past Cemaes Bay, where at Wylfa Head there is one of the largest nuclear power stations in the world (an information tower permits a view), to the A5. Turn right to run across the bridge that links Holy Island with Anglesey. Here is Holyhead. The principal attraction is *Holyhead Mountain, reached by following the postings for it and

LLANBERIS LAKE

South Stack. From the mountain there are fine views north to the Isle of Man and back to Snowdonia. Just beyond is one of the most dramatic lighthouses in Britain, the South Stack Light (open Monday–Friday afternoons). Many seabirds may be seen in the area.

Return then to the Menai Strait Bridge on the A5. You may be lucky enough to see the Royal Air Force at work, for to your right as you return to Anglesey from Holy Island is R.A.F. Valley, a training base for the use of Phantom jets, helicopter air-sea rescue units and other aircraft. The Strait is now 18 miles east: run for it, except to divert north on the A5114 2 miles to visit Llangefni, the administrative town of Anglesey. Just before reaching the Menai Strait Bridge (which, when Thomas Telford built it in 1826, was the longest bridge in the world) you will pass through   *Llanfairpwllgwyngyllgogerychwyrndrobwllllantysiliogogogoch (usually shortened to Llanfair P. G.), which has long attracted attention for having the longest placename in the world (despite clear competition from a Maori-named site in New Zealand). To the right, on the shore of the Strait, is a large statue of Lord Nelson.

Crossing the bridge, turn right on the A487 for Caernarvon. The great attraction here, of course, is the massive Caernarvon Castle, which Edward I began to build in 1283 to assure his control over North Wales. In the castle the present Prince Charles was invested as Prince of Wales in 1969.

The Welch Fusiliers Museum, inside, is quite good, and the castle has enough odd turrets and stairways to keep children happy for an hour. However, the castle is the single greatest tourist attraction in Wales, and you will have to battle with the crowds. Further south, just off the A487, is the site of Segontium, a Roman fort, which is well worth visiting. So too is the open-air cattle market, in Castle Square, if it is Saturday.

You will also require lunch, if you are keeping to the short-tour schedule. And for this necessity, Caernarvon is very ill-equipped. Resign yourself to fish and chips, or hot dogs and ice cream from the carts, or arm yourself with bread and cheese to eat as you drive, for every place will be thronged and nothing will be worth the wait. This is equally true of Bangor, to which you should press on, retracing your steps northwards on the A487. Bangor is a relatively attractive town, focused on its university on the hill and its cathedral below. Enter on the Menai Bridge Road and bear left into College Road, where the **Museum of Welsh Antiquities** is worth visiting. There are a few objects of American-related interest here, including a collection of Dr Griffith Evans, a veterinary surgeon who visited field hospitals of the Northern Army during the American Civil War, when he met Abraham Lincoln. Make your way down the hill to the cathedral, which is rather good but difficult to view from a distance. While the building dates from the 16th century, a cathedral has stood on this site longer than anywhere else in Britain. Between the cathedral and the Town Hall is the remarkable *Gardd yr Esgob, a garden in which one finds all the trees, shrubs and flowers mentioned in the Bible (and capable of surviving in the climate of Wales). The 'Bible Walk' is especially worth taking, for here everything is laid out in the order in which it is mentioned in the scriptures. One may purchase a handbook to the garden and walk at either the Town Hall or the Public Library. Just beyond Bangor, off the A5, you may also visit Penrhyn Castle, which includes a very large exhibit of dolls and a railway museum.

Now follow the A55 to Conway, 14 miles away, skirting the edge of the Carnedd Range section of Snowdonia National Park. *Conway was founded by Edward I in 1283, and it is regarded as the best-preserved medieval fortress-town in Britain. The castle (open 9.30–7) is dramatic, and one of those I like best; its thick walls were built in the shape of a Welsh harp. The road crosses the river on a suspension bridge, flung up by Telford in 1827, which is built into the castle battlements. Crossing the river, turn left into the A496 for Great Ormes Head. The road passes along West Shore: Lewis Carroll was inspired to write *Alice in Wonderland* here, and there is a statue of the White Rabbit on the promenade. Follow the postings for the toll road around the Head, and thence into Llandudno, Wales' largest resort. It is not unattractive. Follow The Parade east to Queens Road (the B5115) and right on it to Roumania Drive, then left, right, and right again to the Rapallo House Museum, which contains a traditional Welsh kitchen and rather interesting pictures (open weekdays 10–1, 2–5). Return to the A546 on the seafront, and turn right to Colwyn Bay, on the A55. Angle right onto the B5443 to Gwrych Castle, relatively little known but quite good. Then continue to Abergele, where there is an interesting shop that makes love spoons, to rejoin the A55, turning away from the coast, to St Asaph. Here is one of the smallest cathedrals in Britain, dating from the 15th century. **H. M. Stanley,** he who found Livingstone, once was employed in the workhouse here.

Turn right on the A525 for **Denbigh.** This is the market town of the former Denbighshire (now Clwyd) and there is a fine castle to visit, which incidentally includes a model of the cottage in which H. M. Stanley was born. Continue on the A525 to Ruthin, once a fortified town, where the curfew is still rung every night at 8. In Ruthin Castle you may enjoy a banquet of Tudor food, accompanied by Welsh harp music, if you like that sort of thing. And here, if time is running out, you must turn left on the A494, through Mold, the county town of Flintshire (once the smallest county of Wales, now absorbed into Clwyd), if you are to reach Chester, and the Grosvenor Hotel, by nightfall. Just before the English border, now on the A55, you will pass *Hawarden House (pronounced 'harden'), which was the home of William E. Gladstone, the great Prime Minister. The hall is not open, but you may visit the ruins of the old castle (Fri.– Sun., Easter–Oct., 2–6) and the grounds.

• Alternatively, and not to miss one of the more interesting sections of Wales if you have time, continue south from Ruthin on the A525 to the A542. (Right on the A5104 brings you to **Bryneglwys,** a tiny village where in the parish church is the Yale chapel, which once belonged to the family of that name. It was to be Elihu Yale who provided the gift which led to the founding of Yale University. Shortly before entering the village you will find **Plas-yn-Yale,** the house in which Elihu's father was born.) The A542 continues across the Llantysilio Mountain via the locally famed Horseshoe Pass, and past the attractive ruins of Valle Crucis Abbey, into *Llangollen, at the head of the vale of that name, and site of the International Musical Eisteddfod each summer. The **Old Toll House** on the A5 is associated with 'Mary had a little Lamb', the rhyme being said locally to have originated from an actual event here. (Actually, the verse – by an American, Mrs Sarah Josepha Hale – was published ten years too early for Llangollen's claim.) Plas Newydd, where the Ladies of Llangollen lived, is a black and white timber-framed house common enough in nearby Cheshire but not particularly so here, and is worth visiting. Borrow describes the Vale of Llangollen in detail.

• Now follow the A5 east. At Acrefair is the dramatic *Pont-Cysyllte Aqueduct, built by Telford in 1795–1805 to carry not a railway but a canal across the Dee Valley; the aqueduct is on such a large scale that it is a major and unexpected example of industrial archaeology. Follow the A5 to Chirk, and then right on the B4500 to *Chirk Castle, up the Vale of Ceiriog. Occupied since 1310, and in the hands of the same family since 1595, this rectangular fortress is one of the most interesting in Wales, for it is the only unaltered border castle (open Easter–Sept., Tues., Thurs., Sat., Sun., 2–5). There is a fine clipped yew walk. If time permits, the drive on up the vale at least as far as Llanarmon Dyffryn Ceiriog, well into the Berwyn Mountains, is very attractive. On the way you pass through **Glyn Ceiriog,** 5 miles above the castle. The Hughes Institute here contains a tablet to Thomas Jefferson, because of his Welsh descent, and a memorial to George Borrow is nearby.

• Return to Chirk. (If you bear right on the A5 into the A483, you will reach Welshpool in 23 miles. Here is the beautiful *Powis Castle, built of sandstone, continuously lived in for five hundred years. The gardens are by Capability Brown, and they include a towering Douglas fir. Here, too, is the Welshpool and Llanfair Railway. Discontinued in 1956, the line has made a comeback with rides for tourists covering a round trip of 11 miles in an hour and forty-five minutes, with two or three trains daily in the season. It is the least interesting of the eight such railways in Wales, unless you have specialized knowledge of railwayana. But if you know a banger from a banjo, and if having seen the snip you've taken a snap aboard, you'll enjoy being on the shovel. No, I don't really know what I'm talking about, but Donald J. Smith's *Discovering Railwayana,* a booklet in the 'Discovering' series, will tell you about all of the museums, and railway terms, so that you too may sound like an insider. You might then turn east on the A458 to Shrewsbury.) If you turn left at Chirk, however, follow the A5 to Ruabon, and then right on the A539 into a uniquely detached portion of Flint, cut off from the rest of the county by Denbigh (until the amalgamation of all into Clwyd), you will find Overton, an attractive town. Turn north on the B5059 to Bangor-is-y-coed, and left on the A525 to **Wrexham.** This is the heart of industrial North Wales. St Giles's Church has an exceptional steeple; in its churchyard lies buried Elihu Yale (called by one of the English guidebooks, a Pilgrim Father, which he decidedly was not, since he made his fortune as a merchant in Madras, and is remembered in the name of Yale University solely because of a gift of books). A painting in the church, said to be by Rubens, was given by Yale and the north porch of the church was restored by graduates of the university. A public footpath leads a mile and a half northeast from Wrexham to **Erddig Park,** where Yale lived with his parents. In 1973 the house was deeded to the National Trust, and it is well worth visiting.

• Leave Wrexham north on the A483. The road passes through **Gresford,** which was the scene for 'The Angler' in Washington Irving's *Sketch-Book.* The church here is quite fine, and a visit to its churchyard, adorned by a massive yew, is perhaps as good a final stop in Wales as you could ask. 9 miles beyond is Chester, the Grosvenor Hotel, bed and a chance to drop your hire car and return by rail to London.

WHAT TO READ   Tennyson, Irving, and Dylan Thomas, as the tour suggests, may be read as you travel. Of Thomas, read in particular *Under Milk Wood*, *Portrait of the Artist as a Young Dog* and *In Country Sleep*. Sample the *Mabinogion* while in Wales. Of course, read Richard Llewellyn's *How Green Was My Valley* while here. Perhaps struggle again with Spenser's *Faerie Queen*, now to finish it. It is interesting that such prolific mystery writers as Agatha Christie, John Creasey (who wrote well over 500 books under various names) and Andrew Garve (who ranges far and wide for different settings) seem not to have been attracted to the Welsh countryside. There are dozens of Scottish-based works of detective fiction but few of quality that are set in Wales. However, while staying in a Welsh country hotel, look amongst the shelves for Walter H. Boore's *The Valley and the Shadow*, which is strong on Welsh character types; Christianna Brand's lesser work *Cat and Mouse*; and Eden Phillpotts' *Deed Without a Name*. Phillpotts usually writes of his beloved Devon, but he appears to know Wales too. However, here one's reading must generally be a bit more serious.

Discover Arthur Machen, born at Caerleon and a delightful teller of tales; read Robert Browning, who lived for a time in Llangollen; perhaps above all, wrestle if you never have before with that most complex of poets, Gerard Manley Hopkins, who lived and taught, as a Jesuit convert, at St Beuno's College in St Asaph (on the A55). The River Elwy passes to the west, and of its valley he wrote:

> Lovely the woods, waters, meadows, coombes, vales,
> All the air things wear that build this world of Wales . . .

He felt, Hopkins wrote, the 'instress and charm of Wales', and his poetry is uplifted with that same instress.

16   Scotland

The culture of Scotland is very different from that of England, and you will not travel long or far without realizing this. The Scots (the people) and Scotch (the drink) both travel well, and the ties between America and Scotland are many. Indeed, were one to write of the Highland Clans of Scotland alone – of the Clans Macduff, Hamilton, Stewart, Donald, Morrison, Campbell, Grant, Macpherson, Cameron, Ross, Sinclair, Lindsay (the list numbers over 60 clans) – one would be able to mention hundreds of ancestral sites with close American connections. One must just assume that members of the Hay family in America already know that Delgatie Castle is where they should seek out the Clan Hay society, and that quite possibly members of the Chisholm family do not care – preferring to visit Loch Mullardoch. If one is a Kerr, then it is to the Lowlands and Jedburgh that one goes. Still, although American connections are close, the actual number of specifically American-related sites that still stand in Scotland is relatively small.

As with most of the tours in this book, travel by automobile is assumed. One can see quite a bit of Scotland by rail, and the overnight West Highlands Express from King's Cross Station, in London, to Fort William is a dramatic introduction to the area, especially as the country above Glasgow is seen in the morning's light. You may also travel by rail from Edinburgh to Inverness, via Aberdeen, in comfort. Nonetheless, much of Scotland can be penetrated only by road, and a motor car is essential if you are to see the far north, the islands, or the Lowlands at all well. Accordingly, the following itinerary is laid out as a circuit from Edinburgh, the city where most visitors to Scotland begin their touring. I have

EDINBURGH

suggested a total of ten days (plus at least one for Edinburgh), although more will be required if you wish to explore the islands.

Scotland is changing, and if you have not visited it recently, you will find that the North Sea oil discoveries in particular have already brought their good and their ill, in a quickened economic pace (that is helping to slow the steady outward migration of young Scots to London and south-east England) and in threats to the serenity of the Highlands and coastal areas, which have served as a vital lung for not only Britain but Europe as well. Tourism is also changing, and you will encounter better facilities today than ever before. While really first-rate restaurants are still scarce, a meal in a small country hotel in Scotland is likely to be superior to its counterpart in England or Wales. Skiing has been developed at Aviemore, a fine wildlife park has been opened at Kingussie, the township of Drumbuie has been rescued from the developers, and new visitor facilities – called Landmark, and providing excellent displays on the natural history of the area, as well as selling Scottish books, foods and crafts – have been opened at Carrbridge in the Highlands and Stirling near the Trossachs. There are several well-maintained properties owned by the National Trust for Scotland, which is quite independent of the National Trust in England and Wales. And while not set up as well as one might wish, opportunities to visit Harris tweed mills, or as many as forty-four Highlands and Islands distilleries where the superb unblended malts are made, add a further dimension to touring in Scotland. (There are also three fine unblended Lowland malts.)

You can fly from Heathrow, London, to Edinburgh, to begin the circle tour, or (as I much prefer) approach Scotland more slowly by taking the early morning express from King's Cross Station, London, having the best British Rail breakfast going, and arriving in Edinburgh, 393 miles away, about seven hours later. There are also night trains, if you prefer, with good sleeping car accommodation. I have also twice flown directly to Aberdeen, and twice directly to Inverness, in order to begin touring well to the north. Near the northern tip of Scotland, at Wick, there is a grassy airport from which a daily flight will deposit you back at Edinburgh, if you prefer to drive to John o'Groats – always said to be the northernmost point in Britain – without facing the return journey. You can reach most of the Inner Hebrides by ferries from the mainland, but you will probably want to fly (even though ferries exist) if you wish to visit the Outer Hebrides, or the Orkney and Shetland Islands.

Edinburgh   You can quite fruitfully spend several days in Edinburgh, especially when the Festival is on in late August and early September. A variety of theatre and art shows, opera and music, as well as the Edinburgh Military Tattoo – held each evening within Edinburgh Castle – make this city second only to London in the range of activities available to the visitor at this time of year. Separate guides are published annually to the Festival, and the description here must be limited to those places you would wish to visit whether or not the Festival were a competing attraction.

A city of slightly less than 500,000, Edinburgh is second to Glasgow in size, but it has been the capital and the cultural focus of Scotland since 1437. Its ties with America are legion, for virtually any American writer or statesman who visited Britain sought out, and commented upon, this handsome, greystone citadel of the north. You can walk to most of the places of interest in Edinburgh, so you need not have a car until you are ready to leave the city. If you arrive by train, stay at the Carlton Hotel, a rather ugly but comfortable hostelry directly on North Bridge next to the railway station.

For meals, there are several acceptable restaurants, and two that are outstanding. One is **Prestonfield House** (book) – a taxi is required – and worth visiting for itself as well as for the food. Many famous people have dined here, including Benjamin Franklin. The other is Houstoun House, at Uphall, near Livingston, west of Edinburgh. Both are open for lunch and dinner. I had what I consider to be the finest meal I've ever eaten in Britain at the latter, where you may begin the evening by sampling your way through a number of malt whiskies, and then move on to a set, and always imaginative, menu. You should book, and to reach Houstoun House, take the M8 west past Turnhouse airport, exit at the Livingston interchange, pass under to the north side of the motorway, and follow the signs.

CANONGATE TOLBOOTH, EDINBURGH

Begin with Edinburgh Castle. Dominating the city, the castle offers fine views over Edinburgh. Its oldest part, St Margaret's Chapel, dates from 1100. The Scottish National War Memorial (on the Palace Yard), the Great Hall of James IV, and the Honours of Scotland (the Scottish Crown Jewels) should be seen, and if you are in the castle grounds at 1.00 p.m., go to the Half-Moon Battery to see the daily gun discharged. Oddly, a bit of the Esplanade is Nova Scotian territory. Both the Royal Scots Regimental Museum and the **Scottish United Services Museum** are within the castle, and the latter contains many objects relating to the activities of the Scottish regiments in the American Revolution. In the Naval Section there is a display on John Paul Jones.

Now walk the Royal Mile, the collective name for the ancient streets which form the main route down the hill from the Castle to Holyrood-house. The sites here include **Old St Paul's** (where there is a Samuel Seabury chapel); Lady Stair's House, where there are exhibits on Scott, Stevenson and Burns; Riddle's Court, where David Hume lived; Brodie's Close, where the original of Stevenson's Dr Jekyll and Mr Hyde (Deacon William Brodie) resided; and **St Giles' Cathedral,** the High Kirk of Edin-burgh, where John Knox was the minister – thirty-nine of the Colours of former Scottish regiments, including those that served in the American Revolution, hang from the pillars of the interior. Note the cobbles in the area by the cathedral that mark the site of Old Tolbooth, a prison referred to as the 'Heart of Midlothian'; the old Mercat Cross; Gladstone's Land (open Mon.–Fri., 2–5), an old house with fine wooden ceilings; the Parliament House, in which the Act of Union with England was agreed to in 1707; and the **Museum of Childhood.** Several American toys, Mc-Guffey's Readers, and books for American Indian children are included here.

At the end of the High Street, still on the Royal Mile, is the John Knox House, containing relics relating to Knox. You then enter Canongate, where many restored houses attest to the city's desire to maintain its char-acter. Adam Smith is buried in Canongate churchyard. Nearby is an excellent shop where you may purchase mohair blankets, a particularly good buy in Scotland. The walk ends at Holyroodhouse, begun about 1500. You may tour the grounds, and if the Queen is not in residence, see the State Apartments. Most interesting of all is the Royal Portrait Gallery and the rooms of Mary, Queen of Scots. Holyrood Abbey stands in ruins nearby. Above rises Arthur's Seat, an easy climb with fine views.

Now a quick taxi to Greyfriars Church, where you may begin a second walking tour. It was in the churchyard here that the National Covenant – to resist the Anglican faith as interpreted by Charles I – was signed. The church is better known for the statue of Greyfriars Bobby, a terrier, which stands outside: when Bobby's master died and was interred in the churchyard, the dog watched over the grave for fourteen years, and was buried next to his master by the city. To the south is the new part of the **University of Edinburgh** – the old library, now a Senate chamber, is worth seeing if the caretaker will unlock it for you. James Blair, founder of the College of William and Mary, and James Geddes, founder of Iowa State University, studied here. To the north is the exceedingly fine Royal Scot-tish Museum, covering a range from the Stone Age to space flights (open weekdays 10–5, Sun. 2–5). Beyond, off George IV Bridge, is the National Library of Scotland, dating from 1682, with two million books and varied permanent exhibits.

Continue northwest, across the Royal Mile, and down The Mound, with views over the new city. From here one can sometimes sense why Edin-burgh was called Auld Reekie, even though the industrial smoke is now quite modest. To the right is the Royal Scottish Academy and **National Gallery.** The former holds exhibitions of the work of current members of the Academy, while the Gallery contains fine Old Masters, Cézannes, the National Collection of Scottish art to 1900, and work by John James Audubon, Benjamin West and other Americans. It is open weekdays 10–5, and until 8 during the Festival.

You are now on Princes Street, a handsome road running along opposite the castle. To the right is the 200-foot spire of the memorial to Sir Walter Scott; immediately to the left is the oldest floral clock in the world, requiring 25,000 flowers to complete it. Follow the West Princes Street Gardens to Castle Street, which runs north at right angles to Princes Street; here, at no. 30, Kenneth Grahame, of *The Wind in the Willows*, was born; and at no. 39 Sir Walter Scott wrote most of his Waverley novels. Turn left one block into Charlotte Square, the most handsome square in the city and a triumph of the New Edinburgh, designed in 1792 by Robert Adam. The north side is especially handsome and, with its returned ends, better than anything in London. Lord Lister, who pioneered antiseptic surgery, lived at no. 9; Earl Haig was born in no. 24. The National Trust of Scotland has its offices in the square, and you may buy pamphlets on each of the Trust properties to be visited. South Charlotte Street, which runs out of the square to Princes Street, is the birthplace (no. 16) of Alexander Graham Bell. A quarter-mile to the southwest, off Queensferry Street, is **St Mary's Cathedral,** the seat of the Scottish Episcopal Church, which is a separate self-governing branch of the Anglican Church, and the second largest ecclesiastical structure in Scotland. Samuel Seabury, first bishop of the American Episcopal Church, was associated with this church (although not on its present site, as the present building dates from 1874). He is recalled in a print in the Kirkland Memorial, inside.

Return through Charlotte Square and walk the length of George Street, where there are especially good shops, to St Andrews Square. Leave the square from the northeast corner; one block north is the **Scottish National Portrait Gallery.** Open weekdays 10–5, Sunday 2–5 (to 8 during Festival weekdays), this gallery shares space with the National Museum of Antiquities. If you have wondered what Robert Burns, Thomas Carlyle, Flora Macdonald – who sailed for America in 1774 – James Boswell, David Hume, or the Earl of Dunmore (colonial governor of New York and Virginia) looked like, this is the place to find out. There are four good John Singer Sargents, as well as work by other American artists.

Strike east on York Place; Sir Henry Raeburn lived at no. 32. Next comes Picardy Place; at no. 11, Sir Arthur Conan Doyle was born. To the right is the Roman Catholic Cathedral. Now return west along Queen Street, through the Queen Street Gardens, and Hanover Street, to Heriot Row, where at no. 17 Robert Louis Stevenson lived from 1857 until 1879.

Return to Hanover Street and catch a bus running north; get out near no. 8 Howard Place, the house where Stevenson was born. 200 yards ahead, off Inverleith Row, is the entrance to the Royal Botanic Garden and Arboretum. (Opposite the entrance is a modest hotel, Inverleith House, which we have always found comfortable and inexpensive.) Here too is the **Scottish National Gallery of Modern Art,** housing the National Gallery's 20th century collection (open weekdays 10–6, Sun. 2–6). Here there is work by Matisse, Picasso, Giacometti, and several Americans including Jackson Pollock, Robert Motherwell and Peter Hurd. In summer the gallery remains open until dusk, and it is a good place to finish the day, before having a leisurely dinner or going to the Tattoo.

• Two interesting excursions may be taken from Edinburgh, to the east and to the south. The first, to the Border Country and to Abbotsford, the home of Sir Walter Scott, is not described in detail here, but you may have a quick taste of it by leaving Edinburgh south on the A702, thence on the A701 and the A703 to Milton Bridge where the Scottish Infantry regiments maintain a museum, and thus on to Peebles. Here at the heart of Peeblesshire (sometimes called Tweeddale) one is in what may be called John Buchan country, and anyone who has thrilled to his novels will want to explore the area with care. He passed his holidays at his grandparents' house, The Green, in Broughton (west on the A72, south on the B712, and right on a country road) and his uncanny ability to invoke the feel and smell of the Scottish landscape came from these years. *John Burnet of Barns* is based on Barns house in the village. From Peebles drive east on the A72 to Innerleithen. Here is Traquair House, the longest-inhabited mansion in Scotland. Its old brewhouse has been restored to what it was 200 years ago. The ale, over twice as strong as most, is unique to the house, which itself is one of the most interesting in Scotland (open July 1–Sept. 30, daily except Fri., 1.30–5.30; also Sun. from mid-May, and Wed. and Sat. in June). Then continue to Selkirk.

• Or you may explore the farmlands of East Lothian for a quiet day. Drive east from Edinburgh on the A1 and the A198 to Gullane. Here is Muirfield golf course, home of the Honourable Company of Edinburgh Golfers, and thought to be the oldest golf club in the world. (La Potinière is a fine restaurant.) The green countryside of East Lothian is known as the Holy Land of Golf. Return on the A6137 to Haddington, the handsome county town which is well worth walking in. Then follow the B6369 to **Gifford,** where John Witherspoon, signer of the Declaration of Independence for New Jersey and President of Princeton, was born. (Beyond is Yester Castle and a lonely country road across the Lammermuir Hills to Duns, thence via the A6105 and the B6364 to **Kelso,** ancestral home of William Hooper.) Return to Edinburgh from Gifford on the B6355, past Winton House, to the A1 at Tranent.

FIRST DAY

Leave Edinburgh going west on the A90, following postings for Queensferry. At the city's edge, divert right for **Lauriston Castle** (posted), the early home of John Law, the speculator responsible for the famous Mississippi bubble. The castle contains an excellent collection of Blue John ware and wool mosaics (open April–Oct., daily except Fri. 11–1, 2–5; Nov.–March, Sat.–Sun., same hours). Continue on to Queensferry in West Lothian; drive through the village and under the railway bridge, in order to see both it and the highest and longest road bridge in Britain, capable of taking the world's heaviest load. The Hawes Inn at Queensferry is where the abduction of David Balfour was planned in Stevenson's *Kidnapped*. Continue west, now on the A904, to Hopetoun House at Abercorn. Seat of the Marquis of Linlithgow, this is Scotland's finest mansion, and the gardens – styled on Versailles – are also handsome. The house holds paintings by Rembrandt, Rubens and Titian, excellent Chippendale, and fine silks (open May 3–Sept. 21, daily except Thurs.–Fri., 1.30–5.30).

Proceed on the A904 through B'ness (actually Borrowstounness), which lies at the eastern end of the Antonine Wall, a Roman fortification stretching west to the River Clyde. Beyond is Kinneil House, a 16th century structure with good wall and ceiling paintings. Behind the house is James Watt's steam engine, for he experimented in the park here. Turn back briefly, then right on the A706 to Linlithgow, here to see the Palace (open April–Sept., daily, 9.30–7, Sun. 2–7; Oct.–March, close 4) in which Mary, Queen of Scots, was born. Then return to the Forth Road Bridge (this time to cross it) by taking the B9080 from Linlithgow to Kirkliston, and following the postings.

When crossing the bridge, watch for postings for **Dunfermline.** Scotland's capital for six centuries, this hilly town contains the graves of many of Scotland's kings, including Robert the Bruce. Dunfermline Abbey Church should be visited, especially for its nave; go also to Pittencrieff Park, given to the city by Andrew Carnegie, the American industrialist who was born here. The cottage of his birth is a museum, and the birthplace memorial on Moodie Street contains A. H. Sorson's painting of the blast furnace of the Carnegie Steel Company in Pittsburgh in 1910. Leave Dunfermline on the A994, joining the A985, to Culross. Much of this Royal Burgh is under the protection of the National Trust of Scotland, and its red-tiled buildings and cobbled streets are among the most attractive in the country.

You must then choose between two routes running from Culross to Dundee. The first is the more interesting, and will require the rest of the day. The second is more leisurely and would also permit reaching beyond Dundee for the night.

Option One Turn back on the A985 toward Dunfermline, continue to its junction with the M90, and thence onto the A92 for **Kirkcaldy.** John Paul Jones anchored here in 1779, demanded £200,000 not to destroy it, and was driven away by adverse winds. Adam Smith was born in Kirkcaldy in 1723; his authorship of *The Wealth of Nations,* the first great free trade classic, in 1776, is regarded here as an event at least as significant as the Revolution that occurred in the same year. A plaque commemorates him in the High Street. Robert Adam, the architect, was born here, and Thomas Carlyle lived in the Kirk Wynd. **The Kirkcaldy Museum and Art Gallery,** on War Memorial Square, contains work by local and American artists, including Howell Dyer and Henry Muhrmann. (If you continue along the coast on the A955 to East Wemyss, where the castle of Shakespeare's Macduff stands, and then on the A915, you reach Lower Largo, where there is a statue to Alexander Selkirk. It was Selkirk's lonely five years on Juan Fernandez island, beginning in 1704, which formed the basis for the story of Robinson Crusoe.)

From Kirkcaldy, follow the A92 inland to its junction with the A912, then go left to Falkland, to visit the handsome Falkland Palace. Now owned by the Queen, this palace (open late March to mid-Oct., weekdays 1–6, Sun. 2–6) was a hunting lodge of the Stuarts. The Royal Tennis Court is the oldest in Scotland (1539) and the State Apartments are worth seeing. Continue then to the A91, thence to St Andrews.

St Andrews is set apart from all else in Scotland by its water-girt ruined cathedral, dating from the 12th century; fine ruined castle; ancient (1410) university (which gave Benjamin Franklin the honorary doctorate by which he was known as 'Dr Franklin'); and the Royal and Ancient Golf Club (1754). Golfers come from around the world to play the Old Course here, and anyone may do so for a fee. There is a good restaurant on the top floor of the Old Course Hotel, which looks out across the course. James Wilson was born at **Carskerdo,** near St Andrews, in 1742; it was he who most powerfully developed the argument, while speaking for the colony of Pennsylvania, that Parliament was capable of unconstitutional acts, and he was a major proponent of independence.

Dundee, on the far side of the Firth of Tay, north of St Andrews, is Scotland's fourth largest city. It is best known for Dundee marmalade, first made by Mrs Keiller in 1797, for Dundee cakes, and for jute manufacturing. Camperdown House (with a golfing museum) and the **City Art Gallery and Museum** on Albert Square, containing a huge painting by John Singleton Copley of the Battle of Camperdown, are worth visiting. While the cathedral, opposite the university, is dour, the Shipping and Industrial Museum on Barrack Street is quite interesting.

You may spend the night in Dundee, at the modern Angus Hotel, or move on 12 miles on the A930 to Carnoustie, for a rather better bed and meal at the Bruce Hotel near the famous golf links. Even if you are

not a golfer, take time to see this course, which is often said to be one
of the two or three finest in the world. For breakfast, have Arbroath
smokies – salted, smoked haddock.

Option Two   If golf and St Andrews do not attract, continue west from
Culross on the country road to Kincardine, birthplace of John Dewar,
of whisky fame, inventor of the vacuum bottle in which you may carry
the national drink of Scotland with you (but make it coffee for the road).
Turn right on the A977, then left on the A907, to visit Alloa, the main
town of Scotland's smallest county, Clackmannan. (10 miles would carry
you to its far side, near Stirling.) At Alloa, bear north on the A908 and
the A91 into Kinross, on Loch Leven, the county town for Kinross-shire.
In the lake are the ruins of Loch Leven Castle, from which Mary, Queen
of Scots, escaped in 1568.

Now pick up the M90 just west of Kinross, to run north (soon on the
A90) to Perth, the Fair City. The castle contains **The Black Watch
Regimental Museum,** one of the best in Scotland. Since the Black Watch
played an important role in both the Seven Years' War and the American
Revolution (during the latter, in India), the museum holds many relevant
objects (open May 1–Sept. 3, Mon.–Fri., 10–12, 2–4.30, closing 3.30
rest of the year). The Black Watch Pipe Band played at the funeral of
John F. Kennedy. Branklyn Gardens are said to be the finest small gardens in Scotland. (20 miles further west are the fine Drummond Castle
Gardens.) Just north of Perth is Scone, coronation place of Scotland's
kings (the last, Charles II, in 1651). Alas – say Scottish Nationalists –
the Stone of Scone is in Westminster Abbey.

You can now drive from Perth east to Dundee on the A85, 22 miles,
and rejoin the main tour described under Option One.

SECOND DAY

Whether beginning in Dundee or Carnoustie, start the day with a drive to
Glamis (pronounced 'Glarms') the attractive town for Glamis Castle
(open May–Sept., Sun.–Thurs., 2–5.30) which contains excellent portraits, furniture and weapons. Princess Margaret was born here in 1930,
and Shakespeare called Macbeth the Thane of Glamis. In the village
itself are several restored cottages, in which the Angus Folk Museum
teaches you about farm life (open Easter–Sept., daily 1–6). Follow the
A928 north to Kirriemuir, where J. M. Barrie was born at 9 Brechin
Road (open April –Oct., daily 10–12.30, 2–6, and by appointment: Kirriemuir 2646). He is buried in the cemetery here. Author of sentimental
tales about country towns, glens and crofts, Barrie is most famous as a
playwright – author of *The Little Minister* (in which Kirriemuir appears
as Thrums), *Quality Street, The Admirable Crichton,* and of course
Peter Pan, the boy who won't grow up. The house was saved only when

GLAMIS CASTLE

it was reported that it was to be taken down stone by stone and rebuilt as a museum in the United States.

Now take the A926 east to Forfar, county town of Angus, in the Vale of Strathmore, and thence on the B9134 to Brechin. Stop to see the cathedral, then go north on the A94 and the B966 to Edzell Castle and Gardens (open April–Sept., weekdays 9.30–7, Sun. 2–7; Oct.–March, close 4), ancestral stronghold of the Lindsays. The walled garden is unique. Continue east on the B966 through Fettercairn and the green Howe of the Mearns. Turn left on the B974 as far as the old Clatterin' Brig, immediately right on a country road down Strath Finella and thence to the coast at Inverbervie. North on the A92 is Dunnottar Castle, the most dramatic ruin on the eastern side of Scotland, set on a rock in the sea and reached by a path from the shore. Scott's *Old Mortality* was based on a stonemason who worked in the churchyard here. North again is Aberdeen.

Aberdeen, Scotland's third largest city, is built of granite, and it is at once clean-lined and dour. Among notable Americans born here was General Hugh Mercer, founder of Mercersburg, Pennsylvania, who fell in the Battle of Princeton in 1777. Make sure you see the Cathedral of St Andrew's, and the famous Church of St Nicholas, divided into two churches by a transept. Two old town-houses may be viewed: Provost Skene's (the better) and Provost Ross'. The architecture of both Marischal (Mercer studied here) and Gordon's colleges should be seen, and next to the latter is the **Aberdeen Art Gallery and Regional Museum** (once a school where Lord Byron studied) which includes Epstein bronzes, several John Singer Sargents and work by other American artists. North on the A92 is the major portion of the old university and the handsome old St Machair's Cathedral.

You will probably wish to spend the night not far beyond Aberdeen. If taking the first alternative for the third day (below) leave Aberdeen north on the A92, then left on the B999 to Pitmedden. Here is a fine 17th century garden maintained by the National Trust. In four parterres with elaborate designs, 30,000 annuals are planted each year in May. The grounds are open all year and daily, 9.30 to dusk. A mile north is Tolquhon Castle, seat of the Forbes family. The night can then be spent most happily in Old Meldrum, 5 miles west on the B920, in the Meldrum House Hotel, open from April 1 to mid-November.

If taking the second alternative (below) leave Aberdeen southwest on the A93 to Banchory, a Deeside town where you may see how lavender is distilled at the lavender water factory, and from an observation platform watch salmon leap the rapids in the spring. The Tor-na-Coille and Raemoir Hotels are both good. Before reaching Banchory you pass Crathes Castle, a fairytale structure with fine painted ceilings and attractive gardens.

THIRD DAY

Option One   From Old Meldrum take the B922 south to Inverurie, then the A96 northwest to the B9002, thus left to Leith Hall. Built in 1650, the hall has been the home of the Leith and Hay families ever since (open May–Sept., weekdays 11–1, 2–6, Sun. 2–6; gardens all year 11–dusk). Beyond, join the A97 right to Huntly, where the ruined castle is the ancestral stronghold of the Gordon chiefs. Turn northeast on the A97 to the B9025, then turn east to Turriff. Delgatie Castle, 2 miles northeast, is the headquarters of the Clan Hay. Drive north on the A947, then right on the B9105 past Craigston Castle to the A98, east to New Pitsligo, and north on an unnumbered country road to Pennan, felt by many to be the most attractive fishing village on the coast of Scotland. From here drive west on the B9031 to Macduff.

Follow the A98 to Banff and beyond turn left on the A95 for Keith. Just short of Keith a road right takes you to **Newmill,** birthplace of James Gordon Bennett, founder of the New York *Herald,* which was the first newspaper to exploit sensational journalism, use headlines, and incorporate maps into news items. The Strath Isla distillery at Keith is the oldest in Scotland. (Dufftown, 10 miles southwest on the B9014, is also famous for its distilleries.) Follow the A941 north from Dufftown to join with Option Two at Craigellachie; continue north on the A941, then right on the B9015 to Fochabers, to spend the night in the pleasant Gordon Arms Hotel, which serves traditional Scottish dishes.

Option Two   At Banchory turn north on the A980 to Craigievar Castle (open May–Sept., Wed, Thurs, Sun., 2–7, also Sat. in July–Aug.), virtually unaltered since 1626. Return down the A980 to a country road marked for Aboyne (on the A93) where you rejoin the River Dee highway, and continue up the Dee to Ballater. Cross the river to the B976 and hold to the bank of the Dee as far as Balmoral Castle (one views it best after crossing the river to the north bank again, and driving a mile further west on the A93). The castle is a royal residence, not open to the public. Where the B976 rejoins the A93 is Crathie Parish Church, opened in 1895, in which there are many royal memorials and mementoes to Queen Victoria and her consort, Prince Albert. Then continue on westwards to Braemar, where the Royal Highland Gathering is held each September.

At Braemar the A93 turns abruptly south, to climb over the mountains via the Devil's Elbow, through the Spittal of Glenshee, to Blairgowrie, 34 miles away. Just beyond Blairgowrie take the A923 west to Dunkeld, in the Strath Tay, the point at which you begin the climb up the Tay and Tummel to the pass of Killiecrankie. South of Dunkeld via the A984 is **Murthly Castle,** where you may see two of Alfred Jacob Miller's paintings of Sir William Drummond Stewart. Dunkeld's ruined cathedral dates from the 9th century. From here proceed north on the A9 (the Atholl Way) to Pitlochry, a holiday resort with a summer festival theatre, hydropathic baths and a salmon ladder. You then enter the Pass of Killiecrankie, where on the higher ground above in 1689 Viscount Dundee (Scott's 'Bonnie Dundee') won a Jacobite victory and lost his life in the doing. The National Trust maintains an information post in the pass. At Blair Atholl the Way ends. From Dunkeld the roadside has been planted with many types of trees, including some Oregon cypress just south of Pitlochry. These plantations end at **Diana's Grove,** a unique collection dating from 1880, next to the car park at Blair Castle. The imposing castle is one of the finest in Scotland, although its castellation dates only from the 19th century (open May to mid-Oct., weekdays 10–6, Sun. 2–6, also Sun.–Mon. in April); it is the home of the Chiefs of the Name of Murray.

Continue now on the A9 to the top of Glen Garry, through the Forest of Atholl, over the Grampians and into Newtonmore. Here is the Clan Macpherson House and Museum (open daily 10–12, 2–6, except Sun.). Left and southwest on the A86 is **Cluny Castle.** Duncan Macpherson, who fought with the Fraser Highlanders in the war against the American colonies, is buried nearby. Further north on the A9 is Kingussie, where the excellent Highland Folk Museum (open daily May–Sept. except Sun., 10–1, 2–5) contains exhibits relating to domestic life. At Aviemore, north again, the British have developed a thoroughly modern skiing resort

BALMORAL CASTLE

with all the facilities one expects. The impact of the wide highway and modern developments as you drive east on the B951 and then up the slopes of Cairngorm into the Glen More National Forest Park is not an entirely happy one. At the end of the road a chairlift will take you nearly to the summit for views over the Cairngorm Mountains.

Soon after Aviemore, turn right on the A95 to proceed down the Strathspey. This winding, green valley is the heart of the Scotch whisky industry, and if you are interested, it is the place to sample the widest variety. The stream is regarded as one of the finest for fishing in Scotland. The 'capital' of the district is Grantown-on-Spey, founded in 1776 by Sir James Grant. The hill of Craigellachie is the traditional gathering place for the Clan Grant; its meaning, 'Stand Fast', provides the name for one of Grant's best whiskies. There are several good hotels in Grantown, with the Palace and the Grant Arms both quite pleasant. Craigellachie, where you unite with Option One, above, is 24 miles ahead on the A95.

FOURTH DAY

Now head towards Inverness, via the A941 and Elgin, along the northern edge of Moray and Nairn. At **Elgin** there is a fine ruined cathedral, once called the Lantern of the North; Alexander Graham Bell was a schoolmaster here, at Weston House Academy. Beyond Forres, about 4 miles after crossing the river, is Macbeth's Hillock where Macbeth met the three weird sisters. 2½ miles further on the right is a fine 17th century doocot (dovecote) after which one reaches Nairn, a handsome town with my favorite Scottish hotel, the Clifton. Leave Nairn south on the B9090 to reach Cawdor Castle, built by its Thane in 1454, the seat of the Campbell clan, and still privately inhabited. Ahead lies Culloden – left on the B9091 into the B9006, 8 miles – the best-marked battle site in Britain. Here the troops of George II, commanded by his son, the Duke of Cumberland, defeated those of Bonnie Prince Charlie on April 16, 1746, cutting the Highland force to pieces and pursuing it savagely. Only here is one able to gain a full picture of the meaning of the Rising of 1745 ('The "Forty-Five"'). Visit the Clava Stones, nearby – ancient stone circles dating from 3000 B.C., and the best set of prehistoric cairns in Scotland.

Inverness, known as the Capital of the North, is a bustling town of 30,000. General Ulysses S. Grant was an honorary burgess here. At the Caledonian Hotel in Church Street, you can usually count on a haggis. See the castle, the Inverness Museum and Art Gallery (open Mon.–Sat. 9–5) and the statue of Flora Macdonald on the Esplanade. There is a Highland Craft shop in Abertarff House, in Church Street, and across the river and the Caledonian Canal is the 19th century cathedral.

Loch Ness lies to the south via the A82, and a pleasant drive down one side and up the other offers views from all angles, as well as the best opportunity to look out for the Loch Ness monster. The loch is 24 miles long, a mile wide, and 800 feet deep. Just beyond Drumnadrochit is ruined Urquhart Castle; it was from near here that one of the only possibly authentic photographs of the monster was taken. A mile further on is a cairn to John Cobb, opposite the point where the racing driver's speed boat blew up, and just ahead may be caravans of the **Loch Ness Phenomenon Group,** which has devoted several years to monitoring the lake in search of the monster. A portion of the project is American-manned and financed. At Fort Augustus, double back on the east side of the loch, first on the A862 and then the B852, which rejoins the A862 at Dores. Coming into Inverness you encounter Pringles Holm Tweed Mills, where you may buy tweeds and tartans and also see them woven.

Leave Inverness west on the A9 via Beauly (the ruined priory is worth visiting) and Muir of Ord to Dingwall, county town for Ross and Cromarty. (At Muir of Ord you may turn right, if you have time, to explore the Black Isle, a low-lying agricultural area. The A832 runs to Fortrose, where there is a ruined 12th century cathedral, and on to Cromarty, a tiny town of rambling roses and narrow streets. You then circuit back down the Isle on the B9163 to **Balblair.** The Rosses of Balblair included Colonel George Ross, one of the signatories of the Declaration of Independence, and John Ross, husband to Betsy. Continue to join the A9 again at Cononbridge.)

FIFTH DAY

It is at Dingwall that the road to the 'far north' begins. There is much of interest in the region to the north and west of Inverness, and there are several good local guide books that provide detailed commentary. American-related sites are few. The few towns along the A9 include Milton, with **Balnagown Castle,** stronghold of the Chiefs of Ross, and the ancestral home of Betsy Ross. Dornoch, via the A949, is the site of the last legal execution for witchcraft in Scotland (1722) and of a fine little 13th century cathedral. This is the county town for Sutherland, and with fewer than 1,000 people is the smallest such in Britain. Wick, further north on the coast, is the flight departure point for the Orkney and Shetland Islands, or back to Inverness.

• The Orkney Islands lie across the Pentland Firth from the mainland. You may either fly to Kirkwall Airport or go by ferry from Scrabster (beyond Thurso) to Stromness. The trip takes two and a half hours, and the return journey can be made the next day. This leaves sufficient time for a drive around the whole of the island somewhat beguilingly called Mainland.

• The Orkneys and Shetlands were settled by Norsemen and ruled by them until 1468, when Norway ceded them to Scotland. The Orkneys consist of some sixty-five islands, thirty of them inhabited, with a population of 18,000. While the Orkney islanders farm, the Shetland islanders fish. There are over one hundred Shetlands, only fifteen inhabited, with another 18,000 people.

• On Orkney, you should visit Kirkwall to see St Magnus's Cathedral, founded in 1137, and Tankerness House, with a museum and art gallery. On the south side of the island is the great natural inlet of Scapa Flow, where the *Royal Oak* was sunk in World War II by a German submarine, taking nearly 800 men down with her. It was here that seventy-four vessels of the German fleet were scuttled in 1919. 9 miles northwest of Kirkwall, off the A965, is Maes Howe, the best Stone Age tomb of its type in Britain.

• You reach the Shetland Islands by flying into Sumburgh Airport at the southern tip of Mainland (yes! again) where you can hire a car for the 75-mile drive to the top of the island. You can also come by ferry from Kirkwall (8 hours) or Aberdeen (12 hours). The airfield is closer to the Arctic Circle than it is to London, and in any season warm clothing is needed.

• South of Sumburgh, 24 miles, is Britain's remote, inhabited Fair Isle, with a population of 50. Twice a week a supply boat sails to it from Grutness. The entire island is a National Trust property famed for bird-watching, and for the world's most exclusive woolly, the Fair Isle sweater. You can probably afford a tea cosy.

John o' Groats is traditionally said to be the northernmost point in Britain. Further west is Dunnet Head, actually the most northerly point, with a chilling view. Beyond Thurso the A836 narrows down to a single track road and, for 100 miles, dips, churns, and thrusts its way through a difficult landscape. The County of Sutherland, the most sparsely settled part of Britain, has a population of seven people per square mile (well below the level usually defined as a 'frontier') against the British average of 586. After Durness you pass through extensive peat-cutting lands. Beyond Unapool, turn right on the B869, along the edge of some of the oldest mountains in the world. At Lochinver, turn south to Inverkirkaig, where the road deteriorates badly. Passing through the Inverpolly Nature Reserve you emerge on an unnumbered road (right) to Achiltibuie, opposite the Summer Isles. (Boats leave every morning to circle the isles.) The Summer Isles Hotel is a good spot for the night.

SIXTH DAY

Now strike inland to find the A835, then south to Ullapool, the largest community – but still less than 1,000 – in this vast region. The road runs past the **Lael Forest Garden,** which contains 150 species of trees and shrubs, including many American. Turn seawards again on the A832, past Gruinard Bay – the island offshore was the scene of germ warfare experiments in World War II, and it is still contaminated with anthrax – to the **Inverewe Gardens.** Begun in 1865, these are the most famous gardens in Scotland (open daily 10–dusk all year). Several pleasant hours can be passed here, especially in spring; there are over 75 different species in a special plot devoted to American plants.

Beyond Poolewe the road to Loch Torridon via the A832 and the A896 is especially beautiful. Drive the unnumbered road to the Applecross Hotel over one of the highest (2053 feet) and the steepest (1 in 4 gradient) climbs in Britain, the Pass of the Cattle. Then retrace the route to follow the A896 to the A890, and take the lovely Loch Carron road to the A87. Turn east briefly to the enchanting scene of Eilean Donan Castle, readily recognizable from the many posters of it issued by the Travel Authority. Built in 1220, rebuilt in 1932, it contains the MacRae clan museum (open Easter–Oct., daily 10–12.30, 2–6). Now go back along the A87 to Kyle of Lochalsh.

• Two islands above all others are places of pilgrimage for travellers: Skye and Iona. The first lies directly across the narrow kyle (or strait) of Lochalsh, and is reached in ten minutes by a ferry that operates every half-hour. On Skye, drive especially the dead-end road to Elgol, through some of the best of the island's Ice Age evidence, the always gloomy Cuillin Hills. See the distillery for Talisker, at Carbost, which you may tour by calling ahead; and **Dunvegan Castle,** headquarters of the Clan

Macleod (open April–Oct., daily except Sun., 2–5, July to mid-Sept. open at 1). John Paul Jones attacked the castle during his raids on the Scottish coast. Beyond Uig the road passes the grave of Flora Macdonald (right) and Duntulm Castle, ruined Clan Macdonald stronghold.

From Kyle of Lochalsh, head for Invergarry, 45 slow miles southeast, on the A87. South of Invergarry the road skirts the great Caledonian Canal, begun in 1803 by Thomas Telford. Just before Spean Bridge stands the Commando Memorial, three grim figures looking upon the land where the Commandos of World War II were trained. Divert right on the B8004 to Gairlochy, and on the B8005 past Clunes. An avenue of beeches planted here in 1745 for Bonnie Prince Charlie, called the Dark Mile, still brackets the road, and at Loch Arkaig the prince is said to have buried his fortune in gold. Return now on the B8004 to the A830 and Fort William, the unofficial capital of the Western Highlands. Above it stands Ben Nevis, at 4406 feet the highest peak in Britain. The A82 south of Fort William circuits Loch Leven (or there is a ferry) to Glencoe, where a previous booking will reward you with rooms at the King's House, the oldest inn in Scotland.

• From Fort William you may turn again to the sea. Northwest of Fort William the A830 winds 45 miles west to Mallaig (from which another ferry departs for Skye). This is the famous Road to the Isles of the song, and you may circuit to Mallaig, Ardnamurchan, across the isles of Mull and Iona, and back across to Glencoe in an exceedingly long day (325 miles, and 5 ferry trips later) passing through the clan lands of the Cameron and past Glenfinnan, where Bonnie Prince Charlie raised the standard of revolt. You cross to Mull by ferry, thence to Ulva, where you can negotiate for a boat to Staffa, 10 miles away. This is the most dramatic cave-ridden and cliff-broken island in Britain; Fingal's Cave is remembered in Mendelssohn's Hebridean overture. From Ulva the B8073 runs into the B8035, south, which then joins the A849 for the drive west to the ferry for Iona. St Columba landed here in 563 and so brought Christianity to Scotland. A place of pilgrimage then and now, it can be crowded, even though so remote. The Lipchitz sculpture of the Virgin Mary, set here in 1959, has been controversial ever since.

SEVENTH DAY

Glen Coe, up the A82, may be the most famous of Scotland's glens. It was certainly one of the bloodiest. Here a 13,000-acre National Trust property encloses most of the sites associated with the massacre in 1692 of forty members of Clan Macdonald by soldiers under the leadership of a Campbell. At Bridge of Orchy, take the B8074 to the A85 and then go west through the Pass of Brander – successfully taken by Robert

Bruce in 1309 in battle against 2000 MacDougalls in ambush – to reach Oban, the port of the Western Isles, a focus for Gaelic culture, and site of the tiny 'Cathedral of the Isles'. You can also reach Iona by passenger ferry from here. At Oban the A816 begins, passing south through Argyll where the Lowlands begin.

• South of Lochgilphead (on Loch Fyne) via the A83 is Campbeltown (from which Flora Macdonald sailed for America in 1774). From Tarbert, on this road, a ferry runs to Islay (pronounced Eye-la) the southernmost of the Inner Hebrides. It is bleak and peat covered. The ferry lands at **Port Ellen,** birthplace of Alexander McDougall, founder of the first modern shipyard in the American Pacific Northwest. Southwest is the Mull of Oa. Here on the cliffs stands a memorial to **American soldiers and sailors** who lost their lives when the *Tuscania* and *Otranto* were torpedoed in World War I. The A846 runs up the island to Bowmore, its capital. The entire area is noted for its distilleries, and especially for the rich Laphroaig. At Port Askaig a ferry crosses to Jura.

From Lochgilphead, continue on the A83 to Inveraray, where the castle once contained fine interiors, tapestries, Scottish weapons and paintings. Home of the Dukes of Argyll, headquarters of the Clan Campbell, and one of the most interesting castles in Scotland, it was gutted by fire in 1976.

• Although relatively near Glasgow, the extensive Cowal peninsula – south from Inveraray via the A815 – is one of the least settled and most roadless sections of Scotland. The circuit of 120 miles carries you down Loch Fyne, then by the A886 to the southern end of the Kyles of Bute, north again on a new road across the peninsula to **Holy Loch,** where American Polaris submarines are based, then to Dunoon (where you may cross the Firth of Clyde by ferry). Then continue to Glasgow or make your way north to Loch Lomond.

Loch Lomond is the best known of Scotland's lakes, because of its proximity to Glasgow, because of the many songs and stories woven about 'its bonnie, bonnie banks', and because it is the largest of the lochs. The eastern shore is protected by the Queen Elizabeth National Forest Park, and Ben Lomond, 3192 feet high, lies within the park also. You may drive along the loch's western length, going south on the A82 through Luss, a lovely town well worth a stop. The road is neither the high nor the low road of the song, which refers in fact to the journey of the spirit after death (the low road) and of the person in life (the high road). At the base of the lake, turn east on the A811. (Just south is Bonhill, birthplace of Tobias Smollett. 4 miles further south is Dumbarton, a county town with a good ruined castle.) After 10 miles on the A811, bear left on the A81 and then the A821 to The Trossachs, which means 'bristly country', and which are oddly shaped peaks, not unlike the Dolomites that so appealed to the romantic imagination of the 19th century. This is perhaps the oldest 'standard tour' in Scotland, and the lake walks, rock climbing and general amenities (especially at Loch Katrine, site of Scott's *Lady of the Lake*) are well developed. Meet the A84 at the Pass of Leny; turn north here to a country road, left, posted for Balquhidder (pronounced Balwhidder) on Loch Voil, burial place of Rob Roy. Just north on the A84 is the Lochearnhead Hotel, an excellent spot for afternoon tea, dinner, or the night. Or you might drive another 30 miles along the north shore of Loch Earn on the A85, right on the B827, right again on the A822 into the A9, south through Dunblane – where there is a fine Gothic cathedral famed for its Ruskin Window (open weekdays 10–5) – to **Bridge of Allan,** where George Inness, the American painter, died. The Queens Hotel offers good accommodation. Stirling is just ahead.

EIGHTH DAY

Stirling is the site of one of the finest castles in Europe, Stirling Castle (open April, May, Sept., daily 10–6.45; June–Aug., to 9; winter to 4), seat of the Scottish kings since 1451. Inside is the fine regimental museum of the Argyll and Sutherland Highlanders. West of Stirling on the A84 is **Blair Drummond,** where Benjamin Franklin planted trees that are still standing, while he was a guest of Lord Kames. Just off the A80 south is the site of the National Trust park for the Battle of Bannockburn, with an information post where you can learn how Robert the Bruce turned back an English army that outnumbered his by three to one. Just beyond, pick up the motorway, M9, which becomes the A80 past Cumbernauld New Town. Planned in 1956 as an overspill town for Glasgow, it was long hailed as a model for town planners the world over. It is interesting to visit, both as a possible environment for the future, and because of the evidence of extensive vandalism that suggests something about how people feel when they live in totally planned and antiseptic communities. Then follow the A80 to the M8, thence into Glasgow, exiting at the cathedral.

Glasgow is a teeming city of well over a million people, and is the third largest in Britain. It is a creature of the Industrial Revolution and is thus a heaven for industrial archaeologists or for those who like the Victorian period. There is much that is handsome and modern, and yet somehow the image of the Gorbals, Britain's most famous slum, hangs over the city. Glasgow is of particular interest to those who follow architectural history, since fourteen buildings designed by Charles Rennie Mackintosh (1868–1928), the Frank Lloyd Wright of British architecture, still stand (the Glasgow Information Bureau, on George Square, will supply both a guide to the city and a map of locations of the Mackintosh buildings).

The cathedral is small but important, being the only undamaged survivor of the Gothic churches of southern Scotland. Opposite it is Provand's Lordship House, the only pre-Reformation house left in the city. See also the **Old Glasgow Museum,** in People's Palace, devoted to the history of the city (open daily 10–5, Sun. 2). Exhibits on Sir Thomas Lipton, who five times tried to capture the America's Cup with his yachts, are here. George Square is the area in which **Bret Harte** worked when he was American Consul in Glasgow in the 1880's. He lived at 35 Burnbank Gardens. The **University of Glasgow,** designed by Sir Gilbert Scott, is worth visiting. James Wilson, who signed the Declaration of Independence for Pennsylvania, studied here. **The Hunterian Museum and University Art Collection** (open Mon.–Fri. 10–5, Sat. 10–12) on the campus is an outstanding small gallery. Of great importance are the James McNeill Whistlers, no few than seventy-six oils, hundreds of drawings and many letters, as well as work by over forty modern Americans, including Leonard Baskin, Thomas Hart Benton, Alexander Calder, Willem de Kooning, Roy Lichtenstein, Robert Motherwell, Claes Oldenburg, Larry Rivers, Ben Shahn and Grant Wood.

Down the hill and across the River Kelvin stands the massive **Glasgow Art Gallery and Museum** (open daily 10–5, Sun. 2–5). It is especially good for weapons, shipbuilding, and for its fine Dutch, French and Flemish Old Masters, including pictures by Rembrandt, Raphael, Rubens, Botticelli, and Corot. Dali's 'Christ of St John of the Cross' is here, as are the works of several American painters, including Sargent, West and Whistler (only thirteen this time). At Clydebank, 5 miles west, headquarters of shipbuilding on the Clyde, is John Brown's shipyard, where the *Lusitania, Queen Mary,* and both *Queen Elizabeth*s were built.

To the south, Hampden Park, the largest football stadium in Europe, holds 163,000, dwarfing even the huge American bowls. 8 miles southeast in Blantyre is the **Scottish National Memorial** to David Livingstone, embracing his birthplace, a museum and fine grounds (open daily 10–6, Sun. 2–6). There are H. M. Stanley relics as well. Also south is Pollok House, containing perhaps the best collection of Old Spanish Masters in Britain, including El Greco, Goya and Murillo, as well as excellent Chippendale and Sheraton, and good silver (open daily 10–5, Sun. 2–5). Just west is **Paisley,** world-famous for thread-making. John Witherspoon, signer of the Declaration of Independence, was a minister here. The Museum and Art Gallery contains the largest collection of Paisley shawls to be found. Just beyond Paisley you pick up the M8 north and west, until it becomes the A8 along the southern bank of the Clyde into Greenock, birthplace of James Watt and still an industrial city. Here take the A78 along the shore to Skelmorlie to spend the night at the very pleasant Manor Park Hotel, which, however, thinks it an amenity to offer '4-day laundry'. Offshore is the Island of Bute, reached by ferry from Wemyss Bay, just north of Skelmorlie.

NINTH DAY

Distances in the southern Lowlands are less great, and you can circuit the major communities and all the shrines west of Peebles (for which, see the tours out of Edinburgh) to reach Turnhouse Airport, Edinburgh, in under 300 miles, or one very long day's drive. This, of course, allows no time for diversions. The route outlined here is nearer 400 miles, and it requires two days.

Continue south on the A78 through Largs. Skelmorlie Aisle here is a ruined church with superb carvings. (The A760, then a country road right, brings you to **Beith.** John Witherspoon was a church minister here as well.) From Ardrossan, south again on the A78, you can take a ferry (June–Sept.) to the Island of Arran. Edgar Allen Poe lived in **Irvine,** south again on the mainland, for a period of time. Turn inland here on the A71 to **Kilmarnock.** Here is the largest distillery in the world, begun in 1820 by Johnny Walker, a grocer. The Dick Institute's museum includes a large collection of American coins, and there is a Robert Burns museum in Kay Park. Follow the A77 southwest to Ayr, through the heart of Robbie Burns country. His birthplace is preserved in Alloway, 2 miles south of Ayr on the B7024, and the old Brig o' Doon is there too. A good Burns Museum stands in Ayr's High Street.

• In Tarbolton, northeast of Ayr, is The Bachelors' Club, associated with Burns. Further on is Auchinleck, the site of Auchinleck House, the home of the father of James Boswell; it was here that the American scholar Chauncey B. Tinker found the famous *London Journal*, which tells how Boswell first met Samuel Johnson.

From Ayr take the coastal road, the A719, south to **Culzean Castle** (pronounced 'Cullane', and open March and Oct., 10–4; April–Sept. to 6). Built in 1777, this may well be the finest Adam house in Scotland. It contains the National Guest Flat (closed to visitors) which was set aside for General Dwight D. Eisenhower in 1946 for his lifetime. The gardens are also famous, and the estate is a country park which is open to dusk. In Kirkoswald, nearby, Souter Johnnie's Cottage is a National Trust museum to Burns.

Continuing down the coast, the A77 runs through Ballantrae (made famous by Stevenson) and the village of **Cairnryan,** the site of the assembly of the floating dock (Mulberry Island) used in the invasion of Normandy in 1944. Stranraer is the main town of Wigtownshire. Take the A75, the A747, and the A746 to Whithorn. This is St Ninian's country, and many ancient sites attest to his influence. The oldest Christian memorial in Scotland is preserved in the Whithorn Museum, and 3 miles southeast on the A750 is the Isle of Whithorn (not an island) on which St Ninian landed in 387, bringing Christianity with him. The Steam Packet Hotel, which has only five rooms and offers dinner sharply at 8, is an unusually cozy place to pass your last night in Scotland.

TENTH DAY

Run north up the coast on the B7063 and the B7004, join the A746 and the A714 to Wigtown, county town of Wigtownshire. (This county, together with Kirkcudbrightshire, is the ancient province of Galloway.) On the right, before reaching town, are the ruins of Baldoon Castle, setting for Sir Walter Scott's *Bride of Lammermoor*. Rejoin the A75 at Newton Stewart, and follow it to the coast at Creetown. Rising to the northeast is Cairnsmore of Fleet, which figured prominently in John Buchan's *The Thirty-Nine Steps* (the lonely country road so important to the chase sequence in the book still exists, posted for Upper Rusko). The coastal road to Gatehouse of Fleet was reckoned by many, including Thomas Carlyle, to be the handsomest drive in the Lowlands; it also features in Scott's *Guy Mannering*. At Gatehouse of Fleet you may visit the Murray Arms, where Burns wrote his 'Scots' wha hae', while north on the B796 is Rusko Castle, home of the Young Lochinvar who came out of the West in Scott's poem. Beyond Gatehouse on the A75 divert right on the A755 to Kirkcudbright (pronounced Kur-coo-bree), an excellent crafts town and good for walking in. This area is also known as the Stewartry. Here is a **Tolbooth** preserved as a memorial to John Paul Jones, who was imprisoned in it in 1773. Follow the A711 to Dundrennan; Mary, Queen of Scots, spent her last night in Scotland in the abbey (now ruined) here. Continue to the B736, thence northwest to Castle Douglas. West is Threave Castle, on an island in a lake, stronghold of the Black Douglases, Lords of Galloway.

Leave Castle Douglas on the A745 to Dalbeattie, thence on the A710 along the coast to **Kirkbean.** The parish church has a font presented by the United States Navy, because a country road right reaches **Arbigland,** where the yellow cottage in which John Paul Jones was born still stands. The A710 continues to Dumfries, largest city of southwestern Scotland. Burns wrote 'Auld Lang Syne' here and also died in the town; he is buried in an ugly mausoleum in St Michael's cemetery, and his home in Burns Street is a museum. North of the town on the A76 is the ruined Lincluden Abbey. (Further north, via the A76 and the B729, is Dunscore, 6 miles west on a narrow country road – ultimately posted for Corsock – is the site of **Craigenputtock Farm,** where Thomas Carlyle wrote *Sartor Resartus*, and where he entertained Ralph Waldo Emerson.) From Dumfries run east on the A75 through Annan – Scott's *Redgauntlet* was set here – and north on the B722 for Ecclefechan, left. Here Thomas Carlyle was born in 1795, in a house now a museum, and he is buried in the churchyard. Continue north on the A74 to the A701, and follow this over the height of land beyond the Devil's Beef Tub, past the source of the River Tweed, and left on the B7016 to Biggar. Gladstone Court Museum here is a re-created street of Victorian shops.

• Alternatively, leave Moffat on the A708, past the Grey Mare's Tail, one of the highest waterfalls in Scotland, to Cappercleuch. Here a country road runs west up Megget Water to join the A701 at Tweedsmuir, well below Biggar. This route is nearly twice as long but more attractive.

From Biggar follow the A72 west to the A73 northwest, to Lanark, a mill town. A mile south is **New Lanark,** built by David Dale in 1784 and later organized as the first socialist community in Britain by his son-in-law Robert Dale Owen. New Harmony, Indiana, was to spring from these roots. From Lanark take the A706 north 16 miles to Whitburn to pick up the M8, the motorway that carries you east to Turnhouse (Edinburgh) Airport, and the end of the Scottish tour.

WHAT TO READ   Obviously Robert Louis Stevenson, Sir Walter Scott, Thomas Carlyle, James Boswell, J. M. Barrie, Robert Burns and John Buchan should be one's constant companions while in Scotland. But you might also remember that the Highlands are a popular background for the novel of the chase, for spy thrillers, and for nature and hunting (or stalking) stories. Examples include some of the work of Fred Hoyle, Ian Stuart, Josephine Tey and Len Deighton (*Spy Story*). Sir Compton Mackenzie and George Orwell both lived in Barr, Naomi Mitchison at Carradale. Eric Linklater came from the Orkney Islands and Arthur Conan Doyle was born in Edinburgh. John Galt is now being rediscovered as a novelist; his home was Greenock, and his *Annals of the Parish* is a good place to start. If you missed Dorothy Sayers' *Five Red Herrings*, set in Galloway, read it now.

Many more Americans claim a Scots background than are entitled to it. The majority of Americans who can sustain the claim originate in the Lowlands, while most of the tartans about which Americans inquire are from the Highlands. In 1979 a researcher discovered 180 pipe bands in the United States; of the 3,500 members, a third had no family ties whatever to Scotland. Lowlanders dismissed clans and tartans as relics of a culture they disliked, yet most Americans seek out shops that will sell them tartan ties, shirts, even kilts. This attests to the presumption of close American ties to Scotland, whatever the scholars and the statistics may tell us. Indeed, there are many true ties that cannot be recounted here, from the development of Glasgow by the tobacco trade to the strong commitment of Scots abolitionists after 1833 to ending slavery in the United States. Those interested in the American tie to Scotland may wish to read William R. Brock's *Scotus Americanus*, which focuses on the 18th century and incorporates all significant known information to 1982.

17 Northern Ireland

Officially, the nation is called the United Kingdom of Great Britain and Northern Ireland. Still, most people believe the northern third of John Bull's 'other island' to be an entirely different land, and in many basic ways it is. The history of that land called Ulster by those of Protestant persuasion, or the Six Counties by those (generally but not necessarily Roman Catholic) who think of it as more rightfully a part of Ireland itself (which, to add confusion to the terminology, is officially the Republic of Eire), is a dark and bloody one, not filled with leprechauns at all. Guide books to Britain rightly omit Northern Ireland entirely – although if they cover 'the British Isles' they will usually include the land whose capital is Belfast.

This is not the place to attempt to explain, or even to recite, the tangled history of those six counties, or to tell how Protestant oppressed Catholic, and Catholic oppressed Protestant, over centuries of warfare. Some argue that the 'problem of Northern Ireland' rests upon its relatively clear class distinctions; others as clearly state that Ulster is the site of a religious war, and that the only reason some apologists attempt to cast the conflict into political terms is that they are ashamed, in the 20th century, to fight a war over religion. Of course, if one accepts that religion is a form of ideology, one may take both explanations at face value. Nonetheless, to attempt any easy explanation, to suggest that the problem of Northern Ireland, or of the Partition of Ireland (capitalized to share political nuance with Kashmir, Cyprus, Pakistan, Korea or Germany), may be laid at the doorstep of the British Parliament in Westminster, or on the stoop of the intransigent Irish, or behind the arras in Dublin, simply will not do. The problem is enormously complex, ever changing, and an excellent example of why most historians argue that belief in collective guilt is not a useful tool for analysis.

For the tourist who wishes to avoid the grim realities of the 1980's, Northern Ireland is best omitted. This is unfortunate, and at odds with one thrust of this guide – to lead its readers to American-related sites. For given the massive emigration out of the entire Emerald Isle, there are many places in Northern Ireland which relate to America. Of the seven foreign-born **signers of the Declaration of Independence,** three came from Northern Ireland (although their precise places of birth are unknown): James Smith and Charles Thomson, for Pennsylvania, and Matthew Thornton, for New Hampshire. Indeed, were the island to be taken as a whole, a full and separate guide would be required. Still, one must recognize that however physically attractive the countryside is, most visitors will not choose to remain for long, or to drive in the border region more than they must. If one has less than a month for the whole of the United Kingdom, I would recommend against going to Northern Ireland at this time. If one has more than a month, the Six Counties should be given three to four days (the latter especially if one includes Eire's County Donegal in the tour, which forms a logical geographical entity with Northern Ireland).

One further word of caution: do not miss Northern Ireland simply from fear. Much of it is beautiful, and even the grim areas of Belfast or Londonderry are instructive. If one minds one's business, avoids pubs and other public gathering places, and stays away from border roads (and of course passes no comments on the local scene), a visit will in all likelihood be tranquil. Only at border crossings, in certain sections of Belfast, and at the ferry terminals or Aldergrove (Belfast) Airport will one have the British military presence brought obtrusively to mind.

It is via that airport or those ferry terminals that you will arrive, unless you drive north from Dublin. I would recommend flying to Belfast and renting a car at the airport. You may, if you wish, with some prior arranging, take the car into the Republic, and a pleasant circular tour may be made from Belfast through County Londonderry into the Republic, then south via Sligo to Galway, Limerick, and the south of Ireland. You may then leave your car at Dublin and fly back to London, or drop your car on the west coast of Ireland at Shannon and return directly to the United States. The following itinerary is limited to Northern Ireland, however.

FIRST DAY

Belfast, the capital of Northern Ireland since the Partition in 1921, is an ugly city of 440,000 people, some 38 miles north of the border of the Republic of Ireland. If one drives out any of the three major arteries heading west from the city center – the Crumlin Road, the Shankhill Road or the Falls Road – one can quickly see the tiny row houses in which hatreds, frustrations and envies fester. The A52 brings one into Belfast from the airport via the Crumlin Road, which becomes Donegall (spelled with two *l*'s in Belfast) Street. On the left is the Protestant St Anne's Cathedral, begun in 1898 and completed in 1959. It is not of great interest. One then enters the High Street – the quays are to the left in four short blocks, so park where you can in order to walk about the city's center. This area was the heart of Belfast at the end of the 18th century, when Wolfe Tone (who came in 1791) and others made the town headquarters of the Society of the United Irishmen, and thus of Irish Republicanism, a movement much inspired both by the French Revolution and by the publication of Thomas Paine's *The Rights of Man*. At the eastern end of High Street is St George's Church, the first Church of Ireland parish church in Belfast. Beyond is the custom house, built in 1857, and the **docks** from which thousands of emigrants departed for America. Approximately a quarter-mile north of the custom house is Corporation Square; here is the **Seamen's Church,** dating from 1857, which is locally said to be in the 'Moby Dick style'. Return to the High Street, turn west, and at Castle Square turn south into Donegall Square, to see the more imposing of the city's public buildings, none of them outstanding. Outside the City Hall, in the square, is a **monument to the United States Army,** noting that the first contingent to set foot in Europe in World War II arrived here in 1942.

After you retrieve your car, drive west (be careful of the rather complex one-way road system) to Castle Street at the square, and proceed to its junction with Albert Street, then left, and left again at the second turn, to find the grimy and depressing St Peter's Church, in Derby Street. This is the Roman Catholic cathedral, in the heart of the Falls Road district. To the extent that the British army, the local inhabitants and the methodically placed barbed wire will permit, the location offers an opportunity to see the denominational housing segregation of Belfast at work.

Continue south and east again on Albert Street (or head due south from Donegall Square) into Dunham Street, and turn right to continue across Donegall Road into University Road. Beyond, on the left, is the Queen's University of Belfast, founded in 1845. The campus center is of red-brick mock-Tudor. Just beyond is the entrance to the Botanic Gardens Park, and the **Ulster Museum & Art Gallery.** The museum provides a quick overview of Northern Ireland, with archaeological, geological, technical and historical collections. The art gallery includes work by Turner, Lawrence and Sickert, and by Americans Mark Fisher, David Winfield Scott and Edith Scott.

One should not leave Belfast without seeing Stormont, the seat of Northern Ireland's Parliament. The massive administration building for the Six Counties, Dundonald House, was completed in 1963. To reach it, return to central Belfast, bear east on High Street across the bridge over the River Lagan, and follow the A20 for just over 3 miles. Continue another mile and a half through Dundonald (where there is a Norman motte, or fort), and on a mile and a half beyond Dundonald Church to Greengraves, where one finds the Kempe Stones. This is an exceptionally well preserved megalithic protal dolmen, a single-chambered grave with a massive capstone. (Northern Ireland has done much to preserve its prehistoric, ancient and medieval ruins, with well over a hundred National Monuments in the comparatively small area of Ulster. Most are of little interest to the tourist, unless one is especially interested in archaeology. Some can be observed really well solely from the air. Only a few of the most striking are mentioned here.

Carry on to Newtownards, a well-planned town where one should visit the ruined 13th century Dominican friary. Continue on the A20 towards Grey Abbey, now well out into the attractive greenery of County Down. At North East Refuge, just off the road, one may look over Strangford Lough, the largest wildlife preserve in Great Britain or Ireland. Before Grey Abbey one reaches the **Mount Stewart Gardens,** probably the handsomest in Northern Ireland and certainly the most interesting. On the grounds of the home of the Marchioness of Londonderry, 80 acres of garden exploit the climate of the peninsula of the Ards to great effect, and since 1921 they have been developed so as to rival the gardens of Cornwall and Devon. There are, of course, many American plants. Especially attractive is the Ladies' Walk (open April 1–Oct. 31, daily except Tues., 2–6). Just beyond the gardens, but quite separate, is the small Temple of the Winds, also a Northern Ireland National Trust property, which belonged to Robert Steward, the Baron Londonderry.

At Grey Abbey turn east for Ballywalter, crossing the Ard peninsula in 5 miles, and from there north on the A2 to Bangor. Here is an odd tower, built about 1637, which incorporates Scottish features. In the sixth century Bangor was a city of saints and scholars, with a monastery in which 'The Voyage of Brim', one of the oldest of Irish poems, was written down. Viking attacks destroyed the religious community, and today it is simply a pleasant seaside town. At Cultra Manor is the Ulster Folk and Transport Museum. There are seven traditional dwellings here, together with other representative buildings. And if you have booked in advance, you will pass your first night back in Belfast, arriving just in time for dinner at the Wellington Park Hotel, 21 Malone Road. For dinner, begin with the North Sea platter.

SECOND DAY

The circuit of Northern Ireland, which will bring one back to Belfast, may be made under some pressure in two days, and comfortably in three.

An additional day should be added in either circumstance if, as geography suggests, one wishes to tour County Donegal, in the Republic, as well. Food and lodgings throughout this area are plain, with little that bears explicit recommendation. It would be best to avoid Londonderry for the night, which suggests stopping for a short stay at Portstewart (where the Carrig-na-Cule Hotel is said to be good) or a hard drive through to Bundoran, in the Republic but quite near the border, where the Great Southern Hotel serves one well enough.

Leave Belfast going north on the A2, holding to the coast to **Carrickfergus.** Arthur Dobbs, a colonial Governor of North Carolina, came from here. The castle, on the rocks above the harbor, is one of the finest remains in Northern Ireland; it was begun in 1180 and garrisoned until 1928. Just offshore, John Paul Jones (in the *Ranger*) fought his successful engagement against H.M.S. *Drake* in 1778. This was the first action in European waters by an American vessel. On the road leading north from the railroad station one finds **North Gate;** nearby is the inn which provided a living for the ancestors of Andrew Jackson before his father emigrated to America in 1748. 3 miles northeast of town on the Bellahill Road is Dalway's Bawn, a National Monument, the best preserved of Ulster Plantation's bawn and flanker-towers of the 17th century. The road – the B90 – continues via **Ballycarry** (site of the first Presbyterian church in Ireland, founded in 1613) back to the A2. James Orr, the revolutionary poet who escaped to America in 1798, is buried here. Continue on to **Larne** (from which the ferry leaves for Stranraer), home of the Irish-American writer James MacHenry. 4 miles north on the coastal road, at Carncastle, are the ruins of Ballygalley Castle, now incorporated into a hotel. This is the best preserved of the Scottish baronial castles in Ireland; it dates from 1625.

• If time permits, turn inland at Larne on the A8 for a 55-mile circuit which will rejoin the coastal road above Glenarm, adding some 41 miles to your journey. At Ballynure, bear right on a country road for **Ballyeaston,** the ancestral home of Andrew Johnson, whose grandfather emigrated about 1750. Jog left, just beyond, on the B94, then right on the B93, to Antrim, a small town which gives its name to the county. Theodore Roosevelt's mother had ancestral ties here. 1 mile north is the Antrim Round Tower, a National Monument, the most perfect of the towers in Northern Ireland. Nearby is a bullaun, or font-like basin, which is probably of pre-Christian origin; it is the oldest relic of Christianity in Ireland, having been adopted as a repository for holy water. Continue north on the A26 to Ballymena, a Presbyterian town that has provided an unusually large number of emigrants to Canada. 3 miles northwest, on the B62, is **Cullybackey.** Here is the home of the Reverend William Arthur, father of Chester Arthur, the twenty-first President of the United States. Some guide books suggest that Chester was born here in 1830 (which would have made him ineligible to be President), but his father apparently emigrated about 1820. The house is a National Monument. Return to Ballymena, and proceed down one of the several green and beautiful Antrim Glens, via the A42, to the coastal road (or the A2) just above Glenarm.

The coastal drive for the next 38 miles, to Portrush, is slow and often spectacular as one looks out over the North Channel. The handsomest part of the journey lies directly ahead, around Garron Point and into Red Bay, marked by its red sandstone and in spring by many waterfalls. (The A43 diverts left up the best known of the glens, the Glenariff. If time permits take this route to the head of the glen, 6 miles, and then return via the B14, off the slope of the highest hill in Antrim.) 2 miles west of Cushendall is Ossian's Grave – up the Glenaan Road – no doubt based on myth but an attractive place of pilgrimage nonetheless. North, via the B92, is Cushendun, an excellent spot for a late lunch at the hotel if you have been able to resist the detours. The village and the beach belong to the National Trust, and the area is worth careful exploration (purchase the National Trust pamphlet in the town first). On the River Dunn west of the village **Harvard University** has excavated stone-age tools. Then continue via the low-gear and quite narrow Torr Head road along the coast, under the crest of Carnanmore, to rejoin the A2 at Ballyvoy.

Just beyond is Ballycastle. On the shore here Marconi transmitted his first wireless message across to Rathlin Island. Before reaching the town one encounters the ruins of Bunamargy Friary. From Ballycastle one may take a motorboat (on Mon., Wed., and Fri., in good weather) across the dangerous Valley of the Sea to Rathlin Island, on which Robert Bruce was a fugitive. It is here that Bruce most likely watched the steadfast spider which inspired him to return to his cause. Beyond Ballycastle, keep on the coastal road, now the B15, past White Head to Ballintoy. One passes the path to Carrick-a-Rede, clearly marked, by which one may walk out to a basalt stack connected to the mainland by a challenging and ever-swaying bridge built of fishermen's rope. The view, even if you do not dare the crossing, is superb. One then continues on to touch the A2 again, and diverts once more for the coast on the B146 to reach the Giant's Causeway.

No doubt this is the most famous sight in Northern Ireland. First made widely known in 1786, this great basaltic formation has continued to capture the romantic imagination ever since. The area is pockmarked with caves, which figure prominently in a number of picturesque novels set in the region. Allow an hour here, at the least, so that you may walk down the slope and out onto the dramatic area where some 50,000 polygonal basalt columns have cooled to take incredible shape. Properly called Clochan na bhFomharagh (and pronounced – just – Clow-chan-anna-vow-ree), the whole of the causeway and foreshore is now a National Trust property.

Nightfall approaches. Portstewart is only a few miles ahead, but Bundoran is a full 110 miles, a long stretch in this country. Stopping will be less frequent now, and one may make the distance, arriving in time for a latish dinner, but unless truly pressed for time it is best to proceed slowly. The coastal road returns to the A2 at Bushmills, noted for the distillery of that name. (North on the B66 3 miles is **Conogher.** Here James McKinley, grandfather of President William McKinley, was born in 1783. Only an outhouse remains.) Further on the A2 is Dunluce Castle, a romantic ruin, originally built about 1300. One then arrives at Portrush, a pleasant (and in summer crowded) resort town on the border of County Derry. Just beyond is Portstewart, a good place to spend the night.

The A2 continues on to Coleraine, a river port on the Bann, seat of the New University of Ulster. Follow the A2 along the coast to the Downhill ruins and Mussenden Temple, a summerhouse library built by the Bishop of Derry, Lord Bristol. Bristol was a frequent traveller on the Continent, and many hotels bear his name (rather than that of the city in England). Just beyond, a road – posted Gortmore – strikes sharply up the mountain to a spectacular viewing point. This road continues across the summit of **Binevenagh,** with superb views out to sea and down the green slope of the hills. Many settlers came to America from this area, and it is said that the high ground, being rockiest, was deserted first, usually by Catholics, slowly leaving the more fertile land to the Protestants.

Follow the postings for Limavady (where you may enjoy a good dinner at Blades Restaurant, if you have called first, and if you are willing to drive after dark to reach your bed for the night). Thackeray wrote of 'Sweet Peg of Limavady', and one of New Zealand's most famous Prime Ministers came from here – for this region supplied many emigrants to Australasia and Canada as well. (If time permits, take the B68 up the **Roe,** a most attractive valley, to Dungiven. Ancestors of James Monroe lived near here. Then follow the A6 into Londonderry.) The A2 proceeds along the coast to Londonderry; 11 miles beyond Limavady one crosses a bridge; to the right is a ruined small fort. Nearby, on farmland, **Amelia Earhart** landed her plane in 1932 after becoming the first woman to fly across the Atlantic. One then descends to the River Foyle and into Londonderry.

Londonderry has been a sad town, and it is all the more so today. Most people call it simply Derry. It is the second largest city in Ulster, and it was an important manufacturing point. Today its dramatic old walls – perhaps the best preserved in all of the U.K. – contain a city at war with itself, and one cannot recommend lingering for long. Settlement began with a monastery founded by St Columb in 546; it was demolished by Sir Henry Docwra, when he turned the defenses of Gaelic Ulster and captured Derry in 1600 (the ruins may be seen in St Columb's Park, to the right as one enters the city before crossing the river). In 1613 James I granted Derry to the citizens of London, who put the walls around it and made it into a Protestant plantation. Since then the city, sited as it is on the left bank of the Foyle (which otherwise forms the boundary between the Republic and Ulster) has played a central role in every Irish rebellion, and for those interested in the history of modern Ireland, it is a bleak place of dour pilgrimage.

Today Craigavon Bridge is likely to be patrolled by the military, and one should exercise care in the town center. The places of greatest interest are the old city wall (bear right across the bridge, along the river front, then sharp left into Orchard Street, and sharp right through Ferry Gate); St Columb's Cathedral, built between 1628 and 1633 on the high ground, reached by turning left immediately inside the gate and driving as far as possible, then walking directly ahead; and St Eugene's Cathedral, a massive structure in Gothic Revival (1873), which is rather better outside than in. If one bears right at the cathedral and continues along French Street into Northland Road, one comes to the structures of Magee University College. Just beyond, turn right on Rock Road, then left on Strand Road into the A2, for a 5-mile drive to **Culmore,** where local tradition has it – apparently incorrectly – that Amelia Earhart landed that aeroplane.

Return across the River Foyle to the right bank, and turn southwest on the A5 to **Strabane,** 14 miles distant. An agricultural center on the border with the Republic, Strabane was the birthplace of two men directly connected with the American Revolution: John Dunlap, who issued the first American daily newspaper, *The Pennsylvania Packet*, in 1771, and who acted as the printer for the Declaration of Independence; and Guy Carleton (Lord Dorchester), the Governor of Quebec who defended it against the Americans on Lake Champlain in 1775–6, and the man who was officially the commander-in-chief of British troops in the last years of the war. The printing press where Dunlap was an apprentice still stands on Main Street. Called Gray's, it also is the site of the apprenticeship of James Wilson, grandfather to Woodrow Wilson, who emigrated in 1807. (If you leave Strabane on the B72 and divert right 2 miles, you will come to **Dergalt,** where the house of James Wilson is a National Monument.)

If you wish to remain entirely in Northern Ireland, head south from Strabane on the A5 for Omagh, 20 miles away. This would mean missing the best parts of County Fermanagh, or force upon you a series of backtrackings. So it is best to cross the border into County Donegal, and follow route 18 through Donegal and Ballyshannon to Bundoran, 53 miles in all. If you have stayed overnight somewhere before reaching this stretch you will be able to admire the Blue Stack Mountains to the right, but if you are restricting yourself to the Six Counties and to the three

days suggested here, this portion will have to be driven at speed and in
the gathering dark to arrive before the last orders for dinner are accepted
at 9.00 P.M. at the Great Southern Hotel in Bundoran.

THIRD DAY

This could be a rather more leisurely day than the previous one, although
to complete the remainder of the circuit in a single day will still require
sacrificing some comfort and the time to let the landscapes of Fermanagh,
Tyrone and Armagh creep up on one. Return to Ballyshannon on route
18, and turn east towards Belleek and the Northern Irish border. Belleek
is famous for its extremely delicate luster-finish china, which many regard as among the most beautiful in the world. The pottery is open to
the public, and one may purchase pieces here, except on weekends. Just
beyond lies Ulster's only National Park, Lough Erne, based on the Lowes
Lough, a large and attractive expanse of water, dotted at its lower end
with many small islands, and surrounded by crumbling ruins and ancient
Irish archaeological sites. If you have time to explore with any care,
purchase a copy of Mary Rogers' book, *Prospect of Erne*, first. The
road to the south shore (the A46) is the shorter – 23 miles to Enniskillen –
while the road along the north shore (the A47) is the more attractive,
especially if one also follows the A35 through Kesh and the B82 along
the shore – 33 miles in all.

Enniskillen is the county town of Fermanagh, on the River Erne, be-
tween the Lower and Upper Loughs Erne, and it is perhaps the best base
in Northern Ireland for an extended stay, in order to explore the lakes,
the green countryside and the many prehistoric remnants on the land.
Its strategic location made Enniskillen a Protestant stronghold, and St
Macartan's Cathedral is Protestant (and modest). Enniskillen Castle is a
National Monument, but the two principal sights undoubtedly are the
Portora Royal School, just northwest of the city, which such figures as
Oscar Wilde and Samuel Beckett attended; and Castlecoole, also a National Trust property, the seat of the Earl of Belmore. This is regarded as
the finest Classical mansion in Ireland, dating from 1789. 9 miles southwest of Enniskillen, on the A32, is another National Trust property,
Florence Court, built in 1764, the seat of the Earls of Enniskillen. It is
early Georgian in appearance, and except for some excellent plaster work,
is less interesting than Castlecoole.

Leave Enniskillen north on the A32, 27 miles to **Omagh,** county town
for Tyrone. The birthplace of Thomas Mellon, founder of the Mellon
National Bank in the United States – and precursor of the great Mellon
fortune and many benefactions to the study of British culture – is in a
farmhouse here. At **Deroran,** nearby, was the ancestral home of President

James Buchanan. (South on the A5 and then via the B83 is **Clogher,** a tiny village, the smallest seat of a cathedral in the United Kingdom, yet one of the most ancient. The Roman Catholic see of the diocese is now across the border in Monaghan, and Clogher's is a Church of Ireland structure, built in 1818. Ancient monuments – dolmen, long-chambered cairns, pillarstones, etc. – abound in this area.) For a particularly attractive hill drive, leave Omagh on the B48 north, to Gortin, thence to Plum Bridge, then right on the B47 through the Glenelly Valley – often said to be the most beautiful drive in Ulster – to the B162, and then south to Cookstown. (Or continue via the B47 and the B41, and the A29, to **Maghera,** birthplace of Charles Thomson, secretary to the first United States Congress – it was he who wrote out the Declaration of Independence – and of his brother William, who led the Third Regiment of South Carolina in the Revolutionary War; thence on the A29 south to Cookstown, a diversion that adds 6 miles. Southwest of Cookstown on the B4 is **Pomeroy,** birthplace of General James Shields of the Mexican and Civil Wars.)

Continue on the A29 south to Coalisland, then via the A45 into the A4, ignoring the signs for the motorway. Turn east, and very shortly left, on the B196, to drive to the edge of Lough Neagh. Immediately offshore is **Coney Island,** from which the New York amusement park takes its name. Continue on the B196 until the road rejoins the A4. Near here, at 'The Riches' in **Milltown,** was the birthplace of Stonewall Jackson's grandfather, who went to America in 1765. Join the motorway here, going east, for **Lurgan,** birthplace of James Logan, an early founder and Governor of Pennsylvania; then return on the motorway west four exits, and leave south on the B131, then right on the B28, to Ardress House, a stunningly simple and attractive manor house with superb interior plasterwork.

Turn south to Armagh, the ecclesiastical capital of Ireland, at the junction with the A29. This is the seat of both Protestant and Catholic metropolitan bishoprics, and after Belfast and Londonderry the most important city in the Six Counties to visit. With only 10,000 population, Armagh offers pleasant walking, and the hilly site provides attractive views. Gilbert Tennent, a founder of the Log College at Neshaminy, which was the inspiration for **Princeton University,** came from Armagh, and the legendary Brian Boru is buried here. The buildings are not old, for the town was totally destroyed in 1566. The Protestant cathedral is well worth visiting, especially for its monuments, and the Catholic cathedral, at the head of a flight of steps to the north, features lavish interior decoration. In Ogle Street, south of the Protestant cathedral, is a plaque marking the birthplace of St Malachy. 2 miles west off the A28 is Navan Fort, an ancient hill fort, the Isamnium of Ptolemy's Geography, or Emania, palace of the kings of Ulster's legends for 600 years, scene of the heroic *Ulster Cycle* of tales.

Now head southeast on the A28, and divert right on the B133 beyond Markethill, to Bessbrook. Here is **Derrymore House,** a National Trust property, small and thatched. Built by Isaac Corry after his election for Newry in 1776, the house was one of the sites in 1778 of the organization of the Irish Volunteers to protect Ireland from invasion by the Americans, Spaniards and French, who were then in alliance. Just ahead is Newry, where St Colman's Cathedral may reasonably be overlooked in favor of following the A2 along Carlingford Lough, past the Narrow Water Castle on the right, which is worth a visit, to **Warrenpoint.** Just beyond is an obelisk to the British general, Ross, who burned Washington in the War of 1812. Continue around the base of the Mountains of the Mourne, along the coastal road, across Bloody Bridge – scene of a massacre of Planters in 1641 – through Newcastle, to Clough, then right on the A25 to Downpatrick.

Here is the cathedral and market town from which the county of Down takes its name; here St Patrick is said to have founded a cathedral; here his relics were allegedly discovered. The present cathedral dates from 1790 to 1827; south in its graveyard is a stone, engraved 'Patric', which was said to be the grave of the saint – he actually died at Saul, 2 miles northeast, but his grave has long been lost. North on the A7, at Saintfield, is Rowallane House; the attraction here is the fine garden, which is especially handsome under summer twilight.

Now Belfast – or Aldergrove Airport, if you are dropping off your car and taking a night flight to London, Edinburgh or Dublin – lies ahead. For Belfast, continue straight on the A7 to the A24 to the city. For the airport, take the B6 from Saintfield to Lisburn, perhaps pausing to step into Christ Church Cathedral to see the memorial to **William Smith Dobbs,** killed by John Paul Jones off Carrickfergus. You might also turn left on the A1 for Dromore, there to view yet one more cathedral, or turn right on the A1 for Dunmurry, now a suburb of Belfast, where one may see perhaps the best Ulster Barn Church, the First Presbyterian, built in 1779. (In either case, ignore the motorway.) To reach the airport, continue through Lisburn on the A30, thence via the A26 through **Crumlin** – near here Wolfe Tone left for America – to Aldergrove.

WHAT TO READ   The whole of Ireland is rich in literature and folklore, and it probably is a mistake to restrict one's reading solely to those writers who relate to the Six Counties. After all, it was William Allingham who wrote those famous lines:

> Up the airy mountain,
> Down the rushy glen,
> We daren't go a-hunting
> For fear of little men.

And Allingham came from Ballyshannon, as near the border as it ought
not to matter. Surely this is the moment, casting political boundaries
aside, to refresh oneself on William Butler Yeats, James Joyce – no!
perhaps one *must* save him for Dublin – Oliver Goldsmith, and fresh
above all, Arthur Young's *Tour in Ireland*, published in 1780, to show
what change (and yet what little change) two hundred years brings.

A concluding word

No guide book can truly guide, for the genuinely thirsty traveller wants to taste all for himself. Hundreds of times before, Americans have tried to tell themselves what Britain means to them, but the more one discovers of it, whether guided or not, the more ambivalent one becomes. Perhaps this is Britain's greatest appeal – one can never quite make up one's mind. William Dean Howells, in his *Seven English Cities*, said that 'England is . . . to the American always a realm of faery', and this must be so, both because of the many echoes one discovers of America's past, and because of the overlay of sentiment, emotion, childhood literature, and perhaps just plain bias, that intervenes between us and 'the real Britain'.

Britain has often been looked to as an example to be emulated; equally often, as a horrible example to be avoided. It is, of course, precisely neither, for since that moment in 1776 when America chose a different path, the two histories, however frequently interwoven, have nonetheless been distinct. The common language – in truth, quite possibly better spoken today in America than in England by the general populace – and the common law will continue to be ties that bind. Americans will continue to watch Britain to see where she turns on the tides ahead. As Ralph Waldo Emerson said, when speaking in Manchester, '. . . I feel in regard to this aged England, with the possessions, honours, and trophies, and also with the infirmities of a thousand years gathering around her, irretrievably committed as she now is to transitions of trade, and new and all but incalculable mores, fabrics, arts, machines, and competing populations – I see her not dispirited, not weak, but well remembering that she has seen dark days before. . . . I see her in her old age, not decrepit, but young . . .'. For whose, after all, is the young country? And in the country of the young, what may not be accomplished?

Index

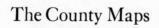
The County Maps

POST-1974 COUNTIES

SHETLAND

ORKNEY

WESTERN
ISLES

HIGHLAND

GRAMPIAN

TAYSIDE

CENTRAL

FIFE

STRATHCLYDE

LOTHIAN

BORDERS

LONDON
DERRY

ANTRIM

TYRONE

DUMFRIES &
GALLOWAY

NORTHUMBERLAND

TYNE & WEAR

FERMANAGH

ARMAGH

DOWN

CUMBRIA

DURHAM

CLEVELAND

ISLE
OF MAN

NORTH
YORKSHIRE

LANCASHIRE

WEST
YORKSHIRE

HUMBERSIDE

MERSEYSIDE

GREATER
MANCHESTER

SOUTH
YORKS

CHESHIRE

DERBY

NOTTINGHAM

LINCOLN

CLWYD

GWYNEDD

SHROPSHIRE

STAFFORD

LEICESTER

NORFOLK

POWYS

W.
MIDLANDS

WARWICK

NORTHAMPTON

CAMBRIDGE

SUFFOLK

HEREFORD
&
WORCESTER

BUCKINGHAM

BEDFORD

HERTFORD

ESSEX

DYFED

GLOUCESTER

OXFORD

GREATER
LONDON

GWENT

W.
GLAMORGAN

MID-
S.

AVON

BERKSHIRE

SURREY

KENT

WILTSHIRE

HAMPSHIRE

WEST
SUSSEX

EAST
SUSSEX

SOMERSET

DEVON

DORSET

ISLE OF WIGHT

CORNWALL